Ezekiel

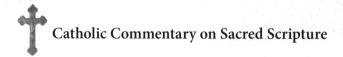

Catholic Commentary on Sacred Scripture

Ezekiel

Daniel A. Keating

Baker Academic
a division of Baker Publishing Group
Grand Rapids, Michigan

© 2024 by Daniel A. Keating

Published by Baker Academic
a division of Baker Publishing Group
Grand Rapids, Michigan
BakerAcademic.com

Printed in the United States of America

Library of Congress Cataloging-in-Publication Data
Names: Keating, Daniel A., author.
Title: Ezekiel / Daniel A. Keating.
Description: Grand Rapids, Michigan : Baker Academic, a division of Baker Publishing Group, [2024] |
    Series: Catholic commentary on sacred scripture | Includes bibliographical references and index.
Identifiers: LCCN 2023056582 | ISBN 9781540965868 (paperback) | ISBN 9781540967770 (casebound) |
    ISBN 9781493446117 (ebook) | ISBN 9781493446124 (pdf)
Subjects: LCSH: Bible. Ezekiel—Commentaries.
Classification: LCC BS1545.53 .K43 2024 | DDC 224/.407—dc23/eng/20240220
LC record available at https://lccn.loc.gov/2023056582

Imprimatur:
Printed with Ecclesiastical Permission
Most Reverend Earl Boyea, March 14, 2024
Lansing, Michigan

Cover art of mosaic from Basilica of Sant'Apollinare in Classe, Ravenna, Italy, showing Abel, Melchizedek, Abraham, and Isaac; De Agostini, A. De Gregorio, Superstock

Baker Publishing Group publications use paper produced from sustainable forestry practices and postconsumer waste whenever possible.

24 25 26 27 28 29 30   7 6 5 4 3 2 1

Contents

Illustrations

Editors' Preface

The Church has always venerated the divine Scriptures just as she venerates the body of the Lord. . . . All the preaching of the Church should be nourished and governed by Sacred Scripture. For in the sacred books, the Father who is in heaven meets His children with great love and speaks with them; and the power and goodness in the word of God is so great that it stands as the support and energy of the Church, the strength of faith for her sons and daughters, the food of the soul, a pure and perennial fountain of spiritual life.

Second Vatican Council, *Dei Verbum* 21

Did not our hearts burn within us while he talked to us on the road, while he opened to us the Scriptures?

Luke 24:32

The Catholic Commentary on Sacred Scripture Old Testament series aims to serve the ministry of the Word of God in the life and mission of the Church. Since the Second Vatican Council, Catholics have demonstrated an increasing hunger to study Scripture in depth and in a way that reveals its relationship to liturgy, evangelization, catechesis, theology, and personal and communal life. This series responds to that desire by providing accessible yet substantive commentary on the books of the Old Testament, drawn from the best of contemporary biblical scholarship as well as the rich treasury of the Church's tradition. These volumes seek to offer scholarship illumined by faith, in the conviction that the ultimate aim of biblical interpretation is to discover what God has revealed and is still speaking through the sacred text. Central to our approach are the principles taught by Vatican II: first, the use of historical and literary methods to discern what the biblical authors intended to express; second, prayerful theological reflection to understand the sacred text "in accord with the same Spirit by whom it was written"—that is, in light of the content and unity of the whole Scripture, the living tradition of the Church, and the analogy of faith (*Dei Verbum* 12).

The Catholic Commentary on Sacred Scripture is written for those engaged in or training for pastoral ministry and others interested in studying Scripture to understand their faith more deeply, to nourish their spiritual life, or to share the good news with others. With this in mind, the authors focus on the meaning of the text for faith and life rather than on the technical questions that occupy scholars, and they explain the Bible in ordinary language that does not require "translation" for preaching and catechesis. Although this series is written from the perspective of Catholic faith, its authors draw on the interpretation of Protestant and Orthodox scholars and hope these volumes will serve Christians of other traditions as well.

A variety of features are designed to make the commentary as useful as possible. Each volume includes the biblical text of the Revised Standard Version, Second Catholic Edition (RSV-2CE). This translation follows in the English Bible tradition largely embodied in the King James Version and conforms to Vatican guidelines given in *Liturgiam authenticam* (2001). Each unit of the biblical text is followed by a list of references to relevant Scripture passages, Catechism sections, and uses in the Roman Lectionary. The exegesis that follows aims to explain in a clear and engaging way the meaning of the text in its original historical context as well as its perennial meaning for Christians. "Reflection and Application" sections help readers apply Scripture to Christian life today by responding to questions that the text raises, offering spiritual interpretations drawn from Christian tradition or providing suggestions for the use of the biblical text in catechesis, preaching, or other forms of pastoral ministry. "In the Light of Christ" sections illustrate how certain passages prefigure, prophesy, or point forward to Christ and the new covenant.

Interspersed throughout the commentary are Biblical Background sidebars that present historical, literary, or theological information and Living Tradition sidebars that offer pertinent material from the postbiblical Christian tradition, including quotations from Church documents and from the writings of saints and Church Fathers. The Biblical Background sidebars are indicated by a photo of urns that were excavated in Jerusalem, signifying the importance of historical study in understanding the sacred text. The Living Tradition sidebars are indicated by an image of Eadwine, a twelfth-century monk and scribe, signifying the growth in the Church's understanding that comes by the grace of the Holy Spirit as believers study and ponder the word of God in their hearts (see *Dei Verbum* 8).

A glossary is located in the back of each volume for easy reference. The glossary explains key terms from the biblical text as well as theological or exegetical terms, which are marked in the commentary with a cross (†). A list of suggested resources, an index of pastoral topics, and an index of sidebars are included to enhance the usefulness of these volumes. Further resources can be found at the series website, www.CatholicScriptureCommentary.com.

It is our desire and prayer that these volumes be of service so that more and more "the word of the Lord may speed on and triumph" (2 Thess 3:1) in the Church and throughout the world.

Mary Healy
Mark Giszczak
Peter S. Williamson

Abbreviations

ACCS 13	Ancient Christian Commentary on Sacred Scripture: Old Testament, vol. 13, *Ezekiel, Daniel,* ed. Kenneth Stevenson and Michael Glerup (Downers Grove, IL: IVP Academic, 2008)
ACW	Ancient Christian Writers
ca.	approximately
Catechism	*Catechism of the Catholic Church* (2nd edition)
CCSS	Catholic Commentary on Sacred Scripture
d.	died
ESV	English Standard Version
fig.	figure
Lectionary	*The Lectionary for Mass* (1998/2002 USA edition)
NABRE	New American Bible Revised Edition
NIV	New International Version
NRSV	New Revised Standard Version
NT	New Testament
OT	Old Testament
RSV-2CE	Revised Standard Version, Second Catholic Edition (2006)

Books of the Old Testament

Gen	Genesis	1 Kings	1 Kings	Ps(s)	Psalms
Exod	Exodus	2 Kings	2 Kings	Prov	Proverbs
Lev	Leviticus	1 Chron	1 Chronicles	Eccles	Ecclesiastes
Num	Numbers	2 Chron	2 Chronicles	Song	Song of Songs
Deut	Deuteronomy	Ezra	Ezra	Wis	Wisdom of Solomon
Josh	Joshua	Neh	Nehemiah		
Judg	Judges	Tob	Tobit	Sir	Sirach
Ruth	Ruth	Jdt	Judith	Isa	Isaiah
1 Sam	1 Samuel	Esther	Esther	Jer	Jeremiah
2 Sam	2 Samuel	Job	Job	Lam	Lamentations

Bar	Baruch	Obad	Obadiah	Hag	Haggai
Ezek	Ezekiel	Jon	Jonah	Zech	Zechariah
Dan	Daniel	Mic	Micah	Mal	Malachi
Hosea	Hosea	Nah	Nahum	1 Macc	1 Maccabees
Joel	Joel	Hab	Habakkuk	2 Macc	2 Maccabees
Amos	Amos	Zeph	Zephaniah		

Books of the New Testament

Matt	Matthew	Eph	Ephesians	Heb	Hebrews
Mark	Mark	Phil	Philippians	James	James
Luke	Luke	Col	Colossians	1 Pet	1 Peter
John	John	1 Thess	1 Thessalonians	2 Pet	2 Peter
Acts	Acts	2 Thess	2 Thessalonians	1 John	1 John
Rom	Romans	1 Tim	1 Timothy	2 John	2 John
1 Cor	1 Corinthians	2 Tim	2 Timothy	3 John	3 John
2 Cor	2 Corinthians	Titus	Titus	Jude	Jude
Gal	Galatians	Philem	Philemon	Rev	Revelation

Bibliographic Note

The following frequently cited works are cited in full on first occurrence in the book and in shortened form thereafter. Other sources are cited in full on first occurrence in each chapter.

Alter, Robert. "Ezekiel." In *The Hebrew Bible*, vol. 2, *Prophets*, 1047–197. New York: Norton, 2019.

Block, Daniel I. *The Book of Ezekiel: Chapters 1–24*. New International Commentary on the Old Testament. Grand Rapids: Eerdmans, 1997.

———. *The Book of Ezekiel: Chapters 25–48*. New International Commentary on the Old Testament. Grand Rapids: Eerdmans, 1998.

Eisemann, Moshe. *Yechezkel/Ezekiel: A New Translation with a Commentary Anthologized from Talmudic, Midrashic, and Rabbinic Sources*. 3 vols. New York: Mesorah Publications, 1977, 1979, 1988.

Greenberg, Moshe. *Ezekiel 1–20*. Anchor Bible 22. New York: Doubleday, 1983.

———. *Ezekiel 21–37*. Anchor Bible 22A. New York: Doubleday, 1997.

Joyce, Paul M. *Ezekiel: A Commentary*. Library of Hebrew Bible/Old Testament Studies 482. New York: T&T Clark, 2007.

Levey, Samson H., trans. *The Targum of Ezekiel*. Aramaic Bible 13. Wilmington, DE: Michael Glazier, 1987.

Milgrom, Jacob, and Daniel I. Block. *Ezekiel's Hope: A Commentary on Ezekiel 38–48*. Eugene, OR: Cascade Books, 2012.

Rosenberg, A. J., trans. *The Book of Ezekiel*, vol. 1. Mikraoth Gedoloth. New York: Judaica Press, 1991.

———. *The Book of Ezekiel*, vol. 2. Mikraoth Gedoloth. New York: Judaica Press, 2000.

Introduction to Ezekiel

Ezekiel is a wonderful, challenging, and perplexing book. There is no disguising the fact that the prophet Ezekiel does extreme things at the prompting of the Lord and speaks severe words to a people gripped by sin and rebellion. Some readers are put off by the unrelenting words of judgment or scandalized by the explicit sexual imagery used to describe the unfaithfulness of God's people. In this book we encounter "the vivid, surreal, and sometimes shocking character of his visions and extended †allegories."[1] But Ezekiel is also a glorious book, brimming with hope and the promise of God's action through his Word and Spirit. The topography of Ezekiel is marked by deep, dark valleys but also illuminated by bright, soaring peaks. For the adventurous reader, ready to traverse both peaks and valleys, Ezekiel offers a breathtaking landscape to explore. Above all, Ezekiel confronts us with the power of God's word: a word that spoke to the people of Ezekiel's time and continues to speak to us today.

Authorship

As the book opens, we are told that "the word of the LORD came to Ezekiel the priest, the son of Buzi, in the land of the †Chaldeans by the river Chebar; and the hand of the LORD was upon him there" (1:3). Ezekiel the prophet, who is also a priest, is identified as the author of the book that bears his name.[2] Ezekiel's name means "God strengthens" or "may God strengthen." Apart from just two verses (1:2–3), the entire book is spoken in the first person singular, in the voice of Ezekiel himself.

1. John Bergsma and Brant Pitre, "Ezekiel," in *A Catholic Introduction to the Bible*, vol. 1, *The Old Testament* (San Francisco: Ignatius, 2018), 837.
2. The name "Ezekiel" appears only once more in the book, when the Lord God tells the people, "Thus shall Ezekiel be to you a sign" (Ezek 24:24).

Until the early twentieth century, readers and scholars alike assumed that the author of this book was the prophet Ezekiel, a priest from the people of Israel who lived among the exiles in Babylon at the beginning of the sixth century BC. However, in the early twentieth century, scholars began to challenge Ezekiel's authorship of the book, arguing for multiple authors and editors and for a complex process of composition that may have taken several centuries to complete. More recently, the scholarly trend has returned to seeing the prophet Ezekiel himself as the primary author of the book, as the one who *spoke* these words to the people and who gathered them and *wrote* them down, even if later editors, followers of Ezekiel, may have had a hand in collecting and organizing these †oracles to produce the book of Ezekiel as we now have it.[3]

We cannot determine with certainty whether Ezekiel is (or is not) the sole or main source of all the sayings in the book, but the unity of style and content throughout the book gives good grounds for receiving it as the product of this remarkable sixth-century BC prophet. Throughout this commentary, we will operate with the assumption that Ezekiel is the author of the prophecies and sayings in the book that bears his name.

Historical Context

The prophet Ezekiel carried out his ministry in one of the darkest and most difficult periods in the history of Israel. The powerful empire of Assyria had conquered and carried off into exile the northern kingdom of Israel (722 BC) and left the southern kingdom of Judah weakened and vulnerable. In the late seventh century BC, the kingdom of Judah and its capital at Jerusalem were threatened by a new power, the Neo-Babylonian kingdom and its powerful general and king, Nebuchadnezzar.[4] The tiny kingdom of Judah was caught between two competing powers—Egypt and Babylon—wavering between an alliance with one and an alliance with the other. It was in this period that the prophet Jeremiah, an older contemporary of Ezekiel, began to prophesy challenging words to the kings and nobles in Jerusalem.

Around 609 BC, Pharaoh Neco of Egypt placed Jehoiakim, a son of Josiah, on the throne of Judah. But this alliance with Egypt did not last long. Nebuchadnezzar asserted his influence in Palestine, and Jehoiakim came over to

---

3. For a summary of scholarly trends over the past century regarding the authorship of Ezekiel, see Paul M. Joyce, *Ezekiel: A Commentary*, Library of Hebrew Bible/Old Testament Studies 482 (New York: T&T Clark, 2007), 7–16. The Greek translation of Ezekiel, probably made in the second century BC, differs at points from the Hebrew version we possess. Modern translations of Ezekiel are normally made from the Hebrew text, but the Greek text is regularly consulted for understanding obscure passages. See Joyce, *Ezekiel*, 44–49, for a thorough discussion of the textual history of Ezekiel.

4. The name of this great general and king appears in two forms in the Hebrew Bible, "Nebuchadnezzar" and "Nebuchadrezzar." The latter spelling is less common and appears only in Jeremiah and Ezekiel; the former spelling is more common and is the usual way of referring to him. Except in scriptural quotations, this commentary adopts the form "Nebuchadnezzar."

his side (ca. 605 BC) and "became his servant three years" (2 Kings 24:1). The book of Daniel adds that this change of allegiance happened because Nebuchadnezzar besieged Jerusalem and forced Jehoiakim to surrender (Dan 1:1–7). The result was that Daniel and other young men of Judah were sent into exile into Babylon. According to the book of Daniel, this was a first deportation of exiles to Babylon.

Three years later, however, Jehoiakim rebelled against Nebuchadnezzar and set the stage for a further siege against the city of Jerusalem in 597 BC (2 Kings 24:1–2). Jehoiakim himself died before the siege occurred, but his eighteen-year-old son Jehoiachin was forced to surrender to the Babylonians and was taken by Nebuchadnezzar into exile along with a majority of the leading people of Judah. Ezekiel was among these exiles taken to Babylon in 597 BC. He would spend the rest of his life in exile, prophesying to the people both before and after the destruction of Jerusalem in 586. This makes Ezekiel's prophetic ministry unique. Unlike the other prophets from Israel, he did all of his prophesying in a foreign land (in Babylon, modern-day Iraq).

When Nebuchadnezzar conquered Jerusalem in 597, he appointed a new king, Zedekiah, to rule over Judah. But Zedekiah, too, made the fateful choice to rebel against Babylon (ca. 589 BC), and thus he set in motion the final act of Babylon's triumph over Jerusalem. In 587, Jerusalem was besieged, and after eighteen months, when the city fell, Nebuchadnezzar decided to burn the temple and destroy the city and its fortifications. A third and final deportation occurred, with more people taken into exile in Babylon, and the doom prophesied by both Jeremiah and Ezekiel came to pass: Judah and Jerusalem were in ruins, and many of its people were either slain or in exile.

Ezekiel began prophesying in 593 and continued for over twenty years (the last recorded prophecy is dated to 571). Before Jerusalem was captured and destroyed, the message of Ezekiel thundered with words of judgment. After the fall of the great city in 586, his message turned sharply toward a promise of restoration. It is against the backdrop of this tragic episode in Israel's history that we read and encounter the words of Ezekiel.

Genre

The predominant genre of the book of Ezekiel is the prophetic †oracle.[5] An oracle is a message spoken by a prophet on God's behalf or in God's name, often framed by an introductory phrase such as "thus says the LORD." The majority of the oracles are given in prose, but Ezekiel also delivers powerful laments in poetic format (for example, in chaps. 19 and 28).

---

5. For the various genres found in the book of Ezekiel, see Daniel I. Block, *The Book of Ezekiel: Chapters 1–24*, New International Commentary on the Old Testament (Grand Rapids: Eerdmans, 1997), 15–17.

Within the general category of prophetic oracle, Ezekiel uses diverse means to convey his message. The book opens with a †call-narrative whereby Ezekiel receives his commission to speak the word of the Lord (1:1–3:27). The call-narrative is common to several of the prophets (see, e.g., Isa 6:1–13; Jer 1:1–10). Like other prophets, Ezekiel also recounts *visions* that he sees as means of conveying God's word. He is considered to be "the most visually descriptive and vision-oriented of the prophets."[6] Ezekiel receives several major visions in the book: the vision of the †divine chariot (the divine presence) in Babylon (1:4–28); the vision of the divine chariot leaving Jerusalem (chaps. 8–11); the vision of the dry bones (37:1–14); and the vision of the new temple and the return of the divine presence to the temple (chaps. 40–44).

Ezekiel makes ample use of *parables* (chaps. 16 and 23) and *allegories* (31:1–9), to such an extent that he is mocked by his fellow exiles for being "a maker of allegories" (20:49). But Ezekiel does not just speak words; he is instructed by God to perform *symbolic actions* that embody God's message for the people. "Sign actions in Ezekiel are really only alternate forms of the prophetic word."[7] For example, he is called to eat a scroll (3:1–3); he is tied up with cords (3:24); he lies upon his left side for 390 days and upon his right side for 40 more (4:4–6); he shaves his head and beard and burns the stubble (5:1–2); and he tunnels through a wall to depict the flight of the king by night (12:1–12).

The most common literary form in Ezekiel is the oracle of judgment. In a judgment oracle, the prophet speaks in the Lord's own voice to chastise or rebuke the people for their sin and unfaithfulness to God. The Lord's opening message to Ezekiel communicates this: "I send you to them; and you shall say to them, 'Thus says the Lord GOD.' . . . And you shall speak my words to them, whether they hear or refuse to hear" (2:4, 7). Time and again Ezekiel is called to announce the Lord's judgment against his own people and against the surrounding nations. But the oracle of judgment is not the final word. Ezekiel also speaks oracles of salvation through which the Lord God promises restoration, the return to the land of Israel, and the renewal of the †covenant.

Structure and Literary Features

Structure

While Ezekiel displays a great variety of themes and topics, the book is divided into two main parts. The first part (chaps. 1–33) focuses on judgment and the *departure* of the presence of the Lord away from Israel and Jerusalem. The

---

6. Ronald E. Clements, *Ezekiel*, Westminster Bible Companion (Louisville: Westminster John Knox, 1996), 13.

7. Ralph W. Klein, *Ezekiel: The Prophet and His Message* (Columbia: University of South Carolina Press, 1988), 35.

second part (chaps. 34–48) emphasizes restoration and renewal, revealed by the *return* of the presence of the Lord to the land and city. Prophecies of judgment and doom predominate before the fall of the city; prophecies of restoration and renewal predominate afterward.[8] The movement from judgment to restoration and the promise of salvation are common to many of the prophets. The hinge between the two main parts is the siege and sacking of the city of Jerusalem (chaps. 24, 33).

It is critical that we as readers recognize these two "movements" of the Lord's action. During the season of judgment, Ezekiel sees visions of the presence of the Lord—the divine chariot—rising up from the city and departing from its midst (10:1–19; 11:22–25). During the time of restoration, Ezekiel witnesses the return of that same divine chariot taking up its abode in the new temple (43:1–7). It is no coincidence that the final line of the book reads, "The LORD is there" (48:35). God's absence and presence is the thread that runs through the book of Ezekiel and serves as the primary structural theme around which Ezekiel organizes his oracles.

The structural feature unique to Ezekiel among the prophets is the dating of many of his oracles. In all, there are fourteen occasions when Ezekiel marks a given prophecy with a precise date (see "Dates of Prophetic Oracles in Ezekiel," p. 31).[9] Generally, they follow one another in chronological order, beginning in 593 BC and ending at 571 BC, though three of the dates are given out of temporal sequence (26:1; 29:17; 33:21), presumably to serve Ezekiel's thematic purposes. From the start of his ministry Ezekiel is painfully aware that he will not be believed or understood, and so he is careful to record and document his prophetic words, so that when the words he speaks come to pass the people will know "that there has been a prophet among them" (2:5; 33:33).

Literary Features

Ezekiel makes use of literary techniques to communicate his message vibrantly and memorably. The first is the practice of restating and reusing earlier themes in later contexts. This "revisiting" serves to underline a given theme but also allows Ezekiel to show how an earlier prophetic word is fulfilled in a later one. For example, Ezekiel is called to be a watchman as part of his initial calling (3:16–21), but this call is revisited when the fall of Jerusalem is at hand (33:1–9), indicating that Ezekiel in fact has been faithful as a watchman in warning the

---

8. There is not a strict division between these two types of prophetic oracles. There are short oracles of salvation and renewal that appear in the first part (11:14–20; 16:59–63; 17:22–24; 20:40–42) and brief oracles of judgment that appear in the second part (34:1–10; 35:1–9; 44:4–8).

9. For the dated oracles, see Ezek 1:2–3; 3:16; 8:1; 20:1; 24:1; 26:1; 29:1; 29:17; 30:20; 31:1; 32:1; 32:17; 33:21; 40:1. The very first date given in the book (in 1:1) is not included in these dated oracles because this date is unique and presents special issues for interpretation (see the commentary on Ezek 1:1).

people of the judgment that was coming. A second example is the declaration (in 18:1–32) that each person will die for his or her own sins, but that the Lord greatly desires that each one should repent and live. This truth is revisited and renewed just at the moment when judgment is falling (33:10–20). Strikingly, the theme of receiving a new heart and a new spirit appears three times in the book. In the first, it stands as a brief promise in the midst of impending judgment (11:19–20); then the people are told to go and get for themselves a new heart and a new spirit (18:31); and finally in a glorious climax, the Lord promises that he will himself provide this new heart and spirit for the people of God (36:24–30).

Ezekiel also strategically repeats ideas to drive his message home and to alert the reader what to expect, and he employs formulas and titles throughout the book that he repeats again and again. Among the most common are the following:

- "thus says the Lord GOD" (125 times)[10]
- "declares the Lord GOD" (85 times)
- "son of man" (93 times)
- "they will know that I am the LORD" (62 times)
- "the word of the LORD came to me" (50 times)
- "for the sake of my name" (7 times)
- "the hand of the LORD was upon me" (7 times)

Through both repetition and revisiting of key themes, Ezekiel brings focus to his diverse oracles, helping readers to keep hold of the overall unity of his message as it unfolds over time.

Theological Themes

1. God-Centered

The book of Ezekiel is intensely focused on God and his sovereign action. Paul Joyce calls this quality "a radical theocentricity that is of an order difficult to parallel anywhere in the Hebrew Bible."[11] What does this mean? The prophet Ezekiel is called to proclaim primarily what *God is going to do*—the judgment that he will bring and the restoration that will follow. Further, the Lord repeatedly

---

10. The title "the Lord GOD" is literally "the Lord †YHWH." The name "YHWH" (often vocalized as "Yahweh") is the proper name of the God of Israel. Traditionally, this name is not pronounced, and in its place the title "Lord" (Hebrew *Adonai*) is spoken. English Bibles commonly put the name "LORD" in small capital letters to indicate that the divine name is being used. In the phrase "the Lord YHWH," however, to avoid saying "the Lord LORD," the word "GOD" is used instead but placed in small capital letters to indicate that this, too, represents the divine name, YHWH.

11. Joyce, *Ezekiel*, 27.

says that he is acting "for the sake of my name" and for "my glory." Certainly, Ezekiel calls the people to hear God's word, to repent, and to follow the ways of the Lord. But the emphasis in this long book is on God, on his glory, and on his initiative to judge, purify, and redeem his people.

2. The Presence of the Lord

From the opening chapter right up to the final verse, Ezekiel draws our attention to the presence of the Lord among his people. This presence is specially signified by the divine chariot that Ezekiel sees in a vision. It first appears when God manifests his presence to Ezekiel in the midst of his exile in Babylon (chap. 1). Then as God judges his people, he indicates his displeasure by withdrawing his presence from the temple and the city of Jerusalem; he withdraws his comfort, protection, and power in the face of persistent disobedience (chaps. 10–11). But this is reversed in the season of restoration: the glorious presence of God returns to the temple (chap. 43). The Lord God does not just bless his people from a distance; he lives among them, even in their exile, and his presence is the source of their life.

3. Judgment and the Call to Repentance

The theme of judgment—of God correcting and chastising his own people—looms large in Ezekiel. Readers need to be prepared: "The first twenty-four chapters of the book of Ezekiel contain one of the most sustained and vehement declarations of judgment to be found anywhere in the prophetic literature of the Hebrew Bible."[12] Drawing on imagery from J. R. R. Tolkien's *The Hobbit*, we could say that this long trek through the oracles of judgment is like the journey through Mirkwood, the dense, dark, seemingly endless forest that makes travelers long for light. There are moments of hope and promise along the way, like shafts of light that break through a thick forest, but the glorious promises of restoration and renewal come only toward the end.

Accompanying the theme of judgment is the call to repentance: to turn away from idolatry and wickedness and to turn back to the Lord and to the following of his commandments. Though the invitation to repentance in Ezekiel is infrequent, it is nonetheless clear and powerful, revealing the heart of the Lord God and his desire that his people "turn, and live" (18:32).

4. Individual and Corporate Responsibility

One of the best-known themes in Ezekiel, declared by the Lord God, is the insistence that a person will be judged only on the basis of his or her own actions,

12. Joyce, *Ezekiel*, 17.

not those of another. The Lord speaks through Ezekiel in the starkest of terms: if someone repents from wickedness and turns to the Lord, that person will live. But if that person then turns away from following the Lord, that person will die (not immediate physical death, but the death of separation from the Lord's blessing). At the same time, there is a strong sense of corporate identity in Ezekiel. The Lord chastises his entire people, and he promises to restore them *as a people*. While no one will suffer condemnation from the Lord for the sins of another, people may experience the *consequences* of another's sin because they are part of a family. In sum, there is a firm commitment to personal responsibility in Ezekiel but an equally strong sense of corporate identification with the people of God.

5. The Word and the Spirit

God's word and his Spirit appear prominently in Ezekiel; they are the two main expressions of divine activity in the book. God's word and Spirit act first of all upon Ezekiel himself. The "word" of the Lord comes to Ezekiel time and again, and he must "eat" this word, digest it, and then speak the word. In the same way, the Spirit comes upon Ezekiel, causing him to rise and stand before the Lord, giving him courage and strength, and inspiring him to speak and act.[13] But God's word and Spirit then move out to impact his people. His word brings both judgment and life. God's Spirit comes to enter the heart and causes the people of God to walk in godly ways. In these instances, Ezekiel is clearly referring to *God's* Spirit, a spirit that comes *from* God. Given the fuller revelation of the Spirit of God (the Holy Spirit) in the New Testament, we are able to perceive here a reference to the person of the Spirit active in Ezekiel's life and prophetic ministry. The Church Father St. Irenaeus (d. ca. 200) speaks of the Word and Spirit of God as the "two hands of God."[14] This description wonderfully applies to the book of Ezekiel: God acts and moves throughout the book through his two hands, his word and Spirit.

6. Visions and Divine Inspiration

Perhaps more than any other prophet, Ezekiel is directly impacted by the Spirit of God. The Spirit enters into Ezekiel and speaks personally to him (2:2; 3:24) and reveals visions before his eyes (8:3; 11:24). He is the charismatic prophet par excellence of the Old Testament. The Spirit's activity that we witness in Ezekiel is enlarged and expanded in the New Testament: the Spirit pours out a variety of gifts on the faithful, inspires the prophets, and presents visions of

---

13. There are fifty-two references to "spirit" in Ezekiel, a frequency matched only by Isaiah in the Old Testament. Block, *Ezekiel: Chapters 1–24*, 50, identifies Ezekiel as "the prophet of the Spirit." For a study of the Spirit in Ezekiel, see James Robson, *Word and Spirit in Ezekiel* (New York: T&T Clark, 2006).

14. For the Son and Spirit as the two hands of God, see Irenaeus, *Against Heresies* 4.pref.4; 5.28.4.

things to come. This sovereign and charismatic activity of the Spirit, present in the Church through the ages, challenges us to understand how the divine Spirit works through human beings in the inspiration of Scripture and in the ongoing manifestations of the Spirit in the life of the Church.[15]

7. Return from Exile, Restoration, Renewal of the Covenant, and the Call to Holiness

This final theme is really the heart of the message of the book. We might ask: What is the purpose of God's sovereign action, his judgments, and his *presence* among his people? Why are his word and Spirit acting in the prophet and in the people? His aim is to bring his people back into relationship with their God, to restore them to their land, to renew the covenant of friendship, to lead them in the path of holiness, and to enable God to dwell among them forever. In other words, Ezekiel reveals God's ultimate purpose for his people: to bring his people back to himself in a covenant of love in which God and his people dwell together forever. This is the main message of Ezekiel as well as the main message of the Bible (see Rev 21:3–4).

Relationship to Other Books of the Bible

1. The Old Testament

Ezekiel never quotes any books of the Old Testament directly, but he was clearly well versed in the †Pentateuch and anchors his message in the Law and in the prophets who came before him. Ezekiel shows clear links to Genesis, especially to the opening chapters. The pattern of the dry bones coming together and then receiving the "breath" of God (Ezek 37) follows the pattern of God forming and breathing life into Adam (Gen 2:7). The rivers that flow through the renewed land of Israel (Ezek 47) mirror the rivers found in the garden (Gen 2:10–14). Ezekiel refers to "Eden" five times, calling it the "garden of God." And he refers by name to some of the great figures from Genesis: Noah, Abraham, Jacob, and Levi.

Ezekiel's connection to Israel's early history is prominent in the book. At several points he refers to Israel's exodus from Egypt. He also speaks about the return from exile, the renewal of the covenant, the design of the temple, and the reapportioning of the land to the twelve tribes. Because of the strong thematic links to this history of deliverance, Ezekiel is sometimes identified as a new or second Moses.[16] In particular, Ezekiel shows a special dependence

---

15. See Vatican II's *Constitution on Divine Revelation* (*Dei Verbum*), 7–11, for how the Spirit of God works through human agents to produce a divinely †inspired word in Sacred Scripture and Sacred Tradition.

16. "All these parallels serve to invest Ezekiel with the authority of a prophet who stands as Moses' worthy successor." Bergsma and Pitre, "Ezekiel," 842.

on the †covenant blessings and curses found in Lev 26 and Deut 28–30. It is almost as if Ezekiel had these passages open before his eyes and was poring over them as he was listening to God's voice and formulating his message to the people. Ezekiel frames the coming judgment and redemption in the language of Leviticus and Deuteronomy.

Finally, Ezekiel shows many connections to his older contemporary, Jeremiah. As a young man, Ezekiel would probably have heard Jeremiah prophesying in Jerusalem during the reign of Jehoiakim. He brought with him into exile his memory of those words. As we shall see, these two great prophets—while each is distinctive—have a great deal in common. Ezekiel takes up and develops many of the themes that characterize the message of Jeremiah.

2. The New Testament

Though Ezekiel is never named or directly quoted in the New Testament, his influence is clear, especially in the †Johannine books. The clearest example is Jesus as the Good Shepherd in John 10, which shows close verbal links to the great shepherd passage from Ezek 34. The New Testament's language of resurrection (e.g., Matt 27:52; Rev 11:11) appears dependent on the dry bones passage in Ezek 37.

Ezekiel's strongest connection to the New Testament is to the book of Revelation: the four living creatures in Rev 4 build on the four living creatures (†cherubim) in Ezek 1; both Ezekiel and John are called to take and "eat" the scroll of God's judgments (Ezek 3; Rev 10); the great and final battle in Rev 20:7–10 makes explicit reference to Gog and Magog, which appear elsewhere only in Ezek 38–39. In short, the †apocalyptic imagery of Revelation draws broadly on Ezekiel.

3. Traditional Jewish Literature

Ezekiel also had an important influence upon traditional Jewish texts that are not part of the biblical †canon. For example, themes and texts from Ezekiel have a place of prominence in the †Dead Sea Scrolls. The †*Targum of Ezekiel*, an †Aramaic translation made in the early centuries after Christ, reveals how Ezekiel was understood by the early †rabbinic Jewish community. We will draw on traditional Jewish interpretation not only for its insights into the text of Ezekiel but also to recognize similarities and differences with respect to traditional Christian interpretation.

Relevance for Christian Life Today

How can a book of prophecies written more than 2,500 years ago, addressed specifically to the people of Israel, be relevant for Christian life today? This can happen only because the Holy Spirit, who inspired Ezekiel to speak and write these words, is the same Spirit that enables these ancient words to speak to us—and to be alive for us—today.

1. A God Who Acts

Ezekiel presents a God who is intensely active and engaged, both among the people of Israel and in the wider world. This is not a †Deist God who sits back and watches from a distance but a God who speaks, who intervenes, and who is deeply concerned for the holiness of his people. This God is a *shepherd* who knows the needs of his flock and is coming to deliver them. Ezekiel communicates powerfully to us today that we have a God who knows us and is involved with our lives.

2. A God Who Chastens, Renews, and Redeems

Ezekiel also shows us a God who has a plan and purpose. He is not just "on call" to make us feel good or to make things go smoothly in our lives. This is a God who has called a people into a covenant of peace and love with himself, and he holds that people to the demands of this high calling. When they fall short, he is ready to chasten, to purify, and to allow them to experience the bitter fruits of their own sin. But his eventual aim is to renew, redeem, and restore—no matter how bad things have become. To those who say, "Our hope is lost" (37:11), God answers with †grace and life to bring even dry bones back from the grave.

3. God's Call to Be a Watchman for the People

Ezekiel himself is a model for us today of the person who hears God's word and speaks that word. Just as Ezekiel was called to be a watchman for the people of Israel, so we are called to be active in speaking God's word to the people of our generation. The same God continues to call people to conversion and repentance today. We, too, are called—in a way suited to our vocation—to watch for the Lord, to be attentive to his working, and to alert the people of our day to his coming.

4. A God Who Changes Us from Within

In Ezekiel, the Lord God acts for the glory of his own name, but his ultimate *purpose* is to renew the hearts of his people and to make them a dwelling place for himself. The goal is the dwelling of God among his people in peace. Ezekiel invites the people of God not just to outwardly obey the commandments but to receive a new heart and a new spirit. This promise of a new heart and new spirit is fulfilled in Christ and through the gift of the Holy Spirit. God has come to dwell in us, to change us, and to befriend us. "Behold, the dwelling of God is with men. He will dwell with them, and they shall be his people, and God himself will be with them" (Rev 21:3).

Outline of Ezekiel

Part 1: Judgment upon Israel, Jerusalem, and the Nations: The Presence
of the Lord Departs (chaps. 1–33)
  A. Ezekiel's Vision of the Divine Presence (chap. 1)
  B. The Call of Ezekiel (chaps. 2–3)
  C. Prophecies against Israel and Jerusalem (chaps. 4–24)
    1. Judgment on the City and the Land (chaps. 4–7)
    2. Judgment on the Temple and the Departure of the Lord's
       Presence (chaps. 8–11)
    3. Oracles and Parables of Judgment against the City and the
       Land (chaps. 12–23)
    4. The End Is at Hand (chap. 24)
  D. Prophecies against the Nations (chaps. 25–32)
    1. The Nations and the City of Tyre (chaps. 25–28)
    2. Egypt (chaps. 29–32)
  E. God's Judgment against Israel Completed: The Fall of Jerusalem
    (chap. 33)[1]
Part 2: Restoration of Israel and Renewal of the Covenant and Temple: The
Presence of the Lord Returns (chaps. 34–48)
  A. Prophecies of Restoration and Renewal of the Covenant (chaps.
    34–37)
    1. The Lord God Comes to Shepherd His People (chap. 34)
    2. A New Heart and a New Spirit (chaps. 35–36)
    3. The Covenant of Peace Renewed (chap. 37)

---

1. Chapter 33 is difficult to place in the overall structure because it acts as a bridge between the two main sections of the book. Along with chap. 24, it brings a conclusion to the long series of judgment oracles and announces the fall of Jerusalem to the Babylonians, but it also opens the door to a new season of blessing and restoration in which the Lord God offers oracles of consolation and return to the land following the fall of the great city.

Dates of Prophetic Oracles in Ezekiel

Biblical Reference in Ezekiel[a]	Year/Month/Day (Ezekiel's dating)	Western Calendar (BC)	Occasion
1:2–3	5th/4th/5th	July 31, 593	Opening vision
3:16	5th /4th /12th	Aug 7, 593	Opening vision (continued)
8:1	6th /6th /5th	Sept 18, 592	Vision of temple abominations
20:1	7th /5th /10th	Aug 14, 591	Inquiry of elders
24:1	9th /10th /10th	Jan 5, 587 (588)	Siege of Jerusalem begins
26:1	11th /9th(?)/1st	Feb–April 586 (587)	Oracle against Tyre
29:1	10th /10th /12th	Jan 7, 587	Oracle against Egypt
29:17	27th /1st /1st	April 26, 571	Egypt and Tyre
30:20	11th /1st /7th	April 29, 587	Oracle against Egypt
31:1	11th /3rd /1st	June 21, 587	Parable against Pharaoh
32:1	12th /12th /1st	March 3, 585	Dirge for Pharaoh, Egypt
32:17	12th / 12th (1st?) /15th	March 18, 585	Lament over Pharaoh
33:21	12th /10th /5th	Jan 8, 585	News of Jerusalem's fall
40:1	25th /1st /10th	April 28, 573	Second temple vision

a. For a concise table of the dates of Ezekiel's prophecies, see Moshe Greenberg, *Ezekiel 1–20*, Anchor Bible 22 (New York: Doubleday, 1983), 8; "Introduction to Ezekiel," in *ESV Study Bible* (Wheaton: Crossway, 2008), 1496.

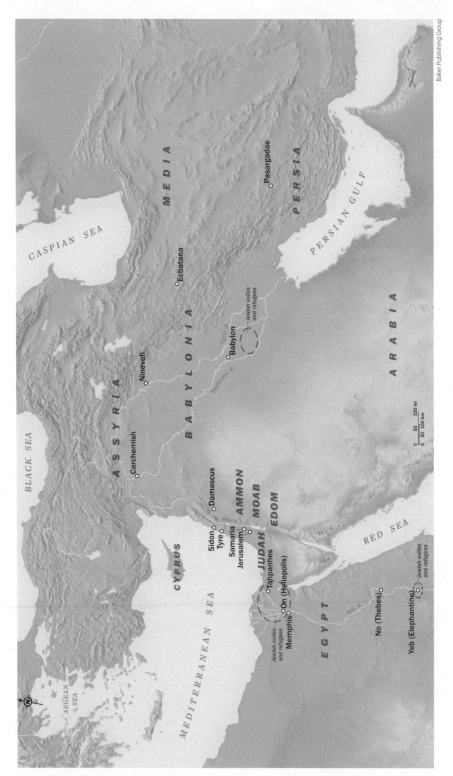

Figure 1. The ancient world of Ezekiel's day

Ezekiel's Vision of the Divine Presence

Ezekiel 1:1–28

The opening three chapters serve as the introduction to the book of Ezekiel and present the main characters in the work: the Lord God, Ezekiel the prophet, and the rebellious people of Israel to whom Ezekiel is being sent.

Chapter 1 throws us in at the deep end. One of the great visions of the Bible opens before our eyes. From his place of exile in Babylon, Ezekiel suddenly beholds a great storm and the emergence of the presence of God in the form of a moving chariot guided by the glorious †cherubim. Even more stunningly, Ezekiel sees something of the glorious divine presence—in the likeness of a human being—seated on a throne above the chariot. As the voice of this figure begins to speak, Ezekiel casts himself down in humility and wonder.

The Word of the Lord Comes to Ezekiel (1:1–3)

¹In the thirtieth year, in the fourth month, on the fifth day of the month, as I was among the exiles by the river Chebar, the heavens were opened, and I saw visions of God. ²On the fifth day of the month (it was the fifth year of the exile of King Jehoiachin), ³the word of the LORD came to Ezekiel the priest, the son of Buzi, in the land of the Chaldeans by the river Chebar; and the hand of the LORD was upon him there.

OT: Num 4:2–3; 1 Sam 15:10; 2 Kings 24:6–8; Ps 137:1; Jer 1:2; Hosea 1:1
NT: Matt 3:16; Mark 1:10; Luke 1:66; Acts 11:21; Rev 4:1
Catechism: God's call on the prophets, 702; the prophetic office of the people of God, 785, 904–7

The opening verses identify the person, the time, and the place where Ezekiel's 1:1–3 visions occurred. God acts *in history*: his word breaks into human events and

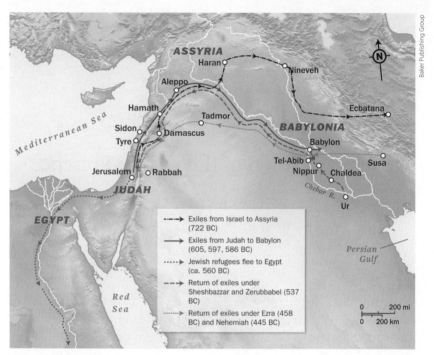

Figure 2. Israel in exile

influences their outcome. Ezekiel is situated right **among the exiles . . . in the land of the †Chaldeans** (that is, the Babylonians). The **river Chebar** is probably located near the ancient Sumerian city of Nippur, southeast of Babylon (see Ps 137:1 for the exiles gathering by the rivers of Babylon).

The date of this opening vision is given in two forms. **The fifth day** in **the fourth month** in **the fifth year** of Jehoiachin's exile works out to July 31, 593 BC. But to what does **the thirtieth year** refer (v. 1)? To compute this date, the Jewish rabbis counted backward thirty years, concluding that Ezekiel received his call in "the thirtieth year" from the beginning of Josiah's reform (see 2 Kings 22:3–13).[1] Another possibility is that it refers to Ezekiel's age (*his* thirtieth year). Ezekiel is identified as a **priest**, and priestly service began at age thirty and continued until age fifty (see Num 4:2–3). If the thirtieth year refers to Ezekiel's age, then the very year he would have begun his *priestly* service in Jerusalem is instead the year he begins his *prophetic* career as an exile in Babylon.[2] Whatever the precise meaning of "thirtieth year," the setting

1. Moshe Eisemann, *Yechezkel/Ezekiel: A New Translation with a Commentary Anthologized from Talmudic, Midrashic, and Rabbinic Sources*, 3 vols. (New York: Mesorah Publications, 1977, 1979, 1988), 72.

2. If the reference to the thirtieth year applies to Ezekiel's age, then the final vision of the book (Ezek 40:1) would have taken place in Ezekiel's fiftieth year, the year that priests were required to retire from active service (Num 4:2–3). See "Introduction to Ezekiel," in *ESV Study Bible* (Wheaton: Crossway, 2008), 1495.

is clear: in the year 593 BC Ezekiel the priest, exiled in the land of Babylon, encounters the Lord God.

This prophetic event is captured in two complementary ways: by *seeing* and by *hearing*. **The heavens were opened** and Ezekiel **saw visions of God**. By spiritual sight Ezekiel sees visions that come from above, from God. But in addition, **the word of the Lord came to Ezekiel** (see Jer 1:2; Hosea 1:1 for parallels). He hears the voice of God. This provides the pattern for the rest of the book: revelation comes to Ezekiel through both seeing and hearing.

We know that Ezekiel is a prophet of God, but in this opening section he is identified also as a priest. This is important for what follows: Ezekiel's concern for the temple and the priestly worship of God is a crucial aspect of his message. Throughout the book he places a notable emphasis on priestly purity among the people of God.

Finally, we are told that **the hand of the Lord was upon him there**, a phrase that appears seven times in the book. Not only did God's *word* come to Ezekiel but the Lord's *hand* pressed heavily upon him. This metaphor indicates that Ezekiel is a man held firmly by God's hand and under his authority.

In the Light of Christ (1:1–3)

Some of the †Church Fathers see a similarity between Ezekiel's opening vision and the baptism of Jesus in the Jordan. Origen of Alexandria (d. 254) speaks of Ezekiel as "a †type of Christ" for the following reasons: both men are thirty years old when they begin their ministries, both experience a vision by a river, and both see the heavens opened and hear the word of the Lord.[3] St. Jerome (d. 420) adds the descent of the Spirit on both figures: just as the Spirit comes upon Ezekiel to enable him to fulfill his prophetic mission (Ezek 2:2), so the Spirit descends upon Jesus for the fulfillment of his †messianic call.[4]

There are also important parallels between Ezekiel's opening vision and the book of Revelation. In Revelation, John is praying on the Lord's Day, and suddenly a door opens into heaven and he is called to come up and see (1:10; 4:1). Like Ezekiel, John receives this revelation through both what he *sees* and what he *hears*. Both Ezekiel and John then proceed to convey in visions a series of severe judgments followed by a picture of a new temple and a new creation in which God will dwell with his people forever. John follows closely in the footsteps of Ezekiel and brings Ezekiel's message to its completion in Christ.

---

3. Origen, *Homily* 1.4, in *Homilies 1–14 on Ezekiel*, trans. Thomas P. Scheck, ACW 62 (New York: Newman, 2010), 32–33.

4. Jerome, *Homilies on Mark* 75 (ACCS 13:2).

The Vision of the Divine Chariot Throne (1:4–28)

---

[4]As I looked, behold, a stormy wind came out of the north, and a great cloud, with brightness round about it, and fire flashing forth continually, and in the midst of the fire, as it were gleaming bronze. [5]And from the midst of it came the likeness of four living creatures. And this was their appearance: they had the form of men, [6]but each had four faces, and each of them had four wings. [7]Their legs were straight, and the soles of their feet were like the sole of a calf's foot; and they sparkled like burnished bronze. [8]Under their wings on their four sides they had human hands. And the four had their faces and their wings thus: [9]their wings touched one another; they went every one straight forward, without turning as they went. [10]As for the likeness of their faces, each had the face of a man in front; the four had the face of a lion on the right side, the four had the face of an ox on the left side, and the four had the face of an eagle at the back. [11]Such were their faces. And their wings were spread out above; each creature had two wings, each of which touched the wing of another, while two covered their bodies. [12]And each went straight forward; wherever the spirit would go, they went, without turning as they went. [13]In the midst of the living creatures there was something that looked like burning coals of fire, like torches moving back and forth among the living creatures; and the fire was bright, and out of the fire went forth lightning. [14]And the living creatures darted back and forth, like a flash of lightning.

[15]Now as I looked at the living creatures, I saw a wheel upon the earth beside the living creatures, one for each of the four of them. [16]As for the appearance of the wheels and their construction: their appearance was like the gleaming of a chrysolite; and the four had the same likeness, their construction being as it were a wheel within a wheel. [17]When they went, they went in any of their four directions without turning as they went. [18]The four wheels had rims and they had spokes; and their rims were full of eyes round about. [19]And when the living creatures went, the wheels went beside them; and when the living creatures rose from the earth, the wheels rose. [20]Wherever the spirit would go, they went, and the wheels rose along with them; for the spirit of the living creatures was in the wheels. [21]When those went, these went; and when those stood, these stood; and when those rose from the earth, the wheels rose along with them; for the spirit of the living creatures was in the wheels.

[22]Over the heads of the living creatures there was the likeness of a firmament, shining like crystal, spread out above their heads. [23]And under the firmament their wings were stretched out straight, one toward another; and each creature had two wings covering its body. [24]And when they went, I heard the sound of their wings like the sound of many waters, like the thunder of the Almighty, a sound of tumult like the sound of a host; when they stood still, they let down their wings. [25]And there came a voice

from above the firmament over their heads; when they stood still, they let
down their wings.

²⁶And above the firmament over their heads there was the likeness of
a throne, in appearance like sapphire; and seated above the likeness of a
throne was a likeness as it were of a human form. ²⁷And upward from what
had the appearance of his loins I saw as it were gleaming bronze, like the
appearance of fire enclosed round about; and downward from what had
the appearance of his loins I saw as it were the appearance of fire, and
there was brightness round about him. ²⁸Like the appearance of the bow
that is in the cloud on the day of rain, so was the appearance of the brightness round about.

Such was the appearance of the likeness of the glory of the Lord. And
when I saw it, I fell upon my face, and I heard the voice of one speaking.

OT: Gen 1:6–20, 26; Exod 3:6; 19:16–20; Sir 49:8
NT: Rev 4:1–8
Catechism: vision of God, 1720, 2519; glory of God, 293–94, 2809; the angels, 328–36

In his vision Ezekiel sees **a stormy wind** coming **out of the north**. The signifi- 1:4
cance of the wind coming from the "north" is unclear. It may just refer to the fact
that the wind in Babylon typically blows from the north, but it could also reflect
an ancient myth that placed the dwelling of the gods in the north (see Isa 14:13;
Ps 48:2).[5] At the center of the storm is a bright cloud with **fire flashing forth**
within, and at the center of the fire is **gleaming bronze**. The imagery of storm,
wind, and fire is common in the Old Testament to describe a †theophany—that
is, God's glorious manifestation to his people. Psalm 97:2–4 provides another
example: "Clouds and thick darkness are round about him. . . . Fire goes before
him. . . . His lightnings lighten the world."

And from the midst of this stormy cloud appears **the likeness of four liv-** 1:5–11
ing creatures. Ezekiel's description of these living creatures comes in parts,
each description building on the previous one. Each living creature is in **the
form of men**, literally "a human likeness" (Hebrew *demut 'adam*), recalling
the making of "Adam" in the image and "likeness" of God (Gen 1:26). But
strikingly, each living creature also has **four faces**: a human face in front,
a lion's face on the right, an ox's face on the left, and an eagle's face behind.
Each living creature has **four wings**—two wings are stretched out and touch
the wings of the others while two wings cover their body. The two wings
covering the body are a sign of modesty and reverence in the presence of the
Lord (see Isa 6:2); the two wings touching the wings of the other living creatures (see 1 Kings 6:27; 2 Chron 3:11) "may imply that they moved in perfect
unison."[6]

---

5. See Greenberg, *Ezekiel 1–20*, 42.
6. Greenberg, *Ezekiel 1–20*, 45.

Jesus as the Fulfillment of the Four Faces of the Living Creatures

LIVING TRADITION

Beginning with St. Irenaeus of Lyons (d. ca. 200), the four faces of the living creatures were applied to Jesus's own life as presented in the four †Gospels. Each Gospel was identified with one of the four faces, though the Fathers differed on which Gospel was paired with which face. St. Jerome's view became the standard account: Matthew was paired with the human face, Mark with the lion, Luke with the ox, and John with the eagle. Pope Gregory the Great eloquently describes how the four "faces" describe the complementary qualities of Christ as revealed in the four Gospels:

> For the Only-Begotten Son of God himself truly became man; he deigned to die like an ox at sacrifice for our salvation; he, through the virtue of his fortitude, rose as a lion. . . . Furthermore, ascending to heaven after his resurrection, he was borne aloft to the heights like an eagle. He is therefore wholly within us at the same time, who became a man in being born, an ox in dying, a lion in rising again, and an eagle in ascending to the heavens.[a]

a. Gregory the Great, *Homilies on the Book of the Prophet Ezekiel*, trans. Theodosia Tomkinson, 2nd ed. (Etna, CA: Center for Traditionalist Orthodox Studies, 2008), 73–74.

What do these faces signify? Each of the four represents the "highest" of its kind: the human being is the greatest of all creatures, made in the image and likeness of God; the bull is the greatest of domestic animals, the lion the greatest of wild animals, and the eagle the greatest of the birds.[7] The ox represents fertility and divinity, the lion strength and royalty, the eagle swiftness and nobility, and the human face dignity, wisdom, and knowledge. These qualities together offer a picture-image of the wisdom and power of God reflected in the faces of the four living creatures.

1:12–14   The creatures were moving. They went **straight forward** without turning right or left. Wherever **the spirit** (Hebrew *ruach*) went, the living creatures would follow. Is it the spirit of the creatures themselves or the Spirit of God directing them? We are not told at this point what this "spirit" is, but the meaning will become clear in a moment. Ezekiel rounds out this opening description by returning to the image of fire: he sees **burning coals of fire** like **torches moving back and forth**, from which lightning bursts forth. This awe-inspiring vision

7. Ralph W. Klein, *Ezekiel: The Prophet and His Message* (Columbia: University of South Carolina Press, 1988), 25. Robert Alter, "Ezekiel," in *The Hebrew Bible*, vol. 2, *Prophets* (New York: Norton, 2019), 1053, describes these as "iconic animals" borrowed from the Babylonian context.

recalls the appearance of the Lord on Mount Sinai with clouds and lightning and flashes of fire (Exod 19:16–20).

The frequency of terms for "likeness," "appearance," "form," and "like" displays the importance of picture language in Ezekiel to convey truths that are beyond normal physical description.[8] In other words, to convey this vision of the throne-chariot and the divine glory, Ezekiel describes things *by analogy*—by resemblance—because what is described cannot be fully understood or seen by human eyes. This use of metaphorical, analogical language is typical of biblical visions of God.

The vision expands: Ezekiel's gaze moves from the four living creatures to the four wheels that are beside them. When he first sees the wheels, they are touching **the earth**. The wheels appear to Ezekiel like **the gleaming of a chrysolite**, a brilliantly green precious stone. As for their construction, Ezekiel perceives in each **a wheel within a wheel**. The precise meaning of this well-known phrase, "wheel within a wheel," is unclear, but it probably indicates that the wheels can go in any direction without needing to turn.[9] The ability to go in any of the **four directions** without needing to turn points to the universal capacity of this †divine chariot. It can travel to the four corners of the earth with ease in any direction. Further, the rims of the wheels are tall and impressive, and there are eyes around the entire rim of the wheels. This bizarre picture of eyes on wheels conveys that the wheels are "all-seeing" in every direction. 1:15–18

The wheels follow the living creatures. They go **wherever the spirit** goes. Now we see that "spirit" here refers to **the spirit of the living creatures** that is **in the wheels**. Whether going forward, going backward, standing still, or rising up, the wheels act in perfect accord with the spirit of the living creatures.[10] 1:19–21

The vision now expands even further, although we (like Ezekiel) do not yet know exactly what we are seeing. Ezekiel's gaze moves above the living creatures, and there he sees **a firmament, shining like crystal, spread out above their heads**. "Firmament," or "dome," is the same word used in the creation account (Gen 1:6–20) to describe what divides the upper part of creation ("the heavens") from the lower part ("the earth and sea"). Here the firmament separates what is created from the very dwelling of God above. 1:22–23

For a moment, Ezekiel's attention is drawn back to the living creatures and their wings that beat actively when the creatures move but are at rest when they stop (vv. 23–25). For the first time Ezekiel's sense of *hearing* is engaged: the beat of 1:24–26

---

8. The term for "likeness" (Hebrew *demut*) occurs fifteen times in Ezekiel (nine times here in chap. 1); the term for "appearance" or "form" (Hebrew *mareh*) occurs thirty-six times.

9. Block, *Ezekiel: Chapters 1–24*, 100, writes: "It is difficult to visualize what Ezekiel saw. Are we to think of a gyroscope, or swiveling casters, or concentric wheels rotating in the same direction and giving the appearance of a disk, or inner and outer wheels operating at right angles to one another? Whatever the case, the prophet seems to envision some sort of four-wheeled chariot."

10. In Jewish mystical tradition, the wheels (Hebrew *ophanim*) were interpreted as angelic beings. This angelic interpretation is reflected in 1 Enoch (61:10; 71:7), where the *ophanim* are portrayed as a class of heavenly beings who, along with the cherubim and seraphim, never sleep but guard the throne of God.

St. Cyril of Jerusalem on the Likeness of the Glory of the Lord

Cyril of Jerusalem (d. 387) picks up on the words "appearance" and "likeness" in Ezekiel's vision to underline that even the appearance of the likeness of God's glory is more than Ezekiel can handle in his mortal nature.

> The prophet saw the likeness of the glory of God (Ezek 1:28); he did not see the Lord, but only the likeness of his glory; he did not even see the glory itself, as it really is, but only its likeness. And yet, though he saw only the likeness of the glory of the Lord, the prophet was so moved that he fell to the ground. If so great a man as the prophet falls to the ground and trembles in the presence of the likeness of the Lord's glory, any man who tries to see God as he really is will surely die.[a]

a. Cyril, *Catechetical Oration 9*, 1, trans. *The Navarre Bible: Major Prophets* (Dublin: Four Courts, 2005), 602–3.

the wings is like the sound of many waters or like a great army going to war. But then Ezekiel returns his attention to what is above the expanse. First he *hears* the sound of **a voice**; we will learn what that voice is saying at the start of chapter 2. Then Ezekiel *sees* **the likeness of a throne**, and seated on that throne is **a likeness as it were of a human form** (NABRE: "a figure that looked like a human being"). Ezekiel is seeing a vision of God, who appears in *something like* a human form, but Ezekiel's repeated use of "likeness" and "appearance" cautions us not to take this visual image too realistically. Still, there is a profound inversion here. In Gen 1:26, man (*'adam*) is described as made in the image and likeness of God; here Ezekiel describes the Lord God as appearing in the likeness of a man (*'adam*).

1:27–28   The upper part of the figure has the appearance of **gleaming bronze**, the lower part has **the appearance of fire**, and all around the figure is a colorful brightness like the rainbow. While Ezekiel is able to perceive the outline of a figure, the main thing he sees is bright, gleaming, colorful light. Finally, we are told what Ezekiel is actually seeing: **such was the appearance of the likeness of the glory of the Lord**. Ezekiel receives a visual picture of the *appearance* of the *likeness* of the *glory* of the Lord. The book of Sirach recounts this vision: "It was Ezekiel who saw the vision of glory which God showed him above the chariot of the cherubim" (Sir 49:8).[11] According to Robert Alter, "Never before in biblical literature has God's 'glory' . . . been given such visual realization."[12]

11. For the identification of the four living creatures with the "cherubim," see the sidebar "The Lord God Seated above the Cherubim," p. 88.

12. Alter, "Ezekiel," 1056.

Once Ezekiel realizes what he is seeing—and in whose presence he finds himself—he falls on his face in awe and fear, and with his eyes now hidden he hears a voice addressing him personally. The similarity to Moses is unmistakable: in his first encounter with God Moses saw the burning bush and heard the voice of the Lord speaking to him, and he, too, "hid his face, for he was afraid to look at God" (Exod 3:6). Like Moses, Ezekiel encounters the "presence" of the Lord outside of the Holy Land, in this case in the pagan region of Babylon, far from the temple in Jerusalem. This appearance of God's presence outside of Israel may have shocked Ezekiel's original audience because they were told in the Scriptures that the Lord would set his presence in a special way in the city of Jerusalem (Deut 12:11; 1 Kings 8:27–30). But now—following the example of God's appearance to Moses in the burning bush and on Mount Sinai—the Lord's glorious presence appears again in a foreign land. The profound truth revealed here is that the presence of the Lord is not limited to the land of Israel and the city of Jerusalem; he is capable of manifesting himself to anyone in any land.

Reflection and Application (1:4–28)

Ezekiel's opening vision is intended to reveal the power and reality of God in a striking, unmistakable way. This follows a pattern of visions given to various figures throughout the Old Testament: to Jacob (Gen 28), to Moses (Exod 34), to Isaiah (Isa 6), to Daniel (Dan 7), and to many others. Likewise, in the New Testament the experience of visions continues: to Peter (Acts 10), to Paul (2 Cor 12), to Stephen (Acts 7), and to John (Rev 1). Now contained within the †canonical Scriptures, these visions have become part of the †inspired revelation of God to the world.

The tradition of the Church also attests to visions given to many of the saints. But do visions continue today, and if so, how should we think about them? God does grant people visions today, and some of them receive official recognition from the Church (for example, the visions given to St. Faustina on God's mercy). But it is essential to grasp the purpose of these visions. They do not add to the deposit of faith, to what the Church calls "public revelation." Instead, visions are "private revelations" that are given in a particular time in order to awaken us to the reality of God and to equip us to respond with insight and faith to the challenges of the day. "It is not their role to improve or complete Christ's definitive Revelation, but to help live more fully by it in a certain period of history" (Catechism 67). When God chooses to impart visions to his people, we should welcome them: they sharpen our sense of God's presence and awaken us to the way he is calling us to act in the world.

The Call of Ezekiel

Ezekiel 2:1–3:27

Now the Lord speaks and calls Ezekiel to his prophetic ministry. The fearful and awesome quality of the divine presence (chap. 1) lends great solemnity to Ezekiel's call. The "word" and "Spirit" of the Lord are present, dynamically interacting with Ezekiel. The call itself is difficult, seemingly hopeless. Ezekiel is commanded to speak to a rebellious, hard-hearted people who will not listen to him. And yet he is called to fulfill this mission by the strength of the Lord. This is high drama right from the start. As readers we are left wondering how all this will work out. Will Ezekiel fulfill his commission? Will the people remain stubborn and refuse to heed his words? And will there be a redemption in the end?

Ezekiel Commissioned to Speak to a Rebellious People (2:1–3:11)

[1]And he said to me, "Son of man, stand upon your feet, and I will speak with you." [2]And when he spoke to me, the Spirit entered into me and set me upon my feet; and I heard him speaking to me. [3]And he said to me, "Son of man, I send you to the sons of Israel, to a nation of rebels, who have rebelled against me; they and their fathers have transgressed against me to this very day. [4]The people also are impudent and stubborn: I send you to them; and you shall say to them, 'Thus says the Lord GOD.' [5]And whether they hear or refuse to hear (for they are a rebellious house) they will know that there has been a prophet among them. [6]And you, son of man, be not afraid of them, nor be afraid of their words, though briers and thorns are with you and you sit upon scorpions; be not afraid of their words, nor be dismayed at their looks, for they are a rebellious house. [7]And you shall speak my words to them, whether they hear or refuse to hear; for they are a rebellious house.

[8]"But you, son of man, hear what I say to you; be not rebellious like that rebellious house; open your mouth, and eat what I give you." [9]And when I looked, behold, a hand was stretched out to me, and behold, a written scroll was in it; [10]and he spread it before me; and it had writing on the front and on the back, and there were written on it words of lamentation and mourning and woe.

[3:1]And he said to me, "Son of man, eat what is offered to you; eat this scroll, and go, speak to the house of Israel." [2]So I opened my mouth, and he gave me the scroll to eat. [3]And he said to me, "Son of man, eat this scroll that I give you and fill your stomach with it." Then I ate it; and it was in my mouth as sweet as honey.

[4]And he said to me, "Son of man, go, get you to the house of Israel, and speak with my words to them. [5]For you are not sent to a people of foreign speech and a hard language, but to the house of Israel— [6]not to many peoples of foreign speech and a hard language, whose words you cannot understand. Surely, if I sent you to such, they would listen to you. [7]But the house of Israel will not listen to you; for they are not willing to listen to me; because all the house of Israel are of a hard forehead and of a stubborn heart. [8]Behold, I have made your face hard against their faces, and your forehead hard against their foreheads. [9]Like adamant harder than flint have I made your forehead; fear them not, nor be dismayed at their looks, for they are a rebellious house." [10]Moreover he said to me, "Son of man, all my words that I shall speak to you receive in your heart, and hear with your ears. [11]And go, get you to the exiles, to your people, and say to them, 'Thus says the Lord GOD'; whether they hear or refuse to hear."

OT: Ps 40:8; Isa 48:4; Jer 15:16
NT: Mark 14:62; Rev 5:1–9; 10:8–11
Catechism: hardness of heart, 1859, 1864, 2840
Lectionary: 2:2–5: 14th Sunday in Ordinary Time (Year B)

Ezekiel's commissioning comes to us in three parts, with two parallel sections flanking a central section. It can be diagrammed like this:

Ezekiel is called to speak to a rebellious people (2:1–7)
Ezekiel is told to eat the scroll of God's word (2:8–3:3)
Ezekiel is called (again) to speak to a rebellious people (3:4–11)

By stating the call twice in similar terms, the Lord hammers home to Ezekiel the enormous challenge of his commission. But by placing the call to eat the scroll at the center, the Lord shines a spotlight on Ezekiel's own obedient response. In contrast to this rebellious people, Ezekiel is called to reject rebellion and faithfully proclaim the word of God.

2:1–2   For the first time in the book the Lord speaks, summoning Ezekiel to stand up before him and listen: **Son of man, stand upon your feet, and I will speak with you.** This is also the first appearance of the phrase "son of man," the most common title by which the Lord addresses Ezekiel (see the sidebar "The 'Son of Man' in the Bible"). Along with the spoken word, the Spirit comes to Ezekiel: **And when he spoke to me, the Spirit entered into me and set me upon my feet.** This is the *Spirit of God* acting upon Ezekiel to strengthen him inwardly so that he can bear up under the difficult word about to be spoken. This is also a kind of preparation for the great vision of the valley of dry bones (Ezek 37), when the Spirit of the Lord will come upon Ezekiel once again to proclaim a time of restoration.

2:3–5   What is the message? Ezekiel is commissioned to speak to the people of Israel, who are identified in shockingly negative terms. They are **a nation of rebels. They and their fathers have transgressed** against the Lord **to this very day.** They are **impudent and stubborn** (literally, "have a hard face and a stubborn heart"; see 3:7–8). This is not an agreeable audience to address. But Ezekiel's call is not based on whether the people respond favorably. Every indication suggests that they will not listen. Nonetheless, Ezekiel is called to deliver God's word to them, and whether they listen or not, **they will know that there has been a prophet among them.** How so? Because the word Ezekiel speaks will come to pass, and so will serve as a witness against the people.

2:6–7   For his part, Ezekiel is told: **be not afraid of them, nor be afraid of their words.** The Lord will protect Ezekiel from the attacks of this rebellious people— from the **briers, thorns,** and **scorpions** that will assail him. The Lord effectively says to Ezekiel: Never mind what they do. Ezekiel is to speak God's word to the rebellious house of Israel whether they receive that word or reject it.

2:8   The very same word that Ezekiel is called to speak to Israel is addressed to Ezekiel himself: **be not rebellious like that rebellious house.** Instead, the Lord tells him: **open your mouth, and eat what I give you.** This is a graphic image of how the word of God is to be received into the heart. Ezekiel has already received the gift of God's word and his Spirit, but he still needs to respond with a willing ear and heart. His own free response to ingest the word is an essential part of being a faithful prophet—that is, an obedient servant of the Lord.

2:9–10   What does the Lord give Ezekiel to eat? **A hand was stretched out to me, and behold, a written scroll was in it.** The scroll is written on the front and back, showing the fullness of judgment that God has decreed against his people.[1] Hauntingly, the words on the scroll are filled with **lamentation and mourning**

---

1. The phrase "written scroll" or "scroll of a book" appears elsewhere in the Bible only in Ps 40:7 and Jer 36:2, 4. Scrolls written on both sides were typically made of papyrus (a plant), making it at least more conceivable for Ezekiel to eat and consume the scroll.

The "Son of Man" in the Bible

The phrase "son of man" (Hebrew *ben-'adam*) appears 93 times in Ezekiel (in 38 of 48 chapters), while occurring just 14 times in the rest of the Old Testament. In several of those instances "son of man" is placed in parallel with "man" (*'adam*), showing that the meaning is something like "mortal human being," one who is descended from Adam, made from the dust of the earth (Gen 2:7; 3:19). Examples occur throughout the Old Testament. From the Law (the †Torah): "God is not *man*, that he should lie, / or a *son of man*, that he should repent" (Num 23:19). From the Prophets: "Blessed is the *man* who does this, / and the *son of man* who holds it fast" (Isa 56:2). From the Psalms: "What is *man* that you are mindful of him, / and *the son of man* that you care for him?" (Ps 8:4). And from the Wisdom literature: "Behold, even the moon is not bright / and the stars are not clean in his sight; / how much less *man*, who is a maggot, / and the *son of man*, who is a worm" (Job 25:5–6). The exception to this meaning is found in Daniel, where "son of man" refers to a humanlike figure who possesses *divine* qualities and who sits at the right hand of God in heaven: "And behold, with the clouds of heaven / there came one like a son of man, / and he came to the Ancient of Days / and was presented before him" (Dan 7:13).

Jesus frequently refers to himself as "the son of man" in each of the four †Gospels. Both meanings of "son of man" apply to him: Jesus is truly a man, a human being, descended from Adam, but he is also the glorious "son of man" who sits at the right hand of God and will come in glory with the clouds of heaven (see Mark 14:62).

---

and woe. The word Ezekiel must speak is a word not of comfort or consolation but of lamentation and definitive judgment.

The Lord then says to Ezekiel: **Son of man, eat what is offered to you; eat** **3:1–3** **this scroll**. Ezekiel is not free to pick and choose the words he will speak. He must eat the entire scroll and ingest all the words that are found in it. And crucially, Ezekiel obeys: this is the act of faith and obedience that the Lord is seeking. **So I opened my mouth, and he gave me the scroll to eat**. But Ezekiel must do more than just take the scroll into his mouth. The Lord tells him: **eat this scroll that I give you and fill your stomach with it**. Ezekiel must receive the word deeply into himself, into his inner parts, so that he can speak this word with power. In a striking way, Ezekiel will be called to embody the word that he receives and speaks.

Surprisingly, Ezekiel discovers that the scroll is **sweet as honey** in his mouth. How can words of mourning and woe be sweet to the taste? Despite the content of the scroll, concerned with coming judgment, the word is still sweet, because it is *God's* word. The word of God is "sweet" and good even when the content of the message is "sour." Ezekiel's older contemporary, Jeremiah, also "ate" the words of God and found them a delight to his heart: "Your words were found, and I ate them, / and your words became to me a joy / and the delight of my heart" (Jer 15:16).

In the Light of Christ (2:8–3:3)

Ezekiel's eating of the scroll finds its direct fulfillment in the book of Revelation (10:8–11). There John is told to take the scroll from the hand of an angel and "eat" the scroll: "Take it and eat; it will be bitter to your stomach, but sweet as honey in your mouth" (v. 9). Just as Ezekiel eats the scroll of God's judgment and finds it sweet in his mouth (but bitter in his stomach), so does John, who now "must again prophesy about many peoples and nations and tongues and kings" (v. 11).

But there is another reference to a scroll that appears earlier in the book of Revelation (5:1–9). This scroll, like Ezekiel's, has words written on the front and back and contains predictions of great judgments to come. But it also has the promise of God's full redemption of the world and of a new creation. Confronted with the words of this scroll, John weeps because no one has been found worthy to open it and bring about its fulfillment. But John is told, "Weep not; behold, the Lion of the tribe of Judah, the Root of David, has conquered, so that he can open the scroll and its seven seals" (v. 5). Jesus Christ, risen and ascended to the right hand of the Father, is now Lord. He has the authority to take the scroll of God's providential judgments and glorious promises and carry its purposes to completion.

3:4–7 The Lord now reaffirms the call to speak a challenging word to **the house of Israel**, a hard-hearted people and—as the Lord will repeat in verse 9—"a rebellious house." Ezekiel is not called to speak to **a people of foreign speech and a hard language**. Ironically, the Lord says that a foreign people would **listen to** Ezekiel despite the language barrier. Israel, in fact, understands Ezekiel's language perfectly well. The problem is not the people's failure to understand what he is saying. The issue is the openness of the heart—this is what determines how the word of God will be heard. The core obstacle is that Israel *as a people* has **a hard forehead** and **a stubborn heart**. Isaiah ran up against the same hindrance: "I know that you are obstinate, / and your neck is an iron sinew / and your forehead brass" (Isa 48:4; see 6:9–10). Israel has turned away from the Lord and is not open to hearing his word.

3:8–11 To match Israel's hardness, the Lord promises Ezekiel that he will give him a **face hard against their faces** and a **forehead hard against their foreheads**. God will equip Ezekiel with the courage and perseverance needed to deliver a "hard

St. Jerome on Eating the Scroll

St. Jerome spiritually applies Ezekiel's eating and ingesting of the scroll to successive stages of meditating upon and memorizing God's word in Scripture. We, too, are called to "ingest" God's word so that it penetrates deeply into our hearts and bears fruit in every season of life. "The eating of the book is the initial reading and the simple history; but when by constant meditation we have stored the Lord's book in the treasure chamber of our memory, our belly is filled spiritually and our bowels are satiated."[a]

a. *Commentary on Ezekiel* 1.3.3b, trans. Thomas P. Scheck, ACW (New York: Newman, 2017), 39.

word" to a people with a "hard heart." There is probably a play on Ezekiel's name here: the word "hard" is closely related to Ezekiel's name, which means "God strengthens" or "God hardens." Once again, the Lord calls Ezekiel to **fear them not**. Who would not be alarmed at the commission to speak a hard word to a hard-hearted people who will refuse to hear this word? Yet Ezekiel is not to be **dismayed** or troubled, just as the Lord said to Jeremiah: "Do not be dismayed by them" (Jer 1:17). The Lord will speak to Ezekiel, who will receive the word in his ears and take it into his heart, and he will be empowered to speak in the Lord's name: **"Thus says the Lord God."**

Ezekiel can be in no doubt about the immensely difficult task facing him. But in direct contrast to this rebellious people, Ezekiel has ears and a heart that are receptive. In Christian terms, he acts as the model disciple: the Spirit is upon him, he has received God's word into his mouth, and he has swallowed that word and taken it into his heart. Now he is ready to act as the servant of the Lord.

Reflection and Application (2:1–3:11)

This section of Ezekiel presents us with a clear contrast of characters. On the one side are the people of Israel: they have hard foreheads and stubborn hearts and refuse to receive God's word. On the other side is Ezekiel himself: he receives God's Spirit and is pliant before God's word, ready to "swallow" God's word deep into his heart. Centuries later the angel Gabriel came to a young woman, announcing God's momentous plan of redemption (Luke 1:26–33). Like Ezekiel, Mary was docile and receptive to God's word. She took that spoken word into her heart, thus enabling the Holy Spirit to overshadow her and bring forth in an utterly unprecedented way the Word of God from her womb. We stand in a similar situation: God's word also comes to us fresh and new. We can be "hardened by the deceitfulness of sin" (Heb 3:13) and refuse to respond, or we can be receptive to God's word through faith and obedience. In the prophet Ezekiel, and preeminently in the Virgin Mary, we have the pattern to follow, the path to adhere to. Obedience to God's word does not free us from difficulty and suffering, but it places us in the hands of God, who will strengthen us to endure and bear fruit through our faith-filled response to God's word.

The Preparation of Ezekiel for His Prophetic Calling (3:12–27)

[12]Then the Spirit lifted me up, and as the glory of the LORD arose from its place, I heard behind me the sound of a great earthquake; [13]it was the sound of the wings of the living creatures as they touched one another, and the sound of the wheels beside them, that sounded like a great earthquake. [14]The Spirit lifted me up and took me away, and I went in bitterness in the heat of my spirit, the hand of the LORD being strong upon me; [15]and I came to the exiles at Telabib, who dwelt by the river Chebar. And I sat there overwhelmed among them seven days.

[16]And at the end of seven days, the word of the LORD came to me: [17]"Son of man, I have made you a watchman for the house of Israel; whenever you hear a word from my mouth, you shall give them warning from me. [18]If I say to the wicked, 'You shall surely die,' and you give him no warning, nor speak to warn the wicked from his wicked way, in order to save his life, that wicked man shall die in his iniquity; but his blood I will require at your hand. [19]But if you warn the wicked, and he does not turn from his wickedness, or from his wicked way, he shall die in his iniquity; but you will have saved your life. [20]Again, if a righteous man turns from his righteousness and commits iniquity, and I lay a stumbling block before him, he shall die; because you have not warned him, he shall die for his sin, and his righteous deeds which he has done shall not be remembered; but his blood I will require at your hand. [21]Nevertheless if you warn the righteous man not to sin, and he does not sin, he shall surely live, because he took warning; and you will have saved your life."

[22]And the hand of the LORD was there upon me; and he said to me, "Arise, go forth into the plain, and there I will speak with you." [23]So I arose and went forth into the plain; and behold, the glory of the LORD stood there, like the glory which I had seen by the river Chebar; and I fell on my face. [24]But the Spirit entered into me, and set me upon my feet; and he spoke with me and said to me, "Go, shut yourself within your house. [25]And you, O son of man, behold, cords will be placed upon you, and you shall be bound with them, so that you cannot go out among the people; [26]and I will make your tongue cleave to the roof of your mouth, so that you shall be mute and unable to reprove them; for they are a rebellious house. [27]But when I speak with you, I will open your mouth, and you shall say to them,

'Thus says the Lord God'; he that will hear, let him hear; and he that will
refuse to hear, let him refuse; for they are a rebellious house.'

OT: Lev 8:33; Job 2:13; Jer 20:9
NT: Matt 11:15; Mark 4:9; Luke 8:8; James 1:13
Catechism: warning against spiritual danger, 1033, 1056, 1852; God's call on the prophets, 702
Lectionary: 3:17–21: Feast of St. John Vianney, Common of Pastors

We might think that at this point Ezekiel is fully equipped and ready to begin   3:12–14
his public prophetic ministry to the people. But the Lord has more to do and
say to Ezekiel before he begins his prophetic task among the exiles.

Once again **the Spirit** comes upon Ezekiel and lifts him up. **As the glory of
the Lord** rises **from its place**, Ezekiel hears the wings of the †cherubim and the
moving wheels of the †divine chariot, which together make **the sound of a great
earthquake**. The first thing we are told is that the Spirit lifts Ezekiel up and takes
him away, but now he goes **in bitterness in the heat of** his **spirit** because **the
hand of the Lord** is strongly upon him. The word of God was initially sweet
in Ezekiel's mouth but is now bitter to his stomach. What is happening here?
The word ingested by Ezekiel—the scroll—is a word of severe and unrelenting
judgment upon the people, and so burns bitterly within Ezekiel's own spirit.
Jeremiah also experienced God's word of judgment like a fire inside him: "There
is in my heart as it were a burning fire shut up in my bones" (Jer 20:9).

The second thing we are told is that the Spirit brings Ezekiel to the com-   3:15
pany of **the exiles** at a place called **Telabib**, by **the river Chebar**, where we
first encountered Ezekiel (1:1).[2] Though the text does not state so explicitly, it
appears that Ezekiel—who is already in exile in Babylon—is led by the Spirit
to this particular place where other exiles are gathered. In his first public "act"
Ezekiel sits silent among the exiles for **seven days**. Just as Job sat silently for
seven days after many calamities befell him (Job 2:13), so Ezekiel remains silent
and motionless for seven days, mourning the great judgment that is to come.
Seven days is also the period set aside for the ordination of a priest (Lev 8:33),
so these seven days may also point to a period of solemn preparation for the
prophetic ministry of the priest, Ezekiel.[3]

At the end of seven days of waiting and preparation, **the word of the Lord**   3:16–17
once again comes to Ezekiel.[4] The Lord God tells Ezekiel that he has made him
to be **a watchman for the house of Israel**. The role of a watchman is to stay
alert and then to give warning to the town or city regarding the danger he sees.

2. Telabib (pronounced "Tel-Aviv") is an Akkadian name and means "mound of the flood." The
modern city of Tel-Aviv in Israel draws its name from this reference in Ezekiel (see Alter, "Ezekiel," 1059).

3. John B. Taylor, *Ezekiel: An Introduction and Commentary*, Tyndale Old Testament Commentaries
(Downers Grove, IL: InterVarsity, 1969), 68, proposes that Ezekiel may have regarded these seven days
"as the preparation for his ordination to a prophetic priesthood."

4. The phrase "the word of the Lord came to me" occurs fifty times in Ezekiel. It is the standard
introduction to a new prophetic oracle.

In this case, the need to "watch" arises not simply from the danger of an enemy who comes to attack but from the approach of God's word, which comes in judgment: **whenever you hear a word from my mouth, you shall give them warning from me**. It is a *prophetic* watchman's role.[5]

3:18–19   The Lord then presents two test cases to Ezekiel to show what it means to be a watchman. In the first case (vv. 18–19), a *wicked* person is walking on a path to destruction. If the Lord gives a word of **warning** but Ezekiel fails to speak that word to the wicked person, then that person will **die in his iniquity**, but the responsibility for his death will fall to Ezekiel: **his blood I will require at your hand**. "His blood" here is a reference to the loss of this person's *life*. The point is that the Lord will hold Ezekiel responsible for the loss of this person's life if Ezekiel does not warn him of his danger. If, however, Ezekiel warns the wicked person but that person still refuses to repent, then he will die, but Ezekiel will be free of responsibility: **you will have saved your life**.

3:20–21   The second case involves a *righteous* person who turns away from the right path and **commits iniquity**. This person **shall die for his sin** if Ezekiel does not warn him, but Ezekiel will be held responsible. If, however, Ezekiel gives the warning and this person turns away from sin, then that person shall live and Ezekiel will have delivered himself from responsibility. When the Lord speaks about setting **a stumbling block** before the person turning to a path of sin, this means not that God is the direct source of temptation to sin (see James 1:13), but that God allows the one who is set on sinning to trip and fall in the path he has chosen.

The call to be a watchman, given here at the start of Ezekiel's ministry, will appear again as the †oracles of judgment reach their climax (33:1–9). These two watchman passages function like bookends for Ezekiel's ministry: everything in between (chaps. 4–32) is the catalogue of the words of warning that Ezekiel courageously speaks to a sinful people. This is a solemn responsibility. Ezekiel cannot determine whether people will turn away from their sin and rebellion, but he is responsible now to speak a word of warning to individuals and to the entire nation of Israel.

3:22   In the final act of preparation for his ministry, Ezekiel experiences for the third time **the hand of the LORD** coming upon him (see 1:3; 3:14), and he is told to **go forth into the plain,** where the Lord will speak to him. This unnamed plain (or "valley"), briefly mentioned in 8:4, will be the location for the great vision of the dry bones (37:1–14).

3:23–24   What does Ezekiel see when he arrives in the valley? **The glory of the LORD stood there, like the glory which I had seen by the river Chebar**. As before (1:28), Ezekiel falls on his face before the awesome presence of God. Once again the Spirit enters into Ezekiel and sets him upon his feet. To bear the

---

5. The prophetic role of watchman is also found in Isa 21:6–9; 56:10; Jer 6:17; Hosea 9:8; Hab 2:1.

Caesarius of Arles on Bishops as Watchmen

LIVING TRADITION

Caesarius of Arles (d. 452) boldly calls those who hold the office of bishop to fulfill the call to be watchmen and faithfully tend the sheep. Caesarius warns that it is all too easy for those with pastoral responsibility to concern themselves with other matters and avoid or neglect their role as watchmen.

If we carefully heed the lessons that are read at the consecration of bishops, we have a means of rousing ourselves to the greatest compunction. What Gospel text is it, except the one I mentioned a little while ago? "Peter, Peter, tend my sheep," and again, "feed my lambs." Did Christ say, cultivate the vineyards by your presence, arrange the country estates yourself, exercise the cultivation of the land? He did not say this, but "feed my sheep." Now what kind of prophetic text is read at the consecration of a bishop? It is this: "I have made you a watchman for the house of Israel." It did not say a steward of vineyards or country estates or the manager of fields; doubtless it is a watchman of souls.[a]

a. *Sermons* 1.11 (ACCS 13:26).

weight of the Lord's word, Ezekiel needs the strengthening power of the Holy Spirit.

What is Ezekiel told to do? To shut himself up within his house and to be **bound** with **cords** so that he **cannot go out among the people**. This is an exceptionally perplexing direction for someone called to speak publicly to the people! How is Ezekiel to carry out his ministry when bound with cords inside his own house? If this refers to a literal binding with ropes, it was probably a temporary symbolic gesture indicating to both Ezekiel and his audience that he was "bound" by God's word and not free to do as he pleased.   3:25

Further, the Lord tells Ezekiel: **I will make your tongue cleave to the roof of your mouth, so that you shall be mute and unable to reprove them**. Not only is Ezekiel bound with ropes to his chair, but his tongue is bound within his own mouth. This muteness is a sign of the rebelliousness of the people: Ezekiel's inability to speak is a reflection of their inability to hear. But then crucially the Lord adds that when he speaks to Ezekiel, Ezekiel's mouth will be opened, and he will be able to speak God's word to them (whether they listen or not).   3:26–27

Elsewhere, Ezekiel is told that he will be mute until the fall of the city (24:27; 33:22). How can we reconcile this promise of muteness with the Lord's previous call to speak, and even more so the Lord's solemn charge that Ezekiel must warn the people as a watchman? We might conclude that Ezekiel's inability to speak lasted for seven years (from 593 until the fall of the city in 586), but it is better to see this muteness as partial, relating to Ezekiel speaking *on his own*.

Only when God opens his mouth in prophecy, only when God speaks with him (v. 27), is Ezekiel able to speak. Otherwise he will remain mute—he will have nothing to say—until the judgment has fallen.

In the Light of Christ (3:27)

In the final verse of chapter 3, the Lord tells Ezekiel: "He that will hear, let him hear; and he that will refuse to hear, let him refuse." There is a striking echo of this language in the words that Jesus himself speaks. Seven times in the Gospels, normally at the conclusion of a parable, Jesus says: "He who has ears to hear, let him hear."[6] Asked by his disciples why he speaks so often in parables, Jesus explains that he does this to sift the hearts of his hearers. Those whose hearts are open will hear and understand; those whose hearts are closed to his word will not understand—the word will not find a home inside them. Just as Ezekiel was derisively called "a maker of parables" (20:49 ESV), so too was Jesus a maker of many parables. It is probable that Jesus was intentionally echoing Ezekiel when he ended his parables with the words, "He who has ears to hear, let him hear."

Reflection and Application (3:16–27)

In every period of history, it seems that God raises up certain individuals to be "watchmen" for his people. Ezekiel and Jeremiah had this role laid upon their shoulders in a season of great crisis for the nation of Israel. If their example tells us anything, it shows that being a "watchman" is a genuinely difficult task. It means opening one's ears to hear God's voice and then finding the courage to speak the word that one hears. Those who "watch" for God's word in this way will experience opposition. The biblical prophets are the exemplars of what a watchman must be, and we hold them in great admiration for their sacrificial service. In our own day, each of us can probably identify certain people who are fulfilling this role: hearing God's voice, discerning the times and seasons, and speaking that word broadly in a public setting.

But what about the rest of us who are not called to a public ministry as Ezekiel was? Are we not called to hear God's word and then speak that word in our own settings and circumstances? Each of us, in our own way, is invited to hear and discern God's voice, and to speak what we hear to those around us: to those in our families, in our workplaces, in our schools. This does not mean that we are responsible to point out everyone's faults and failings! We need to discern when

6. Matt 11:15; 13:9, 43; Mark 4:9, 23; Luke 8:8; 14:35. See also Rev 2–3 for this phrase.

to speak and how we are to speak. But we may have a word of exhortation or warning that could prevent or rescue someone from stumbling and falling. The apostle Peter calls *all* the faithful to be "good stewards of God's varied †grace" and encourages the one who speaks to do so "as one who utters oracles of God" (1 Pet 4:10–11). This is not just for the great prophets in Ezekiel's day and ours. By the power of the Holy Spirit, each of us can hear and speak the "oracles of God" and so bring God's life-giving word to those around us.

Judgment on the City and the Land

Ezekiel 4:1–7:27

We have now arrived at the first major section of the book. Ezekiel has beheld the glorious and awe-inspiring vision of God's presence, received his call, and been prepared for a hard task. From this point all the way through chapter 24 we are in the terrain of God's word of judgment against Israel and Jerusalem. If we are going to walk this road with the prophet, we, too, need to be prepared to hear a challenging word delivered again and again in diverse ways until the judgment against the people, land, and city reaches its culmination.

This first major subsection (chaps. 4–7) focuses on judgment against the city of Jerusalem and the land of Israel. It opens (4:1–5:4) with four prophetic actions by Ezekiel that dramatize the coming judgment upon the Holy City and the people.

Dramatizing the Fall of Jerusalem (4:1–5:4)

¹"And you, O son of man, take a brick and lay it before you, and portray upon it a city, even Jerusalem; ²and put siegeworks against it, and build a siege wall against it, and cast up a mound against it; set camps also against it, and plant battering rams against it round about. ³And take an iron plate, and place it as an iron wall between you and the city; and set your face toward it, and let it be in a state of siege, and press the siege against it. This is a sign for the house of Israel.

⁴"Then lie upon your left side, and I will lay the punishment of the house of Israel upon you; for the number of the days that you lie upon it, you shall bear their punishment. ⁵For I assign to you a number of days, three hundred and ninety days, equal to the number of the years of their punishment; so long shall you bear the punishment of the house of Israel. ⁶And when you have completed these, you shall lie down a second time, but on

your right side, and bear the punishment of the house of Judah; forty days I assign you, a day for each year. ⁷And you shall set your face toward the siege of Jerusalem, with your arm bared; and you shall prophesy against the city. ⁸And behold, I will put cords upon you, so that you cannot turn from one side to the other, till you have completed the days of your siege.

⁹"And you, take wheat and barley, beans and lentils, millet and spelt, and put them into a single vessel, and make bread of them. During the number of days that you lie upon your side, three hundred and ninety days, you shall eat it. ¹⁰And the food which you eat shall be by weight, twenty shekels a day; once a day you shall eat it. ¹¹And water you shall drink by measure, the sixth part of a hin; once a day you shall drink. ¹²And you shall eat it as a barley cake, baking it in their sight on human dung." ¹³And the LORD said, "Thus shall the people of Israel eat their bread unclean, among the nations where I will drive them." ¹⁴Then I said, "Ah, Lord GOD! behold, I have never defiled myself; from my youth up till now I have never eaten what died of itself or was torn by beasts, nor has foul flesh come into my mouth." ¹⁵Then he said to me, "See, I will let you have cow's dung instead of human dung, on which you may prepare your bread." ¹⁶Moreover he said to me, "Son of man, behold, I will break the staff of bread in Jerusalem; they shall eat bread by weight and with fearfulness; and they shall drink water by measure and in dismay. ¹⁷I will do this that they may lack bread and water, and look at one another in dismay, and waste away under their punishment.

⁵:¹"And you, O son of man, take a sharp sword; use it as a barber's razor and pass it over your head and your beard; then take balances for weighing, and divide the hair. ²A third part you shall burn in the fire in the midst of the city, when the days of the siege are completed; and a third part you shall take and strike with the sword round about the city; and a third part you shall scatter to the wind, and I will unsheathe the sword after them. ³And you shall take from these a small number, and bind them in the skirts of your robe. ⁴And of these again you shall take some, and cast them into the fire, and burn them in the fire; from there a fire will come forth into all the house of Israel."

OT: Lev 26:26, 33, 39; Num 14:34; Deut 23:12–14; Isa 50:4; 53:6
NT: 1 Pet 2:21–25; 1 John 2:2
Catechism: God's punishment and judgment of sin, 211, 679, 1472–73, 2054

Ezekiel begins his public ministry not with words but with actions. The Lord tells him to act out symbolically the coming siege against the city of Jerusalem. Let's recall that Jerusalem was besieged by and surrendered to the armies of Babylon in the recent past (in 597), leading to the exile of many, including Ezekiel. Ezekiel is now called to depict a further siege of the city by the same Babylonian armies. To accomplish this, Ezekiel is told to **take a brick and lay it before you, and portray upon it a city, even Jerusalem**. This mimics a practice current at

4:1–3

that time in Babylonian society: "The practice of sketching a city plan on a clay brick is confirmed by several exemplars discovered by archeologists."[1] Next, the prophet is to build **siegeworks** and **plant battering rams against** the city from every side, portraying what the Babylonians will do when they besiege the city. Typically a siegework was a tower, mound, or ramp of wood, stones, and earth that would enable a besieging army to approach and shoot projectiles into a city and eventually to penetrate its defenses by means of battering rams. The prophet is told to construct a scale model of these devices. Strikingly, Ezekiel is then told to **take an iron plate, and place it as an iron wall between you and the city**, and set his face toward it and **press the siege against it**. The iron plate symbolizes God's own determined judgment against the city, a wall set up between the Lord and his people. All this is to be **a sign for the house of Israel**.[2] The sobering, ominous reality is that the Lord God has set *himself* against his own people and city, and the prophet is not going to take up a posture of interceding for the city.

4:4–8   The second †sign-act graphically portrays the punishment that will fall upon Israel. Ezekiel is told: **lie upon your left side, and I will lay the punishment of the house of Israel upon you**. The word translated "punishment" can also mean "iniquity" or "guilt." Here we see Ezekiel's priestly identity coming into play. This is a priestly-prophetic action. He is representationally bearing the punishment of the whole people in symbolic solidarity with them.[3]

The length prescribed for this "lying down" is astounding: Ezekiel is assigned **three hundred and ninety days** to lie on his left side to **bear the punishment of the house of Israel**, and then further assigned an additional **forty days** to lie on his right side, to **bear the punishment of the house of Judah**. Each day represents one year of their punishment.[4] But what do the numbers 390 and 40 signify? Some commentators see a distinction between the punishments imposed on the two kingdoms, the northern kingdom of Israel and the southern kingdom of Judah. But since the northern kingdom was only in existence for just over two hundred years, this is unlikely. Moreover, the phrase "house of Israel" in Ezekiel normally refers to the whole people (north and south), not just the northern kingdom. Probably it is best to correlate the 390 years with the history of disobedience of the *entire* people of Israel since the founding of the first temple, and to see the forty years as a symbolic representation of the unfaithfulness of Judah (the southern kingdom) in the recent past.[5] The numbers,

1. Block, *Ezekiel: Chapters 1–24*, 171.

2. The word "sign" appears four times in Ezekiel (4:3; 12:6, 11; 24:24). In the latter three occurrences, Ezekiel himself, through his prophetic action, is the "sign" to the people.

3. For Old Testament priests bearing the iniquity or punishment of the people, see Exod 28:38; Lev 10:17; Num 18:1.

4. In Num 14:34, because of the unbelief of the people of Israel, the Lord assigns forty *years* of wandering in the wilderness as a symbolic punishment for the faithless forty *days* of scouting the land.

5. Alter, "Ezekiel," 1061, observes that 390 years approximates the time from the building of the first temple until its destruction by the armies of Babylon.

then, represent two periods of disobedience (the second one contained in the first), and the overall meaning is that the coming siege of the city is the outcome and culmination of a long history of disobedience.[6]

It is hard to imagine how Ezekiel could lie upon his side for well over one year, just in terms of bodily health and functions. It is at least possible that Ezekiel spent only some portion of each day in this prone posture. Nor is it clear whether the Lord God placed literal cords upon Ezekiel to keep him in place. But however Ezekiel carried out this demanding sign-act, he was not silent during it. The Lord tells him to **prophesy against the city**, even as he continues visually to set his face against the model of Jerusalem he has set up. In this opening scene, then, Ezekiel joins together his acts and his words to signal the Lord's impending judgment on the Holy City.

In the Light of Christ (4:4–8)

Is Ezekiel, lying on his side and bearing the punishment of the people, a †type of Christ, who bore our iniquities and atoned for our sin through the cross? Most commentators, ancient and modern, conclude that Ezekiel was *not* atoning for the sins of the people through this action. To the contrary, it is quite clear throughout the book of Ezekiel that the people themselves will suffer severe punishment for their grievous sins against the Lord. Instead, by this act of lying on his side Ezekiel was *embodying* the punishment due to the people for their long history of disobedience.

Still, Ezekiel's action—and the language used to describe it—point us toward what Christ would accomplish through his sacrificial death. Ezekiel was told to "bear" the "punishment/iniquity" of the people. These are precisely the terms used to describe how the priests of the Old Covenant bear the iniquity of the people (Exod 28:38; Lev 10:17; Num 18:1). On the solemn Day of Atonement, the priest confesses over the head of the goat all the sins of the people, and thus "the goat shall bear all their iniquities" (Lev 16:22) and bear them out of the camp. In the great Servant Song of Isa 53 we see similar language used to depict the iniquity-bearing role of God's servant: "All we like sheep have gone astray; . . . and the LORD has laid on him the iniquity of us all" (Isa 53:6). As the apostle Peter tells us, this prophecy of the servant is fulfilled in Christ (1 Pet 2:21–25). By symbolically bearing the iniquity of the house of Israel, Ezekiel did not bring about atonement (and so forgiveness) for the people, but his prophetic-symbolic action points us to the one who did—Jesus Christ, who "is the atoning sacrifice for our sins" (1 John 2:2 NRSV).

---

6. It is probably not a coincidence that the two periods (390 and 40) add up to 430 years: this is the number of years that Israel dwelt in Egypt, where they were enslaved (Exod 12:40–41). The later period of disobedience corresponds to the earlier period of slavery.

4:9–11   To fill out the picture, Ezekiel is told in the third sign-act to prepare food and drink for the days he will lie on his side. These represent the famine rations that the people will be forced to use during the upcoming siege of the city. The six kinds of food—**wheat and barley, beans and lentils, millet and spelt**—are combined to make bread. They represent a siege diet when no single ingredient would be available in large quantity: "The use of so many kinds of flour symbolizes a besieged people scraping the bottom of their barrels."[7] Water is likewise to be measured out carefully day to day. Using modern measurements, Ezekiel's rations amount to about eight ounces of bread per day and less than one liter of water—these are indeed famine rations.

4:12–15   The worst hardship for Ezekiel, though, is not the short supply of bread and water. It is the command to bake the barley cake **on human dung**, signifying that during the siege the people of Israel shall **eat their bread unclean**. Because human dung was declared unclean by the law of Moses (Deut 23:12–14), bread cooked on human dung would also be unclean. Ezekiel bursts out in his complaint to the Lord: **Ah, Lord God! behold, I have never defiled myself**. Never before has Ezekiel (the priest) defiled himself with unclean food. In response to Ezekiel's genuine concern for ritual purity, the Lord God concedes Ezekiel's request and allows him to bake the bread using **cow's dung** (which was not unclean) for fuel.

4:16–17   To conclude, the Lord reveals to Ezekiel the meaning of this sign-act: it is meant to show that the Lord **will break the staff of bread in Jerusalem**, requiring the people to measure out the short rations of bread and water carefully. In consequence, the people will **in dismay** recognize this lack of bread and water as judgment upon them and **waste away under their punishment**. The language used here closely resembles the wording of the †covenant curses found in Leviticus: "I will break the staff of bread" is taken from Lev 26:26; the phrase "waste away under their punishment" paraphrases Lev 26:39.[8] Ezekiel's listeners (and readers) would be familiar with the covenant blessings and curses promised in Leviticus (and in Deut 28–30). By making use of this biblical language, Ezekiel shows that the judgment about to befall Jerusalem and the people of Israel is in fact a fulfillment of the promise made long ago through Moses. Because of their sustained disobedience, they are receiving the punishment decreed in the law.

To sum up: in this third sign-act, Ezekiel is symbolically enacting beforehand the kind of hardship that the people will face in the siege to come. He is "taking the punishment on himself," not in terms of atonement but in a kind

---

7. Ralph W. Klein, *Ezekiel: The Prophet and His Message* (Columbia: University of South Carolina Press, 1988), 43.

8. The phrase "break [the] staff of bread" occurs also in Ezek 14:13; the idea of wasting or pining away because of iniquities appears also in Ezek 24:23 and 33:10.

Theodoret on the Strangeness of Ezekiel's Symbolic Acts

Theodoret of Cyrus (d. 460), from the Antiochene tradition, is one of only a few early Christian writers to write a commentary on the prophet Ezekiel. Here he proposes that the novelty and strangeness of Ezekiel's prophetic actions serve the divine purpose:

> The ruler of the universe ordered each of these things to be done so that by the strangeness of this spectacle he might gather those who would not be persuaded by speech or give an ear to prophecy and so dispose them to hear the divine †oracles. . . . He arranged this extraordinary novelty to draw everyone by its strangeness to the spectacle and make his counsel persuasive to those who come.[a]

a. *Lives of Simeon Stylites* 12 (ACCS 13:33).

of solidarity that is meant to reveal the Lord's punishment coming upon his people.

In the fourth and final sign-act, Ezekiel is told to shave his head and his beard completely and divide the cut hair into three equal parts. Notably, he is instructed to **take a sharp sword . . . as a barber's razor**, pointing to the weapon of punishment that will come upon Israel. For a priest, shaving one's hair and beard was forbidden, a sign of desecration. By shaving himself in this way, Ezekiel is embracing and embodying the punished state of the people (see the sidebar "Shaving One's Head and Beard," p. 60).

5:1

The three ways that Ezekiel is told to divide and deal with the shaved hair refer to the diverse judgments that will befall Jerusalem and the people of Israel. Here we should recall the model of the city inscribed on the clay tablet with siegeworks against it as the scene for carrying out this action (Ezek 4:1–3). The first **third** that Ezekiel burns **in the fire** points to those who will die within the city by famine and plague (see 5:12); the second **third**, struck **with the sword**, stands for those who will perish by the sword as they seek to escape the city; and the final **third**, scattered **to the wind**, signifies those who are sent into exile—even they will be pursued by the sword of judgment, as is promised in Lev 26:33: "And I will scatter you among the nations, and I will unsheathe the sword after you." The **small number** of hairs that Ezekiel is told to **bind . . . in the skirts of** his **robe** represents the exiles who will survive, but even some of these shall perish **in the fire**. The application of this threefold action is plain: through various means **all the house of Israel** will be punished—none will escape the judgment of the Lord.

5:2–4

Shaving One's Head and Beard

BIBLICAL BACKGROUND

It was a serious matter for the Lord to tell Ezekiel the priest to shave his head and beard. In the law of Moses, priests were forbidden to shave their head or their beard: "They shall not make tonsures upon their heads, nor shave off the edges of their beards" (Lev 21:5). This restriction against shaving head and beard is reflected in the restoration of the priesthood later in Ezekiel (44:20): the priests "shall not shave their heads or let their locks grow long; they shall only trim the hair of their heads." With this prescription in mind, traditional Jewish commentary concluded that Ezekiel must have shaved his head only symbolically because the Lord would not give a command that went against the †Torah. More generally, shaving one's head was a sign of mourning (Isa 15:2; Jer 48:37) or disgrace (2 Sam 10:4). It was a sign of judgment and humiliation (see Isa 7:20). When the Lord tells Ezekiel to shave his head and beard, he is making Ezekiel once again to be a sign representing the whole people of Israel, who are about to suffer shame, humiliation, and defeat.

Indictment of Jerusalem (5:5–17)

⁵"Thus says the Lord GOD: This is Jerusalem; I have set her in the center of the nations, with countries round about her. ⁶And she has wickedly rebelled against my ordinances more than the nations, and against my statutes more than the countries round about her, by rejecting my ordinances and not walking in my statutes. ⁷Therefore thus says the Lord GOD: Because you are more turbulent than the nations that are round about you, and have not walked in my statutes or kept my ordinances, but have acted according to the ordinances of the nations that are round about you; ⁸therefore thus says the Lord GOD: Behold, I, even I, am against you; and I will execute judgments in the midst of you in the sight of the nations. ⁹And because of all your abominations I will do with you what I have never yet done, and the like of which I will never do again. ¹⁰Therefore fathers shall eat their sons in the midst of you, and sons shall eat their fathers; and I will execute judgments on you, and any of you who survive I will scatter to all the winds. ¹¹Wherefore, as I live, says the Lord GOD, surely, because you have defiled my sanctuary with all your detestable things and with all your abominations, therefore I will cut you down; my eye will not spare, and I will have no pity. ¹²A third part of you shall die of pestilence and be consumed with famine in the midst of you; a third part shall fall by the sword round about you; and a third part I will scatter to all the winds and will unsheathe the sword after them.

¹³"Thus shall my anger spend itself, and I will vent my fury upon them and satisfy myself; and they shall know that I, the LORD, have spoken in my jealousy, when I spend my fury upon them. ¹⁴Moreover I will make you a desolation and an object of reproach among the nations round about you and in the sight of all that pass by. ¹⁵You shall be a reproach and a taunt, a warning and a horror, to the nations round about you, when I execute judgments on you in anger and fury, and with furious chastisements—I, the LORD, have spoken— ¹⁶when I loose against you my deadly arrows of famine, arrows for destruction, which I will loose to destroy you, and when I bring more and more famine upon you, and break your staff of bread. ¹⁷I will send famine and wild beasts against you, and they will rob you of your children; pestilence and blood shall pass through you; and I will bring the sword upon you. I, the LORD, have spoken."

OT: Lev 26:27–33; Deut 28:53–57; Jer 21:5
NT: John 3:17, 19; 2 Pet 3:7, 9; Rev 6:8
Catechism: God's punishment and judgment of sin, 211, 679, 1472–73, 2054

In the remainder of chapter 5, the Lord himself—speaking through Ezekiel—interprets Ezekiel's four prophetic actions. It is a verbal description of what has been visualized in the prophetic actions. Ezekiel is saying to his audience: you have seen my prophetic acts; now this is what they mean.

The city that Ezekiel inscribed on the clay tablet is **Jerusalem**. The Lord **set**   5:5–6
her in the center of the nations, a greatly privileged place that is later called "the center of the earth" (Ezek 38:12). But Jerusalem **has wickedly rebelled against** the statutes and ordinances of the Lord, not only disobeying them, but in the process becoming even *worse* than the nations who did not have the gift of God's law.

Because of this, the Lord solemnly declares: **Behold, I, even I, am against**   5:7–10
you. Could there be words more haunting and terrifying than these? If the Lord is against his own people, what hope do they have of avoiding disaster? The prophecy goes on to say that the magnitude of this punishment will be greater than what has come before or will come after—it will be of exceeding severity: **And because of all your abominations I will do with you what I have never yet done, and the like of which I will never do again**.[9] Because of the desperateness of the siege against Jerusalem, **fathers shall eat their sons in the midst of you, and sons shall eat their fathers**. This dreadful outcome—a famine so horrendous that people consume the bodies of their family members—is just what was predicted in the covenant curses (see Deut 28:53–57; also see Lam 4:10).

Because the leaders and people have **defiled** the **sanctuary** (that is, the   5:11
temple), the Lord says that he will **cut** them **down**. There are two distinct ways

---

9. The term "abomination" appears more than thirty-five times in Ezekiel and refers to actions that are greatly offensive to the Lord and to the law he has given to Israel.

of understanding the Hebrew verb here. The RSV-2CE and NRSV adopt the translation "I will cut you down." This fits the context well: just as Ezekiel symbolically cut off his hair and beard, so the Lord will cut off his people. The ESV and NABRE adopt a different translation, "I will withdraw." This fits with the vision of the withdrawal of the divine presence—the Lord's chariot—which will appear in chapter 10. And this is a dire consequence indeed. The active *presence* of the Lord with his people is a key part of his covenant love for them. Both translations of verse 11 fit the context well and reveal the severity of God's judgment toward his people.

5:12   With verse 12, Ezekiel's division of his shaved hair into three parts receives its interpretation: (1) a third **shall die of pestilence and be consumed with famine**; (2) a third **shall fall by the sword** when the city falls; and (3) a third the Lord **will scatter to all the winds and will unsheathe the sword after them**. No one will be exempt from the thorough, searching judgment of the Lord. There will be no loopholes or exceptions.

5:13–17   The language in this section is perhaps the most impassioned and the most severe in the entire book. The Lord speaks of his **anger, fury**, and **jealousy** and his determination to make his people **a reproach and a taunt, a warning and a horror, to the nations** surrounding Israel (vv. 13–15). This is why he will **execute judgments** upon them through famine, pestilence, the sword, and a fourth means of punishment, wild beasts (vv. 16–17). The determination of the Lord is clear: twice he underlines, **I, the LORD, have spoken** (vv. 15, 17). The *result* of this cycle of severe punishments is that "they shall know that I am the LORD" (v. 13 ESV).[10] In other words, the people will come to recognize the truth and justice of what the Lord has said and done when he brings their due punishment upon them.

What are we to make of this harsh language that describes the Lord God as venting his fury on his people and executing judgments against them with furious rebukes? The particular quality of this section is the passionate severity of the Lord's judgment. It comes like a storm, like a furious attack, so great is his dismay and his determination to demonstrate the destructiveness of sin. Some contemporary commentators see here an unworthy depiction of the Lord, who, like a Greek god, vents his anger and jealousy just like a sinful human being might do. They conclude that Ezekiel uniquely presents a harsh, spiteful God who is concerned only for getting his own way.[11]

There is no escaping the fact that the Lord, through the prophet Ezekiel, expresses deep displeasure and genuine anger here. The sins of the people have piled up, and the Lord is determined to bring a sharp judgment upon his sinful

10. See the sidebar "'Then You Will Know That I Am the LORD,'" p. 187.

11. For an example of this view, see Baruch J. Schwartz, "Ezekiel's Dim View of Israel's Restoration," in *The Book of Ezekiel: Theological and Anthropological Perspectives*, ed. Margaret S. Odell and John T. Strong (Atlanta: Society of Biblical Literature, 2000), 43–67.

The Typical Means of Judgment

When Ezekiel speaks in 5:12 of a threefold judgment by *famine*, *pestilence*, and *the sword*, he is following a common biblical way of speaking. How does judgment typically strike? Through "the sword" of foreign armies, through death-dealing famine, and through wasting disease. This "triad of judgments" occurs four times in Ezekiel (5:12; 6:11–12; 7:15; 12:16) and more than fifteen times in Jeremiah (e.g., Jer 14:12; 21:9; see also 1 Chron 21:12 and Bar 2:25). Sometimes a fourth means of judgment, "wild beasts," is added to the other three. We see this in Ezekiel when he identifies "four deadly acts of judgment" (14:21 NRSV; see also 5:17). The four means—the sword, famine, pestilence, and wild beasts—also are found in Deut 32:23–25. Notably, these four means reappear in the book of Revelation as the main vehicles for God's judgment against the ungodly nations: "They were given power over a fourth of the earth, to kill with sword and with famine and with pestilence and by wild beasts of the earth" (Rev 6:8). In one sense, these acts of judgment are "natural"—that is, they occur through natural causes in our world (e.g., wars, plagues, famines). But from a biblical standpoint, these natural occurrences can be means, allowed by God, through which he accomplishes his purposes in the world. As we see in Ezekiel, one of God's main intentions is to bring his own people—and all peoples—under judgment for sin, with the aim of leading them back into relationship with himself.

people. But this language is not unique to Ezekiel. As we have already observed, Ezekiel seems to be taking his cue from the language of the covenant curses—in this case, Lev 26:27–28 (ESV): "But if in spite of this you will not listen to me, but walk contrary to me, then I will walk contrary to you in fury, and I myself will discipline you sevenfold for your sins." In fact, Ezek 5:5–17 reads like a restatement and expansion of Lev 26:27–33. Ezekiel is adapting the language of the covenant curses in Leviticus to convey the Lord's present word to a disobedient people. Ezekiel also reflects the language of his contemporary, Jeremiah, who spoke in similar language about the Lord's stand against his own people: "I myself will fight against you with outstretched hand and strong arm, in anger, and in fury, and in great wrath" (Jer 21:5).

Furthermore, the statement **Thus shall my anger spend itself, and I will vent my fury upon them** can be understood in two different ways, both of which are consistent with Ezekiel's presentation of God's interaction with his people. In the first way (represented by the ESV translation), the Lord is speaking of venting his full anger upon the people until he is satisfied that they have suffered appropriately: he will "spend" his fury upon them to demonstrate his passion and jealousy. In the second way, this phrase expresses *comfort* because the Lord's anger has come to an end (literally, has come "to rest"), as in Robert Alter's translation: "And my anger shall come to an end, and I will put to rest My wrath against them, and I will repent, and they shall know that I the Lord have spoken in My passion when I bring to an end My wrath against them."[12] When the Bible speaks in terms of God "repenting," it does not mean he is sorry for wrongdoing or failure, but that he has chosen to relent from punishing his people as they deserve.

The God revealed in this book—and within the wider biblical testimony—is a God who seeks the good of his people and who acts with determination to bring them back into relationship with him. His "jealousy" is not like a vacillating human emotion but is a quality of his relentless steadfast love.

Reflection and Application (5:1–17)

Today it is common to hear something like the following: "The God of the Old Testament is a God of wrath and anger, but the God revealed in Jesus is a God of mercy and forgiveness." Those who make this sharp contrast, like the †Gnostics of old, slice off and toss away the Old Testament as unworthy of the "good" God revealed in Jesus. But this judgment is not fair to the Old Testament or the New. Certainly Jesus came, like a physician, to heal the sick and to welcome sinners into the kingdom of God (Mark 2:17). The Son came into the world not to condemn the world but so that the world might be saved (John 3:17) and have life in abundance (10:10). But the New Testament speaks frequently of judgment: "And this is the judgment, that the light has come into the world, and men loved darkness rather than light, because their deeds were evil" (John 3:19). Even in this present age of the world, God is sifting people's hearts through the preaching of the †gospel. And we know from the words of Jesus himself that he will come again and carry out a final judgment upon all (Matt 25:31–46; John 5:28–29).

Likewise, the Old Testament is not about a God of wrath, anger, and punishment, but about a God who has created a good world and is determined to redeem that world. When God acts to judge or punish, it is because he is calling people back from the sin that kills. In Ezekiel, we hear this plea in the Lord's own voice: "Have I any pleasure in the death of the wicked, says the Lord GOD, and not rather that he should turn from his way and live? . . . So turn and live" (Ezek 18:23, 32). This is a God who raises up dry bones and breathes new life into them (37:1–14). This is a God who brings his people out of exile, who promises to give them a new heart and spirit (36:26). This is

---

12. Alter, "Ezekiel," 1064. Eisemann, *Ezekiel*, 127, observes that "each of the key verbs in this phrase . . . lend themselves to various interpretations," and he offers examples from Jewish †rabbinic tradition of the two contrastive readings of v. 13.

a God who pledges himself to be their shepherd and to lead them into good pasture (34:11–16). The God of the Old Testament is the same God who is revealed in the New Testament. All his actions—even his severe judgments—are aimed at bringing us back to himself so that we may dwell with him forever.

Judgment against the Mountains of Israel (6:1–14)

¹The word of the Lord came to me: ²"Son of man, set your face toward the mountains of Israel, and prophesy against them, ³and say, You mountains of Israel, hear the word of the Lord God! Thus says the Lord God to the mountains and the hills, to the ravines and the valleys: Behold, I, even I, will bring a sword upon you, and I will destroy your high places. ⁴Your altars shall become desolate, and your incense altars shall be broken; and I will cast down your slain before your idols. ⁵And I will lay the dead bodies of the people of Israel before their idols; and I will scatter your bones round about your altars. ⁶Wherever you dwell your cities shall be waste and your high places ruined, so that your altars will be waste and ruined, your idols broken and destroyed, your incense altars cut down, and your works wiped out. ⁷And the slain shall fall in the midst of you, and you shall know that I am the Lord.

⁸"Yet I will leave some of you alive. When you have among the nations some who escape the sword, and when you are scattered through the countries, ⁹then those of you who escape will remember me among the nations where they are carried captive, when I have broken their wanton heart which has departed from me, and blinded their eyes which turn wantonly after their idols; and they will be loathsome in their own sight for the evils which they have committed, for all their abominations. ¹⁰And they shall know that I am the Lord; I have not said in vain that I would do this evil to them."

¹¹Thus says the Lord God: "Clap your hands, and stamp your foot, and say, Alas! because of all the evil abominations of the house of Israel; for they shall fall by the sword, by famine, and by pestilence. ¹²He that is far off shall die of pestilence; and he that is near shall fall by the sword; and he that is left and is preserved shall die of famine. Thus I will spend my fury upon them. ¹³And you shall know that I am the Lord, when their slain lie among their idols round about their altars, upon every high hill, on all the mountain tops, under every green tree, and under every leafy oak, wherever they offered pleasing odor to all their idols. ¹⁴And I will stretch out my hand against them, and make the land desolate and waste, throughout all their habitations, from the wilderness to Riblah. Then they will know that I am the Lord."

OT: Lev 26:30; Deut 30:1–3; Prov 3:11–12; Isa 55:6–7
NT: Heb 12:5–11
Catechism: the sin of idolatry, 2112–14; God's punishment and judgment of sin, 211, 679, 1472–73, 2054

6:1–2   We continue the same topic—judgment—but change location. Chapters 4 and 5 centered on Jerusalem; now Ezekiel directs his words to **the mountains of Israel**. Just as Ezekiel was called to set his face against the city (4:7), he is called here to **set** his **face** against the mountains and hills of Israel and to prophesy against them.

6:3–4a   What sense does it make to prophesy against inanimate **mountains and . . . hills**? The physical location of the "high places" stands symbolically for the practice of idolatry. From ancient times, it was a common practice for the people to erect altars on the highest places in the land, where they would offer sacrifices, prayers, and incense to idols. The Lord sees this and is determined to bring judgment against this practice: **I will destroy your high places. Your altars shall become desolate, and your incense altars shall be broken**.[13] Notably, Ezekiel will later prophesy about the *restoration* of the mountains and hills (see 36:1–15), indicating God's purpose to restore what has been lost.

6:4b–6   Once again, the covenant curses in Leviticus seem to provide the script for Ezekiel's condemnation of idolatry in the land: "And I will destroy your high places, and cut down your incense altars, and cast your dead bodies upon the dead bodies of your idols; and my soul will abhor you" (Lev 26:30). This is just what the Lord promises here: **I will cast down your slain before your idols. And I will lay the dead bodies of the people of Israel before their idols**. The Lord will destroy all the places where idolatry has been practiced in the land, and the people will fall slain *in the very places* where they have sinned against the Lord. The punishment will be suited to the sin: just as the people prostrated themselves before idols on the high places, so their slain will be **cast down** in death before these same high places.

6:7   The final line, **and you shall know that I am the LORD**, is critically important. Four times in this chapter Ezekiel restates a version of this refrain (vv. 7, 10, 13, 14).[14] Why is it significant that the people "know" that this is the Lord's doing? The Lord's aim is not simply to dispense punishment, but by means of punishment to lead his people to repentance. This is the logic of Deut 30, which provides the background for Ezekiel's words: "And when all these things come upon you, the blessing and the curse, which I have set before you, and you call them to mind . . . ; then the LORD your God will restore your fortunes, and have compassion upon you" (Deut 30:1, 3). The Lord justly punishes the guilty because of their sin—this is an important part of God's revelation of himself (see Ezek 7:9). If the people do not recognize that this disaster has befallen them because of their sin, then they will not repent and turn back to the Lord. Repentance and restoration is the Lord's endgame.

13. Condemnation of the "high places" runs throughout the Old Testament, from the Law to the Prophets and the Wisdom literature. For characteristic denunciation of idolatry practiced on the high places of Israel, see Num 33:52; 1 Kings 14:23–24; Ps 78:58; Jer 19:4–5; Hosea 10:8.

14. For the meaning of this refrain, see the sidebar "'Then You Will Know That I Am the LORD,'" p. 187.

The Covenant Blessings and Curses

BIBLICAL BACKGROUND

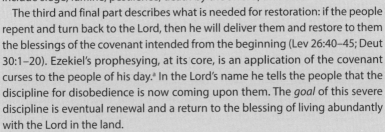

The †covenant blessings and curses, found in Lev 26 and Deut 28–30, are foundational for Ezekiel's understanding of what is unfolding *in his day* between the Lord and his people Israel. Ezekiel never quotes these passages directly—he restates them in his own words—but they clearly provide the lens through which he sees the dire situation of God's people. The statement of the covenant blessings and curses follows a simple structure. The first part states what will happen *if* the people follow the Lord and keep his commandments: they will receive abundant blessings in the land and bear fruit in manifold ways (Lev 26:3–13; Deut 28:1–14). The announcement of the blessings is brief and compact.

The second part narrates the curses—the judgments and punishments—that will befall Israel if they disobey the voice of the Lord and fail to keep his commandments. In both Leviticus and Deuteronomy, the punishments come in stages: if the people do not repent when the Lord disciplines them, then he will send other, more severe judgments (Lev 26:14–39; Deut 28:15–29:29). The punishments include siege, famine, pestilence, death by the sword, and exile.

The third and final part describes what is needed for restoration: if the people repent and turn back to the Lord, then he will deliver them and restore to them the blessings of the covenant intended from the beginning (Lev 26:40–45; Deut 30:1–20). Ezekiel's prophesying, at its core, is an application of the covenant curses to the people of his day.[a] In the Lord's name he tells the people that the discipline for disobedience is now coming upon them. The *goal* of this severe discipline is eventual renewal and a return to the blessing of living abundantly with the Lord in the land.

a. Ezekiel is not alone is applying the covenant curses to the people of Israel. We find a similar application of the covenant curses in 1 Kings 8:46–51; 2 Kings 17:7–23; and Dan 9:3–11.

6:8–10 To counter the potential misunderstanding that the Lord intends to wipe out his people completely, the Lord says, **Yet I will leave some of you alive.**[15] This is *not yet* a word of comfort or a promise of return from exile. God has a purpose for those **who escape the sword, and . . . are scattered through the countries**: they will remember the Lord **among the nations where they are carried captive,** where the Lord will break **their wanton heart,** which has departed from the Lord. "Wanton" can also be translated "lusting" (NABRE) or "whoring" (ESV). This is the first time in Ezekiel when the sin of idolatry is described through the metaphor of prostitution or adultery. This will become a major theme later in the book. The term for "idols," found thirty-eight times

15. The Hebrew text has simply, "and I will leave," which the NRSV translates as "but I will spare some."

in Ezekiel, literally means "dung-balls," indicating the disdain Ezekiel has for the folly of idol worship.

There are two ways to understand the verb "to break" in verse 9. The first (RSV-2CE, NABRE) adopts the *active* form of the verb: the Lord "will break" their adulterous hearts, which have turned away from him. The second (ESV, NRSV, NIV) adopts the *passive* form of the verb: the Lord himself "is broken" by the adulterous acts of his people. Both readings fit the context, but the second reading shows how God's own heart is broken by the unfaithfulness of his people, a theme that echoes across the Scripture.[16] Sin is a matter not just of breaking rules but of breaking God's heart.

The result is grave: **they will be loathsome in their own sight for the evils which they have committed**.[17] A deep spirit of repentance and regret will fall upon the exiles, and **they shall know** that it is the Lord God who justly did **this evil to them**. There are two distinct senses of "evil" in verses 9–10. The "evils" that the people committed are moral evils—they are "abominations" in the sight of the Lord. But the "evil" that the Lord has done to them in return is not moral evil, as if the Lord were doing something wicked and against his character. "Evil" here refers to the just punishment, promised by Moses, that God will bring upon the people if they do not walk in his ways: "See, I have set before you this day life and good, death and evil" (Deut 30:15).[18]

6:11–13   This section restates in similar terms the same basic judgment against the mountains of Israel found in 6:1–10. Ezekiel tells his audience of exiles: **Clap your hands, and stamp your foot** as a sign of profound grief and visceral repentance for **all the evil abominations of the house of Israel**. Ezekiel revisits the consequences of the oncoming disaster in terms of the threefold judgment—**by the sword, by famine, and by pestilence**—and grimly depicts the slain lying dead on the mountaintops where **they offered pleasing odor to all their idols**. The "odor" refers to the fragrance that came from the burning of the sacrifices, intended to be pleasing to their gods. Ezekiel's condemnation of idolatry here is reminiscent of the prophet Hosea: "They sacrifice on the tops of the mountains, and make offerings upon the hills, under oak, poplar, and terebinth" (Hosea 4:13).

6:14   Ezekiel concludes: **And I will stretch out my hand against them, and make the land desolate and waste, throughout all their habitations, from**

16. For the Lord grieving over the sin of his people, see Ps 78:40; Isa 5:1–4; Hosea 2:1–23. Jesus also grieves over the hardness of heart among the Jewish leaders of his day (Mark 3:5) and mourns over the Holy City, which is about to reject him (Luke 13:34).

17. The theme of the Lord acting to bring about self-loathing among his people recurs in Ezek 20:43 and 36:31.

18. The prophet Jeremiah makes use of these two distinct senses of "evil" when speaking of the Lord's judgment for wrongdoing: "And if that nation, concerning which I have spoken, turns from its evil, I will repent of the evil that I intended to do to it" (Jer 18:8).

the wilderness to Riblah. God's judgment, in other words, will extend from the far south (the wilderness) to the far north (Riblah, in central Syria). Later it will be at Riblah that the chief leaders of Israel in the revolt against Babylon will be put to death and the exile will begin (2 Kings 25:6, 21; Jer 39:5–6). The chapter closes with the core refrain: **Then they will know that I am the LORD**. The point of God's judgment is to bring his people to a true knowledge of God and his ways that leads to deep repentance.

Reflection and Application (6:1–14)

If we read the sixth chapter of Ezekiel all by itself, it seems to convey only unrelenting judgment and punishment. We might ask: *Where is the good news here?* This is why it is critical to read these announcements of judgment in the wider context of the whole book and of the entire biblical narrative. God allows our disobedient ways to lead to ever-graver consequences until we, like the prodigal son in the pigsty (Luke 15:11–32), awake to our true situation and return to the Lord. In the context of Ezekiel, many of the unfaithful people will perish in the disaster that will soon befall them, but the Lord will preserve a remnant who will learn what it means to repent and be faithful to the Lord.

Hebrews 12 points us toward the attitude we should adopt when we experience suffering and loss. Though the context in Hebrews is less severe and does not involve the same level of disobedience that we find in Ezekiel, the basic message is this: by means of trials and hardships God is, in fact, treating us as *his children*, his sons and daughters. A line taken from the book of Proverbs points us in the right direction: "Do not regard lightly the discipline of the Lord, nor be weary when reproved by him. For the Lord disciplines the one he loves, and chastises every son whom he receives" (Heb 12:5–6 ESV, citing Prov 3:11–12). When trials and hardships befall us, we are encouraged to receive these as "the discipline of the Lord." It is true that "for the moment all discipline seems painful rather than pleasant" (Heb 12:11). But the *point* of this painful discipline is "our good, that we may share his holiness" (12:10). Even more, when we recognize that we are being disciplined and reproved because of our sin, we should receive this as the medicinal treatment of the Lord to bring us true healing. The following lines from the prophet Isaiah wonderfully express how we are called to return to the Lord in repentance and hope: "Seek the LORD while he may be found, / call upon him while he is near; / . . . let [the unrighteous man] return to the LORD, that he may have mercy on him, / and to our God, for he will abundantly pardon" (Isa 55:6–7).

Sounding the Alarm for the Land of Israel (7:1–27)

[1]The word of the LORD came to me: [2]"And you, O son of man, thus says the Lord GOD to the land of Israel: An end! The end has come upon the four corners of the land. [3]Now the end is upon you, and I will let loose my anger upon you, and will judge you according to your ways; and I will punish you for all your abominations. [4]And my eye will not spare you, nor will I have pity; but I will punish you for your ways, while your abominations are in your midst. Then you will know that I am the LORD.

[5]"Thus says the Lord GOD: Disaster after disaster! Behold, it comes. [6]An end has come, the end has come; it has awakened against you. Behold, it comes. [7]Your doom has come to you, O inhabitant of the land; the time has come, the day is near, a day of tumult, and not of joyful shouting upon the mountains. [8]Now I will soon pour out my wrath upon you, and spend my anger against you, and judge you according to your ways; and I will punish you for all your abominations. [9]And my eye will not spare, nor will I have pity; I will punish you according to your ways, while your abominations are in your midst. Then you will know that I am the LORD, who strike.

[10]"Behold, the day! Behold, it comes! Your doom has come, injustice has blossomed, pride has budded. [11]Violence has grown up into a rod of wickedness; none of them shall remain, nor their abundance, nor their wealth; neither shall there be preeminence among them. [12]The time has come, the day draws near. Let not the buyer rejoice, nor the seller mourn, for wrath is upon all their multitude. [13]For the seller shall not return to what he has sold, while they live. For wrath is upon all their multitude; it shall not turn back; and because of his iniquity, none can maintain his life.

[14]"They have blown the trumpet and made all ready; but none goes to battle, for my wrath is upon all their multitude. [15]The sword is without, pestilence and famine are within; he that is in the field dies by the sword; and him that is in the city famine and pestilence devour. [16]And if any survivors escape, they will be on the mountains, like doves of the valleys, all of them moaning, every one over his iniquity. [17]All hands are feeble, and all knees weak as water. [18]They clothe themselves with sackcloth, and horror covers them; shame is upon all faces, and baldness on all their heads. [19]They cast their silver into the streets, and their gold is like an unclean thing; their silver and gold are not able to deliver them in the day of the wrath of the LORD; they cannot satisfy their hunger or fill their stomachs with it. For it was the stumbling block of their iniquity. [20]Their beautiful ornament they used for vainglory, and they made their abominable images and their detestable things of it; therefore I will make it an unclean thing to them. [21]And I will give it into the hands of foreigners for a prey, and to the wicked of the earth for a spoil; and they shall profane it. [22]I will turn my face from them, that they may profane my precious place; robbers shall enter and profane it, [23]and make a desolation.

"Because the land is full of bloody crimes and the city is full of vio-lence, [24]I will bring the worst of the nations to take possession of their houses; I will put an end to their proud might, and their holy places shall be profaned. [25]When anguish comes, they will seek peace, but there shall be none. [26]Disaster comes upon disaster, rumor follows rumor; they seek a vision from the prophet, but the law perishes from the priest, and coun-sel from the elders. [27]The king mourns, the prince is wrapped in despair, and the hands of the people of the land are palsied by terror. According to their way I will do to them, and according to their own judgments I will judge them; and they shall know that I am the LORD."

OT: Gen 6:13; Num 17:8; Jer 18:18; Zech 1:18
NT: Matt 6:20–21; 1 Cor 7:30–31
Catechism: God's punishment and judgment of sin, 211, 679, 1472–73, 2054; sin manifested in violence, 1851

In this chapter, Ezekiel truly takes up his role as watchman for Israel. His mes-sage is full of alarm, of staccato-like sayings declaring that judgment is about to fall on the entire land of Israel. It is also the first time in the book that Ezekiel makes use of poetic form, sensing perhaps that the medium of poetry is best suited to capture the sharp cry of alarm in his message.

The defining word for this section is "end." It appears five times in the first **7:1–4** six verses and reappears once more at the end of the chapter (v. 24) to tie the message together. **An end! The end has come upon the four corners of the land. Now the end is upon you**. The people's sins have piled up, the Lord's anger will be unleashed, and nothing can stop it. The term "end" recalls Gen 6:13: "I have determined to make an end of all flesh; for the earth is filled with violence through them." There is also an echo of the words of the prophet Amos: "The end has come upon my people Israel; I will never again pass by them" (Amos 8:2). In the same spirit, Ezekiel declares that the Lord is acting to "end" the sins and transgressions of his people in the land. He **will judge** them for their abominations and **will punish** them for their evil ways. The consequence and goal (once again) is that the entire people **will know that I am the LORD**.

To intensify the gravity of the alarm, Ezekiel adds the phrase **disaster after** **7:5–9** **disaster** (v. 5, restated in v. 26). As with an ominous drumbeat, Ezekiel repeats the certain coming of this disaster: **Behold, it comes. An end has come, the end has come; it has awakened against you. Behold, it comes. Your doom has come to you. . . . The time has come**.[19] Ezekiel's audience could be in no doubt that a devastating cataclysm was about to fall upon the people and the land.

In this section, the theme of judgment continues but is now carried by the **7:10–13** term "day": **Behold, the day! Behold, it comes! . . . The time has come, the day**

19. There is a wordplay in v. 6 between the word "end" (Hebrew *qets*) and the verb "awake" (Hebrew *qits*). The rabbis concluded that the "end" of Israel would cause them to "awaken" to their own sin (Eisemann, *Ezekiel*, 142–43).

draws near. Reference to the "day" recalls the common prophetic announcement of "the day of the Lord," which refers universally to a day of judgment.[20] Ezekiel then underlines the pride and violence of the people. In contrast to the budding and blossoming of Aaron's rod (Num 17:8), their rod produces blooms of arrogance. The result is that the economy of the nation of Israel will be destroyed and their wealth will perish: **None of them shall remain, nor their abundance, nor their wealth**. "The collapse of the economy will be total, rendering all business transactions futile."[21] This collapse applies not just to a select few but to **all their multitude; it shall not turn back**. No amount of wealth gained through violence will be able to deliver the people in that day.

In the Light of Christ (7:10–13)

When Paul instructs Christians in the city of Corinth about how they should conduct themselves, he uses paradoxical language: "those who mourn as though they were not mourning, and those who rejoice as though they were not rejoicing, and those who buy as though they had no goods" (1 Cor 7:30). Paul is probably drawing here on Ezek 7:12–13: "Let not the buyer rejoice, nor the seller mourn. . . . For the seller shall not return to what he has sold." Paul is not applying this verse from Ezekiel in exactly the same sense that it has for the prophet, but using similar terms he redirects the meaning to teach the early Christians how they are to conduct themselves in view of the return of Jesus. For Ezekiel, because the day of the Lord's judgment is at hand, buying and selling (and rejoicing and mourning) will soon come to an end. For Paul, because "the appointed time has grown very short" and "the form of this world is passing away" (1 Cor 7:29, 31), Christians should not treat this world and its riches as their true and lasting home. Their primary investment is in the coming kingdom where, as Jesus says, "neither moth nor rust consumes and where thieves do not break in and steal. For where your treasure is, there will your heart be also" (Matt 6:20–21).

7:14–16   Now we hear of the desperate state of the people of Israel under siege in Jerusalem. The first calamity is the inability to fight against the besieging foe: **they have blown the trumpet and made all ready; but none goes to battle**. They stand helpless, unable to muster arms against the hosts of Babylon. Next, the triad of judgments is about to befall them: **the sword is without,**

20. The Greek version (†Septuagint) of Ezek 7:10 includes the full phrase, "day of the Lord." For the phrase "day of the Lord" in the Old Testament prophets, see, for example, Isa 13:6; Jer 46:10; Joel 1:15; Amos 5:20; Zeph 1:7.
21. Block, *Ezekiel: Chapters 1–24*, 259.

pestilence and famine are within. Those who remain in the city will be devoured by disease and hunger; those who seek to flee or fight will die by the sword outside the walls. **And if any survivors escape** from these disasters, they will be left to wander about the hills, **moaning** in grief because of their iniquities.

Ezekiel stresses that all without exception will become helpless: **all hands are feeble, and all knees weak as water.** The people will cover themselves in **sackcloth** and go about in deep shame for the doom that has fallen upon them. Even the rich, who seek to take refuge in their wealth, will be powerless: **their silver and gold are not able to deliver them in the day of the wrath of the Lord**. The prophet Zephaniah echoes this message: "Neither their silver nor their gold / shall be able to deliver them / on the day of the wrath of the Lord" (Zeph 1:18). Once again the punishment fits the crime. The rich and powerful sought after great wealth (silver and gold) and used it to make **abominable images** of false gods. But these gods cannot save them. Their silver and gold will become **an unclean thing to them** because it cannot deliver them from this great crisis. The result is that this foreign nation (Babylon) will occupy and **profane** the Holy City and its people. | 7:17–21

As terrible as this is, the most dire consequence is what the Lord God will do: **I will turn my face from them**. This is the most momentous and tragic result of their sin. The glorious presence of God among his people is the source of all his blessings; his departure—turning away his face—is the cause of all their calamities. The people have repeatedly turned away from the Lord; now the Lord will turn away from them by removing his blessing, protection, and presence. | 7:22–23a

The chapter closes as it began: Ezekiel sums up what is about to befall Jerusalem and the land of Israel. Why has the Lord decreed this punishment? **Because the land is full of bloody crimes and the city is full of violence**. Here the social sins of Israel are brought into the light. Because the people—and especially the leaders—have committed grave injustice against their own people, the Lord will send them into exile. | 7:23b–24

When this calamity happens, **they will seek peace, but there shall be none**. The Lord will do to them as they have done to others: **according to their way I will do to them, and according to their own judgments I will judge them**. Ezekiel foretells a judgment on *all* the main groupings within the people of Israel (prophets, priests, elders, and king/prince). The prophet Jeremiah was rejected by similar groups among the people: "Come, let us make plots against Jeremiah—for the law shall not perish from the priest, nor counsel from the wise, nor the word from the prophet" (Jer 18:18). Rejecting this false boasting, Ezekiel declares that in vain **they seek a vision from the prophet,** while **the law perishes from the priest, and counsel from the elders**. No one will be able to save them in that day. The prophets will give no vision, the priests will not | 7:25–27

"Shekinah" in Jewish and Christian Tradition

LIVING TRADITION

The biblical text of Ezek 7:22 reads, "I will turn my face from them." But the †*Targum of Ezekiel*—an early †Aramaic translation—rephrases this: "And I will make my †Shekinah depart from them."[a] In the same way, where Ezek 1:1 reads, "And I saw visions of God," the Targum renders this: "And I beheld . . . a vision of the glory of the Shekinah of the Lord."[b] "Shekinah" is a postbiblical Hebrew word meaning "dwelling" or "presence" that became popular in early †rabbinic Judaism. "Shekinah" is closely related to two biblical words, "to dwell" (Hebrew *shakan*) and "dwelling" or "tabernacle" (Hebrew *mishkan*). In Exod 29:45 (ESV), the Lord says, "I will dwell [*shakan*] among the people of Israel and will be their God." In Ps 26:8 the psalmist rejoices, "O Lord, I love the habitation [*mishkan*] of your house, / and the place where your glory dwells." The fact that Ezekiel witnessed the divine presence (the Shekinah) *outside* of Israel in the land of exile (Ezek 1:1–3) was a source of great comfort to the Jewish people after the destruction of both the first temple (in 586 BC) and the †second temple (in AD 70). Though the temple—the place of God's glorious presence—was gone, the Shekinah of the Lord could still dwell among his people.

The use of the term "Shekinah" to identify the glorious presence of God has also come into use in Christian writing and preaching. Speaking of the Christian liturgy, Joseph Ratzinger (Pope Benedict XVI) uses the term "Shekinah" to show how God's glory is manifested in the reserved eucharistic presence of Christ in the tabernacle:

> The Ark was seen as an empty throne, upon which the Shekinah—the cloud of God's presence—came down. . . . In fact, the tabernacle is the complete fulfillment of what the Ark of the Covenant represented. It is the place of the "Holy of Holies." It is the tent of God, His throne. Here He is among us. His presence (*Shekinah*) really does now dwell among us—in the humblest parish church no less than in the grandest cathedral.[c]

a. Samson H. Levey, trans., *The Targum of Ezekiel*, Aramaic Bible 13 (Wilmington, DE: Michael Glazier, 1987), 34.
b. Levey, *Targum of Ezekiel*, 20.
c. Joseph Ratzinger, *The Spirit of the Liturgy* (San Francisco: Ignatius, 2018), 84, 89.

uphold the law, the elders will fail in counsel, the king/prince will mourn and be in despair, and all the people will be paralyzed **by terror**.

Once again, when all these things come to pass, the Lord's purpose will come about: **they shall know that I am the Lord**. The people will understand their own grievous sin and the Lord's punishment of their sin, but they will also recognize God's abiding disposition to bring his people back to himself and dwell among them once more.

Reflection and Application (7:1–27)

Ezekiel lived in momentous times, when nations were rising up against nations and God's own people were receiving a sharp judgment from the Lord God. The foundations were not only shaken but seemingly destroyed beyond repair. Ezekiel's prophetic message in this chapter expresses the special *urgency* of those times and the need to respond promptly with faith, repentance, and obedience. But do we not live in similar times? All around us we see the shaking among the nations of the earth; we are witnessing a large-scale abandonment of God and his ways in our broader culture; and we can recognize an acute judgment upon the Church for the failures and sins of her children. Trusting in our "silver and gold" to deliver us will not work. All around us we can see the fragility and insufficiency of wealth and possessions. These did not save the people in Ezekiel's day, and they will not save us in ours.

How, then, are we to respond? By hearing God's word in faith, repenting of our own sin and the sins of God's people, and returning to the obedience of holiness in all its manifestations. In his day, Ezekiel heard and acted on the word of the Lord to him. He is a model of the person who hears and obeys, even when others are turning away in droves. Jesus himself provides us with counsel for such alarming times. His advice could be summed up in terms drawn from his final discourse to his disciples: Be alert and be awake, but do not be alarmed! We are to "keep alert" and read the signs of the times, so that we are not unprepared (Mark 13:33 NRSV). We are also to "keep awake" for the Lord's coming, bearing fruit in every season (13:35 NRSV). But Jesus also tells us: "Do not be alarmed" (13:7)—that is, do not panic or give way to fear. Christ is reigning over all these events, and he will hold us secure. Even in the midst of great trials, he will watch over us and enable us to bring the witness of the gospel to many (13:9–10).

Judgment on the Temple
and the Departure of the Lord's Presence
Ezekiel 8:1–11:25

With chapter 8 we begin a new subsection of the book that runs through chapter 11. Moshe Greenberg summarizes it like this: "These four chapters offer a panorama of the crimes of the Jerusalemites and the divine intervention to punish them."[1] The focus of these four chapters is the Lord's judgment upon the temple in Jerusalem, climaxing in the departure of the Lord's glorious presence. Many in Israel presumed that God never would abandon his own temple and city—that in the end he would, of course, save them from Israel's enemies.[2] This presumption is shattered by the vision of the Lord's †divine chariot rising up and leaving the temple and the city.

Opening and closing "bookends" show the thematic unity of chapters 8–11. In the prologue (8:1–4), Ezekiel, seated among the exiles in Babylon, is transported in vision by the Spirit *to* Jerusalem, where he sees the appearance of the divine glory. In the epilogue (11:22–25), these events are reversed: Ezekiel, beholding the divine glory departing from Jerusalem, is transported by the Spirit *away from* Jerusalem back to Babylon, where he finds himself seated once again among the exiles. Within these bookends Ezekiel gives voice to a series of prophetic †oracles that express God's severe judgment upon the temple and the Holy City.

The Abominations in the Temple (8:1–18)

---

[1]In the sixth year, in the sixth month, on the fifth day of the month, as I sat in my house, with the elders of Judah sitting before me, the hand of the

---

1. Greenberg, *Ezekiel 1–20*, 204.
2. The prophet Jeremiah was threatened with death because he dared to prophesy the destruction of Jerusalem (Jer 26:11).

Lord GOD fell there upon me. ²Then I beheld a form that had the appearance of a man; below what appeared to be his loins it was fire, and above his loins it was like the appearance of brightness, like gleaming bronze. ³He put forth the form of a hand, and took me by a lock of my head; and the Spirit lifted me up between earth and heaven, and brought me in visions of God to Jerusalem, to the entrance of the gateway of the inner court that faces north, where was the seat of the image of jealousy, which provokes to jealousy. ⁴And behold, the glory of the God of Israel was there, like the vision that I saw in the plain.

⁵Then he said to me, "Son of man, lift up your eyes now in the direction of the north." So I lifted up my eyes toward the north, and behold, north of the altar gate, in the entrance, was this image of jealousy. ⁶And he said to me, "Son of man, do you see what they are doing, the great abominations that the house of Israel are committing here, to drive me far from my sanctuary? But you will see still greater abominations."

⁷And he brought me to the door of the court; and when I looked, behold, there was a hole in the wall. ⁸Then said he to me, "Son of man, dig in the wall"; and when I dug in the wall, behold, there was a door. ⁹And he said to me, "Go in, and see the vile abominations that they are committing here." ¹⁰So I went in and saw; and there, portrayed upon the wall round about, were all kinds of creeping things, and loathsome beasts, and all the idols of the house of Israel. ¹¹And before them stood seventy men of the elders of the house of Israel, with Jaazaniah the son of Shaphan standing among them. Each had his censer in his hand, and the smoke of the cloud of incense went up. ¹²Then he said to me, "Son of man, have you seen what the elders of the house of Israel are doing in the dark, every man in his room of pictures? For they say, 'The LORD does not see us, the LORD has forsaken the land.'" ¹³He said also to me, "You will see still greater abominations which they commit."

¹⁴Then he brought me to the entrance of the north gate of the house of the LORD; and behold, there sat women weeping for Tammuz. ¹⁵Then he said to me, "Have you seen this, O son of man? You will see still greater abominations than these."

¹⁶And he brought me into the inner court of the house of the LORD; and behold, at the door of the temple of the LORD, between the porch and the altar, were about twenty-five men, with their backs to the temple of the LORD, and their faces toward the east, worshiping the sun toward the east. ¹⁷Then he said to me, "Have you seen this, O son of man? Is it too slight a thing for the house of Judah to commit the abominations which they commit here, that they should fill the land with violence, and provoke me further to anger? Behold, they put the branch to their nose. ¹⁸Therefore I will deal in wrath; my eye will not spare, nor will I have pity; and though they cry in my ears with a loud voice, I will not hear them."

OT: Exod 24:9–11; Deut 4:19
Catechism: the sin of idolatry, 2112–14; God's punishment and judgment of sin, 211, 679, 1472–73, 2054

8:1–3a   The date of this prophetic †oracle is September 18, 592 BC, fourteen months after Ezekiel's inaugural vision (see chap. 1). He is sitting in his own house in Babylon, **with the elders of Judah sitting before** him. The elders represent the leaders among the tribe of Judah who were sent into exile in 597. We are not told why they were seated before Ezekiel, but it is probable that they came seeking a sign or prophetic word from him. With no forewarning, Ezekiel once again experiences God intervening: **the hand of the Lord God fell there upon me.**[3] Ezekiel sees **a form that had the appearance of a man**, with fire below the waist and gleaming metal above. The Hebrew text has "the appearance of fire," while the Greek text (the †Septuagint) has "the appearance of a man." Most modern translations follow the Greek because of the parallel with the Hebrew text of Ezek 1:26–27, which speaks of a "likeness . . . of a human form" surrounded by fire. In either case, what Ezekiel sees is a vision—parallel to what he saw in his first vision—of the Lord God, who puts out **the form of a hand** and takes hold of Ezekiel by his hair. Ezekiel is exquisitely careful throughout the book to formulate his visual descriptions of God with the language of "form" and "likeness" so that we recognize that these are not to be taken as literal descriptions of God.

8:3b   At the same time, Ezekiel recounts that **the Spirit lifted me up between earth and heaven, and brought me in visions of God to Jerusalem**. For the second time in the book, Ezekiel says that he saw "visions of God."[4] He was not carried bodily from Babylon to Jerusalem but was taken by the Spirit "in visions" to the temple precincts. What Ezekiel sees there is **the image of jealousy, which provokes to jealousy**—that is, an idol to a foreign god, right in the heart of the Lord's temple, which provokes the jealous, spousal love of God for his people. The remainder of chapter 8 recounts the gory details of this idolatry within the very temple of God.

8:4   Crucially, Ezekiel sees—right next to this idolatrous image—**the glory of the God of Israel . . . like the vision that I saw in the plain**. Ezekiel wants his listeners and readers to recognize what he is seeing: this is a vision of the same all-seeing chariot of God's divine presence that he saw in chapter 1. The battle lines are drawn: the temple cannot contain both the Lord's glorious presence and the worship of a false god. One or the other must go.

8:5–6   Strikingly, the Lord now "poses as a tour guide leading Ezekiel around the temple complex."[5] In the first leg of the tour (vv. 5–6), Ezekiel is told to look across to the northern gate, leading into the inner court of the temple. There he sees the **image of jealousy**, a reference to a false god lodged at the center of the temple. And the Lord asks him: **Do you see what they are doing . . . to drive me**

---

3. For the "hand of the Lord" coming upon Ezekiel, see also 1:3; 3:14, 22; 33:22; 37:1; 40:1.
4. The first time Ezekiel saw "visions of God" is recounted in Ezek 1:1; the third and final time occurs in Ezek 40:2.
5. Block, *Ezekiel: Chapters 1–24*, 283.

Figure 3. Marduk, patron god of the city of Babylon, depicted on the Ishtar Gates

far from my sanctuary?[6] This brazen act of idolatry in sight of the altar of incense provokes the Lord to take leave of his own sanctuary. "The very place which was to be the source of Israel's holiness became the witness of their depravity."[7] But this is only the beginning. Ezekiel is told: **you will see still greater abominations**.

The second leg of the tour (vv. 7–13) is more involved. Ezekiel is escorted to **8:7–10** the entrance of the inner court of the temple, where he sees a hole in the temple wall. The Lord then tells Ezekiel to dig into this hole. He finds an entrance to an inner room, where he beholds all sorts of engravings to various and sundry false gods—idolatry is multiplied right within the inner courts.

Further, Ezekiel beholds **seventy men of the elders of the house of Israel** **8:11–13** offering incense (that is, worship) to this multitude of idols.[8] This is in direct contrast to the seventy elders of Israel who worshiped and ate with Moses on Mount Sinai, inaugurating the †covenant the Lord made with his people (Exod 24:9–11).[9] These elders that Ezekiel beholds are repudiating the covenant and have abandoned all allegiance to the Lord. They say to one another, **the LORD does not see us, the LORD has forsaken the land**. This verse carries an ironic

6. An alternate reading of v. 6, due to the ambiguity of the grammar, has the people removing *themselves* from the Lord's sanctuary, rather than driving the Lord away through their idolatrous practice (see Alter, "Ezekiel," 1072).

7. Eisemann, *Ezekiel*, 159.

8. Just one person among the seventy elders, Jaazaniah son of Shaphan, is named, presumably their leader. He is linked with the family of Shaphan, known for loyalty to the Lord (2 Kings 22:8–10; Jer 26:24), and his failure is therefore all the more grievous.

9. See also Num 11:16, 24–25 for the seventy elders of Israel. Rabbi David Kimchi (d. 1235) highlights the contrast between these seventy elders and their forerunners from Moses's day: the seventy men are "the seventy members of the Sanhedrin, to show him that these very elders, given by God to instruct the people of Israel in the good way, were now misleading them." A. J. Rosenberg, trans., *The Book of Ezekiel*, vol. 1, Mikraoth Gedoloth (New York: Judaica Press, 1991), 54.

double meaning. On the one hand, these elders are pursuing other gods because they believe that the Lord has abandoned them and no longer *sees* their need; on the other hand, by acting in secret they somehow think that the Lord does not *see* their abominable idolatry. The first conviction is ironically true: because they have abandoned the Lord and the covenant, he no longer "sees" them in the sense of watching over them for their good. The second is terrifyingly false. Four times in this chapter (vv. 6, 12, 15, 17) the Lord asks Ezekiel whether he "sees" the abominations being committed: the Lord certainly sees the people's idolatry and will punish it without pity (v. 18).

8:14–15   The third leg of the temple tour (vv. 14–15) is brief in the extreme. Returning to the north gate of the inner temple, Ezekiel observes **women weeping for Tammuz**. This is the only instance of "Tammuz" in the Bible. The name refers to an ancient Mesopotamian rite that centered on the shepherd-king and the god of vegetation and celebrated the cycles of the agricultural year by ritually enacting the dying and rising of the god. According to Moshe Greenberg, "Wailing for Tammuz . . . was a woman's rite practiced widely over the Near East through the centuries."[10] It is one more example of idolatry finding an entrance in Israel.

8:16–18   The fourth and final leg of the tour (vv. 16–18) brings Ezekiel to the inner court of the temple, where he beholds **twenty-five men**—presumably priests within the altar area—**with their backs to the temple of the LORD . . . worshiping the sun toward the east**. In the ancient world the sun was widely worshiped as a deity, but in Israel worship of the sun was explicitly forbidden (Deut 4:19; 17:2–3).[11] According to Moshe Eisemann, "By turning their backs to the *Shekinah* and bowing to the sun, they proclaimed their belief in a blind determinism from which God's providence was excluded."[12] All these acts of faithless idolatry provoke the Lord to righteous anger.[13] The chapter closes with these unsparing words: **I will deal in wrath; my eye will not spare, nor will I have pity**.

God's Judgment upon the City (9:1–11)

---

[1]Then he cried in my ears with a loud voice, saying, "Draw near, you executioners of the city, each with his destroying weapon in his hand." [2]And behold, six men came from the direction of the upper gate, which faces north, every man with his weapon for slaughter in his hand, and with them was a man clothed in linen, with a writing case at his side. And they went in and stood beside the bronze altar.

---

10. Greenberg, *Ezekiel 1–20*, 171.

11. For the worship of the sun in the ancient world, see Greenberg, *Ezekiel 1–20*, 172; Block, *Ezekiel: Chapters 1–24*, 298.

12. Eisemann, *Ezekiel*, 166 (modified).

13. In v. 17, the phrase "they put the branch to their nose" is obscure but probably indicates a visual sign of derision.

The Catechism on Punishments for Sin

The Catechism explains the nature of punishment for sin as arising from the nature of sin itself and shows how through repentance and conversion we can be freed from the punishment of sin.

To understand this doctrine and practice of the Church, it is necessary to understand that sin has *a double consequence*. Grave sin deprives us of communion with God and therefore makes us incapable of eternal life, the privation of which is called the "eternal punishment" of sin. On the other hand every sin, even venial, entails an unhealthy attachment to creatures, which must be purified either here on earth, or after death in the state called Purgatory. This purification frees one from what is called the "temporal punishment" of sin. These two punishments must not be conceived of as a kind of vengeance inflicted by God from without, but as following from the very nature of sin. A conversion which proceeds from a fervent charity can attain the complete purification of the sinner in such a way that no punishment would remain.[a]

a. Catechism 1472.

[3]Now the glory of the God of Israel had gone up from the cherubim on which it rested to the threshold of the house; and he called to the man clothed in linen, who had the writing case at his side. [4]And the LORD said to him, "Go through the city, through Jerusalem, and put a mark upon the foreheads of the men who sigh and groan over all the abominations that are committed in it." [5]And to the others he said in my hearing, "Pass through the city after him, and kill; your eye shall not spare, and you shall show no pity; [6]slay old men outright, young men and maidens, little children and women, but touch no one upon whom is the mark. And begin at my sanctuary." So they began with the elders who were before the house. [7]Then he said to them, "Defile the house, and fill the courts with the slain. Go forth." So they went forth, and killed in the city. [8]And while they were killing, and I was left alone, I fell upon my face, and cried, "Ah, Lord GOD! will you destroy all that remains of Israel in the outpouring of your wrath upon Jerusalem?"

[9]Then he said to me, "The guilt of the house of Israel and Judah is exceedingly great; the land is full of blood, and the city full of injustice; for they say, 'The LORD has forsaken the land, and the LORD does not see.' [10]As for me, my eye will not spare, nor will I have pity, but I will repay their deeds upon their heads."

[11]And behold, the man clothed in linen, with the writing case at his side, brought back word, saying, "I have done as you commanded me."

OT: Exod 12:7–13; Jer 44:7
NT: 1 Pet 4:17
Catechism: the sin of idolatry, 2112–14; sealing of the faithful in baptism and confirmation, 1216, 1272–74; 1293–96

The subject of this chapter is the active judgment of God against the Holy City and its people. In the vision that Ezekiel sees, the Lord God employs executioners to go throughout the city, but first he puts a mark on the foreheads of all those who have not participated in these idolatrous acts—and then all the rest are slain by the command of the Lord.

9:1–2   As this chapter begins, we are still with Ezekiel in the temple area. Ezekiel's tour guide cries out with a loud voice: **Draw near, you executioners of the city, each with his destroying weapon in his hand**. In response, six men emerge with weapons for slaughter accompanied by **a man clothed in linen, with a writing case at his side**,[14] and together they stand ready beside the bronze altar in the inner court of the temple.

9:3   Ezekiel turns our attention back to the glorious presence of the Lord: **Now the glory of the God of Israel had gone up from the †cherubim on which it rested to the threshold of the house**. The presence of God is on the move, departing from the cherubim in the holy of holies and moving to the temple's outer boundary. Even as the Lord executes judgment against the people, his presence begins to move away from the temple. As Paul Joyce observes, "The long withdrawal of the glory from the temple begins here."[15] This is also the first appearance of the name "cherubim" to identify the "living creatures" who pilot the divine chariot (1:5–14; 10:15, 20).[16]

9:4   What does the Lord now do? He tells the man clothed in linen to pass through the city of Jerusalem **and put a mark upon the foreheads of the men who sigh and groan over all the abominations that are committed in it**. The Lord is "marking out" for protection those who grieve over the terrible sins of the people. This recalls the mark made on the doorposts of the Israelites at the first †Passover, when God's avenging angel passed over the marked houses and spared the firstborn of the people (Exod 12:7–13).[17]

9:5–7   The Lord now speaks to the other six men: **Pass through the city after him, and kill; your eye shall not spare, and you shall show no pity**. The executioners come right on the heels of the forehead-marking. And significantly they are told, **begin at my sanctuary**, the heart of the temple itself, where the most grievous

---

14. The linen clothing points to the priestly identity of this figure (see Exod 28:39–42), and the writing case to his role as a scribe. The rabbis concluded that this figure, like a scribe, made the mark on the forehead with pen and ink. In the †rabbinic Jewish tradition, the six "men" were understood to be angels (see Dan 10:5; 12:6), and the seventh figure clothed in linen was identified as the angel Gabriel. See Eisemann, *Ezekiel*, 170; Rosenberg, *Book of Ezekiel*, 1:58–59.

15. Joyce, *Ezekiel*, 102.

16. The words "cherub" (singular) and "cherubim" (plural) appear thirty times in Ezekiel, more frequently than in any other biblical book.

17. According to one Jewish rabbinic interpretation, the righteous received the mark of the Hebrew letter "taw" *in ink* on their foreheads (meaning "you shall live"), while the wicked received the mark of the "taw" on their foreheads *in blood* (meaning "you shall die"). Rosenberg, *Book of Ezekiel*, 1:59.

St. Augustine on the Mark on the Heart

LIVING
TRADITION

St. Augustine provides a spiritual reading of this passage by interpreting the mark on the forehead in Ezekiel as foreshadowing the mark of Christ that is made on the "inner forehead" of the Christian's heart.

> It makes a great deal of difference, you see, where a person keeps the sign of Christ, whether on the forehead or both on the forehead and in the heart. You heard, when the holy prophet Ezekiel was speaking, how before God sent an exterminator of a wicked people, he first sent a marker and said to him, "Go and mark with a sign the foreheads of those who groan and grieve over the sins of my people, which are committed among them." . . . And this is why they have been marked with a sign on the forehead—the forehead of the inner self, not the outer one. There is a forehead of the face, you see, and a forehead of the conscience.[a]

a. *Sermon* 107.7 (ACCS 13:35).

sins of idolatry were being committed.[18] Commanded to **touch no one upon whom is the mark . . . they went forth, and killed in the city** all who were not marked upon their foreheads.

In the Light of Christ (9:4)

The "mark" put on the foreheads of the repentant faithful in the Holy City (Ezek 9:4) is the last letter of the Hebrew alphabet, *taw*. Notably, in the archaic Hebrew script the letter *taw* had the shape of an X or a cross, and this led early Christian writers to link this "marking" in Ezekiel with the sign of the cross given in the baptismal anointing. The book of Revelation draws directly on this passage in Ezekiel when speaking of the sealing of the servants of God on their foreheads, to protect them from the judgment about to fall upon the earth (Rev 7:3; 9:4). In contrast to those who bear the mark of the beast on their foreheads (Rev 14:9; 20:4), those who belong to the Lamb and stand with him are the ones who have his name and the name of his Father written upon their foreheads (14:1; 22:4). The mark of the cross is first of all a sign that protects the Christian faithful from God's judgment upon evildoing, just as the blood of the Passover lamb placed on the doorposts of the Israelites protected them from the avenging angel. But even more, the mark of the cross is a sign of *possession and belonging*. Those

18. The Lord's command that judgment should begin at the sanctuary in the midst of his people recalls the apostle Peter's statement: "For the time has come for judgment to begin with the household of God" (1 Pet 4:17).

marked with the name of Christ upon their foreheads belong to him and share his destiny and mission.

9:8–10   As he sees all this unfolding before his eyes, Ezekiel falls upon his face in supplication and cries out: **Ah, Lord God! will you destroy all that remains of Israel in the outpouring of your wrath upon Jerusalem?** Ezekiel repeats this entreaty in nearly identical words in 11:13: "Ah, Lord God! will you make a full end of the remnant of Israel?" Ezekiel seems to be questioning not the justice of God's judgment against the wicked but rather its *extent*, praying for a remnant to be spared, in order to preserve the heritage of Israel.[19] The Lord answers Ezekiel's plea with stern words: **The guilt of the house of Israel and Judah is exceedingly great**. The entire land is full of bloodshed, and the city replete with injustice. Though the people complain that the Lord has abandoned his people and so does not see their plight, the Lord insists that he sees all too clearly: **my eye will not spare, nor will I have pity**.

9:11   The chapter concludes with the man in linen reporting back to the Lord God: **I have done as you commanded me**, marking the foreheads of those who did not partake of the sins of the people. This itself is an answer to Ezekiel's prayer—the preserving of a faithful remnant even in the midst of great destruction. Jewish and Christian commentators—ancient and modern—have debated whether anyone was actually spared in this vision of God's judgment upon the temple and city. Some conclude that none were spared, not even those marked upon their foreheads. Others read the passage as implying the deliverance of at least a remnant. Given that this vision points to the siege and sack of Jerusalem in 597 and that some people were in fact spared and taken as exiles to Babylon, we are warranted in seeing here the deliverance of a remnant in answer to Ezekiel's prayer, even if the emphasis is on the judgment of those who were not so marked.

The Burning of the City and the Lord's Departure (10:1–22)

[1]Then I looked, and behold, on the firmament that was over the heads of the cherubim there appeared above them something like a sapphire, in form resembling a throne. [2]And he said to the man clothed in linen, "Go in among the whirling wheels underneath the cherubim; fill your hands with burning coals from between the cherubim, and scatter them over the city."

19. Ezekiel's concern for a remnant reflects the Lord's own concern spoken through Jeremiah: "Why do you commit this great evil against yourselves, to cut off from you man and woman, infant and child, from the midst of Judah, leaving you no remnant?" (Jer 44:7).

And he went in before my eyes. ³Now the cherubim were standing on
the south side of the house, when the man went in; and a cloud filled the
inner court. ⁴And the glory of the LORD went up from the cherubim to the
threshold of the house; and the house was filled with the cloud, and the
court was full of the brightness of the glory of the LORD. ⁵And the sound
of the wings of the cherubim was heard as far as the outer court, like the
voice of God Almighty when he speaks.

⁶And when he commanded the man clothed in linen, "Take fire from
between the whirling wheels, from between the cherubim," he went in
and stood beside a wheel. ⁷And a cherub stretched forth his hand from
between the cherubim to the fire that was between the cherubim, and took
some of it, and put it into the hands of the man clothed in linen, who took
it and went out. ⁸The cherubim appeared to have the form of a human
hand under their wings.

⁹And I looked, and behold, there were four wheels beside the cherubim,
one beside each cherub; and the appearance of the wheels was like spar-
kling chrysolite. ¹⁰And as for their appearance, the four had the same likeness, as if a wheel were within a wheel. ¹¹When they went, they went in any
of their four directions without turning as they went, but in whatever direction the front wheel faced the others followed without turning as they went.
¹²And their rims, and their spokes, and the wheels were full of eyes round
about—the wheels that the four of them had. ¹³As for the wheels, they were
called in my hearing the whirling wheels. ¹⁴And every one had four faces:
the first face was the face of the cherub, and the second face was the face of
a man, and the third the face of a lion, and the fourth the face of an eagle.

¹⁵And the cherubim mounted up. These were the living creatures that I
saw by the river Chebar. ¹⁶And when the cherubim went, the wheels went
beside them; and when the cherubim lifted up their wings to mount up
from the earth, the wheels did not turn from beside them. ¹⁷When they
stood still, these stood still, and when they mounted up, these mounted up
with them; for the spirit of the living creatures was in them.

¹⁸Then the glory of the LORD went forth from the threshold of the
house, and stood over the cherubim. ¹⁹And the cherubim lifted up their
wings and mounted up from the earth in my sight as they went forth, with
the wheels beside them; and they stood at the door of the east gate of the
house of the LORD; and the glory of the God of Israel was over them.

²⁰These were the living creatures that I saw underneath the God of Israel by the river Chebar; and I knew that they were cherubim. ²¹Each had
four faces, and each four wings, and underneath their wings the semblance
of human hands. ²²And as for the likeness of their faces, they were the very
faces whose appearance I had seen by the river Chebar. They went every
one straight forward.

OT: Exod 40:34; 1 Kings 8:10–11; Pss 16:11; 84:1–2
NT: 1 Cor 6:19; Heb 4:16; Rev 4:7
Catechism: vision of God, 1720, 1726, 2519; glory of God, 293–94, 2809; the angels, 328–36

10:1–2   In this vision, the divine presence, which has been hovering in the background (8:4; 9:3), now comes to center stage. Ezekiel once again, as in chapter 1, sees the divine chariot mounted upon the cherubim (that is, upon the four living creatures), **in form resembling a throne**. And a voice from the throne speaks to the man clothed in linen, telling him to **go in among the whirling wheels underneath the cherubim**. "Whirling wheels" is a singular term in Hebrew, often translated as "wheelwork" (NRSV, NABRE). Its meaning is unclear, but it may refer to the movement of the "wheels within wheels." There the man clothed in linen is to fill his hands with **burning coals** and **scatter them over the city**. The "burning coals" of fire (first described in 1:13) represent the heavenly counterpart to the fire of the altar of sacrifice in the Jerusalem temple. The "fire" of God's judgment is both punishing and cleansing. It burns up whatever is incompatible with God, but only to prepare a purified receptacle capable of receiving his presence (see Isa 6:6). This action—taking the burning coals from before the presence of the Lord—displays the *priestly* identity of the linen-clothed man: "It is the priestly aspect of the man clothed in linen that qualifies him to enter among the cherubs and handle the heavenly fire blazing among them."[20] The burning coals of fire also recall the destruction of Sodom and Gomorrah (Gen 19:24–25). Jerusalem is to suffer the same fate.[21] The destruction of temple and city by fire—announced here—is preparing the way for the new temple and city, in which the Lord will once again dwell with his people (chaps. 40–48).

10:3–5   Ezekiel then turns our gaze to the vision of the divine chariot: the cherubim are seen standing on the south side of the inner temple while **a cloud filled the inner court**. The cloud represents the glorious presence of God, but instead of resting there, the cloud **went up from the cherubim to the threshold of the house**—that is, the temple—**and the house was filled with the cloud, and the court was full of the brightness of the glory of the LORD**. This movement of the Lord's cloudlike presence duplicates what Ezekiel saw in 9:3. The sharp contrast with past manifestations of God's glory could not be clearer. When Moses finished building the tabernacle, the glory of God—in a cloud—*settled down* and filled it (Exod 40:34). The same occurred for Solomon at the consecration of the first temple (1 Kings 8:10–11). But here the movement is in the opposite direction: the glorious presence of the Lord is *leaving* the temple by increments, not coming to settle and stay there.

10:6–8   The spotlight returns to the man in linen, who walks among the **whirling wheels** of the divine chariot and receives **fire** from one of the **cherubim**. He now fulfills his commission by taking the fire (the burning coals) and going out to scatter it over the city in judgment.

---

20. Greenberg, *Ezekiel 1–20*, 180.
21. For the actual burning of Jerusalem by the Babylonians, see 2 Kings 25:9; 2 Chron 36:19; Jer 39:8.

Ezekiel next provides us with a reiteration of the vision he saw in 1:15–21: **10:9–14**
the **four wheels**, the "wheels within wheels" going in any of the **four directions** without needing to turn, with eyes all around. Why would Ezekiel retell
here with greater detail this vision of the wheels? On the one hand, Ezekiel is
confirming that this is a vision of the *same* divine chariot that he saw at the
beginning of his prophetic ministry. What he saw on the plains of Babylon is
the same divine presence that is now making ready to leave the temple. On
the other hand, by rehearsing the vision of the wheels Ezekiel underlines the
mobility of God's presence: the Lord is not bound to the temple in Jerusalem
but can go where he wills, even to be with his people in exile.

Verse 14 presents several challenges for interpretation. First, it appears that
Ezekiel ascribes the four faces to the wheels themselves—**and every one had
four faces**—but it is better to see this as a reference to the cherubim (referred to
in v. 9), not to the wheels themselves. Second, the first face is identified as the
face of a **cherub**, not an ox (see 1:10 for comparison). Why this substitution?
The reason is unclear. The rabbis accounted for this alteration on the basis of
the sin of the golden calf: because Israel was tempted to worship a calf, the face
was changed.[22] Third, in Ezekiel's description of the four cherubim here, each
cherub seems to possess just one face four times over, rather than each cherub
possessing four *different* faces (as in 1:10–11).[23] This aligns with the presentation of the living creatures in Revelation: "The first living creature like a lion,
the second living creature like an ox, the third living creature with the face of a
man, and the fourth living creature like a flying eagle" (Rev 4:7). John's vision
of the cherubim in Revelation is probably based on the specific rendering of
the four cherubim here in Ezek 10.

To close the chapter, we return to the movement of the divine chariot—and **10:15–19**
so the glorious presence of the Lord—away from the temple. Ezekiel is at pains
to assure his hearers that the four cherubim in this vision are the same as the
four **living creatures** he saw **by the river Chebar** in Babylon. As the cherubim
rise with moving wings, so the wheels of the chariot follow. Because **the spirit
of the living creatures** is **in them**, the wheels are fully docile to this movement.
Crucially, **the glory of the Lord went forth from the threshold of the house**
and migrated to **the door of the east gate of the house of the Lord**. We have
a picture here of a divine chariot, piloted by the four cherubim, with the cloudlike presence of the glory of the Lord seated above, moving by stages from the
inner temple, to the threshold of the inner temple, and finally to the east gate
leading out of the temple. Notably, the divine presence is moving to the *east*,
where Babylon lies, to be present to the forlorn exiles.

22. See Eisemann, *Ezekiel*, 187; Block, *Ezekiel: Chapters 1–24*, 324–25.

23. According to Greenberg (*Ezekiel 1–20*, 182), "The plain sense of [the Hebrew text] is that each
cherub . . . had four of the same faces, but the form of the faces differed for each cherub. This diverges
from 1:10, which gives each creature a set of four different faces."

The Lord God Seated above the Cherubim

BIBLICAL BACKGROUND

In chapter 10, Ezekiel identifies the four living creatures who appeared to him beside the river Chebar (Ezek 1:5) as cherubim (10:15, 20). His vision of the cherubim builds upon an earlier tradition in Israel but develops that tradition significantly. The first appearance of cherubim in the Bible, in terms of biblical order, occurs in the story of the exile of Adam and Eve from the garden: the cherubim guard the entrance against them with a flaming sword (Gen 3:24). But for Ezekiel's purposes, the more significant background to the cherubim appears in the instructions given to Moses for the building of the tabernacle. Two cherubim, made of gold, were attached to the "mercy seat," the lid of the ark of the covenant, with wings that shrouded the invisible presence of the Lord. It is called a "seat" because it was here that the Lord was seated (that is, enthroned) among his people: "There I will meet with you, and from above the mercy seat, from between the two cherubim that are upon the ark of the covenant, I will speak with you" (Exod 25:22). It is called the "mercy" seat because it was from here that God manifested his mercy by atoning for sin. When Moses went to stand before the Lord's presence in the tabernacle, he would hear the Lord's voice speaking to him "from between the two cherubim" (Num 7:89). The Lord God is described as being "enthroned upon the cherubim" seven times in the Old Testament (see, for example, 1 Sam 4:4; Pss 80:1; 99:1). What Ezekiel sees in his vision, however, is not carved, lifeless cherubim attached to the ark of the covenant in a stationary tabernacle. Instead, he sees "living" cherubim acting as the guardians and pilots for the mobile chariot that bears the divine presence.[a]

a. In the Christian tradition, nine ranks of angels were identified from the witness of the Old and New Testaments (see Isa 6:1–3; Ezek 10:15–20; Eph 1:21; Col 1:16). In the hierarchical order of the nine ranks of angels first presented by Dionysius (sixth century) and adopted by St. Thomas Aquinas, the cherubim occupy the second rank after the seraphim.

10:20–22   The chapter concludes with Ezekiel restating that **these were the living creatures that** he **saw underneath the God of Israel** beside the Chebar River in his opening vision (1:1–3). He makes entirely clear that this was a vision of "the God of Israel" that he was beholding. The "living creatures" that he saw in that original vision are now clearly identified as the **cherubim,** each with **four faces** and **four wings,** going straight ahead as they were directed.

By interweaving the narrative of the burning coals and the movement of the divine chariot, Ezekiel conveys that these two actions are occurring simultaneously; both are signs of the Lord's judgment upon his people's sin. The Lord sends his judgment upon temple and city through the burning coals of fire, and at the same time the Lord rises up and removes his presence from his people.

Ezekiel's Chariot in Biblical and Jewish Tradition

Ezekiel's vision of the divine presence borne aloft by a cherubim-propelled four-wheeled vehicle came to be identified as the divine "chariot" (Hebrew *merkabah*) and appears in biblical texts that post-date the book of Ezekiel. The instructions for the construction of Solomon's temple in 1 Chronicles, for example, include the word "chariot" in their description of the ark of the covenant. David gave to Solomon "his plan for the golden chariot of the cherubim that spread their wings and covered the ark of the covenant of the Lord" (1 Chron 28:18). The prophet Daniel alludes to Ezekiel's chariot when describing his vision of the throne of God: "His throne was fiery flames, / its wheels were burning fire" (Dan 7:9). And the book of Sirach straightforwardly speaks of the divine chariot that Ezekiel saw in a vision: "It was Ezekiel who saw the vision of glory / which God showed him above the chariot of the cherubim" (Sir 49:8). In the first century BC, reference to Ezekiel's chariot throne is found in the writings of the Jewish community at Qumran that collected the †Dead Sea Scrolls. Following the destruction of the temple in AD 70, Ezekiel's vision of the divine chariot gave rise to a Jewish mystical tradition, known as †Merkabah mysticism, that developed stages of ascent to God through a spiritualized vision of the divine chariot throne of God.[a]

a. For Ezekiel's chariot in biblical and Jewish tradition, see Greenberg, *Ezekiel 1–20*, 205–6.

Reflection and Application (10:1–22)

Do we take access to God's presence for granted? In Ezekiel's day, many assumed that the Lord God would never abandon his people and his special dwelling place in the temple. Yet Ezekiel witnessed the divine presence—the cloud of God's glory—tragically rising up and leaving the Holy City. The presence of God among his people *is* the central blessing of the covenant. It is God himself—not just what he gives—that provides life for his people. When the Lord told Moses that he would still grant his blessing to Israel but would not "go up" with them into the promised land, Moses refused the offer: "If your presence will not go with me, do not carry us up from here" (Exod 33:15). As the psalmist says, "You show me the path of life; / in your presence there is fulness of joy" (Ps 16:11). To be where God is and to dwell with him is the fullness of life: "How lovely is your dwelling place, / O LORD of hosts! / My soul longs, yes, faints / for the courts of the LORD" (Ps 84:1–2). The presence of God that appeared to Moses and that dwelt in the temple was a great blessing. But how much greater is God's presence among us now that the eternal Son has made his dwelling among us (John 1:14) and made us to be temples of the Holy Spirit (1 Cor 6:19)! How astonishing is the access we now have to our Father through Christ in the Spirit (Eph 2:18)! God has come to dwell in us, and so we also dwell in him. As the Letter to the Hebrews invites us: "Let us then with confidence draw near to the throne of †grace, that we may receive mercy and find grace to help in time of need" (Heb 4:16).

Judgment upon the City (11:1–13)

¹The Spirit lifted me up, and brought me to the east gate of the house of the LORD, which faces east. And behold, at the door of the gateway there were twenty-five men; and I saw among them Jaazaniah the son of Azzur, and Pelatiah the son of Benaiah, princes of the people. ²And he said to me, "Son of man, these are the men who devise iniquity and who give wicked counsel in this city; ³who say, 'The time is not near to build houses; this city is the caldron, and we are the flesh.' ⁴Therefore prophesy against them, prophesy, O son of man."

⁵And the Spirit of the LORD fell upon me, and he said to me, "Say, Thus says the LORD: So you think, O house of Israel; for I know the things that come into your mind. ⁶You have multiplied your slain in this city, and have filled its streets with the slain. ⁷Therefore thus says the Lord GOD: Your slain whom you have laid in the midst of it, they are the flesh, and this city is the caldron; but you shall be brought forth out of the midst of it. ⁸You have feared the sword; and I will bring the sword upon you, says the Lord GOD. ⁹And I will bring you forth out of the midst of it, and give you into the hands of foreigners, and execute judgments upon you. ¹⁰You shall fall by the sword; I will judge you at the border of Israel; and you shall know that I am the LORD. ¹¹This city shall not be your caldron, nor shall you be the flesh in the midst of it; I will judge you at the border of Israel; ¹²and you shall know that I am the LORD; for you have not walked in my statutes, nor executed my ordinances, but have acted according to the ordinances of the nations that are round about you."

¹³And it came to pass, while I was prophesying, that Pelatiah the son of Benaiah died. Then I fell down upon my face, and cried with a loud voice, and said, "Ah, Lord GOD! will you make a full end of the remnant of Israel?"

OT: Gen 45:7; Isa 10:22; Jer 23:3; Mic 3:3
Catechism: the sin of idolatry, 2112–14

Three distinct sections are included in this chapter. The first (vv. 1–13) brings us back to the judgment on the city; the second (vv. 14–21) opens up a word of promise for the exiles; the third (vv. 22–25) concludes the larger section (chaps. 8–11) by narrating the departure of God's glorious presence from the temple.

As chapter 11 begins, the Spirit once again lifts up Ezekiel and brings him   11:1–12
to the east gate of the house of the LORD. There Ezekiel beholds a group of **twenty-five men**, among whom are Jaazaniah and Pelatiah, **princes of the people**—that is, men of the royal family.[24] The Lord tells Ezekiel that they are giving **wicked counsel** to those in the city by claiming that, because they are contained like **flesh** (meat) in a **caldron** (pot), it is not yet time to build up the city.[25] The precise meaning of the image of flesh in a caldron is unclear. It probably reflects the confident presumption of those inside the city that they would be protected by the caldron from the fires raging outside. According to Daniel Block, "The pot is Jerusalem, offering security to those inside."[26] In response, the Lord tells Ezekiel to prophesy against them: because they have shed the blood of many and have not followed the ways of the Lord, they will *not* remain protected within the city like meat in a caldron, but they will be taken out of the city and die: **You shall fall by the sword; I will judge you at the border of Israel; and you shall know that I am the LORD.** This judgment by **the hands of foreigners** is meant to bring home to them their crimes against the Lord and his people.

While Ezekiel is prophesying this word, Pelatiah dies, causing Ezekiel to   11:13
fall to the ground in anguish and cry out: **Ah, Lord GOD! will you make a full end of the remnant of Israel?** We are not told how Ezekiel in faraway Babylon knows that Pelatiah has suddenly died in Jerusalem—he must have seen his death through the vision the Lord gave him. But why would the death of this man, a prince of the people, cause Ezekiel to cry out again (as he did in 9:8), asking the Lord to preserve a "remnant of Israel"? Perhaps the answer lies in his name "Pelatiah," which means "the Lord rescues." It is possible that the death of this man signaled to Ezekiel that the Lord would *not* rescue his people from the disaster rushing to meet them.

Promise of Return and Final Departure of the Lord (11:14–25)

---

[14]**And the word of the LORD came to me:** [15]**"Son of man, your brethren, even your brethren, your fellow exiles, the whole house of Israel, all of them, are those of whom the inhabitants of Jerusalem have said, 'They have gone far from the LORD; to us this land is given for a possession.'** [16]**Therefore say, 'Thus says the Lord GOD: Though I removed them far off**

---

24. The mention of Jaazaniah (see 8:11) and the twenty-five men (see 8:16) ties this section back to chap. 8 and brings this word of judgment against temple and city to its conclusion.

25. The prophet Micah also uses the image of meat boiling in a caldron to signify the Lord's severe judgment of his people (Mic 3:3).

26. Block, *Ezekiel: Chapters 1–24*, 334.

The Preservation of a "Remnant"

BIBLICAL BACKGROUND

Ezekiel's anguished concern for the "remnant of Israel" touches on a consistent theme that occurs throughout the Old Testament. In both Hebrew and Greek, the word that is translated "remnant" means "that which is left over" or "that which remains." Even in the midst of severe judgment or loss, the Lord acts to preserve a remnant of his people through whom he will fulfill his promises. Already with Joseph, Jacob's son, we see the theme of the remnant in play. After revealing himself to his brothers, who sold him into slavery, Joseph speaks of the providence of God: "And God sent me before you to preserve for you a remnant on earth" (Gen 45:7). At a later time, the prophet Isaiah predicts that only a remnant of the multitude of Israel will survive the coming judgment, "for though your people Israel be as the sand of the sea, only a remnant of them will return" (Isa 10:22), but then subsequently announces the glorious return of this remnant: "For out of Jerusalem shall go forth a remnant, and out of Mount Zion a band of survivors. The zeal of the Lord of hosts will accomplish this" (37:32). Jeremiah, an older contemporary of Ezekiel, also predicts the return of the remnant of Israel from captivity in foreign lands: "Then I will gather the remnant of my flock out of all the countries where I have driven them, and I will bring them back to their fold, and they shall be fruitful and multiply" (Jer 23:3). Acting within this tradition, Ezekiel twice cries out to God, wondering if the Lord's severe judgment will "make a full end of the remnant of Israel" (11:13). In the end, a remnant will be preserved, and Ezekiel will live to proclaim the return of the remnant to the land (see 34:11–16).

among the nations, and though I scattered them among the countries, yet I have been a sanctuary to them for a while in the countries where they have gone.' ¹⁷Therefore say, 'Thus says the Lord GOD: I will gather you from the peoples, and assemble you out of the countries where you have been scattered, and I will give you the land of Israel.' ¹⁸And when they come there, they will remove from it all its detestable things and all its abominations. ¹⁹And I will give them one heart, and put a new spirit within them; I will take the stony heart out of their flesh and give them a heart of flesh, ²⁰that they may walk in my statutes and keep my ordinances and obey them; and they shall be my people, and I will be their God. ²¹But as for those whose heart goes after their detestable things and their abominations, I will repay their deeds upon their own heads, says the Lord GOD."

²²Then the cherubim lifted up their wings, with the wheels beside them; and the glory of the God of Israel was over them. ²³And the glory of the LORD went up from the midst of the city, and stood upon the mountain which is on the east side of the city. ²⁴And the Spirit lifted me up and

brought me in the vision by the Spirit of God into Chaldea, to the exiles. Then the vision that I had seen went up from me. [25]And I told the exiles all the things that the LORD had showed me.

OT: Jer 12:7; 32:39
NT: Rom 3:9–18; Eph 2:1–3
Catechism: new heart and new spirit, 711, 1432

Ezekiel now declares a promise of restoration right in the midst of a section   **11:14–16**
dominated by words of judgment.[27] This is a direct response to Ezekiel's cry in verse 13, "Will you make a full end of the remnant of Israel?" The inhabitants of the city are casting scorn upon those already taken into exile and claiming rights to the land for themselves, maintaining arrogantly, **to us this land is given for a possession**. In reply, the Lord turns his eyes toward those in exile and graciously commits himself to their welfare: **Though I removed them far off among the nations, and though I scattered them among the countries, yet I have been a sanctuary to them for a while in the countries where they have gone**. The irony here is deep: just at the point when the Lord is departing from the *sanctuary* in Jerusalem, he promises that he himself has now become a *sanctuary* for his people in exile.[28] This is a remarkable promise: "This statement is without parallel in the Old Testament."[29] The Lord God is not just providing sanctuary *for* his people; he himself has *become* their sanctuary in the gloomy place of their exile. Once again, the central theme of God's presence appears: no matter how dire the situation might be, God can be present to his people who call upon him in humility.

Though the Lord's presence as a sanctuary for the exiles is a great blessing,   **11:17–18**
it is only a temporary measure. And so in addition the Lord promises through Ezekiel a full return from exile accompanied by an inner transformation of heart. The Lord solemnly announces that he **will gather** them **from the peoples** and **will give** them **the land of Israel** once again.

More than this, the Lord promises: **I will give them one heart, and put a new**   **11:19–21**
spirit within them. This astonishing promise will be restated and expanded in Ezek 36:26–27. To accomplish this, the Lord will **take the stony heart out of their flesh and give them a heart of flesh**. The renowned Jewish rabbi Rashi (d. 1105) explains that "heart of flesh" means "a heart that is soft and easily submissive"; Rabbi David Kimchi (d. 1235) understands the "heart of flesh" to

---

27. This is one of four passages in the first part of Ezekiel that speak of hope, promise, and restoration. The other three are found in 16:59–63; 17:22–24; 20:40–44.

28. †*Targum of Ezekiel* renders this verse as already pointing to the establishment of the synagogue in the exile: "Therefore I have given them synagogues, second only to my Holy Temple." Levey, *Targum of Ezekiel*, 41.

29. Block, *Ezekiel: Chapters 1–24*, 349.

be "receptive to rebuke and reproof."[30] The result will be that the people will keep—from the heart—the commands and statutes of the Lord.

This word of hope reaches its climax in the renewal of the covenant promise: **they shall be my people, and I will be their God**. This covenant promise recurs in Ezekiel 37:23, 27. It echoes the foundational promise to Abraham (Gen 17:8), which is restated in the covenant blessings (Lev 26:12). This promise is reiterated in the Prophets and is cited by Paul (2 Cor 6:16) and the author to the Hebrews (Heb 8:10).[31]

"One heart" or "a single heart" stands in contrast to the unreliability and unfaithfulness of a "double heart": "With flattering lips and a double heart they speak" (Ps 12:2). When the psalmist prays, "Unite my heart to fear your name" (Ps 86:11), he is asking for the "single heart" promised here. Ezekiel's words closely mirror those of Jeremiah: "I will give them one heart and one way, that they may fear me forever" (Jer 32:39). This is a remarkable, hope-filled promise, a shaft of bright light in the midst of gloom and darkness on every side.[32]

11:22–23   With these verses, Ezekiel brings the first temple vision (chaps. 8–11) to its ominous and even terrifying conclusion. As the glory of God makes its exit, everything that the people relied on for blessing, provision, and protection is gone. The words of the prophet Jeremiah are fulfilled: "I have forsaken my house, / I have abandoned my heritage" (Jer 12:7). The cherubim lift their wings—with the glory of God hovering over them—and go up from the midst of the city, leaving it behind, and come to stand on the mountain east of the city (the Mount of Olives): **And the glory of the LORD went up from the midst of the city, and stood upon the mountain which is on the east side of the city**. This is the sum total of what Ezekiel reports. The divine chariot—bearing the presence and glory of God—departs eastward, toward the region where the exiles dwell. We will have to wait a long time for the Lord's departure to be reversed. It is not until chapter 43 that the glory of the Lord in the form of the divine chariot returns to the *new* temple and fills it with his presence once again.

11:24–25   In the meantime, Ezekiel himself is lifted up in vision and brought back (by the Spirit of God) to the exiles in †Chaldea, and the vision then leaves him: **Then the vision that I had seen went up from me**. Ezekiel does not hide what he has seen but tells his fellow Jews **all the things that the LORD had showed** him. How did his hearers respond? We are not told, but it seems that Ezekiel's prediction of certain doom for the Holy City was not embraced by his fellow exiles.

---

30. Rosenberg, *Book of Ezekiel*, 1:74.
31. For this covenant promise in the Prophets, see Jer 24:7; 31:33; 32:38; Zech 8:8.
32. Ezekiel will briefly touch again on this promise of a new heart and new spirit (18:31) and then draw out its fuller implications toward the close of the book (36:26–27; 37:14).

St. Augustine on a Heart of Flesh

LIVING TRADITION

St. Augustine explains the meaning of Ezekiel's reference to "a heart of flesh" by linking it to Paul's teaching on the "tablets of flesh" that we receive in the New Covenant through Christ.

> For the prophet [Ezekiel] has said, "I will take from them a heart of stone, and I will give them a heart of flesh" (Ezek 11:19). Let them see whether this does not say the same thing as "not on tablets of stone but on tablets of hearts of flesh" (2 Cor 3:3). For neither a "heart of flesh," which was said in the one place, nor "tablets of flesh," which was said in the other, mean that we should think in a fleshly manner. But because in comparison with a stone, which is without feeling, the flesh has feeling, the stone's lack of feeling signified a heart without understanding, and the feeling of the flesh signified a heart with understanding. . . . Therefore, when the Father is heard within and teaches, so that one may come to the Son, he takes away the heart of stone and bestows a heart of flesh, as he promised by the word of the prophet. For it is thus that he makes them children of the promise and vessels of mercy that he has prepared for his glory.[a]

a. *Against Faustus* 15.4; *Predestination of the Saints* 8.13 (ACCS 13:41–42, modified).

Reflection and Application (11:1–25)

As we read the book of Ezekiel, we see everything through Ezekiel's eyes and are stirred by the things impacting his heart. It is much more difficult to "see" the book through the eyes and ears of Ezekiel's audience: his fellow exiles and (if his message was relayed back to the Holy Land) the Jewish leaders in Jerusalem. How would we, if we were in their shoes, have responded to this sharp word of judgment followed by an astounding word of promise and restoration? From what we can tell, very few of Ezekiel's listeners believed and acted upon his prophetic word. Many probably rejected Ezekiel's words as being too negative; they wanted to hear a word that promised a quick and painless restoration of the land and city. Others may have simply been unsure what to make of this prophet's extreme words and actions: they listened but did not commit themselves in a faith-filled response. They were neither hot nor cold but just waited to see what would happen.

The Lord's promise to give his people "one heart" and "a new spirit" points us to what *we* need in order to respond to God's word. The Scriptures witness to the reality of our stony, sin-scarred hearts (see Rom 3:9–18; Eph 2:1–3). Apart from the grace of God softening our hearts—to become hearts of flesh—we would probably have responded much the same way as those who sat with Ezekiel in exile. We have darkened our own eyes and hearts; only God can restore and renew them: "The human heart is heavy and hardened. God must give man a new heart" (Catechism 1432 [Ezek 36:26–27]). The good news is that in Christ through the Spirit God has done this! To consider Ezekiel's audience—to put ourselves in their shoes—helps us to rejoice with great thanksgiving that God has acted in Christ to give *us* a new heart and spirit, so that we can hear his word and walk in a new way of life.

Oracles and Parables of Judgment against the City and the Land, Part 1

Ezekiel 12:1–15:8

We now begin an extended trek through the most loosely structured section of Ezekiel (chaps. 12–24). The overall theme of judgment runs like a scarlet thread through the uneven terrain of these thirteen chapters. Two parallel passages (12:1–20 and 24:15–27) serve as bookends or frames for the whole. Both describe prophetic †sign-acts in which Ezekiel is commanded to perform a symbolic forewarning of things to come. Both record a question from the audience requesting an explanation for the sign-act. And both identify the prophet himself as a "sign" for the people—the only occasions in the book when Ezekiel himself is identified as a sign. Between these frames, Ezekiel seems to have collected miscellaneous †oracles and parables, one following upon the other, with no discernible sense of order or development.[1]

We will divide this long section into three parts (chaps. 12–15, 16–19, 20–23), with the final chapter (chap. 24) functioning as the conclusion to the first major part of the book.

Ezekiel Acts Out the Coming Exile and Judgment (12:1–20)

[1]The word of the LORD came to me: [2]"Son of man, you dwell in the midst of a rebellious house, who have eyes to see, but see not, who have ears to hear, but hear not; [3]for they are a rebellious house. Therefore, son of man, prepare for yourself an exile's baggage, and go into exile by day in their

---

1. Block, *Ezekiel: Chapters 1–24*, 361: "Between these frames the collection of prophecies forms a fascinating collage, attesting to Ezekiel's remarkable creativity, versatility, and rhetorical power."

sight; you shall go like an exile from your place to another place in their sight. Perhaps they will understand, though they are a rebellious house. [4]You shall bring out your baggage by day in their sight, as baggage for exile; and you shall go forth yourself at evening in their sight, as men do who must go into exile. [5]Dig through the wall in their sight, and go out through it. [6]In their sight you shall lift the baggage upon your shoulder, and carry it out in the dark; you shall cover your face, that you may not see the land; for I have made you a sign for the house of Israel."

[7]And I did as I was commanded. I brought out my baggage by day, as baggage for exile, and in the evening I dug through the wall with my own hands; I went forth in the dark, carrying my outfit upon my shoulder in their sight.

[8]In the morning the word of the LORD came to me: [9]"Son of man, has not the house of Israel, the rebellious house, said to you, 'What are you doing?' [10]Say to them, 'Thus says the Lord GOD: This oracle concerns the prince in Jerusalem and all the house of Israel who are in it.' [11]Say, 'I am a sign for you: as I have done, so shall it be done to them; they shall go into exile, into captivity.' [12]And the prince who is among them shall lift his baggage upon his shoulder in the dark, and shall go forth; he shall dig through the wall and go out through it; he shall cover his face, that he may not see the land with his eyes. [13]And I will spread my net over him, and he shall be taken in my snare; and I will bring him to Babylon in the land of the Chaldeans, yet he shall not see it; and he shall die there. [14]And I will scatter toward every wind all who are round about him, his helpers and all his troops; and I will unsheathe the sword after them. [15]And they shall know that I am the LORD, when I disperse them among the nations and scatter them through the countries. [16]But I will let a few of them escape from the sword, from famine and pestilence, that they may confess all their abominations among the nations where they go, and may know that I am the LORD."

[17]Moreover the word of the LORD came to me: [18]"Son of man, eat your bread with quaking, and drink water with trembling and with fearfulness; [19]and say of the people of the land, Thus says the Lord GOD concerning the inhabitants of Jerusalem in the land of Israel: They shall eat their bread with fearfulness, and drink water in dismay, because their land will be stripped of all it contains, on account of the violence of all those who dwell in it. [20]And the inhabited cities shall be laid waste, and the land shall become a desolation; and you shall know that I am the LORD."

OT: Lev 26:43; 2 Kings 25:4–7; Ps 115:5–6; Isa 6:8–10; Jer 5:21; Lam 1:16
Catechism: unbelief, 678; disobedience, 397, 615, 1850

12:1–3a This chapter is all about the exile that is coming. Like a tidal wave from the sea, the exile will crash suddenly upon the people. It is coming soon and there is no stopping it. Using language that echoes Ezekiel's original call in chapters 2–3, the Lord once again identifies Israel as **a rebellious house** and adds that they **have eyes to see, but see not**, and **ears to hear, but hear not**. Isaiah faced the same challenge in his day (Isa 6:8–10), and Jeremiah confronted the people for their refusal to see and truly listen: "Hear this, O foolish and senseless people, who have eyes, but see not, who have ears, but hear not" (Jer 5:21). The people's inability to see and hear resembles the senselessness of the very idols that they worship. According to the psalm, idols "have . . . eyes, but do not see. / They have ears, but do not hear" (Ps 115:5–6). The people have become like their idols.

Ezekiel, living in exile in Babylon, then receives instructions for undertaking a prophetic action. This prophetic †sign-act applies to those who are living in Jerusalem, but the message is intended primarily for Ezekiel's fellow exiles in Babylon. "Ezekiel, who was included in the first deportation to Babylon, predicts a further exile by means of symbolic actions."[2]

Ezekiel is told to prepare **an exile's baggage** and **go into exile by day in their sight**, and then **go forth . . . at evening in their sight**.[3] In a further instruction, Ezekiel is told to **dig through the wall in their sight**, lift the baggage upon his shoulder, and carry it off in the night with his face covered so that he does not **see the land**. What is going on here? Digging through the wall probably dramatizes a furtive and desperate attempt to escape the siege of the city. The Babylonian armies would have occupied the gates of the city, and so those wishing to flee must resort to digging through a portion of the wall in the hope of making an escape unseen. Ezekiel himself is **a sign for the house of Israel**. He dramatically portrays a man going off into exile.[4] By covering his face and going out into the darkness, Ezekiel indicates the shame of defeat that accompanies loss of the land. And so, Ezekiel faithfully carries out this prophetic action in the sight of the people in exile in the hope that **perhaps they will understand, though they are a rebellious house** (v. 3). Another interpretation of this verse expresses hope that through Ezekiel's prophetic action, "perhaps they will see that they are a rebellious house" (NABRE) that is destined to be sent into exile.

Naturally, Ezekiel's fellow exiles ask, **What are you doing?** The exiles appear to be the losers—they were the ones sent into exile away from the land. But Ezekiel's prophetic actions show that those who remained in the land of Israel will in fact receive the more severe judgment. And so the next morning, the Lord gives Ezekiel the *words* to explain the prophetic *actions*. The sign points

12:3b–7

12:8–14

---

2. "Introduction to Ezekiel," in *ESV Study Bible* (Wheaton: Crossway, 2008), 1514.

3. For an exile's baggage, see Jer 10:17–18; 46:19. According to the Jewish rabbis, an exile's baggage consisted of a bag, a dish, and a mat. See Eisemann, *Ezekiel*, 203.

4. Alter, "Ezekiel," 1080, sees the departure both by day and by night as indicating "the encompassing nature of the departure into exile."

to **the prince in Jerusalem and all the house of Israel who are in it**—that is, Zedekiah, his entourage, and all the people walled up in the siege. Their fate is stated forcefully: **they shall go into exile, into captivity.** The prince shall take his baggage, dig a hole through the wall, and go out into the dark with his face covered in shame. But all this is really the Lord's doing: **I will spread my net over him . . . and I will bring him to Babylon.** Ominously, the prophecy says that Zedekiah **shall not see it** (that is, Babylon). According to the biblical record of the siege, this in fact came true: the Babylonians made a breach in the wall, and Zedekiah fled by night with his nobles through a gate in the wall but was captured and had his eyes put out (2 Kings 25:4–7; Jer 39:4–7). The one who did not "have eyes to see" was "blinded" and exiled to a land he was unable to see.

12:15–16   It is not just the prince but *all the people* who will be scattered into exile, pursued by the sword. The result will be knowledge of the Lord and his just judgment. **They shall know that I am the LORD, when I disperse them among the nations.** It is for this reason—to know that the Lord is God—that a few (the remnant) will be allowed to **escape from the sword, from famine and pestilence.** This is a severe mercy: the nation of Israel will be preserved through the fire of judgment and come to know and confess their grievous sins. The book of Lamentations serves as an eloquent testimony to Israel's heartfelt confession of sin in the midst of their exile: "For these things I weep; / my eyes flow with tears" (Lam 1:16).

12:17–20   Ezekiel is told to perform a second sign: **eat your bread with quaking, and drink water with trembling and with fearfulness.** With this sign comes the word that explains it. Ezekiel represents the people of Israel, who will **eat their bread with fearfulness, and drink water in dismay.** Why? Because the cities will be devastated and the land will have become a desolation. This promise also recalls the †covenant curse from Leviticus: "The land shall be left by them, and enjoy its sabbaths while it lies desolate without them" (Lev 26:43). Through famine and scarcity the **people of the land** will also suffer along with those trapped in the besieged city. Once again, all of them will come to know the truth of the declaration, **I am the LORD.** It is the Lord who has spoken and acted.

The Time of the Vision Is at Hand (12:21–28)

²¹And the word of the LORD came to me: ²²"Son of man, what is this proverb that you have about the land of Israel, saying, 'The days grow long, and every vision comes to nothing'? ²³Tell them therefore, 'Thus says the Lord GOD: I will put an end to this proverb, and they shall no more use it as a proverb in Israel.' But say to them, The days are at hand, and the fulfilment of every vision. ²⁴For there shall be no more any false vision or flattering

The Delay in the Fulfillment of God's Word

BIBLICAL BACKGROUND

In Ezekiel's day, many people concluded that, because the promised judgment was *delayed*, they could set it aside and carry on as normal. They doubted the truth of the prophecies—"every vision comes to nothing"—because they just did not seem to be coming true. A concern that the Lord not delay the fulfillment of his word also marks the prophets. Daniel pleads in prayer: "O LORD, give heed and act; delay not, for your own sake, O my God" (Dan 9:19). Likewise, the prophet Habakkuk admits the need to be patient for God's timing, but assures the people that the Lord will not delay in fulfilling his word: "For still the vision awaits its time; / it hastens to the end—it will not lie. / If it seems slow, wait for it; / it will surely come, it will not delay" (Hab 2:3). Jesus himself, in the parable of the persistent widow, assures us that God our Father will not long delay in bringing justice to those who cry out to him: "Will he delay long over them? I tell you, he will vindicate them speedily" (Luke 18:7–8). We find the same thing happening during the time that the apostle Peter is writing about the return of Jesus in glory (2 Pet 3:1–7). Scoffers will claim that nothing has really changed since the beginning of the world—all this talk about Christ's return is just a groundless myth that can be ignored. Peter, however, defends the "delay" in God fulfilling his promise: "The Lord is not slow about his promise as some count slowness, but is forbearing toward you, not wishing that any should perish, but that all should reach repentance" (2 Pet 3:9). In the scriptural narrative it can seem that God's word is delayed, and his people wonder if it will ever come to pass. But his word-in-action always arrives at just the right time: God is faithful to his word and will bring it to pass at the appointed time.

divination within the house of Israel. ²⁵But I the LORD will speak the word which I will speak, and it will be performed. It will no longer be delayed, but in your days, O rebellious house, I will speak the word and perform it, says the Lord GOD."

²⁶Again the word of the LORD came to me: ²⁷"Son of man, behold, they of the house of Israel say, 'The vision that he sees is for many days hence, and he prophesies of times far off.' ²⁸Therefore say to them, Thus says the Lord GOD: None of my words will be delayed any longer, but the word which I speak will be performed, says the Lord GOD."

OT: Isa 55:11; Dan 9:19; Hab 2:3
NT: Luke 18:7–8; John 17:4; 2 Pet 3:1–9
Catechism: reliability of the word of God, 157, 182

A proverb was circulating among the people of Israel that was dismissive of **12:21–25** prophecies of gloom and judgment: **The days grow long, and every vision comes** to nothing.[5] It seems to the people that these prophecies foretell an impending doom but nothing ever happens, and so they ignore the word. The Lord replies bluntly: **I will put an end to this proverb**. How? By bringing this judgment swiftly and surely upon the people. In response to this dismissive proverb, the Lord says: **The days are at hand, and the fulfilment of every vision**. What the Lord has spoken **will be performed. It will no longer be delayed**. This is a firm and sure promise. Despite their dismissal, the Lord says to the **rebellious house** of Israel that the promised judgment will indeed fall in their days.

12:26–28   The Lord then refutes another claim made by the people—namely, that Ezekiel's vision of judgment is for **many days hence** and for **times far off**. "Even if the word is true," they are saying, "it won't happen in our day."[6] But the Lord rejects this false hope: **None of my words will be delayed any longer.** The word that God has spoken through his prophets **will be performed** speedily and surely.

Reflection and Application (12:21–28)

Three times in the conclusion to Ezek 12 the Lord says that the word he speaks will not be delayed but he will "perform" it: the word "will be performed." Other translations render this "be fulfilled" or "brought about." The verb is simply "to do"—the word that God speaks will "be done." This echoes the great promise in Isaiah, when the Lord says that the word he speaks—that he "sends out"—will not return empty but will accomplish everything that he has planned: "So shall my word be that goes forth from my mouth; / it shall not return to me empty, / but it shall accomplish that which I intend, / and prosper in the thing for which I sent it" (Isa 55:11). When God speaks, what he speaks happens. The opening chapter of Genesis displays this powerfully. "And God said . . . ," and so it was. The creation came into being out of nothing.

We speak many words, but only some of them "come to pass." There is no guarantee that the words we speak will be fulfilled. Our words do not have this inherent power. But God's word is different. When God speaks, it comes to pass as he intended. Most profoundly, God has sent his "Word"—his Son—into the world to accomplish our salvation. And that Word did not return to him empty but accomplished everything the Father intended: "I glorified you on earth, having accomplished the work which you gave me to do" (John 17:4). For our part, we can have full confidence that God's word of promise will come to pass in our own lives, in the Church, and in the world. He will *perform* it.

---

5. The term "proverb" (Hebrew *mashal*) appears eight times in Ezekiel and is used flexibly to refer to sayings, parables, stories, and riddles.

6. In a similar way, King Hezekiah took comfort because he was told that Isaiah's dire prediction, that Babylon would capture and exile the people of Israel, would not happen in his day (2 Kings 20:16–19).

Oracles against False Prophets and Fortune Tellers (13:1–23)

[1]The word of the LORD came to me: [2]"Son of man, prophesy against the prophets of Israel, prophesy and say to those who prophesy out of their own minds: 'Hear the word of the LORD!' [3]Thus says the Lord GOD, Woe to the foolish prophets who follow their own spirit, and have seen nothing! [4]Your prophets have been like foxes among ruins, O Israel. [5]You have not gone up into the breaches, or built up a wall for the house of Israel, that it might stand in battle in the day of the LORD. [6]They have spoken falsehood and divined a lie; they say, 'Says the LORD,' when the LORD has not sent them, and yet they expect him to fulfil their word. [7]Have you not seen a delusive vision, and uttered a lying divination, whenever you have said, 'Says the LORD,' although I have not spoken?"

[8]Therefore thus says the Lord God: "Because you have uttered delusions and seen lies, therefore behold, I am against you, says the Lord GOD. [9]My hand will be against the prophets who see delusive visions and who give lying divinations; they shall not be in the council of my people, nor be enrolled in the register of the house of Israel, nor shall they enter the land of Israel; and you shall know that I am the Lord GOD. [10]Because, yes, because they have misled my people, saying, 'Peace,' when there is no peace; and because, when the people build a wall, these prophets daub it with whitewash; [11]say to those who daub it with whitewash that it shall fall! There will be a deluge of rain, great hailstones will fall, and a stormy wind break out; [12]and when the wall falls, will it not be said to you, 'Where is the daubing with which you daubed it?' [13]Therefore thus says the Lord GOD: I will make a stormy wind break out in my wrath; and there shall be a deluge of rain in my anger, and great hailstones in wrath to destroy it. [14]And I will break down the wall that you have daubed with whitewash, and bring it down to the ground, so that its foundation will be laid bare; when it falls, you shall perish in the midst of it; and you shall know that I am the LORD. [15]Thus will I spend my wrath upon the wall, and upon those who have daubed it with whitewash; and I will say to you, The wall is no more, nor those who daubed it, [16]the prophets of Israel who prophesied concerning Jerusalem and saw visions of peace for her, when there was no peace, says the Lord GOD.

[17]"And you, son of man, set your face against the daughters of your people, who prophesy out of their own minds; prophesy against them [18]and say, Thus says the Lord GOD: Woe to the women who sew magic bands upon all wrists, and make veils for the heads of persons of every stature, in the hunt for souls! Will you hunt down souls belonging to my people, and keep other souls alive for your profit? [19]You have profaned me among my people for handfuls of barley and for pieces of bread, putting to death persons who should not die and keeping alive persons who should not live, by your lies to my people, who listen to lies.

²⁰"Wherefore thus says the Lord GOD: Behold, I am against your magic bands with which you hunt the souls, and I will tear them from your arms; and I will let the souls that you hunt go free like birds. ²¹Your veils also I will tear off, and deliver my people out of your hand, and they shall be no more in your hand as prey; and you shall know that I am the LORD. ²²Because you have disheartened the righteous falsely, although I have not disheartened him, and you have encouraged the wicked, that he should not turn from his wicked way to save his life; ²³therefore you shall no more see delusive visions nor practice divination; I will deliver my people out of your hand. Then you will know that I am the LORD."

OT: Jer 6:14; 14:14; 23:16
NT: John 20:19, 21; Eph 2:14, 17
Catechism: warning against spiritual danger, 1033, 1056, 1852; God's call on the prophets, 702

This chapter is all about false prophets, lying fortune tellers, and charm makers. The previous chapter concluded with the people dismissing the true prophetic messages of Ezekiel. Now we hear about two groups of people (men and women) who are actively misleading the people through false words and omens.

13:1–5   The first target group is **the prophets of Israel** who are prophesying **out of their own minds**. The word "minds" is literally "hearts" and is also translated "thoughts" (NABRE) and "imagination" (NRSV). Instead of listening to the Lord's word, they **follow their own spirit, and have seen nothing**. In contrast to a true prophet—like Ezekiel—who speaks under the †inspiration of the "Spirit," they follow their own "spirit." They should have strengthened the people by going up **into the breaches** and building up **a wall for the house of Israel**, but instead they have acted like **foxes among ruins** who only tear down what is already crumbling. The imagery here is of a people under siege: the walls of their city have been breached, and they lie open to attack. Instead of filling in these breaks in the wall by building it up, the prophets have acted like wild foxes who by scrambling among the ruins of the wall only serve to tear it down even further.[7] The point is that these prophets were meant to strengthen the people to stand in faithfulness to the Lord; instead, their words have contributed to a further dismantling of the people's trust in the Lord and eroded their readiness to rely upon him.

13:6–7   This is the core of their offense: **they have spoken falsehood and divined a lie**. They claim to speak on behalf of the God of Israel, saying, "Thus **says the LORD**," but in fact **the LORD has not sent them**. Because God has not spoken this word through them, they have brought to birth **a delusive vision** and a **lying †divination**. This is a grave indictment.

7. Rabbi David Kimchi (d. 1235) relates this verse to Song 2:15, "the little foxes, that spoil the vineyards," and concludes that these false prophets were breaking down the walls of the people and so destroying the vineyard, which is the people of Israel. Rosenberg, *Book of Ezekiel*, 1:84.

Origen on True and False Spirits

LIVING TRADITION

In his commentary on Ezekiel, Origen of Alexandria (d. 254) contrasts two spirits of prophecy: the first is our own spirit (which is false), and the other is the Holy Spirit of God (who is true): "He who is a false prophet prophesies from his own heart and he walks not after the Spirit of God but after his own spirit. For there is a spirit of man that lives in him—far be it from me that I should walk after it!—but I understand the Holy Spirit of God and will walk after the Lord my God."[a]

a. *Homily* 2.3, in *Homilies 1–14 on Ezekiel*, trans. Thomas P. Scheck, ACW 62 (New York: Newman, 2010), 50.

When the one that you claim to serve—and in whose name you speak—arrives on the scene and says categorically that he did *not* send you and did not give you this word to speak, then you are unmasked and proven fraudulent. Such is the position of these false prophets pretending to speak in God's name. The prophet Jeremiah came up against this same band of prophets and dismissed them in similar language: "The prophets are prophesying lies in my name; I did not send them, nor did I command them or speak to them. They are prophesying to you a lying vision, worthless divination, and the deceit of their own minds" (Jer 14:14).

In this section, the Lord expands his testimony against the false prophets: **My** **13:8–9** **hand will be against the prophets who see delusive visions.** When the Lord called Ezekiel, the Lord's hand came *upon* him, but with the false prophets his hand is *against* them. By removing them from the council of his people and disinheriting them from the land, the Lord removes these false prophets from the †covenant and its blessings. The †*Targum of Ezekiel* and many of the Jewish rabbis viewed this as an eternal disinheritance from the life of the age to come.[8]

What is their great fault? **They have misled** the people, proclaiming *in God's* **13:10–16** *name* that there will be peace, **when there is no peace.** They saw **visions of peace** for Jerusalem **when there was no peace.** Jeremiah, too, faced these false prophets with their deceptive promises of peace: "They have healed the wound of my people lightly, saying, 'Peace, peace,' when there is no peace" (Jer 6:14). The contrast between the false prophets and Ezekiel is stark. Ezekiel is called to be a watchman, to warn the people of the utter disaster that is on their doorstep. The false prophets directly counter this claim, assuring the people that the Lord will deliver them from the dreaded Babylonian armies, that there will be peace

8. *Targum of Ezekiel* translates this passage as follows: "And in the inscription *for eternal life which is inscribed for the righteous* of the House of Israel, they shall not be inscribed" (Levey, *Targum of Ezekiel*, 44). See Eisemann, *Ezekiel*, 219–20.

St. Ambrose on True and False Peace

In this short selection, St. Ambrose (d. 397) offers a spiritual interpretation of Ezekiel's distinction between a true and a false peace—between a true peace, born of love, and a so-called peace that is really only a stumbling block:

> There is a peace that does not have a stumbling block and a peace that does. The one that does not have a stumbling block is from love; the one which does, from pretense. So also the prophet says, "Peace, peace; and where is peace?" Let us therefore run away from the peace of sinners, for they conspire against the guiltless person, they come together to oppress him who is just.[a]

a. *The Prayer of Job and David* 3.3.6 (ACCS 13:47).

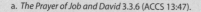

in the land, and that all will be well. The temptation these prophets faced is the same temptation that prophets perennially face: to proclaim what the people wish to hear. And so the people, pleased to hear a message of peace, are given a false assurance instead of being spurred on to repentance.

These false words of assurance are likened to whitewash spread over a collapsing wall (vv. 10–15). The whitewash does nothing to strengthen the wall but only temporarily hides the decay within. But the wall will not stand against the storm the Lord is sending against it. Both the wall and those who **daubed** it **with whitewash** will come to ruin. When this disaster happens, then says the Lord God, **you shall know that I am the LORD**.

In summary, the false prophets make a pretense of building up, but in fact they are tearing down. Ezekiel appears to be tearing down the hopes of the people, but by speaking a true word of judgment he is, in fact, preparing the foundations for true restoration and rebuilding.

13:17–23   Ezekiel now turns his attention to a group of women **who prophesy out of their own minds**.[9] Who are these women? They are fortune tellers selling magical amulets and offering false hope of deliverance to people who pay for their lies. They dabble in magic and witchcraft, invoking demonic powers. Ezekiel accuses them of being **in the hunt for souls**. For small amounts of cash, they spread lies among the people, **putting to death persons who should not die and**

---

9. This is the primary occasion in the Old Testament where the Lord speaks against specifically female false prophets (see also Neh 6:14). Ezekiel does not use the term "prophetess" here, however. The term "prophetess" is used positively of female prophets four times in the Old Testament: of Miriam (Exod 15:20); of Deborah (Judg 4:4); of Isaiah's wife (Isa 8:3); and of Huldah (2 Kings 22:14; 2 Chron 34:22). In the New Testament, Anna is described as a prophetess (Luke 2:36–37), and Philip's four daughters are described as prophesying in the context of Paul's visit to Caesarea (Acts 21:9).

keeping alive persons who should not live. They may not be literally killing people, but through their false words and lying divinations they are drawing people into the path of spiritual death and placing their physical well-being in jeopardy by minimizing the Babylonian threat. We can see here the presence of the demonic, the reality of spiritual warfare, and the need to be on guard against evil powers. Through Ezekiel the Lord declares that he will bring down these "hunters of souls" but will ensure that the souls of their victims **go free like birds**.

The contrast with Ezekiel the watchman is once again striking. He has been called to warn the wicked so that they will turn from their evil ways and live. These false fortune tellers have done the opposite. They have **disheartened the righteous falsely**, while at the same time they have **encouraged the wicked, that he should not turn from his wicked way to save his life**. Because of this, the Lord rebukes them as he did the false prophets: **you shall no more see delusive visions nor practice divination**. Despite their lying visions, the Lord in the end will deliver his people from these false prophets, and as a result they shall know that he is the Lord.

A central focus of this chapter is the Lord's intense and personal concern for his people. He identifies the people of Israel as "my people" seven times. Coupled with the reference to "the righteous" in verse 22, all this shows that the Lord is deeply committed to the welfare of all his people but especially to those who cling loyally to him in desperate times. We see here a brief expression of what will break out into the open in the latter part of Ezekiel: despite the great sins of the people, the Lord himself will come to rescue them from the hand of their enemies.

In the Light of Christ (13:8–16)

Both Jeremiah and Ezekiel rail against false prophets in their day who are proclaiming, "Peace, peace," when there is no peace (Hebrew *shalom*). The truth revealed throughout the Bible is that true peace will come only when we are in right relationship with God and one another. When wickedness abounds, there can be no peace: "'There is no peace,' says the LORD, 'for the wicked'" (Isa 48:22). Further, the Lord God himself is the source of our peace: "May the LORD give strength to his people! / May the LORD bless his people with peace!" (Ps 29:11). The prophecies of the †Messiah identify peace (*shalom*) as one of the core fruits of his reign (Isa 9:7). In contrast to the false prophets who proclaim a specious peace, Isaiah predicts a day when true peace will come to pass: "Peace, peace, to the far and to the near, says the LORD; / and I will heal him" (Isa 57:19). The fulfillment of this promised peace is found in Jesus himself. The apostle Paul, writing with this promise from Isaiah in view, declares Jesus himself as our peace: "For he is our peace, who has made us both one. . . . And he came and preached peace to you who were far off and peace to those who were near" (Eph 2:14, 17). Christ as the one who brings peace is revealed profoundly on Easter day, when he greets his disciples: "Peace to you" (Luke 24:36; see also John 20:19, 21). Twice toward the end of Ezekiel, God promises a renewal of the "covenant of peace" that God will make with his people (Ezek 34:25; 37:26). We have come to know that this promise is fulfilled in Christ alone, who brings about the covenant of peace, and that he himself is the peace that unites us.

Oracle against Elders with Idolatrous Hearts (14:1–11)

[1]Then came certain of the elders of Israel to me; and sat before me. [2]And the word of the LORD came to me: [3]"Son of man, these men have taken their idols into their hearts, and set the stumbling block of their iniquity before their faces; should I let myself be inquired of at all by them? [4]Therefore speak to them, and say to them, Thus says the Lord GOD: Any man of the house of Israel who takes his idols into his heart and sets the stumbling block of his iniquity before his face, and yet comes to the prophet, I the LORD will answer him myself because of the multitude of his idols, [5]that I may lay hold of the hearts of the house of Israel, who are all estranged from me through their idols.

[6]"Therefore say to the house of Israel, Thus says the Lord GOD: Repent and turn away from your idols; and turn away your faces from all your abominations. [7]For any one of the house of Israel, or of the strangers that sojourn in Israel, who separates himself from me, taking his idols into his heart and putting the stumbling block of his iniquity before his face, and yet comes to a prophet to inquire for himself of me, I the LORD will answer him myself; [8]and I will set my face against that man, I will make him a sign and a byword and cut him off from the midst of my people; and you shall know that I am the LORD. [9]And if the prophet be deceived and speak a word, I, the LORD, have deceived that prophet, and I will stretch out my hand against him, and will destroy him from the midst of my people Israel. [10]And they shall bear their punishment—the punishment of the prophet and the punishment of the inquirer shall be alike— [11]that the house of Israel may go no more astray from me, nor defile themselves any more with all their transgressions, but that they may be my people and I may be their God, says the Lord GOD."

OT: Deut 13:2–4; 30:19; 1 Kings 22:20–23
NT: James 1:13
Catechism: the sin of idolatry, 2112–14; the call to repentance and conversion, 1427–39

The scene now shifts back to Ezekiel in Babylon, where **certain of the elders of**   14:1–3
Israel have approached him and are seated around him. We are not told why
they have come, but given the Lord's word to them, it seems that they have
come to consult Ezekiel about the word of the Lord. But the Lord God sees into
their hearts: **Son of man, these men have taken their idols into their hearts**
and have fixed a **stumbling block of their iniquity before their faces.**[10] What
does this mean? It is unlikely that they are actually worshiping false gods in
secret (what the elders in Jerusalem were found doing in chap. 8), but they are
allowing idols into their hearts by consulting other spiritual sources (gods)
alongside the Lord in the hope of discovering what is going to happen to them
and their people. The result is that their hearts are not pure as they come to
consult the Lord.

The response of the Lord to these men is striking. He says that he will answer   14:4–8
the elders of Israel, not by giving them what they seek, but in order to **lay hold**
of the hearts of the house of Israel. God wants their hearts returned to him!
They have become **estranged . . . through their idols**, and the Lord wants them
back. And so, God says to them: **Repent and turn away from your idols; and**
turn away your faces from all your abominations. This is one of the few explicit
calls for repentance in the book of Ezekiel. The Lord's goal is to recapture the
hearts of his people. If, however, they continue in their iniquity, the Lord will
set his **face against** them, native Israelite and sojourner alike, and cut them off
from his people. The choice before them is to choose life or death: "I have set
before you life and death, blessing and curse. Therefore choose life, that you
and your descendants may live" (Deut 30:19).

Reflection and Application (14:1–8)

It is all too easy for us to dismiss the sin of idolatry as something that tempted
primitive peoples but does not impact us today. Who in the present time wor-
ships idols of silver and gold? There is, in fact, a notable rise in the practice of
ancient religions and the spread in the modern world of what can properly be
called "idolatry." But Ezekiel takes us to a deeper level when he accuses the
people of his day of "taking idols into their hearts." This is more than merely
an outward show of reverence toward idols; this involves genuine devotion to
the idol in the heart. Just as we can take the law of God into our hearts, so it is
possible to take an idol into our hearts.

The Catechism describes how idolatry can work its way into our hearts
through many means: "Idolatry not only refers to false pagan worship. It remains

---

10. The phrase "stumbling block of iniquity" appears five times in the book and is unique to Ezekiel
(7:19; 14:3, 4, 7; 44:12). It refers to the effects of idolatry: when the people revert to the evil of idolatry,
they set up a stumbling block *in their hearts* that prevents them from hearing and following the Lord.

The "Sojourner" in Israel

Ezekiel refers to the "sojourner" (Hebrew *ger*) five times in the book (14:7; 22:7, 29; 47:22, 23). Concern for the sojourner goes all the way back to Abraham, the father of the people, who wandered throughout the promised land without ever becoming a true resident: "I am a stranger and a sojourner among you" (Gen 23:4). The Lord repeatedly told the people of Israel to treat sojourners among them with love and justice, because the Israelites, too, were once sojourners in a land not their own: "The stranger who sojourns with you shall be to you as the native among you, and you shall love him as yourself; for you were strangers in the land of Egypt" (Lev 19:34). Even in their own land, the people of Israel remain sojourners, because the land fundamentally belongs to the Lord: "For the land is mine; you are strangers and sojourners with me" (Lev 25:23). Who were these strangers and sojourners in Israel to whom Ezekiel refers? They were immigrants from other nations, living in the midst of the people of Israel and partaking fully or partially in Israel's way of life and worship: "You shall have one law for the sojourner and for the native; for I am the LORD your God" (Lev 24:22). Notably, the Lord takes special care for the sojourner and stranger, along with his care for widows and orphans: "He executes justice for the fatherless and the widow, and loves the sojourner, giving him food and clothing. Love the sojourner therefore; for you were sojourners in the land of Egypt" (Deut 10:18–19). By his attention to the sojourners in Israel, Ezekiel imitates the Lord and shows that he is not just concerned for genealogical Israel; he recognizes a place for those from the nations who live among the people of Israel.

a constant temptation to faith. Idolatry consists in divinizing what is not God. Man commits idolatry whenever he honors and reveres a creature in place of God, whether this be gods or demons (for example, satanism), power, pleasure, race, ancestors, the state, money, etc." (2113). Even if we are unlikely to be tempted to worship physical idols, the temptation to *idolatry* is just as strong today as ever. We are perhaps more sophisticated in our choice of idols, but nonetheless we are sorely tempted to put other things in the place of God. Whenever we "divinize" a created thing or being, we fall into the sin of idolatry and rob God of the glory that is due to him alone.

The process of Christian conversion includes the gradual giving up of anything that stands in the place of God. If we are willing, the Lord gently but firmly helps us to remove any idols that we have taken into our hearts. This is for our deep good but also contributes to the glory of God.

14:9–10   In verse 9, the Lord makes a stunning and perplexing claim: **If the prophet be deceived and speak a word, I, the LORD, have deceived that prophet**. How

---

St. John of the Cross on the Lord Deceiving the False Prophet

LIVING
TRADITION

St. John of the Cross explains what it means when the Lord says that he will deceive the false prophet (Ezek 14:1–9):

> [That prophet] will lose the Lord's favor and be deceived. That is what is meant by "I the Lord will answer him myself; and I will set my face against that man": that man will be deprived of God's †grace and favor, which makes it clear that the deception is the result of God's withdrawal. Then the devil will speak and respond according to the man's will and desires, and because he is satisfied, and the sayings and messages that he hears suit him, he will allow himself to be greatly deceived.[a]

a. *Ascent of Mount Carmel* 2.21.13, trans. *The Navarre Bible: Major Prophets* (Dublin: Four Courts, 2005), 645.

---

are we to understand the action of the Lord in this deception? Many commentators conclude that God simply deceives these bad-hearted prophets, matching "insincerity for insincerity."[11] There is precedent for this elsewhere in the Old Testament. In 1 Kings 22:20–23, the prophet Micaiah claims that the Lord God sent an enticing spirit to lead King Ahab astray. More indirectly, in Deuteronomy the Lord permits the activity of false prophets in order to "test" his people to see if they will obey his voice alone (Deut 13:2–4). The Letter of James, however, tells us that "God cannot be tempted with evil and he himself tempts no one" (James 1:13). It is probably best to read this statement of the Lord deceiving the false prophet in this light: God allows sin to have its full consequences, and so allows deception to occur, so that the erring prophet and people may experience the full impact of their sin: **and they shall bear their punishment**.

The end-goal, however, is not punishment but recovery and the renewal of 14:11 the covenant. The Lord says that he acts in this way so that **the house of Israel may go no more astray from me** but instead be purified. The goal is a relationship of covenant love between God and his people: **that they may be my people and I may be their God**.

Certainty of the Coming Judgment (14:12–23)

---

¹²**And the word of the Lord came to me:** ¹³**"Son of man, when a land sins against me by acting faithlessly, and I stretch out my hand against it, and**

---

11. Block, *Ezekiel: Chapters 1–24*, 432. Greenberg (*Ezekiel 1–20*, 254) likewise concludes that this passage ascribes the prophet's error to "divine misguidance."

break its staff of bread and send famine upon it, and cut off from it man and beast, [14]even if these three men, Noah, Daniel, and Job, were in it, they would deliver but their own lives by their righteousness, says the Lord GOD. [15]If I cause wild beasts to pass through the land, and they ravage it, and it be made desolate, so that no man may pass through because of the beasts; [16]even if these three men were in it, as I live, says the Lord GOD, they would deliver neither sons nor daughters; they alone would be delivered, but the land would be desolate. [17]Or if I bring a sword upon that land, and say, Let a sword go through the land; and I cut off from it man and beast; [18]though these three men were in it, as I live, says the Lord GOD, they would deliver neither sons nor daughters, but they alone would be delivered. [19]Or if I send a pestilence into that land, and pour out my wrath upon it with blood, to cut off from it man and beast; [20]even if Noah, Daniel, and Job were in it, as I live, says the Lord GOD, they would deliver neither son nor daughter; they would deliver but their own lives by their righteousness.

[21]"For thus says the Lord GOD: How much more when I send upon Jerusalem my four sore acts of judgment, sword, famine, evil beasts, and pestilence, to cut off from it man and beast! [22]Yet, if there should be left in it any survivors to lead out sons and daughters, when they come forth to you, and you see their ways and their doings, you will be consoled for the evil that I have brought upon Jerusalem, for all that I have brought upon it. [23]They will console you, when you see their ways and their doings; and you shall know that I have not done without cause all that I have done in it, says the Lord GOD."

OT: Gen 6:9; 18:22–33; Deut 32:23–25; Job 1:1; Dan 9:22–23; 10:12–14
NT: Rev 6:8
Catechism: God's punishment and judgment of sin, 211, 679, 1472–73; hardness of heart, 1859, 1864, 2840

14:12–20   This section underlines the certainty of the judgment that is coming upon the land of Israel and the city of Jerusalem. This judgment is going to befall the people because they have sinned against the Lord **by acting faithlessly**. Not even the prayers of three of the most righteous people in the biblical record—**Noah, Daniel, and Job**—would turn aside the judgment that is coming, says the Lord to Ezekiel. The situation is so dire that not even these great intercessors would turn back the acts of judgment that will soon befall the land and the city.

Jeremiah, who is prophesying in Israel at the same time as Ezekiel, renders a similar verdict, declaring that even the intercessory influence of Moses and Samuel would not turn the tide of judgment that is coming: "Though Moses and Samuel stood before me, yet my heart would not turn toward this people" (Jer 15:1). And though Abraham is not mentioned in this context, his "bargaining" with the Lord for the deliverance of Sodom and Gomorrah for the

St. John Chrysostom on the Intercession of Holy People

John Chrysostom (d. 407), a renowned preacher of the early Church, confirms that the prayers of the saints have great power but also points to the need for genuine repentance by the people. "But even if it is Ezekiel who does the pleading, he will be told, 'though Noah comes, and Job and Daniel, they shall deliver neither sons nor daughters. . . .' For it is true that the prayers of the saints have the greatest power, but only on condition of our repentance and amendment of life."[a]

a. *Homilies on the Gospel of Matthew* 5.7 (ACCS 13:55).

sake of ten righteous people (Gen 18:22–33) provides an important biblical example of the influence of the intercession of upright people to impact the Lord's judgment.

The three figures named are Noah, Daniel, and Job. According to Genesis 6:9: "Noah was a righteous man, blameless in his generation." His righteousness did not save the wicked of his generation—they all perished in the flood—but his whole family was delivered from the judgment.[12] For his part, Job "was blameless and upright, one who feared God, and turned away from evil" (Job 1:1).[13] Daniel, a contemporary of Ezekiel in Babylon, was a righteous man and a powerful intercessor whose earnest prayer brought blessing and protection to his people,[14] though scholars question whether the "Daniel" named here is meant to identify Ezekiel's contemporary.[15] While the identity of this "Daniel" remains uncertain, the fundamental point of the text is clear. By bringing forward these three outstanding examples of righteous living, Ezekiel shouts aloud how bad things really are. *Not even these great figures*, if they lived among this people, would turn aside the judgment that is coming. Yes, they would deliver

---

12. For Noah as a righteous man, see also Heb 11:7; 2 Pet 2:5.
13. The Letter of James (5:11) commends Job for his steadfastness under trial.
14. For the effective intercession of Daniel, see Dan 9:22–23; 10:12–14.
15. Some scholars (e.g., Moshe Greenberg, John Taylor) doubt that Ezekiel would have chosen a man of his own generation, a fellow exile in Babylon, to stand in the illustrious company of Noah and Job, while other scholars (e.g., Daniel Block) defend the biblical Daniel as being the most probable candidate. A further issue is that the spelling of the Hebrew name "Daniel" here in Ezekiel is different by one letter from the spelling of the name of the biblical Daniel. Two other figures named "Daniel" are offered as alternatives: (1) the grandfather of Methuselah according to the Jewish work *Jubilees* (4:20); and (2) an ancient Phoenician king, found in ancient Ugaritic texts, known for his righteousness and wisdom—a non-Israelite like Noah and Job (Ezek 28:1–3 shows a link between Daniel and the Phoenician city-state of Tyre).

themselves, but even their presence and their prayer would not turn away God's judgment.

14:21–23 Chapter 14 ends on a note of promise and consolation. Even though the Lord will unleash against his people the **four sore acts of judgment, sword, famine, evil beasts, and pestilence** (see the sidebar "The Typical Means of Judgment," p. 63), yet there will be **survivors** who remain after all the acts of judgment have run their course. **Sons and daughters** will **come forth** to the exiles in Babylon, and their deliverance will be a great consolation from the great grief that has befallen the city. It is unlikely that **their ways and their doings** are in fact righteous before the Lord. Rather, it seems that God decided to spare them in order to preserve a remnant and reveal his mercy right in the midst of his just judgment. The result in any case will be consolation for Ezekiel and his fellow exiles because the Lord has acted to preserve a remnant of his people.

Reflection and Application (14:12–23)

The verdict pronounced against Israel and Jerusalem in chapter 14 can sound hopeless, as if God has determined to punish his people and no one, not even the most holy people, can intervene to stop it. But in fact there is no fatalism in Ezekiel. The Lord makes clear that Noah, Daniel, and Job *would be saved* if they were alive and living among this wicked people. And Ezekiel himself is delivered from death and kept under the Lord's blessing. The point is not that the people are fated to be punished, but that they have become so wicked—so hard of heart and mind—that nothing will now turn them back to the Lord. As a result, the Lord will bring his judgment upon them.

We, too, live in a world where great evils occur, even among the people of God. Shall we give up hope and abandon people to the judgment that seems to be coming upon them? Or shall we not, like Ezekiel, cry out to God on behalf of ourselves and those who have turned away (Ezek 9:8; 11:13)? We are called to be "salt and light" in the world around us (Matt 5:13–14), a "leaven" that brings a blessing upon those we live among (Matt 13:33). We are meant to "seek the welfare of the city" where the Lord has sent us, as Jeremiah counseled the exiles in Babylon (Jer 29:7). In the words of Archbishop Charles Chaput, our calling as Christians is "to make Christ known in the world. To hand on the hope that fills our hearts. To work for God's justice in our nation, honoring all that remains beautiful and good in it. And always to do so knowing that we're on a journey to our final homeland. Longing for that life inspires us along the way."[16]

16. Charles Chaput, *Strangers in a Strange Land: Living the Catholic Faith in a Post-Christian World* (New York: Holt, 2017), 163.

The Parable of the Vinestock (15:1–8)

¹And the word of the LORD came to me: ²"Son of man, how does the wood of the vine surpass any wood, the vine branch which is among the trees of the forest? ³Is wood taken from it to make anything? Do men take a peg from it to hang any vessel on? ⁴Behold, it is given to the fire for fuel; when the fire has consumed both ends of it, and the middle of it is charred, is it useful for anything? ⁵Behold, when it was whole, it was used for nothing; how much less, when the fire has consumed it and it is charred, can it ever be used for anything! ⁶Therefore thus says the Lord GOD: Like the wood of the vine among the trees of the forest, which I have given to the fire for fuel, so will I give up the inhabitants of Jerusalem. ⁷And I will set my face against them; though they escape from the fire, the fire shall yet consume them; and you will know that I am the LORD, when I set my face against them. ⁸And I will make the land desolate, because they have acted faithlessly, says the Lord GOD."

OT: Gen 49:11–12; Ps 80:8–16; Isa 5:1–7; Jer 2:21; 12:10; Hosea 10:1
NT: John 15:1–7
Catechism: God's punishment and judgment of sin, 211, 679, 1472–73; hardness of heart, 1859, 1864, 2840

This short chapter comprises one single parable: the wood of the vine (vinestock) **15:1–4a** serves as an image of the inhabitants of Jerusalem.[17] The plot of the parable is worked out in stages. The Lord asks Ezekiel, **how does the wood of the vine surpass any wood? Is wood taken from it to make anything?** The answer is obvious: it is useful for nothing, it is **given to the fire for fuel**. Thus far, the logic of the parable follows common human experience: the wood of the grapevine cannot be used to build anything, and so once it ceases to bear fruit as a living vine, it is burned in the fire. "The vine alone stands or falls by the harvest which it produces. Its fruits are the noblest of all, but if they fail, there is nothing left. Its wood is unsuitable for any purpose."[18] Jesus makes the same point: vine branches that become disconnected from him "are gathered, thrown into the fire and burned" (John 15:6).

Why does the Lord speak of the vine branch being consumed by **fire** on **15:4b–8** **both ends** and **charred** in the middle? This probably has a historical reference. It may refer to the "burning" of both the northern and southern kingdoms (Israel and Judah) that had already occurred, with Jerusalem itself the charred "middle" waiting its turn in the fire. Or it may refer to the two exiles of the

---

17. In 19:10–14, Ezekiel develops the image of Israel as a fruitful vine that has been pulled up, plucked clean, and burned with fire. For the use of the vine/vineyard as an image of the people of God, see Gen 49:11–12; Ps 80:8–16; Isa 5:1–30; Jer 2:21; 12:10; Hosea 10:1.

18. Eisemann, *Ezekiel*, 238–39.

inhabitants of Jerusalem that had already occurred (ca. 603 and 597 BC), with the third and most devastating exile yet to come. Whatever the case, the point is that right now **the inhabitants of Jerusalem** are like a fruitless vinestock that the Lord will give **to the fire for fuel**. Because the people of Jerusalem **have acted faithlessly** (see 14:13), the Lord has set his **face against them**. Even if they escape from one fire of judgment, they will be consumed by another.

We have come full circle. This larger section (chaps. 12–15) began with the Lord declaring that the inhabitants of Jerusalem will go into exile and the land will become a desolation. It concludes with the same pronouncement: the city will be taken, the people will go into exile, and the land will become desolate. When this happens, the Lord says, the people of Israel **will know that I am the LORD**.

In the Light of Christ (15:1–8)

Twice in his book (chaps. 15 and 19) Ezekiel compares the people of Israel—the children of Abraham—to the wood of the vine that God has planted and made fruitful (19:10). But this choice vine has ceased to bear fruit and is now cast off as fuel for the fire. The metaphor of Israel as a vine (vineyard) has a long history in the Old Testament, beginning with the blessing that Jacob prays over his sons (Gen 49:11–12, 22) and then developing in the Prophets and Psalms. The "vine" stood for the entire people: "You brought a vine out of Egypt; / you drove out the nations and planted it" (Ps 80:8). Isaiah offers an especially poignant lament for the beloved vineyard of the Lord fallen into grave disrepair: "For the vineyard of the LORD of hosts / is the house of Israel, / and the men of Judah / are his pleasant planting; / and he looked for justice, / but behold, bloodshed; / for righteousness, / but behold, a cry!" (Isa 5:7). Jeremiah (2:21; 12:10) and Hosea (10:1–2) each take up the image of the vine to show the unfaithfulness and unfruitfulness of the people.

But this is not the end of the story. When Jesus tells his disciples, "I am the true vine" (John 15:1), he is linking himself to the parables of the vine found in the Old Testament. By claiming to be the "true vine," Jesus declares himself to be the new Israel, who, in contrast to historical Israel, remains faithful and bears fruit. And Jesus says that his disciples are the vinestock planted by the Father, intimately connected to himself: "I am the vine; you are the branches. Whoever abides in me and I in him, he it is that bears much fruit, for apart from me you can do nothing" (John 15:5 ESV). Through faith and baptism, Jesus's disciples, both Jew and †Gentile, are united to him and incorporated into †eschatological Israel (Gal 3:27–29; 6:15–16; Phil 3:3). When Jesus uses the image of vine and branches to describe how his disciples live in him, he is not just using an agricultural metaphor; he is revealing his role in the whole narrative of the history of God with his people. Jesus is the true vine that Israel was meant to be, and we have been grafted into this vine. In him the vine is restored and made fruitful once again to the glory of the Father.

Oracles and Parables of Judgment against the City and the Land, Part 2

Ezekiel 16:1–19:14

In this section, Ezekiel continues his pronouncement of judgment against the holy city of Jerusalem and the people of Israel, but now he uses *parables* as the dominant mode of communication. Chapters 16, 17, and 19 are composed almost entirely of parables that underline the past and present unfaithfulness of Israel. Chapter 18 offers an important interlude in which the Lord God answers the charge of injustice made against him by the people, while at the same time showing his desire that his people repent of their sin and find life. These parables must have been deeply disconcerting to Ezekiel's fellow exiles who were vainly hoping for a speedy return to Israel in peace and blessing. Instead, what they hear from Ezekiel is a series of prophetic rebukes through varied images that lay the fault squarely at the feet of a still-disobedient people.

The Narrative of the Lord's Deliverance of Israel (16:1–14)

---

¹Again the word of the LORD came to me: ²"Son of man, make known to Jerusalem her abominations, ³and say, Thus says the Lord GOD to Jerusalem: Your origin and your birth are of the land of the Canaanites; your father was an Amorite, and your mother a Hittite. ⁴And as for your birth, on the day you were born your navel string was not cut, nor were you washed with water to cleanse you, nor rubbed with salt, nor swathed with bands. ⁵No eye pitied you, to do any of these things to you out of compassion for you; but you were cast out on the open field, for you were abhorred, on the day that you were born.

⁶"And when I passed by you, and saw you weltering in your blood, I said to you in your blood, 'Live, ⁷and grow up like a plant of the field.' And

you grew up and became tall and arrived at full maidenhood; your breasts were formed, and your hair had grown; yet you were naked and bare.

⁸"When I passed by you again and looked upon you, behold, you were at the age for love; and I spread my skirt over you, and covered your nakedness: yes, I pledged myself to you and entered into a covenant with you, says the Lord GOD, and you became mine. ⁹Then I bathed you with water and washed off your blood from you, and anointed you with oil. ¹⁰I clothed you also with embroidered cloth and shod you with leather, I wrapped you in fine linen and covered you with silk. ¹¹And I decked you with ornaments, and put bracelets on your arms, and a chain on your neck. ¹²And I put a ring on your nose, and earrings in your ears, and a beautiful crown upon your head. ¹³Thus you were decked with gold and silver; and your clothing was of fine linen, and silk, and embroidered cloth; you ate fine flour and honey and oil. You grew exceedingly beautiful, and came to regal estate. ¹⁴And your renown went forth among the nations because of your beauty, for it was perfect through the splendor which I had bestowed upon you, says the Lord GOD."

OT: Deut 26:5; Josh 24:2; Ruth 3:9; Isa 62:5; Jer 2:2; Hosea 2:16–19
NT: John 3:29; 1 Cor 11:2; Eph 5:22–33; Rev 19:7
Catechism: the sin of idolatry, 2112–14; disobedience, 397, 615, 1850

In one of the longest chapters in the Bible, Ezekiel unfolds Israel's disobedience through an extended parable: Israel is the beloved spouse of the Lord, a spouse who has wantonly proved unfaithful. Because of the strong rebukes against Jerusalem and the use of explicit sexual imagery, the Jewish community has handled this chapter with great reserve, in practice normally removing it from liturgical reading.[1]

It is important to get an overview of the entire chapter before considering the various parts in greater detail. The first part (vv. 1–14) narrates how the Lord saved Jerusalem as a young, outcast girl, arranged for her upbringing, and then married her and provided for her richly until she reigned as queen. In the second part (vv. 15–34), Jerusalem has become a whore, prostituting herself with the nations and their gods and rejecting the Lord, her husband. In the third part (vv. 35–52), the Lord declares his judgment against Jerusalem: her lovers and enemies will take and destroy her, for she has become worse than her sisters (Sodom and Samaria). In the final part (vv. 53–63), the Lord promises to restore Sodom, Samaria, and Jerusalem, and to renew his †covenant with his people even though they have broken it.

In verses 1–2, the word of the Lord that comes to Ezekiel addresses Jerusalem. **16:1–5** The message, however, is not limited to the city and its inhabitants but applies

---

1. Eisemann, *Ezekiel*, 241–42. †*Targum of Ezekiel* completely rewrites this chapter, reworking the narrative of Israel's history and removing almost all of the sexual imagery. Levey, *Targum of Ezekiel*, 49–54.

to the entire people. The core message is to **make known to Jerusalem her abominations**—this purpose governs the chapter. "Abominations" are grave sins, primarily sins of idolatry against God but also sins against people (e.g., violence, adultery).[2] Then in verse 3, the parable against Jerusalem begins. Shockingly, God describes Jerusalem's parentage in demeaning terms: **your origin and your birth are of the land of the Canaanites; your father was an Amorite, and your mother a Hittite**. The Amorites and the Hittites were prominent Canaanite tribes that practiced all the idolatrous acts that now characterize Israel (see Exod 13:5; Neh 9:8).[3] Israel knew its own history very well, born of Abraham and Sarah and following in the line of Isaac, Jacob, and the twelve patriarchs. But none of this receives any mention here. Instead, the prophet defines Israel in terms of its pagan origins (Deut 26:5; Josh 24:2) rather than its covenantal identity. The prophet unveils Israel's *spiritual* heritage by tying it to the idolatrous nations that inhabited the land of Canaan. Speaking in the Lord's name, Isaiah also points to a spiritual heritage of rebellion: "For I knew that you would deal very treacherously, / and that from birth you were called a rebel" (Isa 48:8; see also Jer 7:25–26). As Daniel Block summarizes, "The prophet hereby announces that contrary to cherished tradition, Jerusalem's spiritual roots derive not from the pious Abraham and Sarah but from pagan peoples whom the Israelites had been charged to drive out."[4]

16:6–7   At her birth, Israel was like a cast-off female infant, fresh from the womb, neither washed nor tended, but left exposed to die. But the Lord, as he **passed by** and saw her **weltering in** her **blood**, said to her, **Live**. This call "to live" is echoed in Ezek 18:32, where the Lord bids Israel to "turn and live." The Lord's aim is not the death of the wicked but the restoration of the repentant sinner to life. As the parable unfolds, the Lord formally adopts Jerusalem as his own child and causes her to **grow up like a plant of the field**, describing her growth in terms of female physical maturity.

16:8–14   In the next episode of the parable, the Lord **passed by . . . again** and claimed Jerusalem as his bride: **I spread my skirt over you, and covered your nakedness** (see Ruth 3:9). Here the covenant of marriage serves as an image of the covenant God made with Israel in the desert: **I pledged myself to you and entered into a covenant with you, says the Lord GOD, and you became mine**. Then, in a second act of provision (vv. 9–13), the Lord bathes Israel, washes off her blood, anoints her with oil, clothes her in fine garments, places a crown

---

2. Ezekiel uses the term "abomination" more than any other Old Testament book, and the greatest frequency appears here in chap. 16.

3. The Amorites were especially seen as hostile to Israel because of their refusal to let Israel pass through their country on the way to the promised land (see Num 21). The Hittites interacted with Abraham and his descendants (Esau married a Hittite woman), and Uriah the Hittite was a faithful soldier in David's army (see 2 Sam 11).

4. Block, *Ezekiel: Chapters 1–24*, 475.

The Spousal Relationship between God and His People

BIBLICAL BACKGROUND

Ezekiel's use of spousal imagery to describe the covenantal relationship between the Lord God and his people occurs frequently in the Bible. Hosea movingly conveys the heartfelt love of the Lord for his people, his bride: "And in that day, says the Lord, you will call me, 'My husband.'... And I will espouse you for ever; I will espouse you in righteousness and in justice, in steadfast love, and in mercy" (Hosea 2:16, 19). Jeremiah follows suit, pointing to Israel's early devotion to the Lord: "I remember the devotion of your youth, / your love as a bride, / how you followed me in the wilderness" (Jer 2:2). Through Isaiah the Lord expresses his delight in the people he has redeemed: "As the bridegroom rejoices over the bride, so shall your God rejoice over you" (Isa 62:5). And the Song of Songs, interpreted by both Israel and the Church as an †allegory of the spousal love between God and his people, portrays the mutual relationship of love in vivid language.

Spousal imagery also appears prominently in the New Testament. John the Baptist refers to Jesus as "the bridegroom" and identifies the world as "the bride" that he has come to save and claim for his own (John 3:29). Paul describes his apostolic work in terms of betrothing the Corinthian church to Christ, in order to present them "as a pure bride to her one husband" (2 Cor 11:2), and he presents marriage as sharing in the mystery of the spousal relationship between Christ and the Church (Eph 5:22–33). Finally, the book of Revelation depicts the culmination of God's salvation as "the marriage of the Lamb," with the Church identified as "his Bride," who "has made herself ready" (Rev 19:7; see also 21:1–4). Despite the unfaithfulness of God's bride, which Ezekiel graphically depicts here in parable, God remains faithful to his espoused people (Israel and the Church), pouring himself out in covenant love.

upon her head, and feeds her with choice foods. This probably refers to Israel's settlement in the land and the rise of the kingship under David and Solomon. The result: she became **exceedingly beautiful, and came to regal estate**. Israel was renowned among the nations because of the beauty and splendor that the Lord bestowed on her. All seemed well.

Jerusalem Prostitutes Herself among the Nations (16:15–34)

[15]"But you trusted in your beauty, and played the harlot because of your renown, and lavished your harlotries on any passer-by. [16]You took some of

your garments, and made for yourself gaily decked shrines, and on them played the harlot; the like has never been, nor ever shall be. [17]You also took your fair jewels of my gold and of my silver, which I had given you, and made for yourself images of men, and with them played the harlot; [18]and you took your embroidered garments to cover them, and set my oil and my incense before them. [19]Also my bread which I gave you—I fed you with fine flour and oil and honey—you set before them for a pleasing odor, says the Lord GOD. [20]And you took your sons and your daughters, whom you had borne to me, and these you sacrificed to them to be devoured. Were your harlotries so small a matter [21]that you slaughtered my children and delivered them up as an offering by fire to them? [22]And in all your abominations and your harlotries you did not remember the days of your youth, when you were naked and bare, weltering in your blood.

[23]"And after all your wickedness (woe, woe to you! says the Lord GOD), [24]you built yourself a vaulted chamber, and made yourself a lofty place in every square; [25]at the head of every street you built your lofty place and prostituted your beauty, offering yourself to any passer-by, and multiplying your harlotry. [26]You also played the harlot with the Egyptians, your lustful neighbors, multiplying your harlotry, to provoke me to anger. [27]Behold, therefore, I stretched out my hand against you, and diminished your allotted portion, and delivered you to the greed of your enemies, the daughters of the Philistines, who were ashamed of your lewd behavior. [28]You played the harlot also with the Assyrians, because you were insatiable; yes, you played the harlot with them, and still you were not satisfied. [29]You multiplied your harlotry also with the trading land of Chaldea; and even with this you were not satisfied.

[30]"How lovesick is your heart, says the Lord GOD, seeing you did all these things, the deeds of a brazen harlot; [31]building your vaulted chamber at the head of every street, and making your lofty place in every square. Yet you were not like a harlot, because you scorned hire. [32]Adulterous wife, who receives strangers instead of her husband! [33]Men give gifts to all harlots; but you gave your gifts to all your lovers, bribing them to come to you from every side for your harlotries. [34]So you were different from other women in your harlotries: none solicited you to play the harlot; and you gave hire, while no hire was given to you; therefore you were different."

OT: Gen 22:1–14; Lev 18:21; 2 Kings 23:10; Isa 57:7–10; Jer 32:35; Hosea 4:13–15
Catechism: the sin of idolatry, 2112–14; disobedience, 397, 615, 1850

16:15–22   Things now turn in a bad direction. Jerusalem **trusted in** her **beauty** and turned away from the Lord (her spouse), playing the whore with the nations round about her. The language of "whoring" and "prostitution" refers primarily to *idolatry*, to following after other gods. Speaking of Judah as a faithless sister, Jeremiah clearly shows this link between idolatry and the imagery of prostitution: "Because harlotry was so light to her, she polluted the land, committing

Child Sacrifice in Israel

BIBLICAL
BACKGROUND

The practice of child sacrifice, which typically meant offering the life of the firstborn son to the god, was practiced in the land of Canaan during the time that Israel journeyed through and then settled in the land. It was strongly denounced in both the Law and the Prophets. Sacrificing one's children by fire is forbidden in Lev 18:21: "You shall not give any of your children to devote them by fire to Molech, and so profane the name of your God" (see also Lev 20:2–5; Deut 18:10). Solomon appears to be responsible for setting up an altar to the god Molech (1 Kings 11:7), but the practice of offering firstborn sons to Molech appears later in the northern kingdom of Israel (2 Kings 17:17). This grisly act was then adopted in Judah by Ahaz (2 Kings 16:3) and Manasseh (2 Kings 21:6). Though child sacrifice was officially banished by Josiah (2 Kings 23:10), both Jeremiah (7:31; 19:5; 32:35) and Ezekiel (16:20–21; 20:26, 31; 23:39) give ample witness to the practice of child sacrifice by fire at the time of the Babylonian invasion. Strikingly, the story of Abraham suggests that sacrificing the firstborn son was at least known and practiced in ancient Canaan. Abraham hears the Lord telling him to sacrifice his only son Isaac, and *he sets out to do this* (Gen 22:1–14). The last-second intervention by the Lord to preserve Isaac's life and to provide a "ram" in his place has traditionally been understood as the Lord's rejection of the practice of child sacrifice in Israel. In this, Israel was to be different from the nations around them. In place of the firstborn son an animal was to be offered in sacrifice (see Exod 13:11–15).

adultery with stone and tree" (Jer 3:9).[5] This involved making images of false gods, offering sacrifices of food and drink to them, and even sacrificing their own **sons** and **daughters**, delivering **them up as an offering by fire** to these false gods. King Josiah tried to banish the practice of child sacrifice (2 Kings 23:10), but Jeremiah's words give evidence that this gruesome practice persisted (Jer 32:35). In the words of Daniel Block: "By offering her offspring Jerusalem proved her Canaanite ancestry beyond doubt. She who had been abandoned by her mother as an infant now sacrificed her own children."[6]

Ezekiel then presses the point, revealing in greater detail the unfaithfulness of **16:23–29** Israel. He shows how Jerusalem **played the harlot with** a succession of empires: the Egyptians, the Assyrians, and finally the †Chaldeans (the Babylonians). Instead of trusting in the Lord, her true spouse, she made alliances with these other regimes, selling herself and welcoming their gods.

5. For idolatry depicted through the imagery of prostitution in the Prophets, see Isa 57:7–10; Jer 2:20; 3:6–10; Hosea 4:13–15.

6. Block, *Ezekiel: Chapters 1–24*, 491.

The Macarian Homilies on Faithfulness to the Spirit

LIVING TRADITION

The Macarian Homilies, written anonymously in the late fourth century, are specially revered in the spirituality of the Eastern Christian tradition. In this selection from *Homily* 15, the author summarizes Ezekiel's case against God's people and applies it to the Christian faithful, offering a stirring call to be faithful to the gift of the Spirit, which God has given:

So also the person who knows God through †grace is warned by the Spirit. Such a one had been cleansed of former sins and adorned with the ornaments of the Holy Spirit and had been made a participator of divine and heavenly food, but yet does not behave in a fitting way with thoughtfulness. She does not persevere in a becoming good will and love toward the heavenly Bridegroom, Christ, and so is cast out and deprived of life of which she once was made a participator. . . . All you who have been made participators of the Spirit of Christ, may you not behave in any matter either small or great in a contemptible way . . . nor treat the grace of the Spirit with abuse so as not to be deprived of life of which you have already been made participators.[a]

a. Pseudo-Macarius, *Homily* 15.4, in *The Fifty Spiritual Homilies and the Great Letter*, trans. George A. Maloney (Mahwah, NJ: Paulist Press, 1992), 109–10.

16:30–34   In a final declaration of Jerusalem's guilt, the Lord speaks about the pitiable disposition of his people: **How lovesick is your heart**. Jerusalem has become **a brazen harlot** who instead of asking payment for her services offers gifts and bribes to her various "lovers" for their attention.[7]

The Lord Declares His Judgment against Jerusalem (16:35–52)

³⁵"Wherefore, O harlot, hear the word of the LORD: ³⁶Thus says the Lord GOD, Because your shame was laid bare and your nakedness uncovered in your harlotries with your lovers, and because of all your idols, and because of the blood of your children that you gave to them, ³⁷therefore, behold, I will gather all your lovers, with whom you took pleasure, all those you loved and all those you loathed; I will gather them against you from every side, and will uncover your nakedness to them, that they may see all your nakedness. ³⁸And I will judge you as women who break wedlock and shed blood are judged, and bring upon you the blood of wrath

7. Isaiah also identifies the city of Jerusalem as a harlot: "How the faithful city has become a harlot" (Isa 1:21).

and jealousy. [39]And I will give you into the hand of your lovers, and they shall throw down your vaulted chamber and break down your lofty places; they shall strip you of your clothes and take your fair jewels, and leave you naked and bare. [40]They shall bring up a host against you, and they shall stone you and cut you to pieces with their swords. [41]And they shall burn your houses and execute judgments upon you in the sight of many women; I will make you stop playing the harlot, and you shall also give hire no more. [42]So will I satisfy my fury on you, and my jealousy shall depart from you; I will be calm, and will no more be angry. [43]Because you have not remembered the days of your youth, but have enraged me with all these things; therefore, behold, I will repay your deeds upon your head, says the Lord God.

"Have you not committed lewdness in addition to all your abominations? [44]Behold, every one who uses proverbs will use this proverb about you, 'Like mother, like daughter.' [45]You are the daughter of your mother, who loathed her husband and her children; and you are the sister of your sisters, who loathed their husbands and their children. Your mother was a Hittite and your father an Amorite. [46]And your elder sister is Samaria, who lived with her daughters to the north of you; and your younger sister, who lived to the south of you, is Sodom with her daughters. [47]Yet you were not content to walk in their ways, or do according to their abominations; within a very little time you were more corrupt than they in all your ways. [48]As I live, says the Lord God, your sister Sodom and her daughters have not done as you and your daughters have done. [49]Behold, this was the guilt of your sister Sodom: she and her daughters had pride, surfeit of food, and prosperous ease, but did not aid the poor and needy. [50]They were haughty, and did abominable things before me; therefore I removed them, when I saw it. [51]Samaria has not committed half your sins; you have committed more abominations than they, and have made your sisters appear righteous by all the abominations which you have committed. [52]Bear your disgrace, you also, for you have made judgment favorable to your sisters; because of your sins in which you acted more abominably than they, they are more in the right than you. So be ashamed, you also, and bear your disgrace, for you have made your sisters appear righteous."

OT: Gen 13:13; 18–19; 2 Kings 17:19; Jer 3:6–14; Hosea 5:3–7
NT: Matt 11:20–24
Catechism: the sin of idolatry, 2112–14; disobedience, 397, 615, 1850

The Lord now declares the punishment that will befall Israel and Jerusalem.   **16:35–43** Because of her idolatry and violence against her own children, Jerusalem will be given into the hands of her former lovers and her enemies alike: **I will gather them against you from every side, . . . and I will give you into the hand of your lovers.** These former lovers—the nations around her—will expose her nakedness[8] and destroy her; that is, they will come against her by military might and conquer her: **They shall bring up a host against you, and they shall stone you and cut you to pieces with their swords**. Thus the Lord will spend his wrath on his people and bring an end to his jealous anger: **Behold, I will repay your deeds upon your head**. The anger (or wrath) of God expressed here is not an emotional outburst or tantrum but is the purifying *love* of God for his people, a love that is determined to cleanse them from their sins of unfaithfulness.[9]

16:44–50   The parable of judgment now circles back to Jerusalem's *spiritual* Canaanite ancestry: **Like mother, like daughter**. Jerusalem has become like her spiritual mother (the Hittites) and her spiritual father (the Amorites). She is also said to possess two spiritual sisters, Samaria and Sodom: **your elder sister is Samaria, who lived . . . north of you; and your younger sister, who lived to the south of you, is Sodom with her daughters**.[10] Samaria was the capital city of the northern kingdom of Israel, conquered and sent into exile for its depravity and idolatry (2 Kings 17:19; Hosea 5:3–7). Sodom was the infamous city destroyed by fire in Abraham's day because of its wicked ways (Gen 13:13; 18–19).[11] The reference to Samaria as Jerusalem's *older* sister, and to Sodom as the *younger* sister, makes no sense in terms of chronology: Sodom was destroyed before Jerusalem or Samaria were in existence, and Jerusalem became the capital city of Judah before Samaria became the capital of the northern kingdom. Modern scholars align with Jewish tradition in seeing these references not in relation to age (older and younger) but in relation to size (larger and smaller). Samaria is the "big" sister to the north, while Sodom is the "little" sister to the south.[12] The point in the end is that Jerusalem has followed their example and has become even worse, and so now bears a similar punishment and greater shame.

16:51–52   In comparison to Jerusalem, these two nations, punished by the Lord because of their sins, now *appear* to be righteous, so bad are Jerusalem's abominations: **you . . . have made your sisters appear righteous by all the abominations which you have committed**. The unfavorable comparison with these obviously sinful nations is intended to shock the people into seeing just how far the nation has fallen and to underline the gravity of their offenses.

---

8. For the punishment of a harlot by exposing her nakedness, see also Isa 3:17; Jer 13:22, 26; Hosea 2:10; Nah 3:5.

9. For understanding the purpose of God's anger or wrath, see the Reflection and Application section for 5:1–17 (p. 64).

10. In a similar way, the prophet Jeremiah accused Samaria and Judah (the northern and southern kingdoms) of being equally faithless sisters, with Judah outdoing the sins of her northern sister (Jer 3:6–14).

11. Isaiah (1:9–10) also makes a spiritual link between the rulers of Judah and the city of Sodom.

12. For the interpretation of the two neighboring cities as "bigger" and "smaller," see Greenberg, *Ezekiel 1–20*, 288–89; Block, *Ezekiel: Chapters 1–24*, 507–8; Eisemann, *Ezekiel*, 267–68; Rosenberg, *Book of Ezekiel*, 1:120.

In the Light of Christ (16:47–52)

Just as Ezekiel pronounces "woe" against the people of his day and compares Judah and Jerusalem unfavorably to wicked "Samaria" and "Sodom," so Jesus denounces the cities in Galilee with a similarly fierce accusation. In Matt 11:20–24, Jesus censures the cities of Chorazin, Bethsaida, and Capernaum, claiming that if the wicked cities of Tyre, Sidon, and Sodom had seen the works that they have seen, these cities would have repented: "But I tell you, it shall be more tolerable on the day of judgment for Tyre and Sidon than for you" (Matt 11:22). When God's own people have become more sinful than the godless nations around them, then things are in a desperate state indeed. Jesus fulfills the role of the watchman-prophet in his day just as Ezekiel had done, exposing the sinfulness of the people by showing how far they have fallen from the Lord and calling them to repentance and a return to faithfulness.

Promise of Restoration and Renewal of the Covenant (16:53–63)

⁵³"I will restore their fortunes, both the fortunes of Sodom and her daughters, and the fortunes of Samaria and her daughters, and I will restore your own fortunes in the midst of them, ⁵⁴that you may bear your disgrace and be ashamed of all that you have done, becoming a consolation to them. ⁵⁵As for your sisters, Sodom and her daughters shall return to their former estate, and Samaria and her daughters shall return to their former estate; and you and your daughters shall return to your former estate. ⁵⁶Was not your sister Sodom a byword in your mouth in the day of your pride, ⁵⁷before your wickedness was uncovered? Now you have become like her an object of reproach for the daughters of Edom and all her neighbors, and for the daughters of the Philistines, those round about who despise you. ⁵⁸You bear the penalty of your lewdness and your abominations, says the LORD.

⁵⁹"Yes, thus says the Lord GOD: I will deal with you as you have done, who have despised the oath in breaking the covenant, ⁶⁰yet I will remember my covenant with you in the days of your youth, and I will establish with you an everlasting covenant. ⁶¹Then you will remember your ways, and be ashamed when I take your sisters, both your elder and your younger, and give them to you as daughters, but not on account of the covenant with you. ⁶²I will establish my covenant with you, and you shall know that I am the LORD, ⁶³that you may remember and be confounded, and never open your mouth again because of your shame, when I forgive you all that you have done, says the Lord GOD."

OT: Job 42:10; Jer 29:14
Catechism: God's redeeming love and covenant faithfulness, 219, 161

16:53–58   The tone of the parable changes noticeably here, moving from sharp condemnation to *consolation* and *renewal*. There remains an element of rebuke and correction, but the thrust of this passage is restoration. The Lord promises to **restore** the **fortunes** of Jerusalem's "sisters" (Sodom and Samaria) but will also bring deliverance to his own people: **I will restore your own fortunes in the midst of them**. The language of "restoring one's fortunes" appears also in Job and Jeremiah. The conclusion to the book of Job reads: "And the LORD restored the fortunes of Job, when he had prayed for his friends" (Job 42:10). Jeremiah, too, promises a day when the fortunes of God's people will be restored: "I will restore your fortunes and gather you from all the nations and all the places where I have driven you, says the LORD" (Jer 29:14). The phrase "restore fortunes" is literally "return [from] captivity." The people's fortunes will be restored when the Lord brings them back from exile and captivity.

There is an unexpected result to this restoration: when the Lord God punishes his own people and then restores them, this will prove to be a kind of **consolation** *to the surrounding nations* (Sodom, Samaria, and those allied with them). They will recognize not only the justice of God in bringing judgment but also his goodness in freely granting restoration to themselves and to the people of Israel.

16:59–63   In this final section, Ezekiel concludes by summing up the point of this long parable. Since Jerusalem has been unfaithful and has broken the covenant between God and his people, the Lord will punish her with justice: **I will deal with you as you have done**. But the emphasis now is on the restoration of the covenant of old: **yet I will remember my covenant with you in the days of your youth, and I will establish with you an everlasting covenant**. This promise of an "everlasting covenant" will be revisited and explained more fully in Ezek 37:26–28.[13] All this, however, will be done in a way that humbles and chastens Jerusalem and keeps her from pride. Sodom and Samaria, Jerusalem's **sisters**, will be given back to her as **daughters**—that is, as dependent on and subordinate to Jerusalem. This will happen not as a reward for Israel's covenant faithfulness but as the sheer unmerited gift of God. In short, the Lord will renew his covenant with his people and forgive their sins, but this will be a reminder of their unfaithfulness and a check against pride.

Reflection and Application (16:1–63)

How can we read the extended parable of this chapter in the light of the new covenant in Christ? The images throughout are severe, expressed in a way

13. For the promise of an "everlasting covenant" in the Old Testament, see also Gen 9:16; 17:7; Exod 31:16; Lev 24:8; 2 Sam 23:5; Isa 24:5; 61:8; Jer 32:40; 50:5.

intended to shock the audience. Some people today criticize chapter 16 for depicting a vengeful God who, like an abusive husband, mistreats his wife[14] and for, at the same time, portraying women as immoral and deserving of spousal abuse. Yet the point of the parable is to show, through a conventional biblical image, that the Lord God is both a king and a bridegroom who has espoused Israel to himself. His people have proved unfaithful and as a consequence have suffered the present season of judgment and loss. But the parable in no way depicts women in general as unfaithful, nor does it encourage or justify any form of abusive behavior against women.[15]

Positively, this extended parable is the Lord's answer to Jerusalem's complaint that the Lord has abandoned his people and forgotten his covenant with them. It is not the Lord who has reneged on the covenant but the people who have been unfaithful by pursuing other nations and their gods. They have turned away and now deserve their punishment; this is the consequence of breaking the covenant. But the Lord's end-goal is to restore *the eternal covenant* and bring his people back to himself in a posture of humility and gratefulness due to his sheer mercy. The Lord is not an abusive God but a merciful spouse toward his people. This long parable, then, narrates the †grace of God in the face of grave sin. The Lord promises to bring his people (and the surrounding nations) back from death and bless them richly with good things.

Parables of Israel's Rise and Decline:
The Great Cedar and the Two Eagles (17:1–24)

---

¹The word of the LORD came to me: ²"Son of man, propound a riddle, and speak an allegory to the house of Israel; ³say, Thus says the Lord GOD: A great eagle with great wings and long pinions, rich in plumage of many colors, came to Lebanon and took the top of the cedar; ⁴he broke off the topmost of its young twigs and carried it to a land of trade, and set it in a city of merchants. ⁵Then he took of the seed of the

---

14. As John Bergsma and Brant Pitre point out ("Ezekiel," in *A Catholic Introduction to the Bible*, vol. 1, *The Old Testament* [San Francisco: Ignatius, 2018], 846), "It is *not* the Lord in these parables who abuses wife-Jerusalem but the pagan Gentile lovers she chose in preference to her Lord-husband. . . . So the Lord's punishment is simply an affirmation of Jerusalem's free will. The abuse Jerusalem receives is actually at the hands of the 'lovers' she pursued by her own choice."

15. "We should remind ourselves that the author intends the audience to be appalled by such imagery, not attracted to it" (John F. Kutsko, "Ezekiel's Anthropology and Its Ethical Implications," in *The Book of Ezekiel: Theological and Anthropological Perspectives*, ed. Margaret S. Odell and John T. Strong [Atlanta: Society of Biblical Literature, 2000], 140). Bergsma and Pitre ("Ezekiel," 846) likewise conclude that Ezekiel does not condone the abuse of women in this passage and that "there is no actual evidence that either of these chapters [16 and 23] has been used in Jewish or Christian tradition as justification for the abuse of women."

land and planted it in fertile soil; he placed it beside abundant waters. He set it like a willow twig, ⁶and it sprouted and became a low spreading vine, and its branches turned toward him, and its roots remained where it stood. So it became a vine, and brought forth branches and put forth foliage.

⁷"But there was another great eagle with great wings and much plumage; and behold, this vine bent its roots toward him, and shot forth its branches toward him that he might water it. From the bed where it was planted ⁸he transplanted it to good soil by abundant waters, that it might bring forth branches, and bear fruit, and become a noble vine. ⁹Say, Thus says the Lord God: Will it thrive? Will he not pull up its roots and cut off its branches, so that all its fresh sprouting leaves wither? It will not take a strong arm or many people to pull it from its roots. ¹⁰Behold, when it is transplanted, will it thrive? Will it not utterly wither when the east wind strikes it—wither away on the bed where it grew?"

¹¹Then the word of the Lord came to me: ¹²"Say now to the rebellious house, Do you not know what these things mean? Tell them, Behold, the king of Babylon came to Jerusalem, and took her king and her princes and brought them to him to Babylon. ¹³And he took one of the royal offspring and made a covenant with him, putting him under oath. (The chief men of the land he had taken away, ¹⁴that the kingdom might be humble and not lift itself up, and that by keeping his covenant it might stand.) ¹⁵But he rebelled against him by sending ambassadors to Egypt, that they might give him horses and a large army. Will he succeed? Can a man escape who does such things? Can he break the covenant and yet escape? ¹⁶As I live, says the Lord God, surely in the place where the king dwells who made him king, whose oath he despised, and whose covenant with him he broke, in Babylon he shall die. ¹⁷Pharaoh with his mighty army and great company will not help him in war, when mounds are cast up and siege walls built to cut off many lives. ¹⁸Because he despised the oath and broke the covenant, because he gave his hand and yet did all these things, he shall not escape. ¹⁹Therefore thus says the Lord God: As I live, surely my oath which he despised, and my covenant which he broke, I will repay upon his head. ²⁰I will spread my net over him, and he shall be taken in my snare, and I will bring him to Babylon and enter into judgment with him there for the treason he has committed against me. ²¹And all the pick of his troops shall fall by the sword, and the survivors shall be scattered to every wind; and you shall know that I, the Lord, have spoken."

²²Thus says the Lord God: "I myself will take a sprig from the lofty top of the cedar, and will set it out; I will break off from the topmost of its young twigs a tender one, and I myself will plant it upon a high and lofty mountain; ²³on the mountain height of Israel will I plant it, that it may bring forth boughs and bear fruit, and become a noble cedar; and under

Figure 4. Assyrian relief depicting the Babylonian breach of Jerusalem's walls

**it will dwell all kinds of beasts; in the shade of its branches birds of every
sort will nest. ²⁴And all the trees of the field shall know that I the LORD
bring low the high tree, and make high the low tree, dry up the green
tree, and make the dry tree flourish. I the LORD have spoken, and I will
do it."**

OT: Num 12:8; Judg 14:2–19; Pss 2:6; 49:4; 78:2; Isa 11:1
NT: Matt 21:9; Luke 1:32, 51–53; Rom 1:3
Catechism: the use of parables, 546; Jesus as the †Messiah of Israel, 436–41, 560, 711–16, 840
Lectionary: 17:22–24: 11th Sunday in Ordinary Time (Year B)

This chapter depicts the recent history of Israel through an extended parable   **17:1–2**
consisting of two eagles, a tree, a vine, and a replanted tree. The Lord tells Ezekiel, **Son of man, propound a riddle, and speak an allegory to the house of
Israel**. The word that is translated †"allegory" (Hebrew *mashal*) is also translated
"parable" (ESV) or "proverb" (NABRE). In Hebrew, verse 2 is literally "riddle
a riddle and parable a parable." The noun and verb in each pair are from the
same root word.

The parable of the cedar and the two great eagles follows, presenting a   **17:3–10**
symbolic story that is both strange and obscure to the listener. **A great eagle**

Riddles and Parables

BIBLICAL BACKGROUND

The prophet Ezekiel, criticized for being "a maker of allegories" (Ezek 20:49), is told here to "propound a riddle, and speak an allegory" to the people of Israel. This pairing of "riddle" and "allegory" occurs also in Pss 49:4 and 78:2: "I will incline my ear to a proverb [*mashal*]; / I will solve my riddle to the music of the lyre" (Ps 49:4); "I will open my mouth in a parable [*mashal*]; / I will utter dark sayings [riddles] from of old" (Ps 78:2; see also Prov 1:6). The two terms are closely related in meaning. A riddle is a "puzzle" that leaves the audience in the dark until the riddle is solved; a parable or allegory is the comparison of one thing to another that, when understood, enables the audience to see something in a new light.[a] Often the two senses are combined in one parable, as here in Ezek 17. In Num 12:8, the Lord God distinguishes Moses from other prophets by the clarity with which the Lord speaks to him: "With him I speak mouth to mouth, clearly, and not in dark speech [riddles]." The classic "riddle" of the Old Testament is the one posed by Samson to the Philistines, "Let me now put a riddle to you. . . . 'Out of the eater came something to eat. Out of the strong came something sweet'" (Judg 14:12, 14).

Why would the Lord speak through riddles and parables? To both conceal and reveal. By presenting the truth in the form of a riddle or parable, the speaker gains the attention of the audience and is able to convey the truth in a new light, while at the same time requiring the audience to search and inquire about the meaning of the riddle or parable. Riddles and parables engage the mind, but at the same time they also test and sift the heart because our response to them often reveals our inner attitude toward the Lord.

a. According to Greenberg, *Ezekiel 1–20*, 309, a riddle in the Bible is an obscure saying intended to produce "opaqueness and mystification," while a parable is the comparison of one thing to another for the sake of "illumination."

plucks the top branch of a tall cedar of Lebanon—a land renowned for its magnificent trees—and plants it **in a city of merchants** (vv. 3–4).[16] The eagle as an image conveys speed and swiftness, but also one who hunts and swoops down upon prey with great skill. This eagle then takes a seedling from the land—a vine—and plants it **in fertile soil**, where it grows and spreads, orienting itself toward the great eagle (vv. 5–6). But then **another great eagle** appears, and the vine *reorients* itself toward this new eagle and is transplanted into good soil, **that it might bring forth branches, and bear fruit, and become a noble vine** (vv. 7–8). To conclude the parable, the Lord asks about the fate of this "plant" that has exchanged one eagle for the other. **Will it**

16. For the use of the image of the eagle, see also 2 Sam 1:23; Job 9:26; Jer 4:13; Lam 4:19; Hab 1:8.

thrive? Will he not pull up its roots and cut off its branches? . . . Will it not utterly wither when the east wind strikes it? At this point, like Ezekiel's hearers, we remain in the dark as to the meaning of this riddle/parable. To what does it refer?

Ezekiel now supplies the interpretation of the parable. The first great eagle represents **the king of Babylon**, Nebuchadnezzar, who **came to Jerusalem, and took her king**, Jehoiachin, **to Babylon**. The cedar represents Israel and Jerusalem, and the topmost twig is Jehoiachin, who was cut off and taken to Babylon. Nebuchadnezzar then chose **one of the royal offspring**—namely, Zedekiah—**and made a covenant with him**, with the result that Zedekiah became Nebuchadnezzar's vassal. **But** Zedekiah **rebelled**, asking for help from **Egypt**, the second great eagle, and so broke his agreement with Babylon. The Lord declares that Zedekiah's change of allegiance will not help him. Because he broke his covenant with Nebuchadnezzar, he will be exiled and die in Babylon—Pharaoh and Egypt will be no help to him.[17]

17:11–15a

Why is God going to punish Zedekiah for breaking a "covenant" with a foreign general? The answer is not entirely clear, but the summary of the same event in 2 Chronicles sheds some light. There the text says that Zedekiah "also rebelled against King Nebuchadnezzar, who had made him swear by God; he stiffened his neck and hardened his heart against turning to the LORD, the God of Israel" (2 Chron 36:13). Zedekiah apparently swore an oath in the Lord's name, and because **he despised the oath and broke the covenant**, he not only broke the second commandment (Exod 20:7) but also hardened his heart against the Lord. For his part, Jeremiah gave an even stronger exhortation for Zedekiah to remain under the "yoke" of Nebuchadnezzar and threatened exile if Zedekiah broke this treaty (see Jer 27:4–15).

17:15b–21

The answer to the Lord's question—**Will he succeed?**—is given on two planes at once. On the human plane (vv. 16–18), Babylon will not overlook this betrayal but will come and destroy Zedekiah for his breaking of the covenant. On the divine plane (vv. 19–21), the Lord sees in Zedekiah's betrayal a much deeper breaking of the covenant: **Surely** it is **my oath which he despised, and my covenant which he broke**. And so the Lord himself will use the armies of Babylon to punish the faithless king (and his people) who have reneged on their covenant relationship with the Lord.[18] As we have seen before, the ancient declaration of the covenant blessings and curses (found in Lev 26; Deut 29–30) provides the context for the Lord's just punishment of those who have been false to his covenant. Once all this comes to pass, the Lord says, **you shall know that I, the LORD, have spoken.**

17. A summary of these historical events is found in 2 Kings 24:11–20 and 2 Chron 36:11–14. The pharaoh named here is either Psammeticus II (594–588 BC) or Hophra (588–569 BC).

18. For the two planes of activity, the human and divine, see Greenberg, *Ezekiel 1–20*, 322–23.

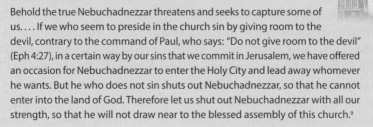

Origen on the Great Eagle
LIVING TRADITION

Origen of Alexandria (d. 254) offers a spiritual interpretation of this parable, seeing in Nebuchadnezzar a figure of the devil, who because of sin and unfaithfulness has power to enter our "city" and lead away the captives. Origen adapts the parable to the Church, calling Christian leaders to "give no room to the devil" and urging them to guard the people of God from captivity by the devil.

Behold the true Nebuchadnezzar threatens and seeks to capture some of us.... If we who seem to preside in the church sin by giving room to the devil, contrary to the command of Paul, who says: "Do not give room to the devil" (Eph 4:27), in a certain way by our sins that we commit in Jerusalem, we have offered an occasion for Nebuchadnezzar to enter the Holy City and lead away whomever he wants. But he who does not sin shuts out Nebuchadnezzar, so that he cannot enter into the land of God. Therefore let us shut out Nebuchadnezzar with all our strength, so that he will not draw near to the blessed assembly of this church.[a]

a. *Homily 12.2*, in *Homilies 1–14 on Ezekiel*, trans. Thomas P. Scheck, ACW 62 (New York: Newman, 2010), 149.

17:22–23   The parable now takes a turn in the direction of hope and restoration.[19] The Lord promises, **I myself will take a sprig from the lofty top of the cedar, ... and I myself will plant it upon a high and lofty mountain**. God himself now takes the place of the "great eagle" of the parable. He is the true king, who determines the destiny of Israel by planting a new "sprig"—his Messiah—on the holy mountain. Ezekiel is prophesying here about the reestablishment of the Davidic king on Mount Zion, which is presented here as a high mountain, not so much physically, but in dignity. It is a reference to the coming Messiah, expressed in parable.[20] Psalm 2, presenting in plain language the message of the parable, makes an equivalent statement about the Messiah to come: "I have set my king on Zion, my holy mountain" (Ps 2:6).

17:24   In this extended parable, the Lord "cuts off" the arrogant, unfaithful "sprig" (17:3) and promises to raise up his own lowly "sprig" (17:22) to be his anointed king, reigning on his holy mountain: **I the LORD bring low the high tree, and make high the low tree, dry up the green tree, and make the dry tree flourish**. The Lord concludes by giving his solemn assurance that this will come to pass: **I the LORD have spoken, and I will do it**. Right here in the midst of the

19. This is one of four †oracles of hope and consolation in the first major part of Ezekiel (see also 11:14–21; 16:59–63; 20:40–44).

20. *Targum of Ezekiel* and the renowned Jewish sage Rashi (d. 1105) interpret Ezek 17:22–24 as referring to the promised Messiah of Israel. See Levey, *Targum of Ezekiel*, 56; Eisemann, *Ezekiel*, 287; Rosenberg, *Book of Ezekiel*, 1:134–35.

parables of judgment, Ezekiel offers a ray of hope by declaring God's intention to establish his reign among his people through the Messiah.

In the Light of Christ (17:22–24)

Both Jewish and Christian tradition understand these final verses of chapter 17 to refer to God's promised Messiah. In the context of the parable, the reference to a "sprig" that God will take and plant in rich soil clearly points to the establishment of a king in the line of David. The term "sprig" is unique to Ezekiel but is parallel to other words (e.g., shoot, branch) used elsewhere in the Prophets to denote the Messiah. Isaiah speaks of a "shoot" and a "branch" that will grow from the stump of Jesse's line (Isa 11:1). Using a different word, both Jeremiah and Zechariah also predict the coming of a righteous "branch" from David's line (Jer 23:5; 33:15; Zech 3:8; 6:12). In Christian understanding, the image of the shoot/branch/sprig sprouting from David's line points directly to Christ Jesus. The angel Gabriel says to Mary about the son to be born from her: "The Lord God will give to him the throne of his father David" (Luke 1:32). He is the Son, "descended from David according to the flesh" (Rom 1:3). He is the one about whom the crowds shout, "Hosanna to the Son of David! Blessed is he who comes in the name of the Lord!" (Matt 21:9).

Ezekiel 17:24 also points to Christ in a further way. The Lord God says that he will cause the "high tree" to be made low and will cause the "low tree" to be made high. In other words, he will cast down the arrogant and faithless king but raise up a lowly one to be his true king, whom he will "plant" on Mount Zion in Jerusalem. This "inversion" of the proud and the humble reflects Mary's prayer (the Magnificat) when she extols the wisdom of God: "He has scattered the proud in the imagination of their hearts, / he has put down the mighty from their thrones, / and exalted those of low degree; / he has filled the hungry with good things" (Luke 1:51–53). The Lord God uses a humble and lowly servant (Mary) to bring about his plan to raise up the Messiah, Jesus, the son of David, as the true and righteous king.

Only the One Who Sins Shall Die (18:1–20)

¹The word of the LORD came to me again: ²"What do you mean by repeating this proverb concerning the land of Israel, 'The fathers have eaten sour grapes, and the children's teeth are set on edge'? ³As I live, says the Lord GOD, this proverb shall no more be used by you in Israel. ⁴Behold, all souls are mine; the soul of the father as well as the soul of the son is mine: the soul that sins shall die.

⁵"If a man is righteous and does what is lawful and right— ⁶if he does not eat upon the mountains or lift up his eyes to the idols of the house of Israel, does not defile his neighbor's wife or approach a woman in her time of impurity, ⁷does not oppress any one, but restores to the debtor his pledge, commits no robbery, gives his bread to the hungry and covers the naked with a garment, ⁸does not lend at interest or take any increase, withholds his hand from iniquity, executes true justice between man and man, ⁹walks in my statutes, and is careful to observe my ordinances—he is righteous, he shall surely live, says the Lord God.

¹⁰"If he begets a son who is a robber, a shedder of blood, ¹¹who does none of these duties, but eats upon the mountains, defiles his neighbor's wife, ¹²oppresses the poor and needy, commits robbery, does not restore the pledge, lifts up his eyes to the idols, commits abomination, ¹³lends at interest, and takes increase; shall he then live? He shall not live. He has done all these abominable things; he shall surely die; his blood shall be upon himself.

¹⁴"But if this man begets a son who sees all the sins which his father has done, and fears, and does not do likewise, ¹⁵who does not eat upon the mountains or lift up his eyes to the idols of the house of Israel, does not defile his neighbor's wife, ¹⁶does not wrong any one, exacts no pledge, commits no robbery, but gives his bread to the hungry and covers the naked with a garment, ¹⁷withholds his hand from iniquity, takes no interest or increase, observes my ordinances, and walks in my statutes; he shall not die for his father's iniquity; he shall surely live. ¹⁸As for his father, because he practiced extortion, robbed his brother, and did what is not good among his people, behold, he shall die for his iniquity.

¹⁹"Yet you say, 'Why should not the son suffer for the iniquity of the father?' When the son has done what is lawful and right, and has been careful to observe all my statutes, he shall surely live. ²⁰The soul that sins shall die. The son shall not suffer for the iniquity of the father, nor the father suffer for the iniquity of the son; the righteousness of the righteous shall be upon himself, and the wickedness of the wicked shall be upon himself."

OT: Exod 34:7; Deut 24:16; 2 Kings 24:3–4; Jer 31:29–30; Lam 5:7
Catechism: call to repentance and conversion, 1427–39

18:1–3 This renowned chapter, one of the best known in Ezekiel, raises the question of whether God is just or not when he punishes his people for their sins. The people state their complaint against God by means of a proverb: **The fathers have eaten sour grapes, and the children's teeth are set on edge**. The point of the proverb is that the sinful deeds of the fathers are transferred to their children, who experience the *penalty* for the evil that their fathers have done. This is also a way of casting off responsibility by blaming one's forebears for the misfortunes that have come upon the people in the present time.[21] But the Lord utterly rejects this proverb and its intended meaning: **As I live, says the Lord God, this proverb shall no more be used by you in Israel.**

The prophet Jeremiah, Ezekiel's older contemporary, also confronted and rejected this proverb: "In those days they shall no longer say: 'The fathers have eaten sour grapes, and the children's teeth are set on edge.' But every one shall die for his own sin; each man who eats sour grapes, his teeth shall be set on edge" (Jer 31:29–30). Ezekiel confirms Jeremiah's rejection of the proverb and explains why it is false. The Lord insists that **all souls** belong to him, both the fathers and the sons, but it is only **the soul that sins** that **shall die.**[22] The sons belong primarily not to their earthly fathers but *to the Lord*—each soul is the Lord's. Therefore it is only the soul who sins that shall die; none shall die because of another's wrongdoing. This is the basic point of this entire section.   **18:4**

To make his point, Ezekiel now offers three case studies as if he were in a court of law. In the first case, the man who **does what is lawful and right . . . shall surely live.** This is a person who refrains from idolatry, sexual immorality, and stealing and who feeds the poor, clothes the naked, lends without interest, and renders true justice. For Ezekiel, righteousness does not merely consist of not violating the commandments but includes being actively generous to one's neighbor. This person is declared **righteous** by his actions, and so he shall live.   **18:5–9**

In the second case, the righteous man's son chooses to turn from his father's ways and walk in the way of sin. He commits all the sins his father abstained from and fails to walk in the way of justice. **Shall he then live?** asks the Lord. No, **he shall surely die; his blood shall be upon himself.** "Death" here is not physical death (for all will die) but separation from the divine blessing. The son turned himself away from the Lord, and so his penalty is deserved; he draws it upon himself.   **18:10–13**

In the third case, the evil man's son (the grandson of the first man) sees the evil his father did and turns back to the Lord's ways. The result: **he shall not die for his father's iniquity; he shall surely live.** Through the example of three generations (a man, his son, and his grandson), Ezekiel demonstrates the falsity of the proverb. The son shall *not* suffer at the hands of the Lord for the sins of his father, nor the father for the sins of his son.   **18:14–18**

Ezekiel restates the case that the Lord has made thus far. The problem with this restatement is that it seems to be directly at odds with the original objection. The people are *now* saying, **Why should not the son suffer for the iniquity of the father?** This surprising new objection reveals the real reason why the people quote the proverb. If the sons suffer for the sins of their fathers, then the   **18:19–20**

---

21. *Targum of Ezekiel* does not translate the proverb literally but simply gives the meaning: "The fathers have sinned and the children have been punished." Levey, *Targum of Ezekiel*, 57.

22. The term "soul" (*nephesh* in Hebrew, *psychē* in Greek) denotes the life of an individual human being.

Personal Responsibility and Generational Sin

BIBLICAL BACKGROUND

How can Ezekiel's prophetic pronouncement—that each person will be judged for his own sin and not for the sins of his parents—be reconciled with passages in the Old Testament that seem to say the opposite? For example, right in the midst of the giving of the Ten Commandments we find this passage: "I the LORD your God am a jealous God, visiting the iniquity of the fathers upon the children to the third and the fourth generation of those who hate me, but showing mercy to thousands of those who love me and keep my commandments" (Exod 20:5–6). It *seems* that the passage is saying that three and even four generations of descendants will be punished for the sins of their fathers.[a] Passages in the historical books would seem to confirm this understanding. In 2 Kings 24:3–4, the author concludes that disaster befell Judah "for the sins of Manasseh, according to all that he had done." And the author of Lamentations boldly claims: "Our fathers sinned, and are no more; / and we bear their iniquities" (Lam 5:7).

Many commentators—ancient and modern—have concluded that Ezekiel is *reversing* an earlier practice and *annulling* the teaching of Moses, by moving away from an era of corporate responsibility and punishment to one in which individual responsibility holds sway.[b] But the picture is more complex than this. In Deuteronomy, Moses declares that each one will be punished only for his or her own sin: "The fathers shall not be put to death for the children, nor shall the children be put to death for the fathers; every man shall be put to death for his own sin" (Deut 24:16). Ezekiel's teaching is in full accord with this law. Further, both 2 Kings and Lamentations acknowledge that the generation that was punished was *also* itself guilty of the sins of their fathers. In other words, it appears that punishment befell the people because they themselves continued the same pattern of sins that their fathers had committed. This is how some †Church Fathers and Jewish rabbis reconcile Exod 20:5–6 with Ezekiel: punishment continued to the third and fourth generation only when those generations also sinned against the Lord as their fathers had done.[c] In any case, Ezekiel certainly underlines personal responsibility for sin and, in the Lord's name, rejects the notion that God punishes someone solely on account of another's sins.

But Ezekiel maintains a corporate sense of responsibility as well: sin *impacts* the entire family and community, and this can include future generations. For example, those born in the exile in Babylon suffer this fate because of the sins of their parents, but God will rescue them and bring them all back to the land (Ezek 39:28). While Ezekiel stresses that the Lord will punish only those who themselves sin, he also prophesies a general judgment on the whole people, even as some (a remnant) are marked out by God for deliverance (see 9:4). In Ezekiel, each person bears responsibility only for his or her own sin, but the Lord still continues to relate to

Israel as a family—as a people—who are the recipients of his judgment and his deliverance.

a. Punishment to the third and fourth generation is stated three more times in the †Pentateuch (Exod 34:7; Num 14:18; Deut 5:9–10).

b. Some Jewish rabbis adopted this view, that because of changing circumstances the teaching of Moses was annulled by the prophecy of Ezekiel. See Eisemann, *Ezekiel*, 288–92.

c. St. Cyril of Alexandria is among the Church Fathers who interpret Exod 20 in this way (*Commentary on John* [9:2–3]). According to many of the Jewish sages, "God visits the guilt of parents only upon unregenerate descendants." Eisemann, *Ezekiel*, 290.

people of Ezekiel's day can shift the blame from themselves to their fathers. The disasters coming upon them, then, are not their fault—not due to their sins and transgressions. They are due to their fathers' sins. It provides a way for them to transfer responsibility away from themselves and onto past evil forefathers (for example, the evil king Manasseh). But the Lord cuts the ground from under them by maintaining that one will be punished only for his or her own sins: **the righteousness of the righteous shall be upon himself, and the wickedness of the wicked shall be upon himself.**

God's Desire That All May Have Life (18:21–32)

[21]"But if a wicked man turns away from all his sins which he has committed and keeps all my statutes and does what is lawful and right, he shall surely live; he shall not die. [22]None of the transgressions which he has committed shall be remembered against him; for the righteousness which he has done he shall live. [23]Have I any pleasure in the death of the wicked, says the Lord God, and not rather that he should turn from his way and live? [24]But when a righteous man turns away from his righteousness and commits iniquity and does the same abominable things that the wicked man does, shall he live? None of the righteous deeds which he has done shall be remembered; for the treachery of which he is guilty and the sin he has committed, he shall die.

[25]"Yet you say, 'The way of the Lord is not just.' Hear now, O house of Israel: Is my way not just? Is it not your ways that are not just? [26]When a righteous man turns away from his righteousness and commits iniquity, he shall die for it; for the iniquity which he has committed he shall die. [27]Again, when a wicked man turns away from the wickedness he has committed and does what is lawful and right, he shall save his life. [28]Because he considered and turned away from all the transgressions which he had committed, he shall surely live, he shall not die. [29]Yet the house of Israel says, 'The way of the Lord is not just.' O house of Israel, are my ways not just? Is it not your ways that are not just?

³⁰"Therefore I will judge you, O house of Israel, every one according to his ways, says the Lord God. Repent and turn from all your transgressions, lest iniquity be your ruin. ³¹Cast away from you all the transgressions which you have committed against me, and get yourselves a new heart and a new spirit! Why will you die, O house of Israel? ³²For I have no pleasure in the death of any one, says the Lord God; so turn, and live."

OT: Deut 30:15–20
NT: Luke 5:31–32; John 10:10; 1 John 2:1
Catechism: call to repentance and conversion, 1427–39; new heart and new spirit, 711, 1432
Lectionary: 18:21–23, 30–32: Mass for remission of sins; 18:25–28: 26th Sunday in Ordinary Time (Year A)

18:21–24   Ezekiel now adds two further case studies to secure his fundamental point, that each person will be held responsible for what he or she has done. In the first case (vv. 21–23), a wicked man who turns from his evil ways and follows the Lord **shall surely live; he shall not die.** Remarkably, none of his past transgressions **shall be remembered against him.** Here we have a case of *repentance*, of turning away from sin and finding life in God.[23] The second case (v. 24) reverses the picture: **a righteous man** who turns from God's ways and does evil shall not live. His righteous deeds will not be remembered; he will die for his sins. This could be a case of *apostasy*, of deciding to turn away from the Lord and his ways, or choosing to sin in a serious manner.

The dichotomy presented here is Ezekiel's version of the "way of life" and "way of death," the two options posed in Deut 30:15–20. There Moses presents the people with two alternatives. If they follow the Lord God, then they "shall live and multiply" (30:16). But if they turn away from the Lord and do evil, then they "shall perish" (30:18). The Lord's deep desire is that his people may live, and so he concludes by calling them to "choose life" (30:19).

18:25–29   The Lord, speaking through Ezekiel, now sums up his case. The people are objecting that **the way of the Lord is not just.** The verb that is translated "is just" or "is fair" is literally "is weighed" or "is measured." Isaiah records a similar complaint by the people: "My way is hidden from the Lord, and my right is disregarded by my God" (Isa 40:27). The people are alleging that God is not *weighing* things fairly in their regard. Perhaps they take offense at God's ways because he does not weigh up good deeds against bad ones over the course of a lifetime. Once again, the Lord turns this objection back upon the people. **Is my way not just? Is it not your ways that are not just?** It *is* just and fair that the one who follows a sinful way should be punished and that the one who repents from sin **shall save his life** (literally, "shall cause his soul to live").

---

23. The verb translated "turn," "return," or "repent" in chap. 18 is a common Hebrew verb (*shub*) used over fifty times in Ezekiel in many contexts.

St. Basil the Great on the Compassion of God   LIVING TRADITION

In the selection that follows, Basil the Great makes allusion to several Old Testament passages that convey God's desire to heal his people, not to see them destroyed. He concludes by referring directly to Ezek 18:32 to show that the Lord desires the sinner to live.

> Remember the compassion of God, how he heals with olive oil and wine. Do not despair of salvation. Recall the memory of what has been written, how he that falls rises again, and he that is turned away turns again, he that has been smitten is healed, he that is caught by wild beasts, escapes and he that confesses is not rejected. The Lord does not want the death of the sinner, but that he return and live.[a]

a. *Letter* 44 (ACCS 13:84).

18:30–32   In these final verses, the Lord reveals his true purpose and heart. He is not simply defending himself from a false charge of injustice—he has no need to defend himself. Instead, his aim is to uncover the true state of his people's sin and call them to repentance and life. God declares that he will in fact judge his people fairly: **I will judge you, O house of Israel, every one according to his ways**. But the endgame that the Lord seeks is repentance and life: **Repent and turn from all your transgressions**. The Lord takes no pleasure whatsoever in punishing his people for their sins. **For I have no pleasure in the death of any one, says the Lord God**. The final words of the chapter—**so turn, and live**—expose the heart of God toward his people.

Astonishingly, the Lord interjects this directive: **get yourselves a new heart and a new spirit!** Back in chapter 11 (v. 19), the Lord promised to give his people a "heart of flesh" and "a new spirit." Now he calls them to "get" for themselves a new heart and spirit. Certainly, this is a genuine call to repent from sin and to seek God for his help and deliverance. This they must do, but what they desperately need they cannot in fact provide on their own. Only God can give new hearts and new spirits. The Lord calls them here to seek and pursue what only the Lord himself can actually supply. Later in the book the Lord reveals the only way that this can come about: "A new heart I will give you, and a new spirit I will put within you" (36:26).

In the Light of Christ (18:30–32)

A question often arises when people are considering the Lord's call here to repent and live. Was repentance under the Old Covenant genuinely effective?

Were people's sins forgiven, and was the †grace of righteousness really communicated, for example, to Ezekiel and those in his day? This raises the broader question of whether the Old Covenant sacrifices that the Lord commanded in the temple were really effective for bringing about the forgiveness of sins. Some theologians over the ages have concluded that grace and forgiveness were *not* genuinely given under the Old Covenant, and they find support for this view from passages in the New Testament that point to the ineffectiveness of Old Covenant sacrifices: "For it is impossible that the blood of bulls and goats should take away sins" (Heb 10:4). They maintain that grace and forgiveness came only through Christ and his perfect sacrifice on the cross. Therefore, the Old Covenant sacrifices and repentance from sin only prefigured the true righteousness that came through Christ.

But other theologians—among whom is St. Thomas Aquinas—draw a different conclusion. They agree that the true and perfect sacrifice for sins came through Christ's sacrifice *alone* and that all genuine forgiveness and true spiritual life comes through him. But they also conclude that grace really was given under the Old Covenant and that people were genuinely forgiven and received grace through the sacrifices in the temple. How can this be? Because Christ's saving work, which happened later in time, was already effective for those who came before him.[24] For Aquinas, the sacrifices and rites of the Old Covenant were not effective *in themselves* to bring about grace and forgiveness, but through genuine faith the people of the Old Covenant were justified and forgiven through the grace of Christ's saving passion and death, which occurred later in time.[25] Paul in fact makes quite clear that Abraham had real faith and was truly justified through that faith even before Christ came (see Rom 4:1–12; Gal 3:8–9). But St. Thomas explains that this justifying faith is effective for Abraham and the people of Israel only because of what Christ accomplished through his saving work.

Reflection and Application (18:1–32)

How does the profound teaching in this chapter apply to us today? First, God's concern for the individual shines through brightly. We are not just part of a large, faceless group or collective, but individual sons and daughters known by their divine Father. He claims each "soul" for his own; he knows us individually and seeks our good that we may live. Second, we are assured that the

---

24. The doctrine of the Immaculate Conception of Mary operates on this same principle: Mary was preserved from original sin by the grace of her Son working beforehand in time (see Catechism 491–92).

25. For Aquinas's treatment of grace and what he calls "the sacraments of the Old Law," see *Summa Theologiae* I-II.62.6; III.70.4.

Lord is *fair* when judging us. He sees our sins, but he also sees our efforts to follow him, and he blesses those who turn to him for life. The Lord invites all to heartfelt repentance and leaves space for us to repent and turn back—and this is very good news for each of us. Third, God is not merely interested in judging us fairly. He wants us to live! He does not keep a scorecard and give an average of our performance over the course of our lives. He *forgives* our sin because he wants to pour out his life into us. Robert Jenson calls chapter 18 "the †gospel by way of Ezekiel, and a central message of all Ezekiel's prophesying."[26]

All this is wonderfully fulfilled in Jesus and the gospel. This is the reason that he came: "Those who are well have no need of a physician, but those who are sick; I have not come to call the righteous, but sinners to repentance" (Luke 5:31–32). The ministry of Jesus in fact fulfills what is proclaimed here in Ezekiel. Jesus has come "that they may have life, and have it abundantly" (John 10:10). This is both a great source of comfort and a spur to leave behind our sins and turn to the Lord. As John reminds us, "If any one does sin, we have an advocate with the Father, Jesus Christ the righteous" (1 John 2:1).

Lamentation for Israel: Parable of the Lioness (19:1–9)

¹And you, take up a lamentation for the princes of Israel, ²and say:

> What a lioness was your mother
>   among lions!
> She lurked in the midst of young lions,
>   rearing her whelps.
> ³And she brought up one of her whelps;
>   he became a young lion,
> and he learned to catch prey;
>   he devoured men.
> ⁴The nations sounded an alarm against him;
>   he was taken in their pit;
> and they brought him with hooks
>   to the land of Egypt.
> ⁵When she saw that she was baffled,
>   that her hope was lost,
> she took another of her whelps
>   and made him a young lion.
> ⁶He prowled among the lions;
>   he became a young lion,

---

26. Robert Jenson, *Ezekiel*, Brazos Theological Commentary on the Bible (Grand Rapids: Brazos, 2009), 148.

and he learned to catch prey;
>   he devoured men.
> [7]And he ravaged their strongholds,
>   and laid waste their cities;
> and the land was appalled and all who were in it
>   at the sound of his roaring.
> [8]Then the nations set against him
>   snares on every side;
> they spread their net over him;
>   he was taken in their pit.
> [9]With hooks they put him in a cage,
>   and brought him to the king of Babylon;
>   they brought him into custody,
> that his voice should no more be heard
>   upon the mountains of Israel.

OT: Num 23:24; 24:9; 2 Kings 23:31–35; 24:8–18; 25:27–30; Jer 22:10–12; 29:2
Catechism: God's punishment and judgment of sin, 211, 679, 1472–73, 2054; the use of parables, 546

This entire chapter is a lamentation in two parts, one based on a parable of a mother lioness and her cubs, the other on a "mother vine" whose branches were once rich but have now withered. In each case what began as something strong and healthy has been cut off and destroyed. The lament appears to include events that have already occurred and events that are going to happen in the near future.

19:1   Ezekiel is told to **take up a lamentation for the princes of Israel**, so we know that this is a lament aimed at the leaders in Jerusalem. The word that is translated "lamentation" "is a technical term for a special kind of musical composition, the dirge, which was composed and sung at the death of an individual, though it is also used of laments at the destruction of a nation or people."[27] This lament is cast loosely in poetic meter to express the songlike quality of the two parables.[28]

19:2–9   The first parable begins by referring to a **mother, a lioness**, who rears a set of cubs. The lion, considered to be the fiercest of wild animals in the ancient world, was a common image for a king. One of the cubs learned to catch his prey and **devoured men**. The nations got wind of this, caught this young lion in a pit, and brought him **with hooks / to the land of Egypt**. When the mother lioness saw that her hope in this cub was lost, she took another of her cubs and established him as **a young lion**. This young cub also **devoured men**, but in addition **ravaged their strongholds, / and laid waste their cities**. Once again

---

27. Block, *Ezekiel: Chapters 1–24*, 592. The term that is translated "lamentation" (Hebrew *kinah*) occurs nineteen times in the Old Testament, ten of which occur in Ezekiel (see also 2 Sam 1:17; 2 Chron 35:25; Jer 7:29; 9:10, 19).
28. Alter, "Ezekiel," 1102.

the surrounding nations came against him, captured him in a pit, and brought him **in a cage**, this time to **the king of Babylon**. Nothing was ever heard of either lion cub again.

Ezekiel does not give the interpretation of this parable, and so we are left to ponder how it relates to actual historical events. The mother lioness may refer to a single figure, Hamutal, the wife of Josiah, who was also called "the queen mother" (Jer 29:2). She was the mother of Jehoahaz and Zedekiah (2 Kings 23:31; 24:18). The first lion cub, which was captured and taken to Egypt, may refer to Jehoahaz, captured by Pharaoh Neco in 609 BC (2 Kings 23:31–35; Jer 22:10–12), while the second lion cub, taken captive to Babylon, may refer to Jehoiachin or to Zedekiah (2 Kings 24:8–16; 25:27–30).[29] The parable does not line up neatly with historical figures, but the point of the parable remains clear: Ezekiel is offering a lament for the decline and subsequent captivity of Judah's kings in Egypt and in Babylon.[30]

Lamentation for Israel: Parable of the Mother Vine (19:10–14)

> [10]Your mother was like a vine in a vineyard
>   transplanted by the water,
> fruitful and full of branches
>   by reason of abundant water.
> [11]Its strongest stem became
>   a ruler's scepter;
> it towered aloft
>   among the thick boughs;
> it was seen in its height
>   with the mass of its branches.
> [12]But the vine was plucked up in fury,
>   cast down to the ground;
> the east wind dried it up;
>   its fruit was stripped off,
> its strong stem was withered;
>   the fire consumed it.
> [13]Now it is transplanted in the wilderness,
>   in a dry and thirsty land.
> [14]And fire has gone out from its stem,
>   has consumed its branches and fruit,

---

29. Alternatively, the lioness may represent the entire tribe of Judah, which has produced the line of kings descended from David, and the lion cubs may refer more generally to the captivity of Judah's royalty by Babylon.

30. The Jewish rabbis disagreed about the precise historical application of the parable, but they concurred that it concerned the fate of the four sons and grandsons of Josiah. See Eisemann, *Ezekiel*, 314.

Jacob's Blessing of Judah

The two parables in Ezek 19 have striking connections to the blessing of Judah by his father Jacob in Gen 49:8–12. As his life drew to a close, Jacob gathered his sons for a final blessing, foretelling what would befall them in the days to come. When Judah's turn arrived, Jacob predicted that all of Judah's brothers would bow down before him, and he identified Judah as both a lion and a lioness:[a] "Judah is a lion's whelp; / from the prey, my son, you have gone up. / He stooped down, he lurked as a lion, / and as a lioness; who dares rouse him up?" (Gen 49:9).[b] The next verse speaks of the ruling "scepter" that Judah will wield: "The scepter shall not depart from Judah, / nor the ruler's staff from between his feet" (49:10). And finally Judah's flourishing is linked to a "vine": "Binding his foal to the vine / and his donkey's colt to the choice vine . . . " (49:11). Ezekiel tells us that his two parables concern "the princes of Israel," which in his day can refer only to the kings of Judah. The terms "lion," "lioness," "scepter," and "vine" in the two prophetic parables clearly make allusion to Gen 49. The context, however, has changed radically. Jacob's blessing in Genesis identifies Judah as a lion/lioness that rules successfully and flourishes; Ezekiel tells the tale of the defeat of lion cubs and their degradation in captivity. Jacob prophesies a blessing of rule and prosperity for the tribe of Judah; Ezekiel sings a song of lament and woe over the fall of Judah's princes. Only in Jesus, "the Lion of the tribe of Judah" (Rev 5:5), is the decline of Judah's kings truly reversed and Jacob's ancient blessing of Judah fulfilled.

a. The lion (or lioness) was recognized proverbially for its strength as the mightiest of wild beasts (Prov 30:30). It was recognized especially for its effectiveness in preying upon others, and so stood as a symbol for invading armies (Pss 7:2; 17:12; Hosea 5:14), but the lion also functioned as a symbol of the monarch or king (Gen 49:9; Prov 20:2; Dan 7:4).

b. The prophet Balaam twice identifies Israel as both a lion and a lioness: "Behold, a people! As a lioness it rises up / and as a lion it lifts itself; / it does not lie down till it devours the prey" (Num 23:24; see also 24:9).

> so that there remains in it no strong stem,
>   no scepter for a ruler.

This is a lamentation, and has become a lamentation.

OT: Gen 49:1–12; 2 Kings 25:1–7
NT: Rev 5:5
Catechism: God's punishment and judgment of sin, 211, 679, 1472–73, 2054; the use of parables, 546

19:10– 14a The second parable also concerns **your mother**, but this time she is **a vine in a vineyard / transplanted by the water**. The **strongest stem** of this vine became a **ruler's scepter** that towered high above the ground with great growth beneath.

But this lush and powerful vine was **plucked up in fury** and **cast down to the ground**. An **east wind** dried up its fruit, the branches were stripped off, and the strong stem of the vine was consumed by fire. The parable then shifts focus, identifying the vine as transplanted **in the wilderness, in a dry and thirsty land**. The fruit is gone, the scepter is lost, and the vine remains only as a weak, unproductive stem.

As with the previous parable, Ezekiel offers no historical interpretation. The vine is best understood as a reference—once again—to the tribe of Judah, while the "scepter" points to Judah's recent line of kings. The "east wind" represents Babylon, and the vine plucked up and cast to the ground probably points to Zedekiah, who was captured on the plains of Jericho, blinded by Nebuchadnezzar, and taken away in exile to "the wilderness"—that is, to Babylon (see 2 Kings 25:1–7).

The chapter concludes: **This is a lamentation, and has become a lamentation,** or "serves as a lamentation." What Ezekiel has "sung" here both expresses a lament and provides a lament for others to use. The two parables of the "mother" (the lioness and the vine) are expressions of deep mourning. The fruitful line of David has been cut down, and the princes have been sent into exile. Ezekiel is called prophetically to mourn over this great loss and to raise a lamentation for the grievous fall of Judah. 19:14b

Oracles and Parables of Judgment against the City and the Land, Part 3

Ezekiel 20:1–23:49

With chapters 20–23, the long series of judgment †oracles and parables against the land and the city comes to an end. Ezekiel presents the same fundamental word of judgment but couches it in new forms. The aim, however, remains the same: to convict the people of Israel of their sin and to forewarn them of the judgment soon to fall.

The Recital of Israel's Unfaithfulness (20:1–17)

¹In the seventh year, in the fifth month, on the tenth day of the month, certain of the elders of Israel came to inquire of the Lᴏʀᴅ, and sat before me. ²And the word of the Lᴏʀᴅ came to me: ³"Son of man, speak to the elders of Israel, and say to them, Thus says the Lord Gᴏᴅ, Is it to inquire of me that you come? As I live, says the Lord Gᴏᴅ, I will not be inquired of by you. ⁴Will you judge them, son of man, will you judge them? Then let them know the abominations of their fathers, ⁵and say to them, Thus says the Lord Gᴏᴅ: On the day when I chose Israel, I swore to the seed of the house of Jacob, making myself known to them in the land of Egypt, I swore to them, saying, I am the Lᴏʀᴅ your God. ⁶On that day I swore to them that I would bring them out of the land of Egypt into a land that I had searched out for them, a land flowing with milk and honey, the most glorious of all lands. ⁷And I said to them, Cast away the detestable things your eyes feast on, every one of you, and do not defile yourselves with the idols of Egypt; I am the Lᴏʀᴅ your God. ⁸But they rebelled

against me and would not listen to me; they did not every man cast away the detestable things their eyes feasted on, nor did they forsake the idols of Egypt.

⁸"Then I thought I would pour out my wrath upon them and spend my anger against them in the midst of the land of Egypt. ⁹But I acted for the sake of my name, that it should not be profaned in the sight of the nations among whom they dwelt, in whose sight I made myself known to them in bringing them out of the land of Egypt. ¹⁰So I led them out of the land of Egypt and brought them into the wilderness. ¹¹I gave them my statutes and showed them my ordinances, by whose observance man shall live. ¹²Moreover I gave them my sabbaths, as a sign between me and them, that they might know that I the LORD sanctify them. ¹³But the house of Israel rebelled against me in the wilderness; they did not walk in my statutes but rejected my ordinances, by whose observance man shall live; and my sabbaths they greatly profaned.

¹⁴"Then I thought I would pour out my wrath upon them in the wilderness, to make a full end of them. ¹⁴But I acted for the sake of my name, that it should not be profaned in the sight of the nations, in whose sight I had brought them out. ¹⁵Moreover I swore to them in the wilderness that I would not bring them into the land which I had given them, a land flowing with milk and honey, the most glorious of all lands, ¹⁶because they rejected my ordinances and did not walk in my statutes, and profaned my sabbaths; for their heart went after their idols. ¹⁷Nevertheless my eye spared them, and I did not destroy them or make a full end of them in the wilderness."

OT: Exod 32:1–10; Lev 18:5; Num 14:28–30; Pss 95:11; 106:6–47
Catechism: God's punishment and judgment of sin, 211, 679, 1472–73, 2054; the sin of idolatry, 2112–14

In chapter 20, the Lord—like a prosecuting attorney—recounts the long history of Israel's unfaithfulness from their sojourn in Egypt up to Ezekiel's day. The same sad story of rebellion presented in †*allegory* in chapters 16 and 23 is here presented as *historical narrative*. The case against Israel, given in five phases (vv. 1–32), is then followed by the Lord's stated determination to purify his people and redeem them from this long history of unfaithfulness (vv. 33–44). The end-goal is a people purified for the Lord. The story told here closely parallels the narrative of Ps 106:6–47, chronicling Israel's rebellion first in Egypt, then in the wilderness wanderings, and finally in the promised land, leading to exile among the nations.

Ezekiel records the date of this prophetic oracle as **the seventh year, in the**   20:1–3
fifth month, on the tenth day of the month (August 14, 591 BC).[1] This falls about one year after the temple vision in 8:1 and five years before the destruction

1. This is the fourth date given in Ezekiel; previous dates appear in 1:1–2; 3:16; 8:1.

of Jerusalem and the temple. As they did previously (8:1; 14:1), **certain of the elders of Israel came to inquire of the Lord, and sat before** Ezekiel. But the Lord rebuffs their inquiry: **Is it to inquire of me that you come? As I live, says the Lord God, I will not be inquired of by you.** The reason for the Lord's rejection of their request is unclear at this point but will be clarified at the close of the narrative (v. 31).

20:4   Instead of answering their inquiry, the Lord tells Ezekiel to **judge them** by recounting **the abominations of their fathers.** We might be tempted to conclude that the Lord is forgetting what he said in chapter 18 and is condemning the sons because of the sins of the fathers, but as we shall see, the Lord underlines the sin and rebellion of each and every generation including the present one. He is bringing judgment not because the fathers sinned but because *all* the generations have been rebellious.

20:5–9   In the first phase of this history (vv. 5–9), the Lord recounts how he chose Israel in Egypt, promising to rescue them from slavery and bring them into **a land flowing with milk and honey, the most glorious of all lands.**[2] He called them to cast off **the idols of Egypt,** but they would not obey. Because of this the Lord was prepared to punish them in Egypt but refrained for the sake of his own name and honor, and despite their unworthiness he brought them out of captivity. Strikingly, Ezekiel presents here a history of idolatry and unfaithfulness *in Egypt* that does not appear elsewhere in the Old Testament record. In the book of Exodus, the Israelites residing in Egypt are reluctant and lack faith in Moses, but the tale of serious unfaithfulness begins in the wilderness after they leave Pharaoh's kingdom.[3] Ezekiel, however, traces the roots of Israel's idolatry all the way back to their time of slavery in Egypt.

20:10–17   In the second phase (vv. 10–17), the Lord narrates how he brought Israel to Sinai in the wilderness, where he gave them his good law: **I gave them my statutes and showed them my ordinances, by whose observance man shall live.** He also gave them the sabbath observance as a sign that the Lord †sanctified them (that is, made them holy and set apart). But once again, they rejected his laws and desecrated the sabbath day (Exod 16:23–30; Num 15:32–36). The Lord was again prepared to **make a full end of them** in the wilderness because of their rebellion (see Exod 32:9–10). But though he spared the people and did not destroy them, he swore that the rebellious generation would not enter the promised land (Num 14:28–30; Ps 95:11). Twice in this section Ezekiel refers to the statutes and ordinances "by which, if a person does them, he shall live" (Ezek

---

2. For Israel as a land "flowing with milk and honey," see also Exod 3:8; 33:3; Lev 20:24; Num 13:27; Deut 6:3; 31:20; Josh 5:6; Jer 11:5; 32:22.

3. Psalm 106:6–7 admits Israel's failure to recall the steadfast love of the Lord in Egypt, but first speaks about Israel's rebellion as occurring at the Red Sea. The incident of the golden calf (Exod 32), with the people's request of Aaron to "make us gods" (32:1), may point to a history of idolatry in Egypt, which the people were all too quick to reclaim when Moses was delayed upon the mountain.

20:11, 13 ESV). This is a clear allusion to Lev 18:5 (ESV): "You shall therefore keep my statutes and my rules; if a person does them, he shall live by them." In short, at Sinai the Lord gave his people good statutes that were meant to be a source of life and blessing for the people, but they rejected his laws and **did not walk in** them.

The Recital of Israel's Unfaithfulness Continued (20:18–32)

[18]"And I said to their children in the wilderness, 'Do not walk in the statutes of your fathers, nor observe their ordinances, nor defile yourselves with their idols. [19]I am the LORD your God; walk in my statutes, and be careful to obey my ordinances, [20]and hallow my sabbaths that they may be a sign between me and you, that you may know that I am the LORD your God.' [21]But the children rebelled against me; they did not walk in my statutes and were not careful to obey my ordinances, by whose observance man shall live; they profaned my sabbaths.

"Then I thought I would pour out my wrath upon them and spend my anger against them in the wilderness. [22]But I withheld my hand, and acted for the sake of my name, that it should not be profaned in the sight of the nations, in whose sight I had brought them out. [23]Moreover I swore to them in the wilderness that I would scatter them among the nations and disperse them through the countries, [24]because they had not executed my ordinances, but had rejected my statutes and profaned my sabbaths, and their eyes were set on their fathers' idols. [25]Moreover I gave them statutes that were not good and ordinances by which they could not have life; [26]and I defiled them through their very gifts in making them offer by fire all their first-born, that I might horrify them; I did it that they might know that I am the LORD.

[27]"Therefore, son of man, speak to the house of Israel and say to them, Thus says the Lord GOD: In this again your fathers blasphemed me, by dealing treacherously with me. [28]For when I had brought them into the land which I swore to give them, then wherever they saw any high hill or any leafy tree, there they offered their sacrifices and presented the provocation of their offering; there they sent up their soothing odors, and there they poured out their drink offerings. [29](I said to them, What is the high place to which you go? So its name is called Bamah to this day.) [30]Wherefore say to the house of Israel, Thus says the Lord GOD: Will you defile yourselves after the manner of your fathers and go astray after their detestable things? [31]When you offer your gifts and sacrifice your sons by fire, you defile yourselves with all your idols to this day. And shall I be inquired of by you, O house of Israel? As I live, says the Lord GOD, I will not be inquired of by you.

> [32]"What is in your mind shall never happen—the thought, 'Let us be like the nations, like the tribes of the countries, and worship wood and stone.'"

OT: Exod 32:9–10; Lev 18:5; Num 14:28–30; 25:1–18; Deut 24:1–4; Ps 95:11
NT: Matt 19:7–10; Mark 10:4–9; Rom 7:12–13
Catechism: God's punishment and judgment of sin, 211, 679, 1472–73, 2054; the sin of idolatry, 2112–14

20:18–24   In the third phase of the narrative (vv. 18–26), the Lord recounts how he spoke to the *children* of those who departed from Egypt, calling them to turn away from their fathers' sins and walk in all the ways of the Lord. But this generation, too, refused to listen: **the children rebelled against me**, as was evident in their idolatrous worship of the Baal of Peor on the verge of the promised land (see Num 25:1–18). Once again the Lord, with justice, could have made an end of them in the wilderness, but he relented. Still, he swore to them that he would **scatter them among the nations and disperse them through the countries** (v. 23). In short, he would send them into exile for their sins, just as the Lord promised through Moses when the people of Israel were about to enter the promised land (see Deut 28).

20:25–26   This section concludes with one of the most perplexing passages in the whole of the Bible. The Lord says through Ezekiel: **Moreover I gave them statutes that were not good and ordinances by which they could not have life; and I defiled them through their very gifts in making them offer by fire all their first-born, that I might horrify them; I did it that they might know that I am the LORD**. We may well ask: How could the Lord give his people "statutes that were not good" and laws "by which they could not have life"?

Ancient and contemporary interpretations of Ezek 20:25 vary widely, but we can identify three main approaches to the words spoken by the Lord, "I gave them statutes that were not good and ordinances by which they could not have life." The first line of interpretation concludes that these words refer *not* to laws actually given by the Lord but either to *the laws of the nations* that ruled Israel in exile (see Ezek 5:7) or to the people's own *evil inclinations* (vv. 28–31). In other words, by rejecting God's law (which does bring life) Israel would be exiled and would become subject to the laws of foreigners (which do not give life). The Lord *gave them* these laws only in the sense that he handed his people over to exile, where they were forced to live under the laws and statutes of foreign nations.[4] This reading, common among the Jewish rabbis and adopted by some modern commentators, takes the exilic context of the passage into account (v. 23) and absolves God from directly giving laws that were not good. The weak point of this interpretation is that it does not easily account for Ezekiel's distinction

---

4. Eisemann, *Ezekiel*, 329, sums up this first interpretation: "Thus the *bad laws* can be said to come from God, since it is he who allowed Israel to be conquered by the alien nations." See also Alter, "Ezekiel," 1107.

between laws that give life (vv. 11, 13) and laws that do not (v. 25), both of which *God gave*, and it requires us to equate the statutes and ordinances that God gave Israel with the laws of foreign peoples. Nevertheless, this is certainly a possible interpretation, in accord with what we know elsewhere about God and his willingness to hand sinful people over to the consequences of their own sin (see Rom 1:24–28).

A second line of interpretation identifies Ezek 20:25 with the Mosaic legislation in general but locates the real problem not in the laws themselves but in the failure of the people to keep the laws because of sin and disobedience. This interpretation, found among the †Church Fathers, interprets this passage through the lens of Paul's teaching that the law itself is holy and good (Rom 7:12) but that, because of sin at work in us, the "good" law worked death in us (7:13). On this view, the problem is with *us*, not with the laws that God gave.[5] This interpretation rightly identifies the fundamental goodness of the law and human inability to keep the law in its fullness, but, even more than the first interpretation, it strains to account for the distinction in Ezek 20 between laws that give life and laws that do not. Paul is referring to the *whole* of the law as good, and to human inability to keep the *whole* of the good law. It is not obvious how Ezekiel's reference to laws that are not good lines up with a Pauline interpretation of the law.

The third line of interpretation claims that Ezek 20:25 is referring to *part* of the law—namely, to the statutes and ordinances given *after* the sin of the golden calf at Mount Sinai. Interpreters who follow this view typically distinguish the Ten Commandments (which bring life) from the detailed legislation that followed Israel's apostasy (which does not bring life). These later laws were a concession to the people's rebellious state and so did not bring about the full life that God intends. This interpretation finds support among the Church Fathers and has been vigorously proposed by some contemporary commentators.[6] This third approach provides the best *contextual* interpretation of the narrative of Ezek 20, but it is hard to find elsewhere in the Bible this kind of distinction between laws given before the golden calf apostasy and laws given afterward. We do not see this kind of distinction described in the law itself, or in the prophets, or in Paul (and the New Testament).

And so the precise meaning of Ezek 20:25 remains unclear. One hint toward its resolution may lie in Jesus's shocking explanation for why Moses allowed

---

5. Among the Church Fathers who adopt this interpretation are Origen, Augustine, and John of Damascus.

6. Among the Church Fathers who adopt this interpretation are Justin Martyr, Irenaeus, and John Chrysostom. Scott Hahn and John Bergsma, "What Laws Were 'Not Good'? A Canonical Approach to the Theological Problem of Ezekiel 20:25–26," *Journal of Biblical Literature* 123 (2004): 201–18, make a carefully argued case that Ezek 20:25 is referring specifically to provisions in the Deuteronomic law code (Deut 12–28).

divorce, though it was not part of the original plan of God: "For your hardness of heart Moses allowed you to divorce your wives, but from the beginning it was not so" (Matt 19:8; see also Mark 10:4–9; Deut 24:1–4). Because of the people's hardness of heart, Moses granted certain kinds of practices—as a concession—that did not express the full purpose of God, and so did not "bring life" to the people.

The meaning of verse 26 is also unclear. Why would the Lord defile them through their gifts "in making them offer by fire all their first-born"? This may refer to the practice of offering the firstborn son in the fire to the god Molech, a practice sharply forbidden in the Old Testament.[7] Though the phrase "by fire" is not in the Hebrew text (it says literally, "in their offering up all their firstborn"), a parallel passage in verse 31 seems to point to this interpretation: "When you offer your gifts and sacrifice your sons by fire . . ."[8] Notably, verse 31 also offers a possible interpretation of verse 26, because it continues, "you defile yourselves with all your idols to this day." In other words, by offering their children in the fire to Molech, the people of Israel "defile themselves." Because God has handed them over to the consequences of their own grave sin, he says that he "defiled them" by these offerings.[9]

Ezekiel 20:25–26 has perplexed Jewish and Christian interpreters through the ages, and there is perhaps no fully satisfactory account of what Ezekiel means by these words. Whatever the precise meaning may be, it is plain that Israel's own generational pattern of sin and rebellion led to the grim state of judgment in which they find themselves.

20:27–32   The long narrative of sin and rebellion now draws to a close. In the final two phases of his case, Ezekiel first accuses the **fathers** of the present generation of having sinned by setting up the worship of false gods throughout the land (vv. 27–29), and then he charges the present generation with worshiping idols and sacrificing their children in the fire to other gods (vv. 30–31). In closing, the Lord solemnly addresses **the house of Israel** and concludes where he began (in v. 3)—**I will not be inquired of by you**—but now he explains why. The Lord will not cooperate with the charade that these elders of Israel are seeking God. He unmasks their pretense and reveals how they—like each of the generations

---

7. According to the law of Moses, all firstborn sons belonged to the Lord and were to be "redeemed" through the sacrifice of an animal (Exod 13:12–13; 34:19–20). Deuteronomy 12:31 expressly forbids the sacrifice of firstborn sons in the fire. Under certain wicked kings of Israel (e.g., Ahaz and Manasseh), child sacrifice was practiced, but both Jeremiah (7:31; 19:5; 32:35) and Ezekiel reject child sacrifice as abominable to the Lord.

8. Hahn and Bergsma, "What Laws Were 'Not Good'?," 210–13, argue that the passage refers not to Molech worship but to the offering of the firstborn of *animals* in sacrifice to the Lord, as prescribed in Deuteronomy.

9. This understanding of v. 26 is a common ⁺rabbinic interpretation. See Eisemann, *Ezekiel*, 329–30; Rosenberg, *Book of Ezekiel*, 1:157–58.

of their ancestors—are really intent in their minds on worshiping idols and being **like the nations** around them.

The Lord's Determination to Purify His People (20:33–49)

³³"As I live, says the Lord GOD, surely with a mighty hand and an outstretched arm, and with wrath poured out, I will be king over you. ³⁴I will bring you out from the peoples and gather you out of the countries where you are scattered, with a mighty hand and an outstretched arm, and with wrath poured out; ³⁵and I will bring you into the wilderness of the peoples, and there I will enter into judgment with you face to face. ³⁶As I entered into judgment with your fathers in the wilderness of the land of Egypt, so I will enter into judgment with you, says the Lord GOD. ³⁷I will make you pass under the rod, and I will let you go in by number. ³⁸I will purge out the rebels from among you, and those who transgress against me; I will bring them out of the land where they sojourn, but they shall not enter the land of Israel. Then you will know that I am the LORD.

³⁹"As for you, O house of Israel, thus says the Lord GOD: Go serve every one of you his idols, now and hereafter, if you will not listen to me; but my holy name you shall no more profane with your gifts and your idols.

⁴⁰"For on my holy mountain, the mountain height of Israel, says the Lord GOD, there all the house of Israel, all of them, shall serve me in the land; there I will accept them, and there I will require your contributions and the choicest of your gifts, with all your sacred offerings. ⁴¹As a pleasing odor I will accept you, when I bring you out from the peoples, and gather you out of the countries where you have been scattered; and I will manifest my holiness among you in the sight of the nations. ⁴²And you shall know that I am the LORD, when I bring you into the land of Israel, the country which I swore to give to your fathers. ⁴³And there you shall remember your ways and all the doings with which you have polluted yourselves; and you shall loathe yourselves for all the evils that you have committed. ⁴⁴And you shall know that I am the LORD, when I deal with you for my name's sake, not according to your evil ways, nor according to your corrupt doings, O house of Israel, says the Lord GOD."

⁴⁵And the word of the LORD came to me: ⁴⁶"Son of man, set your face toward the south, preach against the south, and prophesy against the forest land in the Negeb; ⁴⁷say to the forest of the Negeb, Hear the word of the LORD: Thus says the Lord GOD, Behold, I will kindle a fire in you, and it shall devour every green tree in you and every dry tree; the blazing flame shall not be quenched, and all faces from south to north shall be scorched by it. ⁴⁸All flesh shall see that I the LORD have kindled it; it shall not be

155

quenched." [49]Then I said, "Ah, Lord GOD! they are saying of me, 'Is he not a maker of allegories?'"

OT: Ps 106:47; Isa 40:3–5; 43:16–17; 56:7; Jer 23:7–8; Hosea 2:14
NT: Matt 9:13; Rom 5:8; Heb 12:10
Catechism: God's redeeming love and covenant faithfulness, 219, 1611; call to share in God's holiness, 773, 2012–15

20:33–34   Leaving the past behind, the Lord now promises that **with a mighty hand and an outstretched arm** he will rescue his people from their exile. This is language drawn from the exodus from Egypt but now applied to a "new exodus" of God's people from their exile in foreign lands.[10] Significantly, however, the Lord says that he will rescue his people **with wrath poured out**. This wrath comes not only against the conquering nations but also, given the stern rebuke that precedes and follows, against his own people. The Lord is determined to **be king over** his people, but his deliverance will also include his act of judgment against their persistent sin.

20:35–39   Specifically, the Lord says that he will bring his people out into the **wilderness of the peoples** and there **enter into judgment with** them **face to face**. When the people departed from Egypt, they sinned during their time "in the wilderness." The wilderness will now become the place where God will sift and purify his sinful people. How will this happen? The Lord will cause his people to **pass under the rod** of his discipline, and he will remove all the rebellious people from their midst.[11] The RSV-2CE, following the Greek translation, then reads (v. 37), **and I will let you go in by number**—that is, into the promised land. Most modern translations (e.g., NRSV, NABRE), following the Hebrew text, render this something like "and I will bring you into the bond of the covenant." After sifting and testing his people in the wilderness, the Lord will forgive them and welcome them back into the life of the †covenant, with all its attendant blessings. The Lord is purifying his people "in the wilderness" in order to renew his covenant bond with them. But the oracle concludes with a warning (v. 39): they can choose to reject the Lord's word and continue to pursue their idolatrous ways, but however they respond, the Lord will no longer allow them to **profane** his **holy name**.

20:40–41b   The climax of the chapter now arrives. In this majestic statement, the Lord declares his intention to restore his people to the land so that they will dwell with him on the holy mountain (in Jerusalem) and worship him in a fitting way: **For on my holy mountain . . . there all the house of Israel, all of them, shall**

---

    10. For the return from exile described as a "new exodus" even greater than the first, see Isa 40:3–5; 43:16–17; Jer 16:14–15; 23:7–8.

    11. Rabbi David Kimchi (d. 1235) interprets vv. 35–38 as the Lord's judgment of his people in the wilderness, removing the disobedient before bringing them back to the promised land. Rosenberg, *Book of Ezekiel*, 1:161.

serve me in the land; there I will accept them. This is the goal of God's purifying discipline: a people restored who serve the Lord by offering appropriate and pleasing worship at his holy temple. This promise echoes the words of Isaiah (56:7): "These I will bring to my holy mountain, / and make them joyful in my house of prayer; / their burnt offerings and their sacrifices / will be accepted on my altar; / for my house shall be called a house of prayer / for all peoples."

But there is more. The Lord adds: **I will manifest my holiness among you in the sight of the nations**. When the Lord reveals his holy presence to his people, they will stand in awe and marvel at his holiness, but they will also see by contrast how reprehensibly they have acted toward the Lord. God's holiness will shine a light on their sinfulness and produce that full repentance and contrition so lacking in Ezekiel's present generation of hearers. Once again the Lord says, **And you shall know that I am the LORD**. The Lord God manifests his "name" by showing his sovereign power and mercy and by declaring ahead of time what will come to pass. Because of this, Israel will know that it is their God, the Lord, who has acted (see the sidebar "'Then You Will Know That I Am the LORD,'" p. 187). 20:41c–44

This short section would appear to be a separate and distinct oracle against the nations.[12] It is aimed generally against **the south**, the area of the Negeb wilderness south of Jerusalem where Moab, Edom, and Arabia are located, but no specific nation is named. The Lord declares judgment against this region by means of a fire that will burn up the land in the sight of **all flesh**. Given the context of this oracle, commentators often conclude that this is not directed against a foreign nation but is a word given in symbolic form against the city of Jerusalem itself. Ezekiel's own hearers seem to recognize that this oracle has a symbolic meaning, and so they accuse him of being **a maker of allegories**. In response, Ezekiel voices a complaint to the Lord—**Ah, Lord GOD!**—that his hearers are mocking him for being "a maker of allegories." This is in fact a fitting moniker for Ezekiel: his prophecies are full of parables, riddles, and allegorical stories. His audience appears to be entertained by these symbolic stories but evidently does not take them seriously or give heed to the dire warnings they convey. 20:45–49

Reflection and Application (20:1–44)

Readers of Ezek 20 often fail to see that this long recital of Israel's unfaithfulness is in fact an exposé of God's remarkable *mercy*. At every juncture and with each generation the Lord could have abandoned his people because of their sin, but he relented and did not bring upon them all the judgment that

12. In the Hebrew Bible, this section is part of chap. 21, to which it is more clearly connected by theme.

they deserved. Even the severe punishment about to fall upon them (the coming destruction of the city) will result eventually in the renewal of the covenant between the Lord and his people (Ezek 36–37). A central message of this chapter is that, despite the recurrent unfaithfulness of the people, God is determined to show mercy and restore them to his covenant love. This really is the main story line of the Bible. It is the true narrative, not just about the people of Israel but about the whole human race. When Jesus is faulted for mixing with sinful and seemingly unworthy people, he responds: "For I came not to call the righteous, but sinners" (Matt 9:13). Paul reminds the Romans of the astounding mercy of God, that God loved them even when they were his enemies: "But God shows his love for us in that while we were yet sinners Christ died for us" (Rom 5:8). Even when we scorn the Lord and turn away from him, he patiently woos us back: "Therefore, behold, I will allure her, and bring her into the wilderness, and speak tenderly to her" (Hosea 2:14). Yes, the Lord is prepared to discipline us for our own good, but he does this so that "we may share his holiness" (Heb 12:10).

Judgment against Israel by the Sword (21:1–17)

[1]The word of the LORD came to me: [2]"Son of man, set your face toward Jerusalem and preach against the sanctuaries; prophesy against the land of Israel [3]and say to the land of Israel, Thus says the LORD: Behold, I am against you, and will draw forth my sword out of its sheath, and will cut off from you both righteous and wicked. [4]Because I will cut off from you both righteous and wicked, therefore my sword shall go out of its sheath against all flesh from south to north; [5]and all flesh shall know that I the LORD have drawn my sword out of its sheath; it shall not be sheathed again. [6]Sigh therefore, son of man; sigh with breaking heart and bitter grief before their eyes. [7]And when they say to you, 'Why do you sigh?' you shall say, 'Because of the tidings. When it comes, every heart will melt and all hands will be feeble, every spirit will faint and all knees will be weak as water. Behold, it comes and it will be fulfilled,'" says the Lord GOD.

[8]And the word of the LORD came to me: [9]"Son of man, prophesy and say, Thus says the Lord, Say:

> A sword, a sword is sharpened
>   and also polished,
> [10]sharpened for slaughter,
>   polished to flash like lightning!

Or do we make mirth? You have despised the rod, my son, with everything of wood. [11]So the sword is given to be polished, that it may be handled; it is sharpened and polished to be given into the hand of the slayer. [12]Cry and wail, son of man, for it is against my people; it is against all the princes of

Israel; they are delivered over to the sword with my people. Strike therefore upon your thigh. ¹³For it will not be a testing—what could it do if you
despise the rod?" says the Lord GOD.

¹⁴"Prophesy therefore, son of man; clap your hands and let the sword
come down twice, yes, thrice, the sword for those to be slain; it is the
sword for the great slaughter, which encompasses them, ¹⁵that their hearts
may melt, and many fall at all their gates. I have given the glittering sword;
ah! it is made like lightning, it is polished for slaughter. ¹⁶Cut sharply to
right and left where your edge is directed. ¹⁷I also will clap my hands, and I
will satisfy my fury; I the LORD have spoken."

OT: Exod 8:22–23; Isa 63:7–10
NT: Luke 19:41–44
Catechism: God's punishment and judgment of sin, 211, 679, 1472–73, 2054

The key word for this chapter is "sword."[13] Using the metaphor of a sword of
judgment, Ezekiel announces a time of grief and woe, coupled with a call to
wail and moan, because the Lord's hand of judgment is now raised against the
land. All people—righteous and wicked alike—will go down under the sword
that is unsheathed. The oracles follow one after the other in quick succession,
with a constant theme but shifting focus.[14]

1. The announcement of the sword of judgment (vv. 1–7)
2. The sword of judgment sharpened and prepared (vv. 8–17)
3. The agent of the sword (vv. 18–27)
4. The taunt of the sword (vv. 28–32)

The chapter opens with the same words Ezekiel used to prophesy against the   21:1–7
"south" to close chapter 20—**Son of man, set your face toward . . .** —but now
the target for judgment is **Jerusalem** and **the land of Israel**. Shockingly, the
Lord says that he will **cut off . . . both righteous and wicked**; his sword will be
raised **against all flesh from south to north**.[15] What does this mean, and how
is it consistent with the message of chapter 18, that a person will die only for his
or her own sins? *In this life*, the Lord does not always bring judgment in a way
that neatly discriminates between the righteous and the wicked.[16] The prophet

---

13. The image of the sword also appears, e.g., in chaps. 5, 6, 30, 32.

14. Because of difficulties with grammar and vocabulary, chap. 21 is "one of the most difficult texts
in the book" (Greenberg, *Ezekiel 1–20*, 438). Block, *Ezekiel: Chapters 1–24*, 675, notes the "exclamatory,
repetitious, and garbled state of the text."

15. The ancient versions seemed to have difficulty with the indiscriminate judgment of the righteous
and wicked. The Greek translation (†Septuagint) changes the paired terms to "*unrighteous* and wicked,"
while †*Targum of Ezekiel* rewrites the passage so that the "righteous" are taken off to exile before the
Lord destroys the "wicked." Levey, *Targum of Ezekiel*, 66.

16. When inflicting plagues on Egypt, the Lord begins to discriminate between the Egyptians and
the Israelites only with the fourth plague (see Exod 8:22–23).

Jeremiah provides an example: he followed the Lord wholeheartedly and his life was spared when Jerusalem fell, but he nonetheless suffered the effects of the destruction of Jerusalem and was finally dragged off to Egypt with those who rebelled against the word of the Lord. Sometimes communal solidarity is such that people experience the *effects* of judgment, even if this experience does not reflect God's evaluation of their individual conduct or affect their eternal salvation.

What is Ezekiel's posture in the face of this judgment? The Lord tells Ezekiel to **sigh with breaking heart and bitter grief**.[17] Here the prophet reflects the heart of the Lord, for the Lord also groans over the suffering about to befall his people. God judges and punishes, but he also knows the pain of their suffering as a father knows his children's suffering (see Isa 63:7–10). Jesus likewise wept over Jerusalem because of the judgment for unbelief that was coming upon the Holy City (Luke 19:41–44).

21:8–17 In this section, Ezekiel prophesies the coming of a sword that is **polished** and **sharpened for slaughter**. While these verses are difficult to untangle in the original Hebrew, it is plain that the judgment by the sword will fall on both the people and the princes of the people.[18] It appears that Israel has refused the wooden **rod** of God's correction, and so now deserves the judgment of a sharpened iron sword. Then in verses 14–17, Ezekiel is told to prophesy for the sword to *fall*: it will fall not once but three times; it will cut both to the right and to the left. Wherever Ezekiel turns his face and **clap[s]** his **hands**, there the Lord will turn and bring slaughter upon all—none will escape. Here Ezekiel is not just foretelling the coming judgment; his words and actions function as the prompt for judgment. As he speaks and claps, the judgment will fall.

The Sword of Judgment Unsheathed (21:18–32)

[18]The word of the LORD came to me again: [19]"Son of man, mark two ways for the sword of the king of Babylon to come; both of them shall come forth from the same land. And make a signpost, make it at the head of the way to a city; [20]mark a way for the sword to come to Rabbah of the Ammonites and to Judah and to Jerusalem the fortified. [21]For the king of Babylon stands at the parting of the way, at the head of the two ways, to use divination; he shakes the arrows, he consults the teraphim, he looks at the liver. [22]Into his right hand comes the lot for Jerusalem, to open the mouth with a cry, to lift up the voice with shouting, to set battering rams against

---

17. See Ezek 9:8 for a similar response by Ezekiel to the grievous judgment that is coming on the people.

18. Robert Jenson, *Ezekiel*, Brazos Theological Commentary on the Bible (Grand Rapids: Brazos, 2009), 167, calls this section "a poem with a few lost lines."

the gates, to cast up mounds, to build siege towers. [23]But to them it will seem like a false divination; they have sworn solemn oaths; but he brings their guilt to remembrance, that they may be captured.

[24]"Therefore thus says the Lord GOD: Because you have made your guilt to be remembered, in that your transgressions are uncovered, so that in all your doings your sins appear—because you have come to remembrance, you shall be taken in them. [25]And you, O unhallowed wicked one, prince of Israel, whose day has come, the time of your final punishment, [26]thus says the Lord GOD: Remove the turban, and take off the crown; things shall not remain as they are; exalt that which is low, and abase that which is high. [27]A ruin, ruin, ruin I will make it; there shall not be even a trace of it until he comes whose right it is; and to him I will give it.

[28]"And you, son of man, prophesy, and say, Thus says the Lord GOD concerning the Ammonites, and concerning their reproach; say, A sword, a sword is drawn for the slaughter, it is polished to glitter and to flash like lightning— [29]while they see for you false visions, while they make up lies for you—to be laid on the necks of the unhallowed wicked, whose day has come, the time of their final punishment. [30]Return it to its sheath. In the place where you were created, in the land of your origin, I will judge you. [31]And I will pour out my indignation upon you; I will blow upon you with the fire of my wrath; and I will deliver you into the hands of brutal men, skilful to destroy. [32]You shall be fuel for the fire; your blood shall be in the midst of the land; you shall be no more remembered; for I the LORD have spoken."

OT: Gen 49:10
Catechism: God's punishment and judgment of sin, 211, 679, 1472–73, 2054

Moving from poetry to prose narrative, Ezekiel now adds a prophetic action　21:18–23 to his words of judgment. He is told to draw a map in the dirt with two possible routes **for the sword of the king of Babylon to come.** One leads to the city of Rabbah in the land of the Ammonites; the other goes directly toward Jerusalem.[19] As depicted by Ezekiel, Nebuchadnezzar stands at this crossroads, unsure where to attack first, and he employs three methods of †divination to determine the route appointed by the gods: the shaking out of arrows, inquiry of the gods, and the examination of animal livers. The lot falls to Jerusalem, and so Nebuchadnezzar accosts the Holy City, **to set battering rams against the gates, to cast up mounds, to build siege towers.**

The precise details of verses 24–27 are unclear, but the overall sense of the　21:24–27 message is plain: because of the people's guilt, God will bring punishment upon them and their prince (probably Zedekiah). Their **day has come, the time** of

19. The city of Rabbah, the site of modern-day Amman, is twenty-three miles east of the Jordan River. It is the only Ammonite city named in the Bible, and it sits on the "King's Highway," the major travel route through the land.

their **final punishment**. The Lord will **exalt that which is low, and abase that which is high**, bringing destruction upon the city: **a ruin, ruin, ruin I will make it**. The final line, **there shall not be even a trace of it until he comes whose right it is; and to him I will give it**, points to the coming of a ruler who is the rightful king authorized by God.

This may be an ironic reference to Nebuchadnezzar himself, who is enlisted in the present time as the Lord's own agent to punish his people, but more likely Ezekiel is intentionally making reference to Gen 49:10, a passage well known for describing the future coming of the †messianic king from the tribe of Judah: "The scepter shall not depart from Judah, nor the ruler's staff from between his feet, until he comes to whom it belongs."[20]

21:28–32   The final section of the chapter is difficult to unravel. It concerns the Ammonites, and it probably refers to their taunt against Judah because the **sword** of Nebuchadnezzar had been **drawn for the slaughter** against Judah.[21] Finally, in verses 30–32, the sword that was "drawn for the slaughter" is returned **to its sheath**. This is probably a veiled reference to Nebuchadnezzar and his conquering armies returning home after laying waste Judah and Jerusalem. If so, the Lord God is promising that the conqueror will himself be punished in the land of his origin for wreaking violence upon God's people.

Jerusalem, the City of Bloodshed (22:1–16)

[1]Moreover the word of the LORD came to me, saying, [2]"And you, son of man, will you judge, will you judge the bloody city? Then declare to her all her abominable deeds. [3]You shall say, Thus says the Lord GOD: A city that sheds blood in the midst of her, that her time may come, and that makes idols to defile herself! [4]You have become guilty by the blood which you have shed, and defiled by the idols which you have made; and you have brought your day near, the appointed time of your years has come. Therefore I have made you a reproach to the nations, and a mocking to all the countries. [5]Those who are near and those who are far from you will mock you, you infamous one, full of tumult.

[6]"Behold, the princes of Israel in you, every one according to his power, have been bent on shedding blood. [7]Father and mother are treated with contempt in you; the sojourner suffers extortion in your midst; the fatherless and the widow are wronged in you. [8]You have despised my holy things,

20. Both of these interpretations appear in the Jewish rabbis and are supported by modern scholars. See Moshe Greenberg, *Ezekiel 21–37*, Anchor Bible 22A (New York: Doubleday, 1997), 434–35; Block, *Ezekiel: Chapters 1–24*, 692–93.

21. Some see this oracle as a prophecy against the Ammonites, anticipating the fuller oracle in Ezek 25:1–7. The Ammonite kingdom, lying to the northeast of Israel, was eventually absorbed by "the people of the East" (25:4), probably a reference to desert nomads.

and profaned my sabbaths. ⁹There are men in you who slander to shed blood, and men in you who eat upon the mountains; men commit lewdness in your midst. ¹⁰In you men uncover their fathers' nakedness; in you they humble women who are unclean in their impurity. ¹¹One commits abomination with his neighbor's wife; another lewdly defiles his daughter-in-law; another in you defiles his sister, his father's daughter. ¹²In you men take bribes to shed blood; you take interest and increase and make gain of your neighbors by extortion; and you have forgotten me, says the Lord God.

¹³"Behold, therefore, I strike my hands together at the dishonest gain which you have made, and at the blood which has been in the midst of you. ¹⁴Can your courage endure, or can your hands be strong, in the days that I shall deal with you? I the LORD have spoken, and I will do it. ¹⁵I will scatter you among the nations and disperse you through the countries, and I will consume your filthiness out of you. ¹⁶And I shall be profaned through you in the sight of the nations; and you shall know that I am the LORD."

OT: Lev 18–19; 26:33; Deut 28:64; Nah 3:1
NT: Matt 22:39; Mark 12:31; Luke 10:27
Catechism: God's punishment and judgment of sin, 211, 679, 1472–73, 2054

Ezekiel resumes his prophetic judgments against Israel, now focused on the sin of "shedding blood." Although living in exile in Babylon, Ezekiel directs most of his prophesying toward those living in the land of Israel and the city of Jerusalem. This is because the Lord's message of judgment largely concerns those still living in the land—this is where the judgment will fall. It is possible that summaries of Ezekiel's message were communicated to the people living in Israel. If so, then indirectly he was able to speak to the people living in the land.

In this opening prophetic oracle, Jerusalem—called **the bloody city**—is ar- **22:1–6**
raigned for the double crime of being **a city that sheds blood . . . and that makes idols to defile herself**.²² The expression to "shed blood" means "to commit murder," to take human life unlawfully.²³ Twice more Ezekiel will sum up Israel's major crimes in terms of "shedding blood" and "making idols" (see Ezek 23:37; 36:18). In verse 6, the focus narrows in on the **princes of Israel** who **have been bent on shedding blood**. "The princes" are probably the offspring

---

22. Jerusalem will be called "the bloody city" twice more in Ezekiel (Ezek 24:6, 9). The title "bloody city" is also used by the prophet Nahum to describe Nineveh (Nah 3:1). For the bloodguilt of Israel, see also Ezek 7:23; 9:9.

23. John F. Kutsko, *Between Heaven and Earth: Divine Presence and Absence in the Book of Ezekiel* (Winona Lake, IN: Eisenbrauns, 1999), 71. For Old Testament examples in which "shedding blood" refers to the unlawful taking of a human life, see Gen 9:6; 37:22; Num 35:33; Deut 21:7; 1 Sam 25:31; Ps 79:3; Prov 1:16.

Ezekiel and the Holiness Code

BIBLICAL BACKGROUND

Ezekiel's many allusions to Leviticus—a book focused on priestly identity and practice—confirm Ezekiel's priestly background (see Ezek 1:3). The catalogue of sins in Ezek 22:7–12 is closely correlated to the teaching of the †Holiness Code, found in Lev 17–26, especially chapters 18–19. The following are the sins catalogued by Ezekiel with their counterpart in Lev 18–19: (1) treating father and mother with contempt (Lev 19:3); (2) extortion of one's neighbor, injustice to the sojourner, loaning money at interest (Lev 19:13, 33–36); (3) profaning the sabbath (Lev 19:3, 30); (4) slandering one's neighbor (Lev 19:16); (5) sins of idolatry (Lev 19:4); and (6) various practices against sexual purity (Lev 18:6–20).

Notably, the Holiness Code contains the often-repeated refrain that expresses the *positive* purpose of all these individual commandments: "You shall be holy; for I the Lord your God am holy" (Lev 19:2). Jesus himself refers to a passage from Lev 19 to sum up the second of the great commandments: "You shall love your neighbor as yourself" (Lev 19:18; see Matt 22:39; Mark 12:31; Luke 10:27). The call to holiness, summed up in the commandment to love God and neighbor, remains an essential part of life in the kingdom of God.

of Josiah, but Ezekiel may also have in mind wicked kings who came earlier in the history of Judah.

22:7–16   In verses 7–12, Ezekiel then catalogues the individual sins that the princes and the people have committed. There is no clear thematic order to this string of transgressions. Ezekiel names specific offenses—largely drawn from the lists of transgressions in Lev 18–19—that emphasize two forms of wrongdoing: economic oppression of the vulnerable (sojourners, widows, orphans) and sexual immorality of all kinds. Preferring their sinful practices, the people have disregarded the Lord and his ways: **you have forgotten me, says the Lord God**. Echoing the language of the †covenant curses (Lev 26:33; Deut 28:64), the Lord then declares (vv. 13–16) the punishment that will fall upon them: **I will scatter you among the nations and disperse you through the countries, and I will consume your filthiness out of you**. The people of Israel shall be the cause of their own disgrace among the nations because they have neglected the Lord himself and his commandments that he gave them to follow.[24]

24. The meaning of v. 16, "And I shall be profaned through you in the sight of the nations," is contested. The RSV-2CE follows the Greek, Syriac, and Latin versions (in which God is the one who is profaned), but the Hebrew has "And *you* shall be profaned . . . ," referring to the people as the ones profaned. The rabbis followed the Hebrew text, as do some contemporary translations (ESV) and commentators (Block, *Ezekiel: Chapters 1–24*, 712–13; Greenberg, *Ezekiel 21–37*, 457–58).

Israel, Corrupt and under Judgment (22:17–31)

¹⁷And the word of the LORD came to me: ¹⁸"Son of man, the house of Israel has become dross to me; all of them, silver and bronze and tin and iron and lead in the furnace, have become dross. ¹⁹Therefore thus says the Lord GOD: Because you have all become dross, therefore, behold, I will gather you into the midst of Jerusalem. ²⁰As men gather silver and bronze and iron and lead and tin into a furnace, to blow the fire upon it in order to melt it; so I will gather you in my anger and in my wrath, and I will put you in and melt you. ²¹I will gather you and blow upon you with the fire of my wrath, and you shall be melted in the midst of it. ²²As silver is melted in a furnace, so you shall be melted in the midst of it; and you shall know that I the LORD have poured out my wrath upon you."

²³And the word of the LORD came to me: ²⁴"Son of man, say to her, You are a land that is not cleansed, or rained upon in the day of indignation. ²⁵Her princes in the midst of her are like a roaring lion tearing the prey; they have devoured human lives; they have taken treasure and precious things; they have made many widows in the midst of her. ²⁶Her priests have done violence to my law and have profaned my holy things; they have made no distinction between the holy and the common, neither have they taught the difference between the unclean and the clean, and they have disregarded my sabbaths, so that I am profaned among them. ²⁷Her princes in the midst of her are like wolves tearing the prey, shedding blood, destroying lives to get dishonest gain. ²⁸And her prophets have daubed for them with whitewash, seeing false visions and making up lies for them, saying, 'Thus says the Lord GOD,' when the LORD has not spoken. ²⁹The people of the land have practiced extortion and committed robbery; they have oppressed the poor and needy, and have extorted from the sojourner without redress. ³⁰And I sought for a man among them who should build up the wall and stand in the breach before me for the land, that I should not destroy it; but I found none. ³¹Therefore I have poured out my indignation upon them; I have consumed them with the fire of my wrath; their way have I repaid upon their heads, says the Lord GOD."

OT: Gen 18; Ps 106:23; Isa 1:25; Jer 5:1; Zech 13:9; Mal 3:3
NT: Luke 23:34; Rom 5:8–10; Heb 7:25
Catechism: God's punishment and judgment of sin, 211, 679, 1472–73, 2054; the ministry of intercession, 1368–69, 2577, 2593, 2634–36

In this closing section of the chapter, Ezekiel sums up the Lord's case against his people. In the first part (vv. 17–22), the Lord says that he is going to melt down the dross of his people in the furnace of his just judgment. In the second part (vv. 23–29), the Lord lays out his case against his people, presenting in detail the sins that they have already committed. In the third and final part (vv. 30–31), the Lord looks for a righteous person to stand in the breach but finds no one. The closing line speaks in the past tense about the Lord having poured out his judgment. This is best understood as a promise of what is about to come, spoken in the past tense to communicate the certainty of the Lord's judgment of his people.

22:17–22   Ezekiel now employs a new and different metaphor for the Lord's just anger against his people: they are like the **dross** (the cast-off waste) from purified metal (silver, bronze, tin, lead). The Lord says he will gather his people, like worthless dross, **into the midst of Jerusalem** and melt them in **the fire of** his **wrath**. The image of purifying metal through the smelting process is found elsewhere in the Old Testament to describe the purification from sin (Isa 1:25; 48:10; Zech 13:9; Mal 3:3). But following Jeremiah (6:28–30), Ezekiel employs this image not so much for purification but for judgment and destruction, as Moshe Greenberg observes: "Here, as elsewhere in Ezekiel, fire is not a purifying but a destructive force."[25] The people within the Holy City shall simply be melted down in the fire of God's coming judgment.

22:23–29   In this section, Ezekiel charges all ranks of people within Israel—*princes, priests, prophets, and people*—with grave wrongdoing.[26] **Her princes**, like a roaring lion, have conspired to devour human lives and have seized the property of others.[27] **Her priests** have done violence to the law, they have profaned the holy things of God (the sabbath), and they **have made no distinction between the holy and the common**. In summary, they have failed to lead the people in the way of holiness. **Her princes** (once again) are like wolves who have shed the blood of the people for dishonest gain. **Her prophets** have seen false visions and have lied to the people. Finally, **the people of the land** have practiced extortion and robbery and have oppressed the poor and the sojourner.[28]

22:30–31   Tragically, the Lord says that he sought for an upright person, an intercessor, who would stand before the Lord on behalf of the people—but the Lord found no one: **I sought for a man among them who should build up the wall and stand in the breach before me for the land, that I should not destroy it; but I found none.** Jeremiah also laments the absence of upright people in the city on whose account the people might be spared: "Run back and forth through the streets of Jerusalem, / look and take note! / Search her squares to see / if you can find a man, / one who does justice / and seeks truth; / that I may pardon her" (Jer 5:1). The Lord is grieved because he could find no righteous person—no

---

25. Greenberg, *Ezekiel 21–37*, 468.

26. See Ezek 7:26–27 for a similar catalogue of groups within Israel. In a similar way, Jeremiah speaks against the priests, prophets, and the people (5:30–31; 6:13).

27. The Hebrew version has "prophets" here, reflected in the ESV and Jewish Publication Society translation; the Greek version identifies this first group as "rulers" (and so "princes"), reflected in the RSV-2CE, NRSV, and NABRE translations.

28. Ezekiel's naming of different kinds of metal that are to be smelted down—bronze, tin, iron, lead, and silver (vv. 18, 20)—may be a symbolic reference to these distinct classes of people within Israel. For the identity of the "sojourner" in Israel, see the sidebar "The 'Sojourner' in Israel," p. 110.

prophet, priest, or prince—who was ready to stand in the breach and turn away the coming judgment of the Lord.[29]

Reflection and Application (22:30)

It is shocking to hear that the Lord searched far and wide for *one righteous person* who would stand before him "in the breach" on behalf of the city and the land—but he found no one! Neither Jeremiah nor Ezekiel could find such a person among all the ranks of the people. Standing in the gap—in the breach—is an image of the person who pleads for mercy on behalf of another. Abraham famously negotiated with the Lord to save the wicked cities of Sodom and Gomorrah if only ten righteous people could be found there—but they were not to be found (Gen 18). Moses interceded more successfully before the Lord—he "stood in the breach before him" (Ps 106:23)—to spare the people of Israel after they had worshiped the golden calf. Jesus himself is the great intercessor. Looking upon those who were putting him to death unjustly, he appealed to his Father: "Father, forgive them; for they know not what they do" (Luke 23:34). He offered his life in our place even though we were his enemies (Rom 5:8–10), and we now have an intercessor who "always lives to make intercession" for us (Heb 7:25).

But we are not just the beneficiaries of Christ's intercession. We, too, are called "in Christ" to stand in the breach and pray for God's mercy: for the Church, for our nation, and for the world. We are *participants* now with Christ, members of his body, who are called to "build up" and pray for God's mercy. There is great need for such intercessors. When he searches, may the Lord find many among us who "stand in the breach" before him, who with and in Christ call down his mercy on those in need.

The Unfaithfulness of Israel: Oholah and Oholibah (23:1–21)

¹The word of the LORD came to me: ²"Son of man, there were two women, the daughters of one mother; ³they played the harlot in Egypt; they played the harlot in their youth; there their breasts were pressed and their virgin bosoms handled. ⁴Oholah was the name of the elder and Oholibah the name of her sister. They became mine, and they bore sons and daughters. As for their names, Oholah is Samaria, and Oholibah is Jerusalem.

29. The question arises whether Ezekiel's older contemporary, the prophet Jeremiah, would not have qualified as a "righteous person" who was to be found in the city. As John B. Taylor observes, "Presumably Jeremiah was an exception to Ezekiel's general condemnation, but he had no kingly status and few listened to his words." *Ezekiel: An Introduction and Commentary*, Tyndale Old Testament Commentaries (Downers Grove, IL: InterVarsity, 1969), 170.

⁵"Oholah played the harlot while she was mine; and she doted on her lovers the Assyrians, ⁶warriors clothed in purple, governors and commanders, all of them desirable young men, horsemen riding on horses. ⁷She bestowed her harlotries upon them, the choicest men of Assyria all of them; and she defiled herself with all the idols of every one on whom she doted. ⁸She did not give up her harlotry which she had practiced since her days in Egypt; for in her youth men had lain with her and handled her virgin bosom and poured out their lust upon her. ⁹Therefore I delivered her into the hands of her lovers, into the hands of the Assyrians, upon whom she doted. ¹⁰These uncovered her nakedness; they seized her sons and her daughters; and her they slew with the sword; and she became a byword among women, when judgment had been executed upon her.

¹¹"Her sister Oholibah saw this, yet she was more corrupt than she in her doting and in her harlotry, which was worse than that of her sister. ¹²She doted upon the Assyrians, governors and commanders, warriors clothed in full armor, horsemen riding on horses, all of them desirable young men. ¹³And I saw that she was defiled; they both took the same way. ¹⁴But she carried her harlotry further; she saw men portrayed upon the wall, the images of the Chaldeans portrayed in vermilion, ¹⁵with belts around their waists, with flowing turbans on their heads, all of them looking like officers, a picture of Babylonians whose native land was Chaldea. ¹⁶When she saw them she doted upon them, and sent messengers to them in Chaldea. ¹⁷And the Babylonians came to her into the bed of love, and they defiled her with their lust; and after she was polluted by them, she turned from them in disgust. ¹⁸When she carried on her harlotry so openly and flaunted her nakedness, I turned in disgust from her, as I had turned from her sister. ¹⁹Yet she increased her harlotry, remembering the days of her youth, when she played the harlot in the land of Egypt ²⁰and doted upon her paramours there, whose members were like those of donkeys, and whose issue was like that of horses. ²¹Thus you longed for the lewdness of your youth, when the Egyptians handled your bosom and pressed your young breasts."

OT: 2 Kings 16:8; 17:1–6; Isa 10:10–11; Jer 3:6–11
Catechism: God's punishment and judgment of sin, 211, 679, 1472–73, 2054; the sin of idolatry, 2112–14

Chapter 23 presents an extended allegory in which the northern and southern kingdoms (Israel and Judah) are cast as two sisters, both from Egypt, who have become serial prostitutes deserving of judgment. In this allegory, Ezekiel is especially critical of the various political alliances Israel and Judah have made. These alliances demonstrate infidelity to the Lord since they entail Israel and Judah placing their reliance on other nations and their gods.[30] Ezekiel appears

---

30. Jenson, *Ezekiel*, 191, concludes that despite the prominence of sexual imagery, the allegory in this chapter is "strictly political."

to be taking his cue from the prophet Jeremiah (Jer 3:6–11), who identified the northern and southern kingdoms as two adulterous sisters. In Jeremiah's narrative, after the first sister (faithless Israel) was destroyed because of her infidelity, the second sister (false Judah) did even worse things and is now primed for judgment. Ezekiel's allegory tells the same story in greater detail.

Ezekiel begins by narrating the story of two sisters, Oholah and Oholibah,   23:1–4
who both **played the harlot in Egypt**, though they were wedded to the Lord and bore him sons and daughters. To "play the harlot" in this case was to engage in idolatry (see Ezek 16:20–22). We are told that the first sister, Oholah, represents Samaria, the capital city of the north; the second sister, Oholibah, represents Jerusalem, the capital city of the south.[31] In Hebrew, "Oholah" means "her tent" while "Oholibah" means "my tent is in her." Given that the two sisters represent Samaria and Jerusalem, "her tent" may refer to the idolatrous sanctuary at Shechem in the north, while "my tent is in her" may point to the true sanctuary (temple) of the Lord in Jerusalem. Here and throughout the allegory Ezekiel displays the political and religious conduct of the two sisters in vivid, graphic sexual imagery.[32] According to Moshe Eisemann, "It is as though the prophet understood that a time had come in which the only hope of reaching the people lay in tearing aside the cushioning layers of acceptable language and exposing them brutally to the depths of their degradation."[33]

In verses 5–10, Ezekiel tells the sordid story of Oholah. She **doted on her**   23:5–10
lovers the Assyrians and defiled herself with their idols. These acts of idolatry are characterized in terms of lewd sexual promiscuity. In turn, Assyria punished its former lover, **seized her sons and her daughters** and **slew** her **with the sword**. This brief allegory depicts the historical alliance of the northern kingdom with the Assyrian Empire and the destruction and exile that Assyria brought upon the northern kingdom in 722 BC. The allegory passes over the actual historical cause of this destruction—namely, the revolt by the northern kingdom from Assyria (2 Kings 17:1–6).

Ezekiel continues the allegory by turning to the second sister, Oholibah   23:11–21
(who represents Jerusalem). Ezekiel continues to use the imagery of prostitution and sexual lust to depict Jerusalem's alliances with the Assyrians and the Babylonians, characterized by worship of foreign deities. According to the allegory, Oholibah witnessed her sister's unfaithfulness and its consequences, but instead of repenting she carried on with her own prostitution **worse than that of her sister**. Like her sibling, **she doted upon the Assyrians** (2 Kings

---

31. This identification of the two sisters is similar to the allegory presented in chap. 16, where Ezekiel names Samaria and Sodom as the two unfaithful "sisters" of Jerusalem. The prophet Isaiah (10:10–11) also designates "Jerusalem and Samaria" as the two centers of idolatry in the land.

32. †*Targum of Ezekiel* retains the metaphor of two sisters and the language of love/marriage but removes all explicit sexual imagery and makes idolatry the primary sin. Levey, *Targum of Ezekiel*, 70–74.

33. Eisemann, *Ezekiel*, 388.

16:8)—that is, Jerusalem gave herself to the gods of the Assyrians—but then turned her attentions even more flagrantly to the Babylonians. When she grew disgusted with them—that is, when she broke her alliance with Babylon—she returned to the place of her birth and carried on her immorality, her covenant unfaithfulness, with the nation of Egypt. The response of the Lord to this long and serial pattern of idolatrous unfaithfulness is "disgust": **I turned in disgust from her, as I had turned from her sister.**

Judgment Pronounced against Oholibah (23:22–35)

²²Therefore, O Oholibah, thus says the Lord GOD: "Behold, I will rouse against you your lovers from whom you turned in disgust, and I will bring them against you from every side: ²³the Babylonians and all the Chaldeans, Pekod and Shoa and Koa, and all the Assyrians with them, desirable young men, governors and commanders all of them, officers and warriors, all of them riding on horses. ²⁴And they shall come against you from the north with chariots and wagons and a host of peoples; they shall set themselves against you on every side with buckler, shield, and helmet, and I will commit the judgment to them, and they shall judge you according to their judgments. ²⁵And I will direct my indignation against you, that they may deal with you in fury. They shall cut off your nose and your ears, and your survivors shall fall by the sword. They shall seize your sons and your daughters, and your survivors shall be devoured by fire. ²⁶They shall also strip you of your clothes and take away your fine jewels. ²⁷Thus I will put an end to your lewdness and your harlotry brought from the land of Egypt; so that you shall not lift up your eyes to the Egyptians or remember them any more. ²⁸For thus says the Lord GOD: Behold, I will deliver you into the hands of those whom you hate, into the hands of those from whom you turned in disgust; ²⁹and they shall deal with you in hatred, and take away all the fruit of your labor, and leave you naked and bare, and the nakedness of your harlotry shall be uncovered. Your lewdness and your harlotry ³⁰have brought this upon you, because you played the harlot with the nations, and polluted yourself with their idols. ³¹You have gone the way of your sister; therefore I will give her cup into your hand. ³²Thus says the Lord GOD:

> "You shall drink your sister's cup
>   which is deep and large;
> you shall be laughed at and held in derision,
>   for it contains much;
> ³³you will be filled with drunkenness and sorrow.
> A cup of horror and desolation,
>   is the cup of your sister Samaria;

³⁴you shall drink it and drain it out,
    and pluck out your hair,
    and tear your breasts;

for I have spoken, says the Lord God. ³⁵Therefore thus says the Lord God:
Because you have forgotten me and cast me behind your back, therefore
bear the consequences of your lewdness and harlotry."

OT: Isa 31:1; 51:17; Jer 2:18; Hosea 7:11; Hab 2:15–17; Zech 12:2
NT: Rev 14:10; 16:19
Catechism: God's punishment and judgment of sin, 211, 679, 1472–73, 2054; the sin of idolatry, 2112–14

And so the Lord's judgment will now fall upon the second sister, Oholibah,   **23:22–30**
who represents Jerusalem. **I will rouse against you your lovers from whom
you turned in disgust, and I will bring them against you from every side.** All
her former paramours (Babylon, Assyria, and others) will oppose Jerusalem
and besiege her. The metaphor of the unfaithful wife recedes in verses 22–25,
while the reality of military siege comes into the foreground: **they shall come
against you from the north with chariots and wagons and a host of peoples.**
These nations will punish Oholibah (Jerusalem) with the sword and devour the
city and its people with fire.

Then in verses 26–30, the imagery of sexual infidelity returns to center stage.
The attack by the surrounding nations will **put an end** to the **lewdness** and
harlotry of this unfaithful sister. Jerusalem, the unfaithful spouse, will be left
naked and bare because she **played the harlot with the nations, and polluted**
herself **with their idols.**

The imagery now shifts to drinking a cup of judgment. The Lord promises   **23:31–35**
Oholibah that, because of her infidelities, she will drink the cup of her sister,
Oholah: **you shall drink your sister's cup / which is deep and large.** This **cup
of horror and desolation** will be manifested historically in the sack and exile
of the city of Jerusalem.³⁴ All this will come upon faithless Jerusalem, says the
Lord, **because you have forgotten me and cast me behind your back.** The
kings and princes who engaged in these political alliances with the surrounding
nations presumably justified them as strategic coalitions that were necessary to
preserve the nation from destruction. The Lord, however, sees these alliances
very differently. Repeatedly through the prophets the Lord told Israel's leaders to refrain from these pacts with the nations, because they proceeded from
lack of trust in the Lord to provide for his people. Isaiah questioned why they
were running to Egypt for help instead of relying on the Lord: "Woe to those
who go down to Egypt for help / and rely on horses, . . . / but do not look to

---

34. The metaphor of "drinking a cup" is commonly used by the prophets to give a graphic description of the judgment of God for sin and idolatry. See Isa 51:17, 22; Jer 25:15–17; Hab 2:15–17; Zech
12:2. The book of Revelation (14:10; 16:19) also uses this metaphor to portray the judgment of God.

the Holy One of Israel or consult the LORD!" (Isa 31:1).[35] For Israel, a nation specially called into being by the Lord, these shifting political alliances are acts of infidelity to the covenant between God and his people. Israel abandoned its first love and sold itself to other lovers.

Summation of the Case against Oholah and Oholibah (23:36–49)

[36]The LORD said to me: "Son of man, will you judge Oholah and Oholibah? Then declare to them their abominable deeds. [37]For they have committed adultery, and blood is upon their hands; with their idols they have committed adultery; and they have even offered up to them for food the sons whom they had borne to me. [38]Moreover this they have done to me: they have defiled my sanctuary on the same day and profaned my sabbaths. [39]For when they had slaughtered their children in sacrifice to their idols, on the same day they came into my sanctuary to profane it. And behold, this is what they did in my house. [40]They even sent for men to come from far, to whom a messenger was sent, and behold, they came. For them you bathed yourself, painted your eyes, and decked yourself with ornaments; [41]you sat upon a stately couch, with a table spread before it on which you had placed my incense and my oil. [42]The sound of a carefree multitude was with her; and with men of the common sort drunkards were brought from the wilderness; and they put bracelets upon the hands of the women, and beautiful crowns upon their heads.

[43]"Then I said, Do not men now commit adultery when they practice harlotry with her? [44]For they have gone in to her, as men go in to a harlot. Thus they went in to Oholah and to Oholibah to commit lewdness. [45]But righteous men shall pass judgment on them with the sentence of adulteresses, and with the sentence of women that shed blood; because they are adulteresses, and blood is upon their hands."

[46]For thus says the Lord GOD: "Bring up a host against them, and make them an object of terror and a spoil. [47]And the host shall stone them and dispatch them with their swords; they shall slay their sons and their daughters, and burn up their houses. [48]Thus will I put an end to lewdness in the land, that all women may take warning and not commit lewdness as you have done. [49]And your lewdness shall be repaid upon you, and you shall bear the penalty for your sinful idolatry; and you shall know that I am the Lord GOD."

OT: Isa 54:5, 8; Hosea 2:16, 19–20
NT: Rev 21:2–3
Catechism: God's punishment and judgment of sin, 211, 679, 1472–73, 2054; the sin of idolatry, 2112–14

---

35. For the prophetic critique of Israel running to foreign nations for help, see also Jer 2:18; Hosea 7:11.

The final section of the allegory (vv. 36–49), which poses significant challenges for the interpreter,[36] presents a summation of the case against the two sisters, Oholah and Oholibah. At the same time, Ezekiel really zeroes in on the second sister, who represents Jerusalem.[37] The allegory is about both sisters (Samaria and Jerusalem), but the northern kingdom had already been defeated and its people taken away into exile more than a century before. The point of this section, according to Moshe Greenberg, is that "Oholibah's addiction to infidelity, in which she outstripped her sister, will bring down on her devastation more terrible than her sister's."[38] The focus, therefore, is Jerusalem in the present time, who has followed in the errant ways of her northern sister, Samaria.

Ezekiel is told to **declare to them their abominable deeds**. And so he lists   23:36–39
the sins of the two sisters: they have practiced idolatry, the worship of false gods (v. 37); they have committed a further abomination by offering their children by fire to these gods, brazenly appearing in the Lord's own sanctuary on the day they offer their children (vv. 37, 39); they have broken the sabbath commandment (v. 38); and they have consorted with foreign leaders, engaging in alliances that display lack of trust in the Lord (vv. 40–42).[39]

Ezekiel highlights (again) the wanton and seductive practices of the two   23:40–45
sisters. The nations treated them as nothing more than harlots, and **thus they went in to Oholah and to Oholibah to commit lewdness**. In response, **righteous men shall pass judgment on them** for their unfaithful practices. Who are these "righteous men"? Some commentators identify them with the nations (Assyria and Babylon), but more likely they are a righteous remnant in Israel represented by figures such as Ezekiel and Jeremiah.

The statement in verse 48, **thus will I put an end to lewdness in the land,**   23:46–49
that all women may take warning and not commit lewdness as you have done, seems to step away from the primary allegory and offer a moral lesson for women in general. In the allegory, the two sisters represent two cities whose faithless, disobedient leaders are primarily men (kings, princes, priests, and prophets). Throughout this extended allegory, Ezekiel mainly has Israel's male leaders in his sights; they are the primary offenders who need to repent. But here, attention is turned to "all women," who may learn from this allegory to avoid *actual* adultery and prostitution because of the great harm and judgment that it brings. Here Ezekiel is not accusing the women of his day (or women

36. Greenberg (*Ezekiel 21–37*, 490) describes this section as "remarkable for its incoherence, its linguistic oddities, and the disconcerting changes in number and person." Jenson (*Ezekiel*, 195) calls it simply "a literary and logical chaos."

37. At points in this section, the third-person *plural* address to the two sisters (they, them) is succeeded by the second-person *singular* address (you, vv. 40–41), possibly indicating that the main target of criticism is really the second sister, Oholibah, representing Jerusalem.

38. Greenberg, *Ezekiel 21–37*, 491.

39. For the sin of offering up children in the fire to false gods, see the commentary on Ezek 16:15–34 and the sidebar "Child Sacrifice in Israel," p. 123.

in general) of being seductive or adulterous; he concludes the allegory by calling women, like the men he has primarily been addressing, to be upright and faithful to the Lord.

The chapter concludes where it began: with a prediction of the dire punishment that lies in store for the faithless sisters, Samaria and Jerusalem. The phrase **sinful idolatry** in the closing verse captures the heart of the chapter: God's people, both north and south, have proved perennially unfaithful to the Lord through their constant practice of idolatry and now must **bear the penalty** of their sin.

Reflection and Application (23:1–49)

The graphic sexual language of this chapter has shocked its readers from ancient times up until today. Because of explicit references to sexual acts and body parts, as well as sexual violence, Ezek 23 was not considered appropriate for normal reading in the traditional Jewish community, especially among the young. But concerns have also been raised about the sexual violence against women that chapter 23 depicts and (in the eyes of some readers) justifies. Corrine Patton, however, concludes that "this is not a text that portrays sexual violence against women as a good thing. The metaphor would not work if the male audience were not shocked."[40] Furthermore, it is not the Lord God who carries out this violence against the sisters (see especially vv. 26–29), but the nations that they consorted with. The irony is that, though the people and the city are portrayed allegorically as unfaithful women, those actually charged with the major crimes are men (kings, princes, prophets, elders). Patton concludes: "This text does not substantiate domestic abuse; and scholars, teachers, and preachers must continue to remind uninformed readers that such an interpretation is actually a misreading."[41]

It is important to recognize that the positive image, standing in the background to this chapter, is the faithful marriage covenant between God and his people. This is what God seeks in his relationship with his people. This image of the marriage covenant is expressed profoundly by the prophets. Isaiah, for example, beautifully paints the deliverance of Israel in terms of the Lord restoring a cast-off wife: "For your Maker is your husband, / the LORD of hosts is his name. . . . / In overflowing wrath for a moment / I hid my face from you, / but with everlasting mercy I will have compassion on you, / says the LORD, your Redeemer" (Isa 54:5, 8). Hosea likewise portrays God speaking tenderly to his

---

40. Corrine L. Patton, "'Should Our Sister Be Treated like a Whore?' A Response to Feminist Critiques of Ezekiel 23," in *The Book of Ezekiel: Theological and Anthropological Perspectives*, ed. Margaret S. Odell and John T. Strong (Atlanta: Society of Biblical Literature, 2000), 232.

41. Patton, "Should Our Sister Be Treated like a Whore?," 238.

people, as to his beloved bride: "And in that day, says the LORD, you will call me, 'My husband.' . . . And I will espouse you for ever; I will espouse you in righteousness and in justice, in steadfast love, and in mercy. I will espouse you in faithfulness" (Hosea 2:16, 19–20). In the same way, the grand finale of the book of Revelation portrays eternal life through the image of Jesus coming to dwell with his bride, the Holy City and its people: "And I saw the holy city, new Jerusalem, coming down out of heaven from God, prepared as a bride adorned for her husband" (Rev 21:2). The tragic and calamitous failure of God's people to remain faithful to the Lord in Ezekiel's day underlines the great destiny of the people of God, to be forever wedded to the Lord God in love and holiness.

The End Is at Hand

Ezekiel 24:1–27

With this chapter, the first main section of the book concludes. It brings us to the brink of God's judgment—namely, the siege of Jerusalem by the Babylonians—and prepares the reader for the imminent destruction of the city. There are three distinct parts to chapter 24. The first part (vv. 1–14) opens with the date when Jerusalem was besieged and promises that the city will be consumed by fire. The second part (vv. 15–24) recounts the death of Ezekiel's wife and the Lord's command that he is not to mourn outwardly for her. The third and final part (vv. 25–27) speaks of a day soon to come when a messenger will arrive among the exiles announcing the fall of the Holy City.

The Siege Is Begun: Israel Will Be Consumed (24:1–14)

¹In the ninth year, in the tenth month, on the tenth day of the month, the word of the LORD came to me: ²"Son of man, write down the name of this day, this very day. The king of Babylon has laid siege to Jerusalem this very day. ³And utter an allegory to the rebellious house and say to them, Thus says the Lord GOD:

> Set on the pot, set it on,
>   pour in water also;
> ⁴put in it the pieces of flesh,
>   all the good pieces, the thigh and the shoulder;
>   fill it with choice bones.
> ⁵Take the choicest one of the flock,
>   pile the logs under it;
> boil its pieces,
>   seethe also its bones in it.

⁶"Therefore thus says the Lord GOD: Woe to the bloody city, to the pot whose rust is in it, and whose rust has not gone out of it! Take out of it piece after piece, without making any choice. ⁷For the blood she has shed is still in the midst of her; she put it on the bare rock, she did not pour it upon the ground to cover it with dust. ⁸To rouse my wrath, to take vengeance, I have set on the bare rock the blood she has shed, that it may not be covered. ⁹Therefore thus says the Lord GOD: Woe to the bloody city! I also will make the pile great. ¹⁰Heap on the logs, kindle the fire, boil well the flesh, and empty out the broth, and let the bones be burned up. ¹¹Then set it empty upon the coals, that it may become hot, and its copper may burn, that its filthiness may be melted in it, its rust consumed. ¹²In vain I have wearied myself; its thick rust does not go out of it by fire. ¹³Its rust is your filthy lewdness. Because I would have cleansed you and you were not cleansed from your filthiness, you shall not be cleansed any more till I have satisfied my fury upon you. ¹⁴I the LORD have spoken; it shall come to pass, I will do it; I will not go back, I will not spare, I will not repent; according to your ways and your doings I will judge you, says the Lord GOD."

OT: Lev 17:3; 2 Kings 25:1; Jer 39:1–2; 52:4; Zech 8:19
NT: Luke 19:41–44
Catechism: God's punishment and judgment of sin, 211, 679, 1472–73, 2054; sin manifested in violence, 1851

This prophetic †oracle begins with the date on which the city of Jerusalem was   **24:1–2** besieged by Nebuchadnezzar: **the ninth year, in the tenth month, on the tenth day of the month** (January 5, 588 BC).[1] This day was "seared indelibly upon Israel's consciousness" and became the first of the four fast days observed by Israel during the coming exile and beyond.[2] Ezekiel of course is in Babylon, far from the siege of the city, but the Lord reveals to him prophetically what is taking place on this day. The Lord tells Ezekiel to **write down the name of this day, this very day**, because the ominous opening of the siege signifies the doom of the city.[3] Ezekiel receives this information by divine revelation, though

1. This date is alternately reckoned one year later, January 5, 587 BC, on the basis of the years of Zedekiah's reign, rather than the years of Ezekiel's exile ("Introduction to Ezekiel," in *ESV Study Bible* [Wheaton: Crossway, 2008], 1534). The date given here is identical to that found in 2 Kings 25:1 and Jer 52:4. The method used to denote this date is different from all others in Ezekiel, probably because the date was so well known that Ezekiel follows the standard dating method found elsewhere (e.g., 2 Kings 25:1).
2. Eisemann, *Ezekiel*, 412. The four fast days commemorating the destruction of the first temple are based on Zech 8:19, and they recall the following four events: (1) the beginning of the siege of Jerusalem (tenth day of the tenth month); (2) the breaching of the walls of Jerusalem (ninth day of the fourth month); (3) the destruction of the temple (ninth day of the fifth month); and (4) the death of Gedaliah, the last Jewish leader in the Holy Land (third day of the seventh month).
3. Rabbi David Kimchi (d. 1235) writes that "God told Ezekiel to write down that date and show it to the exiles" so that later when they hear that the siege did in fact begin on that day, "they will know that there was a prophet among them." Rosenberg, *Book of Ezekiel*, 1:204.

the news of the fall of the city (Ezek 33:21–22) will come by human messenger following a siege that lasts a year and a half.[4]

24:3–5   Ezekiel is called once again to articulate **an** †**allegory** or parable—the last of his parables in the book—against **the rebellious house** of Israel.[5] The parable describes a cooking pot filled with water and all the parts (meat and bones) of an animal chosen from the flock, which is then set over a raging fire until the elements in the pot are thoroughly boiled.

24:6–13   The Lord then gives the interpretation of the parable. The boiling pot is the city of Jerusalem, **the bloody city** (see 22:2). Because Jerusalem poured out innocent blood in its streets, by condemning the innocent to death and not protecting the needy, the Lord in the same way will pour out the blood of its inhabitants through the besieging armies.[6] **Woe to the bloody city!** says the Lord. Like a pot that is burned until the pot itself melts with its contents and rust within it, so the Lord will cause the city to be utterly consumed. This melted pot is a dreadful but accurate image of what the Babylonian armies will do to the city and its populace during and after the long siege. The Lord has **wearied** himself by repeated efforts to call his people to repentance (v. 12) and says that he **would have cleansed** his people, but they were unwilling (v. 13). Because of this, a fire will now entirely consume the uncleanness that reigns in the city.

24:14   This is no idle threat but a certain and irreversible judgment. In a kind of crescendo, this section ends with the strongest and direst of declarations. The Lord assures his people through the words of Ezekiel that he has firmly determined on the judgment of the city: **I the LORD have spoken; it shall come to pass, I will do it; I will not go back, I will not spare, I will not repent**. The final act of judgment has begun and will not be drawn back until the city is consumed.

In the Light of Christ (24:1–14)

Just as Ezekiel, with great anguish, predicts the siege and fall of the city of Jerusalem to conquering armies, so Jesus weeps over the city of Jerusalem and predicts its demise. The Lord God, speaking through Ezekiel, says, "I would have cleansed you and you were not cleansed" (24:13). Prophets were sent calling for repentance—not least Jeremiah himself—but the city and its leaders would not listen. Therefore, the city is set for destruction. In a similar way, Jesus approaches

---

4. For the siege of Jerusalem lasting approximately one and a half years, see 2 Kings 25:1–3; Jer 39:1–2.

5. Ezekiel addresses Israel as a "rebellious house" fourteen times in the book.

6. In the law of Moses, the blood of an animal sacrifice was not to remain exposed but to be poured out and covered over (see Lev 17:13). Because Jerusalem has poured out innocent blood openly in its streets, the Lord will leave the people's blood exposed in recompense for the blood they have shed.

Jerusalem in the final days of his life and weeps because of the great ruin that will befall the city (Luke 19:41). Why? Because the people and its leaders will not receive the offer of repentance and new life that Jesus has come to bring. They did not recognize and respond to the day of God's visitation (19:44). Jesus, too, predicts a great siege and utter ruin: "For the days shall come upon you, when your enemies will cast up a bank about you and surround you, and hem you in on every side, and dash you to the ground, you and your children within you, and they will not leave one stone upon another in you" (19:43–44). In a stark and striking way, Ezekiel foreshadows Jesus's own anguished prophecy of judgment against the Holy City.

The Death of Ezekiel's Wife: No Time for Mourning (24:15–27)

[15]Also the word of the LORD came to me: [16]"Son of man, behold, I am about to take the delight of your eyes away from you at a stroke; yet you shall not mourn or weep nor shall your tears run down. [17]Sigh, but not aloud; make no mourning for the dead. Bind on your turban, and put your shoes on your feet; do not cover your lips, nor eat the bread of mourners." [18]So I spoke to the people in the morning, and at evening my wife died. And on the next morning I did as I was commanded.

[19]And the people said to me, "Will you not tell us what these things mean for us, that you are acting thus?" [20]Then I said to them, "The word of the LORD came to me: [21]"Say to the house of Israel, Thus says the Lord GOD: Behold, I will profane my sanctuary, the pride of your power, the delight of your eyes, and the desire of your soul; and your sons and your daughters whom you left behind shall fall by the sword. [22]And you shall do as I have done; you shall not cover your lips, nor eat the bread of mourners. [23]Your turbans shall be on your heads and your shoes on your feet; you shall not mourn or weep, but you shall pine away in your iniquities and groan to one another. [24]Thus shall Ezekiel be to you a sign; according to all that he has done you shall do. When this comes, then you will know that I am the Lord GOD.'

[25]"And you, son of man, on the day when I take from them their stronghold, their joy and glory, the delight of their eyes and their heart's desire, and also their sons and daughters, [26]on that day a fugitive will come to you to report to you the news. [27]On that day your mouth will be opened to the fugitive, and you shall speak and be no longer mute. So you will be a sign to them; and they will know that I am the LORD."

OT: Lev 26:18–19; Deut 12:5; 1 Kings 8:27; Ps 48:2; Sir 24:11; Jer 16:5
NT: Rev 21:1–4, 22–25
Catechism: warning against spiritual danger, 1033, 1056, 1852; God's call on the prophets, 702

24:15–18   In this episode, Ezekiel himself becomes the mournful sign of the judgment about to befall the city and the land. A sign of desolation is played out in his own life.[7] The Lord tells Ezekiel to prepare for the imminent death of his wife: **I am about to take the delight of your eyes away from you at a stroke.** We are not told the circumstances surrounding this death, but it appears that it was unanticipated. Then shockingly the Lord instructs Ezekiel not to mourn his loss outwardly: **you shall not mourn or weep, nor shall your tears run down. Sigh, but not aloud; make no mourning for the dead.** In short, Ezekiel is to refrain from the normal mourning customs: crying aloud, removing one's head covering and sandals, uncovering one's face, and receiving bread from fellow mourners. No doubt staggered by this prediction of personal loss, Ezekiel then speaks with his fellow exiles **in the morning**, and then **at evening**, as the Lord foretold, his wife dies.

24:19–21   And so on the morning following the death of Ezekiel's wife, the people approach Ezekiel and ask what all this means: **Will you not tell us what these things mean for us, that you are acting thus?** The Lord's word comes directly to Ezekiel in answer to their question: The Lord is about to profane his own sanctuary in Jerusalem, the city which is **the pride of** their **power, the delight of** their **eyes, and the desire of** their **soul.** Like Ezekiel, they are about to lose their "bride," the delight of their eyes, suddenly and completely. The phrase "pride of your power" comes from Lev 26:19, embedded within the †covenant curses that will fall upon a disobedient Israel: "And if in spite of this you will not listen to me, then I will chastise you again sevenfold for your sins, and I will break the pride of your power" (Lev 26:18–19). What the Lord promised through Moses is now coming to pass in the time of Ezekiel. The Lord has removed his glorious presence from the beloved city (Ezek 11:22–23), abandoning it to the destructive power of the invading Babylonian armies.

24:22–24   Like Ezekiel, the people in exile who hear this news of Jerusalem's loss will not be given time and space to mourn the loss properly. Instead, they will **pine away in** their **iniquities and groan to one another.** As summed up by Moshe Greenberg, "No mourning rites implying social solidarity and sympathy are to be performed, only private, isolated groaning and moaning."[8] Jeremiah, too, spoke of a severe judgment coming upon the city and land that would give no space for mourning: "Do not enter the house of mourning, or go to lament, or bemoan them; for I have taken away my peace from this people, says the LORD, my steadfast love and mercy" (Jer 16:5). The death of Ezekiel's wife, coupled with the complete lack of normal public expressions of mourning, presents a terrifying sign to the exiles of what is soon going to befall them. When this happens, says

---

7. For the other †sign-acts that Ezekiel is called to perform in the book, see 4:1–5:17; 12:1–28; 21:19–20.
8. Greenberg, *Ezekiel 21–37*, 509.

Jerusalem the Holy and Beloved City

The comparison of Ezekiel's wife to the holy city Jerusalem may seem highly exaggerated to us, but the analogy would have resonated strongly with the people of Israel in Ezekiel's day. Jerusalem was much more than the capital city of the people; it represented the †covenant between God and his people and was a sign of his faithful presence among them. From the time when David conquered it, Jerusalem became "the city of the great King" (Ps 48:2). But even more, it was the place prophesied by Moses where the Lord God would "put his name" to dwell among his people (Deut 12:5). In a unique and special way, God set his dwelling in this city and became accessible to his people through the temple in Jerusalem. Solomon, the builder of the first temple, was keenly aware that the Lord God was not contained within the temple itself: "But will God indeed dwell on the earth? Behold, heaven and the highest heaven cannot contain you; how much less this house which I have built!" (1 Kings 8:27). Nonetheless, Jerusalem and its temple represented the place where the glory and the presence of God came to dwell (Sir 24:11). And so the expressions that Ezekiel uses here to describe Jerusalem—the pride of your power, the delight of your eyes, the yearning of your soul, your stronghold, joy, and glory—accurately capture just how precious the city was to the people of Israel. Even in exile the people yearned for the restoration of their holy city, as the psalmist says: "If I forget you, O Jerusalem, let my right hand wither! Let my tongue cleave to the roof of my mouth, if I do not remember you, if I do not set Jerusalem above my highest joy!" (Ps 137:5–6).

Because Jerusalem was the very dwelling place of the Lord among his people, it seemed inconceivable to many that he would ever depart from the Holy City or allow it to be conquered by Israel's enemies. How could the God of Israel possibly allow his own land to be conquered and his people taken off into exile? But Ezekiel declares that, according to the covenant curses announced by Moses (Lev 26; Deut 28–29), the Lord will abandon his own city because the people's continual and grievous sin has driven him away. The God of Israel is not being defeated but is allowing Israel's enemies to conquer them because of Israel's grievous unfaithfulness. And so Ezekiel sees in vision the glory of the Lord departing from the temple by stages, leaving it open to destruction by the invading armies of Nebuchadnezzar. But this is not the end of the story. Ezekiel also sees in vision the return of the Lord in his glory to the Holy City and temple, where he will once again dwell and reign among his covenant people in peace (Ezek 43:1–5; 47:1–12; 48:35). The book of Revelation brings this vision to fulfillment: in the new creation, God will dwell with his bride, the new Jerusalem, and will fill his people with his glory and light for all eternity (Rev 21:1–4, 22–25).

the Lord, then they **will know that I am the Lord God** (for the meaning of this phrase, see the sidebar "'Then You Will Know That I Am the Lord,'" p. 187).

24:25–27   These final verses function as a bridge, leading up to the fall of the city. The announcement of the city's demise will be delayed until chapter 33, but here we are led right to the brink. This final word is for Ezekiel himself. On the day that the Lord takes the Holy City away from the people—**their stronghold, their joy and glory, the delight of their eyes and their heart's desire**—a fugitive fleeing from the city will (eventually) arrive to announce the news to the exiles in Babylon. On that day, says the Lord, Ezekiel's **mouth will be opened**—he will no longer be required to keep silent. This prophecy recalls the Lord's word to Ezekiel in 3:26–27, that Ezekiel will be mute and unable to speak except for the prophetic words given to him directly by the Lord. These two references to Ezekiel's muteness—the first inaugurating Ezekiel's silence, the second signaling its end—show that this long section of judgment against Israel has come to a close. With the loss of the city, the dark journey through seemingly endless oracles of judgment will conclude. This, too, will be a sign to the people: that the judgment has fallen as predicted and a new season of the Lord's action is now opening up before them.

In Ezek 24 we have an end and a beginning. Just as these final verses link us back to the very beginning of Ezekiel's ministry and so bring to a close this long section on judgment (chaps. 4–23), so they also prepare the way for the glorious promise of the Lord's coming visitation to renew and restore his people (chaps. 34–48).

Prophecies against the Nations, Part 1: The Nations and the City of Tyre

Ezekiel 25:1–28:26

As readers, we would now be expecting to hear news that the city of Jerusalem has fallen to the Babylonian armies. But Ezekiel defers this announcement to chapter 33 and inserts here a long series of †oracles against the surrounding nations (chaps. 25–32), two of which are city-states (Tyre and Sidon).[1] In a sense, Ezekiel is giving us a glimpse into the future, since a majority of the oracles are dated after the fall of Jerusalem.[2] The oracles appear in uneven lengths: the first four nations named—Ammon, Moab, Edom, and Philistia—receive just a few verses each. Then Ezekiel records three chapters of oracles against the city of Tyre and four chapters against the Egyptians, with a short oracle against Sidon tucked in between. Tyre and Egypt are clearly the focus of Ezekiel's ministry of prophetic judgment. Many readers wonder why there is no word of judgment against Babylon. Perhaps, given Ezekiel's residence in Babylon, judgment against Babylon was simply not part of what the Lord †inspired Ezekiel to prophesy. That assignment was given to other prophets who lived beyond the reach of the powerful king of Babylon (see Isa 13–14; Jer 51–52).

The prophetic oracles are grouped topically (by nation), not chronologically (by date), and Ezekiel appears to have arranged the oracles according to the number seven. *Seven* nations are named by Ezekiel as coming under judgment.[3]

---

1. Ezekiel himself may have arranged the order of the oracles in this section, but it is possible that a later editor took Ezekiel's recorded oracles against the nations and arranged them in the present †canonical order.

2. Seven of the oracles are dated (26:1; 29:1, 17; 30:20; 31:1; 32:1, 17), with dates ranging over twenty-five years, from 587 to 562.

3. Ezekiel may be taking inspiration from the register of seven nations, named in Deut 7:1, that Israel was called to supplant in the promised land.

Seven of the oracles are given specific dates. *Seven* distinct oracles are directed against Tyre,[4] as well as *seven* against Egypt.[5] This cluster around the number seven is unlikely to be coincidental. The number seven signifies fullness or completeness. By arranging the oracles into groups of seven, Ezekiel is signaling the completeness of the coming judgment against the nations who have set themselves against the Lord and his people.

We might ask: What purpose do these oracles against the nations serve? Why are they included at all? They demonstrate that, though the Lord is about to judge his own people severely for their many sins, he will also bring judgment against the opponents of Israel for their own wickedness and contempt of Israel (and of Israel's God), just as the Lord promised to do: "And the LORD your God will put all these curses upon your foes and enemies who persecuted you" (Deut 30:7). Thus, these oracles show that the Lord God of Israel also rules over all the nations.[6]

At the same time, the oracles against the nations function as "indirect messages of hope" for Israel.[7] Structurally, the single message of hope for Israel found in this section occurs *precisely* at the midpoint of the oracles against the nations (at Ezek 28:24–26)[8] and announces the return of Israel to the land following the judgment upon the nations: "They shall dwell securely, when I execute judgments upon all their neighbors who have treated them with contempt" (28:26). The central purpose of these oracles, then, is to convey hope to Israel, that despite their own sins the Lord God will in the end overcome Israel's foes and restore his people to their land.

Oracles against Four Nations (25:1–17)

[1]The word of the LORD came to me: [2]"Son of man, set your face toward the **Ammonites, and prophesy against them. [3]Say to the Ammonites, Hear the word of the Lord GOD: Thus says the Lord GOD, Because you said, 'Aha!' over my sanctuary when it was profaned, and over the land of Israel when it was made desolate, and over the house of Judah when it went into exile; [4]therefore I am handing you over to the people of the East for a possession, and they shall set their encampments among you and make their dwellings**

4. The seven oracles against Tyre: 26:1–6; 26:7–14; 26:15–18; 26:19–21; 27:1–36; 28:1–10; 28:11–19.
5. The seven oracles of sayings against Egypt: 29:1–16; 29:17–21; 30:1–19; 30:20–26; 31:1–18; 32:1–16; 32:17–32.
6. Oracles against the surrounding nations also appear in Amos (chaps. 1–2), Isaiah (chaps. 13–23), and Jeremiah (chaps. 46–51).
7. Daniel Block, *The Book of Ezekiel, Chapters 25–48*, New International Commentary on the Old Testament (Grand Rapids: Eerdmans, 1998), 3.
8. In chaps. 25–32, there are ninety-seven verses that precede this word of hope and ninety-seven verses that follow.

in your midst; they shall eat your fruit, and they shall drink your milk. ⁵I will make Rabbah a pasture for camels and the cities of the Ammonites a fold for flocks. Then you will know that I am the LORD. ⁶For thus says the Lord GOD: Because you have clapped your hands and stamped your feet and rejoiced with all the malice within you against the land of Israel, ⁷therefore, behold, I have stretched out my hand against you, and will hand you over as spoil to the nations; and I will cut you off from the peoples and will make you perish out of the countries; I will destroy you. Then you will know that I am the LORD.

⁸"Thus says the Lord GOD: Because Moab said, Behold, the house of Judah is like all the other nations, ⁹therefore I will lay open the flank of Moab from the cities on its frontier, the glory of the country, Beth-jeshimoth, Baal-meon, and Kiriathaim. ¹⁰I will give it along with the Ammonites to the people of the East as a possession, that it may be remembered no more among the nations, ¹¹and I will execute judgments upon Moab. Then they will know that I am the LORD.

¹²"Thus says the Lord GOD: Because Edom acted revengefully against the house of Judah and has grievously offended in taking vengeance upon them, ¹³therefore thus says the Lord GOD, I will stretch out my hand against Edom, and cut off from it man and beast; and I will make it desolate; from Teman even to Dedan they shall fall by the sword. ¹⁴And I will lay my vengeance upon Edom by the hand of my people Israel; and they shall do in Edom according to my anger and according to my wrath; and they shall know my vengeance, says the Lord GOD.

¹⁵"Thus says the Lord GOD: Because the Philistines acted revengefully and took vengeance with malice of heart to destroy in never ending enmity; ¹⁶therefore thus says the Lord GOD, Behold, I will stretch out my hand against the Philistines, and I will cut off the Cherethites, and destroy the rest of the seacoast. ¹⁷I will execute great vengeance upon them with wrathful chastisements. Then they will know that I am the LORD, when I lay my vengeance upon them."

OT: Gen 19:36–38; Deut 2:9; Isa 19:23–25; Jer 27:3–11; Obad 13; Jon 4:11
NT: Matt 11:21–24; 23:13–39; Acts 11:18; Rom 11:17–21
Catechism: God's punishment and judgment of sin, 211, 679, 1472–73, 2054

Ezekiel now takes up the same posture against the surrounding nations that the   25:1–7
Lord called him to take against Israel and Jerusalem: **Son of man, set your face toward the Ammonites, and prophesy against them.** The land of Ammon was east of Israel across the Jordan River. Rabbah was the main city, and Amman, the present-day capital of Jordan, located near the ancient site of Rabbah, is named after the Ammonites. According to Gen 19:36–38, the Ammonites were descended from Lot, the nephew of Abraham. Later, Moses was instructed to avoid conflict with the Ammonites when passing through the Transjordan region because they were descended from Lot (Deut 2:9, 19). Subsequently, there was a

long history of conflict between Israel and the Ammonites, recorded in Judges (chaps. 10–11) and 2 Samuel (chaps. 10–12). Along with Judah, the Ammonites were part of a coalition of nations against Babylon in the period directly leading up to Ezekiel's prophetic ministry (see Jer 27:3–11).[9]

But when the armies of Babylon conquered Judah and destroyed the city of Jerusalem, the Ammonites rejoiced, despite their temporary alliance, probably because a potential rival nation had been eliminated, strengthening their own position in the region. Jeremiah indicates that the Ammonites used Judah's downfall to seize land (Jer 49:1). Because the Ammonites rejoiced over the fall of Jerusalem and the land of Israel—they **clapped** their **hands, stamped** their **feet**, and **rejoiced with . . . malice**—they will be handed over to other nations. The Lord God will bring **the people of the East** (probably desert nomads) against them, to inhabit their land and to remove them from their ancient inheritance.[10] When this happens, the Lord says directly to the Ammonites: **Then you will know that I am the Lord.** God's aim is apparently not their utter destruction, for there will be some remaining Ammonites who will come to recognize that the God of Israel has judged them. God's purpose is to humble this proud nation by bringing his just judgment against it.

25:8–11   The next three oracles are shorter and contain less detail. Instead of addressing these nations directly in the first person, Ezekiel reports God's word in the third person. This first oracle is addressed to **Moab**.[11] Moab lay southeast from Israel, on the far side of the Dead Sea. The three cities named in verse 9 are situated on a line running north–south along the western border of Moab. The Moabites, like the Ammonites, were descended from Abraham's nephew Lot (Gen 19:36–38). There was hostility between Moab and Israel when Moses led the tribes around the territory of Moab to enter the promised land (see Num 22–24). But Moab later made a significant contribution to Israel through the beloved figure of Ruth, the great-grandmother of King David.

Because the Moabites vaunted themselves over Israel and said, **Behold, the house of Judah is like all the other nations**, God will bring judgment upon them. By dishonoring Israel they also dishonor the Lord and bring his name into disrepute. Like the Ammonites, Moab, too, will be given over to **the people of the East as a possession** and will cease to exist as a nation.[12]

---

9. Jeremiah (27:3) also names Moab, Edom, Tyre, and Sidon as all participating in the coalition with Judah against Babylon in 594 BC.

10. For biblical references to "the people of the East," see Judg 6:3, 33; 7:12; 8:10; Isa 11:14; Jer 49:28. Both Jeremiah and Ezekiel connect "the people of the East" with camels, flocks, and tents, indicating a nomadic people.

11. The Hebrew text has "Moab and Seir" as the addressee. Seir is normally a synonym for Edom (Gen 32:3; 36:8–9; Ezek 35:15), which is the subject of the following oracle. It is unclear why Seir is named here in the Hebrew text as a nation separate from Edom.

12. In contrast to this brief word of judgment, Jeremiah utters an extended oracle against Moab (Jer 48:1–47), and both Jeremiah (48:27) and Zephaniah (2:8) accuse Moab of taunting Israel after its fall to Babylon.

"Then You Will Know That I Am the LORD"

Four times in chapter 25 Ezekiel repeats the refrain, "Then you will know that I am the LORD." This phrase, with minor variations, occurs more than sixty times in Ezekiel. It is called the "recognition formula" because when the Lord acts to fulfill his word, then the people will *recognize* that it is the Lord who is acting. Though Ezekiel uses this refrain more frequently than the rest of the Old Testament combined, he is drawing on a rich tradition that preceded him, found especially in the book of Exodus. When promising to deliver Israel from the grip of the Egyptians and bring them into the promised land, the Lord concludes by saying, "And you shall know that I am the LORD your God, who has brought you out from under the burdens of the Egyptians" (Exod 6:7). As the deliverance from Egypt unfolds, this refrain appears again and again as evidence that the word God is speaking will come to pass. And so when the Lord turns the water of the Nile into blood, or causes flies and locusts to infest Egypt, or provides bread for his people in the wilderness, he tells the people: "Then you shall know that I am the LORD" (Exod 7:17; 8:22; 10:2; 16:12). In a similar way, when God acts to destroy the Egyptian armies, then "the Egyptians shall know that I am the LORD" (Exod 14:4). Both Israel and foreign nations will learn to recognize that God has acted to fulfill the word he has spoken. The recognition formula appears on occasion in the historical books (1 Kings 20:28) and in the prophets. Isaiah declares that, when God acts to punish the nations that have persecuted Israel, "then all flesh shall know / that I am the LORD your Savior, / and your Redeemer, the Mighty One of Jacob" (Isa 49:26). Likewise, when God tells Jeremiah that he will act to bless the exiles in Babylon, he adds, "I will give them a heart to know that I am the LORD" (Jer 24:7; see also Jer 16:21; Bar 2:31; Joel 3:17).

Ezekiel's frequent use of this refrain shows a strong link to the deliverance of Israel from Egypt. Just as the Lord acted to save his people from Egypt, so he is acting once again: to judge his people, to deliver them, and to punish the surrounding nations. The primary purpose of this refrain is to declare that when God acts to fulfill the word he has spoken—when he does the thing he has promised—then Israel and the surrounding nations will know that the Lord, the God of Israel, has spoken and acted in power.

Ezekiel next turns to the nation of **Edom**, a land lying to the south of Israel. Edom traces its lineage to Esau, the son of Isaac and twin brother of Jacob (Gen 25:19–26). The Old Testament witnesses to an ongoing hostility between the nations of Edom and Israel (Ps 137:7; Jer 49:7–22; Lam 4:21–22). The Edomites are accused here of acting **revengefully** against Judah, having **grievously offended** the Lord by taking vengeance against his people. What

25:12–14

was their offense? Later in the book, Ezekiel will accuse Edom of giving over "the people of Israel to the power of the sword at the time of their calamity" (Ezek 35:5). The prophet Obadiah adds a further offense when he reprimands the nation of Edom for taking advantage of the weakness of Israel when they were fallen: "You should not have entered the gate of my people in the day of his calamity. You should not have gloated over his disaster in the day of his calamity" (Obad 13). In return for this, God promises a just retribution against Edom: **I will lay my vengeance upon Edom by the hand of my people Israel.** The Edomites will fall by the sword of Israel and receive the same penalty that they imposed upon Israel.

25:15–17   This short series of oracles concludes with a word directed against the **Philistines**, a traditional enemy of Israel lying to the west along the Mediterranean Sea. The people called **the Cherethites**, probably originating from the island of Crete, are closely identified with the Philistines (Zeph 2:5). Like the Edomites, the people of Philistia took active vengeance against a weakened and defeated Israel **with malice of heart to destroy in never ending enmity**. The judgment they gave is the judgment they will get: the Lord will bring upon them **great vengeance . . . with wrathful chastisements**. The end result (and goal) of this penalty remains the same: **then they will know that I am the Lord**.

Reflection and Application (25:1–17)

We might be tempted to conclude that these sharp words of judgment against the nations, so prominent in many of the Old Testament prophets, have nothing in common with the mission and ministry of Jesus. But this sharp dichotomy is inaccurate. On the one hand, Jesus consistently proclaims words of firm judgment against those who reject the coming of the kingdom of God (for example, Matt 11:21–24; 23:13–39). On the other hand, the Lord's desire to save the nations and bring them to life-giving repentance is also found in the Old Testament prophets (for example, Isa 19:23–25). The final message of the book of Jonah is a prime example: "And should not I pity Nineveh, that great city, in which there are more than a hundred and twenty thousand persons who do not know their right hand from their left?" (Jon 4:11). Even Ezekiel, focused as he is on the land and the people of Israel, will make room in the renewed Israel for aliens who live in Israel to be enfolded into the inheritance of the tribes (Ezek 47:21–23).

In Jesus, the †Messiah of Israel, the promises to Israel are extended to all the nations, that they, too, should repent and find new life: "Then to the †Gentiles also God has granted repentance unto life" (Acts 11:18). This is not the appearance of a "new God" in contrast to the "old," but the fulfillment of all that

was promised in the Law and the Prophets. In Jesus and the preaching of the
†gospel, the "judgment" on the nations paradoxically reaches its climax and goal.
Through faith, repentance, and baptism the nations are justified and cleansed
by the merciful word of the gospel, are engrafted into Israel (Rom 11:17–21),
and find salvation in the one true God.

Announcement of Judgment upon Tyre (26:1–21)

¹In the eleventh year, on the first day of the month, the word of the
LORD came to me: ²"Son of man, because Tyre said concerning Jerusalem, 'Aha, the gate of the peoples is broken, it has swung open to me; I
shall be replenished, now that she is laid waste,' ³therefore thus says the
Lord GOD: Behold, I am against you, O Tyre, and will bring up many
nations against you, as the sea brings up its waves. ⁴They shall destroy
the walls of Tyre, and break down her towers; and I will scrape her soil
from her, and make her a bare rock. ⁵She shall be in the midst of the sea
a place for the spreading of nets; for I have spoken, says the Lord GOD;
and she shall become a spoil to the nations; ⁶and her daughters on the
mainland shall be slain by the sword. Then they will know that I am the
LORD.

⁷"For thus says the Lord GOD: Behold, I will bring upon Tyre from the
north Nebuchadrezzar king of Babylon, king of kings, with horses and
chariots, and with horsemen and a host of many soldiers. ⁸He will slay
with the sword your daughters on the mainland; he will set up a siege
wall against you, and throw up a mound against you, and raise a roof
of shields against you. ⁹He will direct the shock of his battering rams
against your walls, and with his axes he will break down your towers.
¹⁰His horses will be so many that their dust will cover you; your walls
will shake at the noise of the horsemen and wagons and chariots, when
he enters your gates as one enters a city which has been breached. ¹¹With
the hoofs of his horses he will trample all your streets; he will slay your
people with the sword; and your mighty pillars will fall to the ground.
¹²They will make a spoil of your riches and a prey of your merchandise;
they will break down your walls and destroy your pleasant houses; your
stones and timber and soil they will cast into the midst of the waters.
¹³And I will stop the music of your songs, and the sound of your lyres
shall be heard no more. ¹⁴I will make you a bare rock; you shall be a place
for the spreading of nets; you shall never be rebuilt; for I the LORD have
spoken, says the Lord GOD.

¹⁵"Thus says the Lord GOD to Tyre: Will not the islands shake at the
sound of your fall, when the wounded groan, when slaughter is made in
the midst of you? ¹⁶Then all the princes of the sea will step down from
their thrones, and remove their robes, and strip off their embroidered

garments; they will clothe themselves with trembling; they will sit upon
the ground and tremble every moment, and be appalled at you. [17]And they
will raise a lamentation over you, and say to you,

> 'How you have vanished from the seas,
>   O city renowned,
> that was mighty on the sea,
>   you and your inhabitants,
> who imposed your terror
>   on all the mainland!
> [18]Now the isles tremble
>   on the day of your fall;
> yes, the isles that are in the sea
>   are dismayed at your passing.'

[19]"For thus says the Lord GOD: When I make you a city laid waste, like
the cities that are not inhabited, when I bring up the deep over you, and
the great waters cover you, [20]then I will thrust you down with those who
descend into the Pit, to the people of old, and I will make you to dwell
in the nether world, among primeval ruins, with those who go down to
the Pit, so that you will not be inhabited or have a place in the land of
the living. [21]I will bring you to a dreadful end, and you shall be no more;
though you be sought for, you will never be found again, says the Lord
GOD."

OT: Isa 23:1–18; Jer 27:1–7; Joel 3:4–8; Amos 1:9–10; Zech 9:2–4
NT: Matt 15:21–28; Mark 3:8; Rev 18:9–19
Catechism: God's punishment and judgment of sin, 211, 679, 1472–73, 2054; prayers of lamentation, 2588

Ezekiel now begins a series of seven oracles against the city of Tyre.[13] Tyre
was a great trading city, the "merchant of the nations" in the ancient world
(Isa 23:3), lying to the north of Israel on the Mediterranean coast. During
the reigns of David and Solomon, King Hiram of Tyre had a friendly trading relationship with Israel (see 2 Sam 5:11; 1 Kings 5:1–2). In the time of
Ezekiel, Tyre maintained daughter-villages on the mainland, but the heart of
the city was an island fortress approximately 550 meters off the coast, accessible only by boat. As a result, Tyre was nearly impregnable against military
assault by land.

26:1–6   This opening prophecy against Tyre is brief and follows the form of the
oracles against Ammon, Moab, Edom, and Philistia in chapter 25. Because it
lacks mention of the month, the date of the oracle can only be approximated
to the year 586, probably shortly after news of Jerusalem's fall would have
reached the exiles in Babylon. What is Tyre's fault? Ezekiel represents Tyre

13. For oracles against Tyre found elsewhere in the Prophets, see Isa 23:1–18; Joel 3:4–8; Amos
1:9–10; Zech 9:2–4.

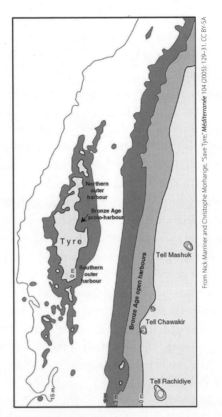

Figure 5. City of Tyre

as saying, **I shall be replenished, now that she is laid waste**. According to Daniel Block, this "suggests that the Tyrians welcomed Judah's demise as an opportunity to expand their own commercial interests."[14] Tyre had taken part in the anti-Babylonian alliance of nations in Jerusalem in 594 (see Jer 27:1–7), but according to Moshe Greenberg, Tyre "did not come to Jerusalem's aid when she revolted."[15] None of the nations in the coalition provided help for Judah in her desperate stand against Babylon. In response to Tyre's actions, the Lord sets himself against the city: **I . . . will bring up many nations against you, as the sea brings up its waves**. In this opening judgment oracle, the prophet predicts the complete destruction of Tyre's island fortress as well as the people dwelling on the mainland.

In the second oracle, Ezekiel depicts in great detail Nebuchadnezzar's siege **26:7–14** of Tyre. This includes the building of siege works, use of battering rams against the walls, attack by armies of horsemen, and the slaughter of people on the

14. Block, *Ezekiel: Chapters 25–48*, 32.
15. Greenberg, *Ezekiel 21–37*, 540.

mainland. The result will be complete devastation: **they will break down your walls and destroy your pleasant houses; your stones and timber and soil they will cast into the midst of the waters**. The city will become **a bare rock** and **shall never be rebuilt**.

Ezekiel's description of this military siege best describes an attack made on the mainland part of the city, but does not portray the kind of siege required for attacking the sea walls of an island fortress (for example, horses cannot be brought up against sea walls). To the best of our knowledge, the predicted destruction of the island city by the armies of Nebuchadnezzar never occurred. According to the Jewish historian Josephus, Nebuchadnezzar besieged the city of Tyre for thirteen years (from 586 to 573), but it appears that he never defeated the city militarily. Instead, an agreement was reached whereby Tyre submitted to Babylonian sovereignty and paid tribute to Nebuchadnezzar, but the city was spared the typical pillaging and destruction, and so remained largely intact. Strikingly, in the latest recorded oracle in the book (dated to the year 571), Ezekiel himself recognizes the failure of the attack on Tyre, acknowledging that "neither he [Nebuchadnezzar] nor his army got anything from Tyre to pay for the labor that he had expended against it" (Ezek 29:18). Tyre certainly suffered a defeat—and so experienced the judgment of the Lord—but apparently not in the devastating manner predicted here initially by Ezekiel.[16] The actual sacking of Tyre occurred more than two hundred years later in 332 BC, when through the determination and tactical ingenuity of Alexander the Great, the island fortress was breached and the inhabitants of the city were either massacred or sold into slavery.

26:15–21   The final section of chapter 26 contains two related oracles against Tyre. In the first (vv. 15–18), the peoples and nations that surround Tyre grieve and lament over the great city's fall. Because the **city renowned, / that was mighty on the sea,** has perished, all the coastal cities who benefited from Tyre's vast trading network tremble and groan in lamentation. This brief lament over Tyre's collapse will be greatly expanded in the next chapter.

The second oracle (vv. 19–21) records God speaking directly against the island city. He will **bring up the deep** over the city, and **the great waters** will swallow it up. The city—like dead human beings—will go down to the pit, to **the nether world**. It is as if the entire city will be buried in the waters and go down to the depths of †Sheol, the place of the dead. According to Daniel Block, "Tyre is now personified, and her demise is presented as the departure of an individual into the dark realm of the dead."[17]

---

16. For understanding the nonfulfillment of this prophetic oracle, see the Reflection and Application section for 29:17–21 (p. 211).

17. Block, *Ezekiel: Chapters 25–48*, 47.

The final phrase of verse 20 is translated in two contrasting ways. One translation, following the Hebrew text, has "but I will set beauty in the land of the living" (ESV). The Jewish rabbis adopted this reading and applied it to the time of the resurrection of the dead in a rebuilt city of Jerusalem.[18] The more common translation, following the Greek †Septuagint, renders this: "you will not . . . have a place in the land of the living." While both translations are true, the second reading better aligns with the overall trajectory of the context, that Tyre will sink beneath the sea and never again see the light of day.

In the Light of Christ (26:15–21)

Though the city of Tyre suffered grievous loss at the hands of the conquering empires (Babylonians and Greeks), in the end it was not utterly destroyed. At the time of Jesus centuries later it remained an active and bustling city of trade and commerce. At one point in his ministry, Jesus leaves Galilee and travels north along the coast: "And Jesus went away from there and withdrew to the district of Tyre and Sidon" (Matt 15:21). There he encounters a Canaanite woman who begs Jesus to deliver her daughter from a severe demon possession. Jesus appears to put her off, saying, "I was sent only to the lost sheep of the house of Israel" (15:24). But she persists, and the reward for her determined faith is the full healing of her daughter: "O woman, great is your faith! Let it be done for you as you desire" (15:28). We also hear of crowds from the region of Tyre and Sidon that, having heard news about Jesus, travel south to encounter him (Mark 3:8). In Ezekiel's day, the city of Tyre came under a sentence of judgment because of their mistreatment of the people of Israel. In the time of Jesus, people from this city seek and find blessing from the Messiah of Israel.

Lament over Tyre, the Beautiful and Glorious City (27:1–25a)

¹The word of the Lord came to me: ²"Now you, son of man, raise a lamentation over Tyre, ³and say to Tyre, who dwells at the entrance to the sea, merchant of the peoples on many islands, thus says the Lord God:

> "O Tyre, you have said,
>   'I am perfect in beauty.'
> ⁴Your borders are in the heart of the seas;
>   your builders made perfect your beauty.

---

18. Eisemann, *Ezekiel*, 446–47; A. J. Rosenberg, trans., *The Book of Ezekiel*, vol. 2, Mikraoth Gedoloth (New York: Judaica Press, 2000), 226.

⁵They made all your planks
    of fir trees from Senir;
they took a cedar from Lebanon
    to make a mast for you.
⁶Of oaks of Bashan
    they made your oars;
they made your deck of pines
    from the coasts of Cyprus,
    inlaid with ivory.
⁷Of fine embroidered linen from Egypt
    was your sail,
    serving as your ensign;
blue and purple from the coasts of Elishah
    was your awning.
⁸The inhabitants of Sidon and Arvad
    were your rowers;
skilled men of Zemer were in you,
    they were your pilots.
⁹The elders of Gebal and her skilled men were in you,
    caulking your seams;
all the ships of the sea with their mariners were in you,
    to barter for your wares.

¹⁰"Persia and Lud and Put were in your army as your men of war; they hung the shield and helmet in you; they gave you splendor. ¹¹The men of Arvad and Helech were upon your walls round about, and men of Gamad were in your towers; they hung their shields upon your walls round about; they made perfect your beauty.

¹²"Tarshish trafficked with you because of your great wealth of every kind; silver, iron, tin, and lead they exchanged for your wares. ¹³Javan, Tubal, and Meshech traded with you; they exchanged the persons of men and vessels of bronze for your merchandise. ¹⁴Beth-togarmah exchanged for your wares horses, war horses, and mules. ¹⁵The men of Rhodes traded with you; many islands were your own special markets, they brought you in payment ivory tusks and ebony. ¹⁶Edom trafficked with you because of your abundant goods; they exchanged for your wares emeralds, purple, embroidered work, fine linen, coral, and agate. ¹⁷Judah and the land of Israel traded with you; they exchanged for your merchandise wheat, olives and early figs, honey, oil, and balm. ¹⁸Damascus trafficked with you for your abundant goods, because of your great wealth of every kind; wine of Helbon, and white wool, ¹⁹and wine from Uzal they exchanged for your wares; wrought iron, cassia, and calamus were bartered for your merchandise. ²⁰Dedan traded with you in saddlecloths for riding. ²¹Arabia and all the princes of Kedar were your favored dealers in lambs, rams, and goats; in these they trafficked with you. ²²The traders of Sheba and Raamah

Figure 6. Tyrian ship

traded with you; they exchanged for your wares the best of all kinds of spices, and all precious stones, and gold. ²³Haran, Canneh, Eden, Asshur, and Chilmad traded with you. ²⁴These traded with you in choice garments, in clothes of blue and embroidered work, and in carpets of colored stuff, bound with cords and made secure; in these they traded with you. ²⁵ᵃThe ships of Tarshish traveled for you with your merchandise."

OT: Ps 50:2; Lam 2:15
Catechism: prayers of lamentation, 2588; the vanity of seeking this world's riches, 1723, 2445, 2556

The chapter begins with a call for lamentation, but surprisingly the first part (vv. 1–25a) is a song *in praise of* Tyre and all its accomplishments: its grandeur, its place among the nations, and all its many trading partners from east and west. The second part (vv. 25b–36) speaks of the sudden fall of Tyre, with all its glory pitching down into the sea and all its former traders and merchants mourning the loss of the great city. A hymn of praise to the city of Tyre turns into a lament for its tragic fall.

Ezekiel is commanded to **raise a lamentation over Tyre** (v. 2), but he begins **27:1–4** by displaying the glory and grandeur of the city. Tyre's claim for itself, **I am perfect in beauty** (v. 3), is confirmed in the next verse by the affirmation that Tyre's builders have indeed **made perfect your beauty** (v. 4). This claim to perfection in beauty points to Tyre's genuinely impressive qualities but also reveals the proud self-satisfaction of the city and the probable cause of its demise. In chapter 16, Ezekiel calls the city of Jerusalem "perfect" in "beauty" through the gift of God: "And your renown went forth among the nations because of your beauty, for it was perfect through the splendor which I had bestowed upon you" (16:14).[19] By making the claim to perfection of beauty, Tyre seems to be exalting itself above the Lord God and his people.[20]

27:5–11   With lavish description, Ezekiel then praises the construction and furnishings of the city, figuratively depicted as a great ship constructed of the finest timber and finely decorated with precious materials originating from cities and lands all across the known world. The vast number of place names displays just how extensive the trading "reach" of this island city was: all the great nations and cities of the earth contributed to the wealth and splendor of Tyre, and **they made perfect** its **beauty**.[21]

27:12–   Ezekiel's praise of Tyre continues by pointing to the glory of its many trading
25a   partners and its **great wealth of every kind**.[22] This catalogue of trading partners spans the map from west to east: As Daniel Block observes, "The prophet's gaze moves successively from Tarshish [probably in Spain] in the farthest west, to Greece and Anatolia [Turkey], down the coast to Syria-Palestine, then on to Arabia, and finally to the cities and nations of Mesopotamia."[23] The expansive list of cities and nations shows the enormous breadth of trade in all directions and highlights the luxury goods from other nations by whose trade Tyre was enriched. The city of Tyre was indeed impressive in every way and seemingly secure in her wealth among the surrounding nations.

Lament over the Fall of Tyre (27:25b–36)

> [25b]"So you were filled and heavily laden
>   in the heart of the seas.
> [26]Your rowers have brought you out
>   into the high seas.
> The east wind has wrecked you
>   in the heart of the seas.
> [27]Your riches, your wares, your merchandise,
>   your mariners and your pilots,
> your caulkers, your dealers in merchandise,
>   and all your men of war who are in you,

19. For Jerusalem as "the perfection of beauty," see also Ps 50:2; Lam 2:15.
20. The Jewish commentator Rashi (d. 1105) sees in Tyre's claim to be "the perfection of beauty" a prideful encroachment on the rightful place of Jerusalem to this claim: "Now you, Tyre, are priding yourself that you have usurped this position." Eisemann, *Ezekiel*, 448.
21. The fact that Ezekiel refers to more than thirty regions and cities not only reveals the extent of Tyre's merchant empire but also shows Ezekiel's wide knowledge of the world of his day.
22. Mention of Tarshish in vv. 12 and 25 marks the beginning and ending of this subsection that describes Tyre's catalogue of trading partners.
23. Block, *Ezekiel: Chapters 25–48*, 81.

> with all your company
>> that is in your midst,
> sink into the heart of the seas
>> on the day of your ruin.
> [28]At the sound of the cry of your pilots
>> the countryside shakes,
> [29]and down from their ships
>> come all that handle the oar.
> The mariners and all the pilots of the sea
>> stand on the shore
> [30]and wail aloud over you,
>> and cry bitterly.
> They cast dust on their heads
>> and wallow in ashes;
> [31]they make themselves bald for you,
>> and put on sackcloth,
> and they weep over you in bitterness of soul,
>> with bitter mourning.
> [32]In their wailing they raise a lamentation for you,
>> and lament over you:
> 'Who was ever destroyed like Tyre
>> in the midst of the sea?
> [33]When your wares came from the seas,
>> you satisfied many peoples;
> with your abundant wealth and merchandise
>> you enriched the kings of the earth.
> [34]Now you are wrecked by the seas,
>> in the depths of the waters;
> your merchandise and all your crew
>> have sunk with you.
> [35]All the inhabitants of the islands
>> are appalled at you;
> and their kings are horribly afraid,
>> their faces are convulsed.
> [36]The merchants among the peoples hiss at you;
>> you have come to a dreadful end
>> and shall be no more forever.'"

OT: Pss 48:7; 138:6; Isa 57:15
NT: Matt 5:5; 20:26–28; Luke 1:52; Rev 18:9–19
Catechism: prayers of lamentation, 2588; the vanity of seeking this world's riches, 1723, 2445, 2556

What is the result of Tyre's impressive trading? The city was **filled and heavily   27:25b–
laden / in the heart of the seas**. The city, like a great trading ship, was filled up   36
with many wonderful things but consequently was overloaded and vulnerable

to flooding and sinking when tossed about by the wind. Tyre was rich, proud, and confident, set for the "fall" that the Lord would bring to humble the great city.

The glory of Tyre vanishes suddenly as the city, like a great ship, sinks beneath the waves into deep water: **The east wind has wrecked you / in the heart of the seas**.[24] All the riches and resources of the city—merchandise, men of war, mariners and crew—**sink into the heart of the seas / on the day of your ruin**. All who witness the demise of the city **wail aloud** and **cry bitterly**, mourning and weeping for the fall of the great city. And they raise a lament: **Who was ever destroyed like Tyre / in the midst of the sea?** The city that **enriched the kings of the earth** now sinks beneath the waves. "She is wrecked by the very elements which brought her prosperity."[25] The Lord pronounces the final doom of the city: **you have come to a dreadful end / and shall be no more forever**. The lament emphasizes the city's uniqueness. "Who was ever destroyed like Tyre?" (v. 32), analogous to "Who is like the LORD our God?" (Ps 113:5), recognizes the godlike quality claimed by this city that has now been brought low. The claim to divinity will reappear in the next chapter and play a central role in Tyre's sin of arrogance.

We might ask: Is this a genuine lament, or is it in fact a kind of ironic lament really meant to accuse the city? There may be elements of both. The Jewish tradition saw Ezekiel's lament as genuine, as giving evidence of God's concern for all the nations of the earth.[26] But there is also probably an element of irony, that the great and beautiful city has been appropriately humbled.

Reflection and Application (27:1–36)

There is a theatrical quality to Ezekiel's portrayal of the glory and the fall of the city of Tyre. The city's magnificence, lauded in †hyperbolic language, stands in sharp contrast to its sudden and utter ruin as it sinks, like a proud and overladen ship, beneath the waves.

Tyre is an example of a consistent pattern we find in the Bible: those that exalt themselves will be humbled, and those who humble themselves will be exalted. In the words of the Virgin Mary, "He has put down the mighty from their thrones, / and exalted those of low degree" (Luke 1:52). The prophets continually warn both Israel and the nations against the sin of pride. One by one the great empires, which for a time acted as masters of the earth, were brought low and disappeared: Assyria, Babylon, Persia, Greece, and eventually the great

---

24. There is an echo here of Ps 48:7: "By the east wind you shattered / the ships of Tarshish."
25. John B. Taylor, *Ezekiel: An Introduction and Commentary*, Tyndale Old Testament Commentaries (Downers Grove, IL: InterVarsity, 1969), 195.
26. Eisemann, *Ezekiel*, 447–48.

city of Rome. The same pattern has occurred throughout history even up to our own day. How many proud nations and empires have fallen quickly and passed from the historical stage in what seems like a moment?

The pride of nations and individuals is really the outworking of the fall. Beginning with the tower of Babel (Gen 11:4), each is an expression of human pride that rises up and disregards God the creator, who brought all things into being in the first place. For the sake of his own glory and for their own good, the Lord will not allow the arrogant to stand in their pride but will bring them low and humble them. Whether we consider the great nations of the earth or individual people (like ourselves!), the Lord is at work—at every level—to humble the proud and raise up the lowly. Jesus recognized the need to teach his own disciples that in order to become great one must become the lowest and the servant of all (Matt 20:26–28). Though this teaching may sometimes seem like a hard word to swallow, it is very good news. In the end it is not the proud and arrogant who will rule the world but the meek who shall inherit the earth (Matt 5:5). As the Lord God says through the prophet Isaiah: "I dwell in a high and holy place, but also with the contrite and lowly of spirit, to revive the spirit of the lowly, to revive the heart of the crushed" (Isa 57:15 NABRE; see also Ps 138:6).

Judgment of the King of Tyre (28:1–10)

¹The word of the LORD came to me: ²"Son of man, say to the prince of Tyre, Thus says the Lord GOD:

"Because your heart is proud,
    and you have said, 'I am a god,
I sit in the seat of the gods,
    in the heart of the seas,'
yet you are but a man, and no god,
    though you consider yourself as wise as a god—
³you are indeed wiser than Daniel;
    no secret is hidden from you;
⁴by your wisdom and your understanding
    you have gotten wealth for yourself,
and have gathered gold and silver
    into your treasuries;
⁵by your great wisdom in trade
    you have increased your wealth,
    and your heart has become proud in your wealth—
⁶therefore thus says the Lord GOD:
"Because you consider yourself
    as wise as a god,

⁷therefore, behold, I will bring strangers upon you,
   the most terrible of the nations;
and they shall draw their swords
   against the beauty of your wisdom
   and defile your splendor.
⁸They shall thrust you down into the Pit,
   and you shall die the death of the slain
   in the heart of the seas.
⁹Will you still say, 'I am a god,'
   in the presence of those who slay you,
though you are but a man, and no god,
   in the hands of those who wound you?
¹⁰You shall die the death of the uncircumcised
   by the hand of foreigners;
   for I have spoken, says the Lord GOD."

OT: Dan 2:19–23; 4:6, 9; 5:13–14
Catechism: the sin of pride, 1866, 2094; the vanity of seeking this world's riches, 1723, 2445, 2556

Ezekiel 28 concludes the oracles of judgment against the city of Tyre, making use of fascinating images drawn from the garden of Eden to show the root of Tyre's pride. The first part (vv. 1–10) is a straightforward judgment of the prince of Tyre for his pride: he has made himself out to be a god, though he is a man, and so the Lord will humble him. The second part (vv. 11–19) is a figurative lament over the king of Tyre set against the backdrop of imagery drawn from the garden of Eden and God's holy mount. Two brief sections conclude this chapter. The first (vv. 20–24) is an oracle against Sidon, the sister city of Tyre. The second (vv. 25–26), like an oasis in the desert, is a poignant promise of hope for Israel: the Lord promises that he will gather his people and bring them back to their own land.

28:1–2   The opening words are aimed directly at the **prince of Tyre**. The Lord accuses him of overweening pride: **your heart is proud** (literally, "lifted up" or "exalted"). This ruler has claimed divine status for himself, saying, **I am a god, / I sit in the seat of the gods, / in the heart of the seas**. The Lord, who is truly God, dismisses this claim: **yet you are but a man, and no god**. Is this word directed at a specific figure in the time of Ezekiel? Probably not.[27] The kings of Tyre were known to claim a divine rank, and so it is likely that this charge is intended as a general rebuke of Tyre's kings.

28:3–5   The prince of Tyre is then compared to the figure of Daniel.[28] The statement **you are indeed wiser than Daniel** may be a genuine acknowledgment in praise

27. We know very little about the prince of Tyre in Ezekiel's day, Ethbaal III, and have no reason to conclude that he was specially identified with this prideful claim.
28. This may be a reference to the biblical Daniel, renowned for his wisdom and gifts of revelation (see Dan 2:19–23; 4:6, 9; 5:13–14), but many scholars believe that Ezekiel is referring either to the grandfather

of the intelligence of the prince of Tyre, but there may also be a hint of sarcasm here, captured in the NABRE translation: "Oh yes, you are wiser than Daniel, / nothing secret is too obscure for you!" In any event, the **wisdom** of this prince has gained him great wealth, causing him to become proud because of his superabundant prosperity.

And so because this *man* considers himself to be **as wise as a god**, the Lord   28:6–10
will bring foreign nations against Tyre that will cast down the city's proud bearing. When the prince himself is killed, then all will see that he is no god: **you shall die the death of the slain / in the heart of the seas**. Ezekiel makes use of an ironic word play here: this man (the prince) who claims in his "heart" to be a god and to rule from the "heart" of the sea will indeed be cast down and destroyed in the "heart" of the sea—that is, sink to the bottom of it. The term for "heart" (Hebrew *lev*) appears eight times in the chapter. This key term reveals the core of the problem—the *heart* of the prince has gone bad and raised itself up against God. In the end, to resolve this heart problem for both Israel and the nations, God will need to give a new heart that is humble and obedient (see Ezek 36:26).

Ezekiel then restates the penalty in store for the king of Tyre: he shall **die the death of the uncircumcised / by the hand of foreigners**. Like Israel, the people of Tyre and Sidon also practiced circumcision. To be cast into the netherworld next to the "uncircumcised" peoples was a sign of humiliation to those nations that practiced circumcision. The final fate of the Tyrian king will show that he is no god.

Lamentation over the King of Tyre (28:11–19)

---

[11]Moreover the word of the LORD came to me: [12]"Son of man, raise a lamentation over the king of Tyre, and say to him, Thus says the Lord GOD:

> "You were the signet of perfection,
>   full of wisdom
>   and perfect in beauty.
> [13]You were in Eden, the garden of God;
>   every precious stone was your covering,
> carnelian, topaz, and jasper,
>   chrysolite, beryl, and onyx,
> sapphire, carbuncle, and emerald;
>   and wrought in gold were your settings
>   and your engravings.

---

of Methuselah according to the Jewish work *Jubilees* or to an ancient Phoenician king from the twelfth century BC known for his great wisdom (see the commentary on Ezek 14:12–21).

> On the day that you were created
> they were prepared.
> [14]With an anointed guardian cherub I placed you;
> you were on the holy mountain of God;
> in the midst of the stones of fire you walked.
> [15]You were blameless in your ways
> from the day you were created,
> till iniquity was found in you.
> [16]In the abundance of your trade
> you were filled with violence, and you sinned;
> so I cast you as a profane thing from the mountain of God,
> and the guardian cherub drove you out
> from the midst of the stones of fire.
> [17]Your heart was proud because of your beauty;
> you corrupted your wisdom for the sake of your splendor.
> I cast you to the ground;
> I exposed you before kings,
> to feast their eyes on you.
> [18]By the multitude of your iniquities,
> in the unrighteousness of your trade
> you profaned your sanctuaries;
> so I brought forth fire from the midst of you;
> it consumed you,
> and I turned you to ashes upon the earth
> in the sight of all who saw you.
> [19]All who know you among the peoples
> are appalled at you;
> you have come to a dreadful end
> and shall be no more for ever."

OT: Gen 1–3; Exod 28:17–20; 39:10–13; Isa 51:3; Joel 2:3
NT: 1 John 3:8
Catechism: the sin of pride, 1866, 2094; the vanity of seeking this world's riches, 1723, 2445, 2556

28:11–12   In the final word directed against Tyre (vv. 11–19), Ezekiel offers **a lamentation over the king of Tyre** ("king" here is a synonym for "prince" in the previous section). Ezekiel speaks about the king of Tyre figuratively, using language drawn from Adam, the primal man, in the garden of Eden. No other Old Testament author makes such extensive use of the imagery of the creation and fall in Gen 1–3.

The qualities that Ezekiel assigns to the king of Tyre are stunning. He is **the signet of perfection, / full of wisdom / and perfect in beauty**. This is high praise indeed! A "signet" is a seal, often fixed to a ring made from a fine jewel.[29]

29. For the use of "signets" in the Old Testament, see Gen 38:18; Exod 28:11; 1 Kings 21:8; Jer 22:24.

Here the "signet" or "seal" is a sign revealing the identity and character of the Tyrian king. The description of the king of Tyre as "the signet of perfection" is probably intended as an echo of Adam and Eve being made in the image and likeness of God (Gen 1:26–27).

Furthermore, this king dwelt **in Eden, the garden of God**, where he had access to precious gems. The king, who dwelt **on the holy mountain of God**, was given **an anointed guardian †cherub** to guard him.[30] Additionally, this king—like Adam—was blameless in all his ways until the day when unrighteousness was found in him. Because of this, God cast him away from the mountain of God. All this took place because his **heart was proud** and his wisdom became corrupted. This glorious figure, who began with such promise, is cast to the ground, exposed before all the nations, and destroyed by fire. It is the story of the rise and fall of Tyre's king, figuratively portrayed against the backdrop of the creation and fall of Adam.

The scene of Adam in the garden provides the imaginative backdrop for the magnificent endowments and tragic fall of the king of Tyre, and the parallels between the Tyrian king and Adam in the garden of Eden are striking and unmistakable. Like Adam, the king of Tyre dwelt in *Eden*, the *garden* of God.[31] All this was prepared for him on the day of his *creation*. A *guardian cherub* was there in the garden with him, and the king *walked in righteousness* right up until the day when pride claimed his heart. Because of his pride, like Adam he was cast out of the garden and brought to ruin. All this recalls the figure of Adam in the garden.

While the parallels are many, there are also contrasts. The precious gems fixed on the Tyrian king's clothing are in sharp contrast to the naked state of Adam (and Eve) in the garden. Notably, the list of gems generally matches the precious stones sewn into the high priest's garments (see Exod 28:17–20; 39:10–13), and so links the figure of the prince of Tyre to the high priest. The precise meaning of this link between the king of Tyre and the high priest is unclear, but it is striking that the high priest bore on his garments the "signets" of the twelve tribes of Israel (Exod 39:6, 14), and that the high priest's crown bore an inscription "like the engraving of a signet, 'Holy to the Lord'" (Exod 39:30). This link between the king of Tyre and the high priest may also be based on Ezekiel's belief that Adam himself originally possessed a high priestly role in creation.

Two details in Ezekiel's story find no parallel in Genesis: the garden of Eden is situated on **the mountain of God**, and the king of Tyre walks in the **midst**

---

30. The main alternate translation, "you were an anointed guardian cherub" (ESV), points toward the identification of the king of Tyre with the figure of †Satan, who was a fallen angel.

31. Outside of Genesis and Ezekiel, the place name "Eden," signifying a garden, appears only in Isa 51:3 and Joel 2:3.

The Fall of Satan

The early Christian tradition consistently applied the description of the king of Tyre to the figure of Satan and treated this passage as providing additional biblical testimony to the prehistorical fall of the devil from †grace (supplementing 1 John 3:8). While Ezekiel probably understood himself to be prophesying about the king of Tyre, the unique statements made about this king make it likely—as early Christian tradition suggests—that the prophet's words have a †fuller sense, intended by God, but not fully grasped by the human author.[a]

Origen of Alexandria (d. 254) concludes that the words Ezekiel speaks cannot possibly depict a mere human being, and so must be understood of a high and lofty angel: "These statements, therefore, from the prophet Ezekiel concerning the prince of Tyre must relate, as we have shown, to an adverse power, and they prove in the clearest manner that this power was originally holy and blessed, and that he fell from this state of blessedness and was cast down to the earth." St. Ambrose (d. 397) draws the same conclusion from the elevated qualities attributed to this figure: "That the devil existed even in paradise we are informed by the prophet Ezekiel, who in discussing the prince of Tyre says, 'You are in Eden, the garden of God.' The prince of Tyre stands for the devil."[b]

a. Traditional Jewish interpretation of Ezek 28 does not apply it to the figure of Satan but interprets the exorbitant claims as signs of the (false) self-deification of the Tyrian king. See Rosenberg, *Book of Ezekiel*, 2:239–44.

b. Origen, *On First Principles* 1.5.4; St. Ambrose, *On Paradise* 2.9 (ACCS 13:94, 96).

of the stones of fire.[32] Ezekiel freely adapts the details of the Genesis story to show how great were the endowments of the king of Tyre and how devastating his subsequent fall through pride.[33]

Oracle against Sidon and Israel's Restoration (28:20–26)

[20]The word of the LORD came to me: [21]"Son of man, set your face toward Sidon, and prophesy against her [22]and say, Thus says the Lord GOD:

"Behold, I am against you, O Sidon,
     and I will manifest my glory in the midst of you.

32. The significance of the king of Tyre walking "in the midst of the stones of fire" is unclear. The "stones of fire" may have some connection to "the coals of fire" that surround the presence of the Lord in the temple (Ezek 1:13) and may point to the purifying presence of God.

33. The Jewish rabbis understood Ezekiel's account here as giving further details about the original story in Genesis (see Greenberg, *Ezekiel 21–37*, 590). Scholars today debate whether Ezekiel is freely adapting the Genesis story or whether he is drawing on a more ancient and expansive tradition concerning the garden of Eden not recorded in Genesis.

> And they shall know that I am the LORD
>   when I execute judgments in her,
>   and manifest my holiness in her;
> [23]for I will send pestilence into her,
>   and blood into her streets;
> and the slain shall fall in the midst of her,
>   by the sword that is against her on every side.
> Then they will know that I am the LORD.

[24]"And for the house of Israel there shall be no more a brier to prick or a thorn to hurt them among all their neighbors who have treated them with contempt. Then they will know that I am the Lord GOD.

[25]"Thus says the Lord GOD: When I gather the house of Israel from the peoples among whom they are scattered, and manifest my holiness in them in the sight of the nations, then they shall dwell in their own land which I gave to my servant Jacob. [26]And they shall dwell securely in it, and they shall build houses and plant vineyards. They shall dwell securely, when I execute judgments upon all their neighbors who have treated them with contempt. Then they will know that I am the LORD their God."

OT: Gen 35:12; Jer 25:22; 47:4; Joel 3:4; Zech 9:2
NT: Matt 11:21–22; Luke 10:13–14
Catechism: the sin of pride, 1866, 2094; the vanity of seeking this world's riches, 1723, 2445, 2556

Tucked in between the lengthy oracles against Tyre and Egypt is this short oracle against **Sidon**, Tyre's sister city.[34] Like Tyre, Sidon was a mercantile Phoenician city renowned for its extensive trade and abundant wealth. The word of judgment against Sidon follows the same form that Ezekiel uses against the other surrounding nations. The Lord has set himself against Sidon and will **manifest** both his **glory** and his **holiness** through the judgment that he will bring upon this city. When the Lord humbles Sidon through pestilence and conquering armies, **then they will know that I am the LORD**. In contrast to the judgments that God will enact against Israel's neighbors, his own people Israel will no longer be attacked or treated with contempt. A new season of restoration will open up for Israel after the severe punishments they have suffered for their sins. 28:20–24

Here at the exact midpoint of the oracles against the nations Ezekiel plants a word of hope and a promise of restoration for his people, anticipating the abundant promises of restoration to come (Ezek 34–36). Israel has in fact been punished and scattered to the nations, but the Lord will gather up the remnant of Israel and bring them back to the land: **they shall dwell in their own land which I gave to my servant Jacob**. 28:25–26

---

34. Sidon is often placed in parallel with Tyre in both the Old and the New Testaments: see Jer 25:22; 47:4; Joel 3:4; Zech 9:2; Matt 11:21–22; Luke 10:13–14.

This act of restoration will **manifest** the **holiness** of God **in the sight of the** **nations**. How so? By restoring his people, the Lord displays in a public and visible way his faithfulness and †covenant love. The Lord promised long ago that if his people sinned grievously, they would lose their land and be scattered among the nations (Lev 26; Deut 28–29), but he also promised that he would bring them back and plant them once again *in the land*, in fulfillment of his word to Abraham, Isaac, and Jacob.[35] By both restoring his people to the land and bringing judgment against the surrounding nations, the Lord ensures not only that his people **shall dwell securely** in the land, where they will flourish once again, but also that they will know that it is **the LORD their God** who has done this.

---

35. The promise of the land given to Jacob builds upon Gen 35:12 and is a common theme in the Prophets (see Isa 14:1–2; 44:3; 49:8; Jer 30:10; 46:27–28).

Prophecies against the Nations, Part 2: Egypt

Ezekiel 29:1–32:32

We now begin a series of seven †oracles against Egypt that occupy the next four chapters. From the time of Assyria's rise (ninth–seventh centuries BC) through the period of Babylonian ascendency (seventh–sixth centuries BC), Egypt was no longer the dominant power but was continually attempting to become a main player and regain influence in Syria-Palestine, usually unsuccessfully. For their part, Israel and Judah (the northern and southern kingdoms) were perennially tempted to make an alliance with Egypt against the dominant powers of Assyria and Babylon. The prophets consistently warned against this. Egypt was an unreliable ally. For Israel to turn to Egypt amounted to a rejection of the Lord and his power.[1]

Oracles of Judgment against Egypt (29:1–21)

¹In the tenth year, in the tenth month, on the twelfth day of the month, the word of the LORD came to me: ²"Son of man, set your face against Pharaoh king of Egypt, and prophesy against him and against all Egypt; ³speak, and say, Thus says the Lord GOD:

> "Behold, I am against you,
>   Pharaoh king of Egypt,
> the great dragon that lies
>   in the midst of his streams,

---

1. For the biblical testimony against Egypt as an unreliable ally, see Isa 30:1–7; 31:1–3; Jer 37:5–10.

that says, 'My Nile is my own;
   I made it.'
⁴I will put hooks in your jaws,
   and make the fish of your streams stick to your scales;
and I will draw you up out of the midst of your streams,
   with all the fish of your streams
   which stick to your scales.
⁵And I will cast you forth into the wilderness,
   you and all the fish of your streams;
you shall fall upon the open field,
   and not be gathered and buried.
To the beasts of the earth and to the birds of the air
   I have given you as food.

⁶"Then all the inhabitants of Egypt shall know that I am the Lord. Because you have been a staff of reed to the house of Israel; ⁷when they grasped you with the hand, you broke, and tore all their shoulders; and when they leaned upon you, you broke, and made all their loins to shake; ⁸therefore thus says the Lord God: Behold, I will bring a sword upon you, and will cut off from you man and beast; ⁹and the land of Egypt shall be a desolation and a waste. Then they will know that I am the Lord.

"Because you said, 'The Nile is mine, and I made it,' ¹⁰therefore, behold, I am against you, and against your streams, and I will make the land of Egypt an utter waste and desolation, from Migdol to Syene, as far as the border of Ethiopia. ¹¹No foot of man shall pass through it, and no foot of beast shall pass through it; it shall be uninhabited forty years. ¹²And I will make the land of Egypt a desolation in the midst of desolated countries; and her cities shall be a desolation forty years among cities that are laid waste. I will scatter the Egyptians among the nations, and disperse them among the countries.

¹³"For thus says the Lord God: At the end of forty years I will gather the Egyptians from the peoples among whom they were scattered; ¹⁴and I will restore the fortunes of Egypt, and bring them back to the land of Pathros, the land of their origin; and there they shall be a lowly kingdom. ¹⁵It shall be the most lowly of the kingdoms, and never again exalt itself above the nations; and I will make them so small that they will never again rule over the nations. ¹⁶And it shall never again be the reliance of the house of Israel, recalling their iniquity, when they turn to them for aid. Then they will know that I am the Lord God."

¹⁷In the twenty-seventh year, in the first month, on the first day of the month, the word of the Lord came to me: ¹⁸"Son of man, Nebuchadrezzar king of Babylon made his army labor hard against Tyre; every head was made bald and every shoulder was rubbed bare; yet neither he nor his army got anything from Tyre to pay for the labor that he had

performed against it. [19]Therefore thus says the Lord GOD: Behold, I will give the land of Egypt to Nebuchadrezzar king of Babylon; and he shall carry off its wealth and despoil it and plunder it; and it shall be the wages for his army. [20]I have given him the land of Egypt as his recompense for which he labored, because they worked for me, says the Lord GOD.

[21]"On that day I will cause a horn to spring forth to the house of Israel, and I will open your lips among them. Then they will know that I am the LORD."

OT: Ps 95:5; Isa 7:14; 19:18–25; 36:6; Jer 46:26; Jon 3:4–10
NT: Matt 2:13–15; Luke 1:38
Catechism: the sin of pride, 1866, 2094; the messianic promise, 528

The opening prophecy is dated to **the tenth year, in the tenth month, on the**   29:1–2 **twelfth day of the month** (January 7, 587), one year into Nebuchadnezzar's siege of Jerusalem. Jeremiah tells us that right in the middle of this siege, Pharaoh and his army came out of Egypt and traveled toward Israel (Jer 37:3–10). This caused Nebuchadnezzar to lift the siege temporarily, but soon Pharaoh retreated and the siege was renewed. With this failed rescue in the background, Ezekiel is told to set his face against Pharaoh and to prophesy **against him and against all Egypt.**

Egypt is charged with two offenses. The first is a boastful claim to divine   29:3–5 honors and powers. Likened to a **great dragon that lies / in the midst of his streams**, Pharaoh boasts that the vast Nile river **is my own; / I made it.**[2] Rather than acknowledging the Lord as the giver of this rich land and its river, Pharaoh places himself in the position of a god who gives the good land to his people. But as Ps 95:5 says, to shape the land belongs to God alone: "The sea is his, for he made it; / for his hands formed the dry land." By usurping God's sovereign position, Pharaoh falsely exalts himself and so calls down the judgment of the Lord upon himself.

Egypt's second offense is the failure to deliver on the promise of help to   29:6–12 Israel. Pharaoh entices Israel to rebel against Babylon with the promise of aid but consistently fails to render the pledged military assistance. Egypt, therefore, is **a staff of reed** on which Israel leaned but which broke and left **the house of Israel** vulnerable and defenseless against Babylon. The prophet Isaiah, speaking in a different historical context, offers a similar judgment about the folly of relying on Egyptian aid: "Behold, you are relying on Egypt, that broken reed of a staff, which will pierce the hand of any man who leans on it. Such is Pharaoh king of Egypt to all who rely on him" (Isa 36:6). For these reasons, the Lord says that he will take hold of this "dragon" of the Nile, put a hook into its snout, and

---

2. The "dragon" (Hebrew *tannin*) was a name for the crocodile that dwelt in the Nile (Ezek 32:2), but also for the great sea serpent that raged against the Lord (see Ps 74:13; Isa 27:1; 51:9).

The Future Restoration of Egypt

BIBLICAL BACKGROUND

The land of Egypt plays a complex role in the biblical story. In the book of Genesis, Egypt is first of all a place of refuge and relief: Joseph, sold as a slave, rises to prominence in Egypt, and through his prudent provision the family of Jacob is delivered from famine and given a fruitful homeland. In a similar way, Egypt is a refuge for the Holy Family fleeing from the murderous plans of Herod the Great (Matt 2:13–15). However, beginning with the book of Exodus, Egypt represents the place of slavery and oppression *from which* God delivered his people; to seek to return to Egypt is to go backward into slavery. In the time of the great empires, the prophets identify Egypt time and again as the land of false hope for Israel. Israel is continually tempted to find refuge in Egypt—but this always proves to be a false confidence. Nevertheless, despite all its sins and flaws, Egypt is one of the few nations that are promised redemption from the Lord. Ezekiel declares this restoration—"I will restore the fortunes of Egypt" (29:14)—though it means being restored to a position of humility. Jeremiah, too, though highly critical of Egypt, hints at the regathering of Egypt's people: "Afterward Egypt shall be inhabited as in the days of old, says the LORD" (Jer 46:26). But it is Isaiah (19:18–25) who describes the Lord's future blessing upon Egypt in the boldest terms. Isaiah predicts a day when Egypt will turn to the Lord and an altar to the Lord will be built in the land. The Lord will make himself known to the Egyptians and will send them a savior. He will heed their prayer and heal them, and it will be said (shockingly): "Blessed be Egypt my people, and Assyria the work of my hands, and Israel my heritage" (Isa 19:25). Though Egypt is primarily the recipient of God's judgment in the Bible, there will come a time when Egypt will come to know the Lord and be counted among his people. The early Christians could recognize one historical fulfillment of this prophecy when by the fourth century AD the majority of people in Egypt had become Christians.

drag it out into the wilderness, where it will become food for the beasts and the birds.[3] Ironically, Egypt will suffer **forty years** of desolation and loss, just as Judah will (see Ezek 4:6).[4]

29:13–16   In a reversal of fortune, Ezekiel prophesies that **at the end of forty years** the Lord will regather Egypt and bring her back to the land: **I will restore the fortunes of Egypt, and bring them back to the land of Pathros.** "Pathros" is

3. The "fish" of Egypt's streams represent either the Egyptian people or the vassal states that have allied themselves with Egypt.

4. Jeremiah, too, predicted severe judgment upon Egypt (Jer 43:8–13; 46:13–26). There is no record in Ezekiel (or elsewhere in the Old Testament) of the Egyptian people being sent into exile for forty years. Thus, we are not told how this prediction was fulfilled.

the name for upper (that is, southern) Egypt (see Isa 11:11; Jer 44:1). But this restoration is also at the same time a humbling of once-proud Egypt: **It shall be the most lowly of the kingdoms**. Yes, the Egyptians will be restored, but God **will make them so small that they will never again rule over the nations**. In consequence, Israel will no longer be tempted to act unfaithfully against the Lord by looking to Egypt for security or aid.

This short prophetic oracle bears the latest date in the entire book (April 26,   **29:17–21** 571). More than fifteen years after the fall of Jerusalem, the Lord speaks to Ezekiel about how God's word is now being worked out for Tyre and Egypt. Nebuchadnezzar labored hard to gain victory and the spoils of war from Tyre, **yet neither he nor his army got anything from Tyre to pay for the labor that he had performed against it**.[5] To compensate for this loss, the Lord is now handing over Egypt to the Babylonian king, **and he shall carry off its wealth and despoil it and plunder it**.[6] Strikingly, the Lord says that Nebuchadnezzar and his army **worked for me** and so deserve some **recompense** for their long labors. Just as the Lord would later raise up Cyrus to deliver his people and return them to their land (see Isa 45:1–7), so the Lord has used Nebuchadnezzar to execute judgment on his own people and on the surrounding nations. The Lord God is providentially ordering the events of history to bring about his plan.

The chapter concludes with a short word of promise to Israel: **On that day I will cause a horn to spring forth to the house of Israel**. This is best seen as a †messianic promise, but the reference is fleeting and undeveloped.[7] A fuller account of the coming messianic kingdom will appear shortly in chapters 34 and 37.

Reflection and Application (29:17–21)

The final oracle of chapter 29 presents us with an interesting problem. An earlier prophecy (26:1–14) that declared the full destruction of Tyre is now reinterpreted by a later prophecy, in which the prophet acknowledges that Babylon did not fully do to Tyre what seemed to be originally promised. What this shows is that predictive prophecy may be conditional. How things turn out may depend on the response of those addressed. Consider the message that

5. The historical records show that Tyre eventually surrendered to Babylon but bargained for the protection of the city and its wealth. Thus, the Babylonians did not receive the full spoils of war for which they had been hoping. On the siege of Tyre, see the commentary on Ezek 26:7–14.

6. Jeremiah, too, predicted the defeat of Egypt by the Babylonian armies (see Jer 43:8–13). The Jewish historian Josephus confirms Nebuchadnezzar's victories in Egypt (*Antiquities of the Jews* 10.180–84).

7. The verb "spring forth" is used elsewhere in the Old Testament to refer to the †Messiah, the son of David (see Ps 132:17; Jer 33:15; Zech 6:12), and is related to the noun "sprout/branch" that became a messianic code word in postexilic Judah (see Isa 4:2; Jer 23:5; Zech 3:8).

Jonah delivered to the city of Nineveh: "Yet forty days, and Nineveh shall be overthrown!" (Jon 3:4). No condition was attached to this prediction ("if you don't repent"); Jonah just announced the city's doom. Yet the people did in fact hear the word and repent: "And the people of Nineveh believed God; they proclaimed a fast, and put on sackcloth, from the greatest of them to the least of them" (3:5). And the city was spared, to Jonah's chagrin (3:10–4:1). Did God's word fail? No, it produced the intended result, and the outcome was blessing instead of judgment.

In the case of the word spoken against Tyre, Ezekiel is not told why the predicted destruction of the city did not take place, but he now perceives that the action of God has shifted in a new direction. Even when God announces his plan of salvation and declares his promise, he often makes use of the active cooperation of human agents to bring about his plan. Abraham's ready obedience confirmed God's promise and opened the door to God's plan (see Gen 22:15–18). Isaiah announced that "a virgin shall conceive and bear a son" (Isa 7:14), and yet the Lord elicited Mary's active "yes" in order to bring about the †incarnation of the Word for our salvation (see Luke 1:38). Even when prophecy is genuine, we do not know *how* or exactly *when* God will bring his word to pass. But we do know that God is faithful. God's word will bear the fruit he intends, in the world and in our own lives.

The Day of Judgment Coming upon Egypt (30:1–19)

¹The word of the LORD came to me: ²"Son of man, prophesy, and say, Thus says the Lord GOD:

> "Wail, 'Alas for the day!'
> ³For the day is near,
>   the day of the LORD is near;
> it will be a day of clouds,
>   a time of doom for the nations.
> ⁴A sword shall come upon Egypt,
>   and anguish shall be in Ethiopia,
> when the slain fall in Egypt,
>   and her wealth is carried away,
>   and her foundations are torn down.

⁵Ethiopia, and Put, and Lud, and all Arabia, and Libya, and the people of the land that is in league, shall fall with them by the sword.

> ⁶"Thus says the LORD:
> Those who support Egypt shall fall,
>   and her proud might shall come down;

from Migdol to Syene
    they shall fall within her by the sword,
says the Lord GOD.
[7]And she shall be desolated in the midst of desolated countries
    and her cities shall be in the midst of cities that are laid waste.
[8]Then they will know that I am the LORD,
    when I have set fire to Egypt,
    and all her helpers are broken.

[9]"On that day swift messengers shall go forth from me to terrify the unsuspecting Ethiopians; and anguish shall come upon them on the day of Egypt's doom; for behold, it comes!

[10]"Thus says the Lord GOD:
I will put an end to the wealth of Egypt,
    by the hand of Nebuchadrezzar king of Babylon.
[11]He and his people with him, the most terrible of the nations,
    shall be brought in to destroy the land;
and they shall draw their swords against Egypt,
    and fill the land with the slain.
[12]And I will dry up the Nile,
    and will sell the land into the hand of evil men;
I will bring desolation upon the land and everything in it,
    by the hand of foreigners;
I, the LORD, have spoken.

[13]"Thus says the Lord GOD:
I will destroy the idols,
    and put an end to the images, in Memphis;
there shall no longer be a prince in the land of Egypt;
    so I will put fear in the land of Egypt.
[14]I will make Pathros a desolation,
    and will set fire to Zoan,
    and will execute acts of judgment upon Thebes.
[15]And I will pour my wrath upon Pelusium,
    the stronghold of Egypt,
    and cut off the multitude of Thebes.
[16]And I will set fire to Egypt;
    Pelusium shall be in great agony;
Thebes shall be breached,
    and its walls broken down.
[17]The young men of On and of Pibeseth shall fall by the sword;
    and the women shall go into captivity.
[18]At Tehaphnehes the day shall be dark,
    when I break there the dominion of Egypt,

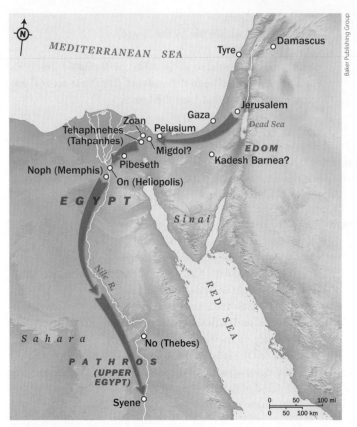

Figure 7. The land of Egypt and the path of the refugees from Judah

> and her proud might shall come to an end;
> she shall be covered by a cloud,
> and her daughters shall go into captivity.
> [19]Thus I will execute acts of judgment upon Egypt.
> Then they will know that I am the Lord."

OT: Isa 13:6; 19:5; Joel 2:1; 3:14; Zeph 1:7
NT: Luke 1:51–52
Catechism: the judgment of God through Christ the Son, 679; the sin of pride, 1866, 2094

30:1–9 Chapter 30 opens with a poetic declaration of the judgment of the Lord against Egypt in the form of a lament (vv. 1–19). Ezekiel is told: **Wail, "Alas for the day!"** Why? Because **the day of the Lord is near**—a day of doom and judgment about to fall on Egypt and the surrounding nations.[8] These nations (Ethiopia, Put, Lud, Arabia, and Libya) represent those who "were either allied with Egypt or

8. For "the day of the Lord" as a time of judgment, see also Isa 13:6; Joel 2:1; 3:14; Zeph 1:7.

214

provided mercenaries to the Egyptians."[9] The catchphrase, **a time of doom for the nations**, aptly sums up the *entire* section of the oracles against the nations (chaps. 25–32): there will be a day of reckoning for the nations when they, too, will be judged. Why are these nations coming under judgment? Because they have all shown support for Egypt: **Those who support Egypt shall fall, / and her proud might shall come down**.

The Lord then speaks to Ezekiel in greater detail about what will happen to   **30:10–19** Egypt: **I will put an end to the wealth of Egypt** through the hand of Nebuchadnezzar king of Babylon. All parts of Egypt will suffer loss. The Nile, the great natural resource of Egypt, will be dried up: "And the waters of the Nile will be dried up, / and the river will be parched and dry" (Isa 19:5). The major cities of Egypt, from north to south, will be devastated.[10] In the process, idols and images will be cast down, and the prince of Egypt (Pharaoh) will be no more. In sum, the Lord will break Egypt's pride and send her people into captivity: **Thus I will execute acts of judgment upon Egypt. / Then they will know that I am the LORD**.

Egypt Broken and Sent into Exile (30:20–26)

---

[20]In the eleventh year, in the first month, on the seventh day of the month, the word of the LORD came to me: [21]"Son of man, I have broken the arm of Pharaoh king of Egypt; and behold, it has not been bound up, to heal it by binding it with a bandage, so that it may become strong to wield the sword. [22]Therefore thus says the Lord GOD: Behold, I am against Pharaoh king of Egypt, and will break his arms, both the strong arm and the one that was broken; and I will make the sword fall from his hand. [23]I will scatter the Egyptians among the nations, and disperse them throughout the lands. [24]And I will strengthen the arms of the king of Babylon, and put my sword in his hand; but I will break the arms of Pharaoh, and he will groan before him like a man mortally wounded. [25]I will strengthen the arms of the king of Babylon, but the arms of Pharaoh shall fall; and they shall know that I am the LORD. When I put my sword into the hand of the king of Babylon, he shall stretch it out against the land of Egypt; [26]and I will scatter the Egyptians among the nations and disperse them throughout the countries. Then they will know that I am the LORD."

OT: Exod 6:6; 17:10–13; Deut 4:34; 5:15; Ps 44:3; Jer 32:21
NT: Luke 1:51–52
Catechism: the judgment of God through Christ the Son, 679; the sin of pride, 1866, 2094

---

9. Alter, "Ezekiel," 1141.
10. Ezekiel refers to eight Egyptian cities or regions, six of them near (or in) the northern delta (Memphis, Zoan, Pelusium, On, Pibeseth, and Tehaphnehes) and two in southern Egypt (Pathros, Thebes).

The Strong Arm of the Lord

BIBLICAL BACKGROUND

The "arm" is a common biblical symbol for strength, power, and authority, especially in military prowess. When the Lord declares through Ezekiel that he will break both of Pharaoh's arms, he is demonstrating that he is stronger than Pharaoh, who vainly boasted about the strength of his arm. The phrase "with a strong hand and an outstretched arm" occurs as a constant chorus in the Old Testament to describe God's deliverance of Israel from Egypt: "You brought your people Israel out of the land of Egypt with signs and wonders, with a strong hand and outstretched arm, and with great terror" (Jer 32:21). The symbolic power of the strength of the arm is visually displayed as Aaron and Hur hold up the arms of Moses, enabling Israel to be successful in battle (Exod 17:10–13). For their part, the people of Israel had to be reminded that it was not their own "arm" that won the promised land but the strong right hand and arm of the Lord (Ps 44:3). Ezekiel is told to act out the coming siege against Jerusalem with his "arm bared," showing that God's strength is now enlisted against his own people (Ezek 4:7). The symbolism of the strong arm continues in the New Testament. The great prayer of Mary (the Magnificat) employs the symbol of the "arm" to show the culmination of God's deliverance now revealed in Jesus the †Messiah, the incarnate Son of God: "He has shown strength with his arm, / he has scattered the proud in the imagination of their hearts, / he has put down the mighty from their thrones, / and exalted those of low degree" (Luke 1:51–52).

30:20–24   In this next oracle (vv. 20–26), dated to **the eleventh year, in the first month, on the seventh day of the month** (April 29, 587), the Lord declares that he has already **broken the arm of Pharaoh**, and that soon he will break both of Pharaoh's arms, **both the strong arm and the one that was broken**. The word "arm" is the key term in this prophecy. The arm (or hand) was the instrument of rule and warfare, a symbol of power and strength. The Lord himself is described as acting "with a mighty hand and an outstretched arm" (Ezek 20:33, 34).[11] Here the Lord promises to **strengthen the arms of the king of Babylon** (Nebuchadnezzar) but **break the arms of Pharaoh**. As Isaiah and Jeremiah clarify, the Lord is making use of Babylon not because of Babylon's goodness or uprightness but to serve the Lord's purpose of judgment against both Egypt and his own people in Jerusalem (see Isa 47:1–7; Jer 28:8–12). In the Lord's providential timing, Babylon will also come under judgment for its many offenses.[12]

11. For the strong arm of the Lord, see also Exod 6:6; Deut 4:34; 5:15.
12. For God's judgment against Babylon, see Isa 13–14; Jer 51–52.

The already-broken arm of Pharaoh probably refers to Pharaoh Hophra and   30:25–26
his unsuccessful attempt to break the Babylonian siege of Jerusalem in 588 (see
Jer 37:4–10). According to ancient inscriptions, Hophra touted himself as the
"possessor of a strong arm."[13] This claim already proved feeble; the strong arm
of Pharaoh was broken before, and *both* his arms will be broken in the days to
come when Babylon defeats Egypt. The final result: the Egyptians will be scattered and dispersed among the nations, just as Israel had been: **I will scatter the
Egyptians among the nations and disperse them throughout the countries.**[14]

Parable of the Judgment against the Great Tree (31:1–18)

[1]In the eleventh year, in the third month, on the first day of the month, the
word of the LORD came to me: [2]"Son of man, say to Pharaoh king of Egypt
and to his multitude:

"Whom are you like in your greatness?
   [3]Behold, I will liken you to a cedar in Lebanon,
with fair branches and forest shade,
   and of great height,
   its top among the clouds.
[4]The waters nourished it,
   the deep made it grow tall,
making its rivers flow
   round the place of its planting,
sending forth its streams
   to all the trees of the forest.
[5]So it towered high
   above all the trees of the forest;
its boughs grew large
   and its branches long,
   from abundant water in its shoots.
[6]All the birds of the air
   made their nests in its boughs;
under its branches all the beasts of the field
   brought forth their young;
and under its shadow
   dwelt all great nations.

---

13. Block, *Ezekiel: Chapters 25–48*, 176.
14. It is difficult to determine how and when this prophecy of Egypt's scattering and exile had a
historical fulfillment, in part or in full. Certainly Egypt has experienced many military defeats, from
the time of Alexander the Great (fourth century BC) until modern times. But it is not evident when the
Egyptian *people* were sent into exile in the way that, for example, the northern and southern kingdoms
of Israel were sent into exile.

7It was beautiful in its greatness,
  in the length of its branches;
for its roots went down
  to abundant waters.
8The cedars in the garden of God could not rival it,
  nor the fir trees equal its boughs;
the plane trees were as nothing
  compared with its branches;
no tree in the garden of God
  was like it in beauty.
9I made it beautiful
  in the mass of its branches,
and all the trees of Eden envied it,
  that were in the garden of God.

10"Therefore thus says the Lord God: Because it towered high and set its top among the clouds, and its heart was proud of its height, 11I will give it into the hand of a mighty one of the nations; he shall surely deal with it as its wickedness deserves. I have cast it out. 12Foreigners, the most terrible of the nations, will cut it down and leave it. On the mountains and in all the valleys its branches will fall, and its boughs will lie broken in all the watercourses of the land; and all the peoples of the earth will go from its shadow and leave it. 13Upon its ruin will dwell all the birds of the air, and upon its branches will be all the beasts of the field. 14All this is in order that no trees by the waters may grow to lofty height or set their tops among the clouds, and that no trees that drink water may reach up to them in height; for they are all given over to death, to the nether world among mortal men, with those who go down to the Pit.

15"Thus says the Lord God: When it goes down to Sheol I will make the deep mourn for it, and restrain its rivers, and many waters shall be stopped; I will clothe Lebanon in gloom for it, and all the trees of the field shall faint because of it. 16I will make the nations quake at the sound of its fall, when I cast it down to Sheol with those who go down to the Pit; and all the trees of Eden, the choice and best of Lebanon, all that drink water, will be comforted in the nether world. 17They also shall go down to Sheol with it, to those who are slain by the sword; yes, those who dwelt under its shadow among the nations shall perish. 18Whom are you thus like in glory and in greatness among the trees of Eden? You shall be brought down with the trees of Eden to the nether world; you shall lie among the uncircumcised, with those who are slain by the sword.

"This is Pharaoh and all his multitude, says the Lord God."

OT: Pss 6:5; 16:10; 49:15; Prov 15:24; Isa 14:9–10; Dan 4:10–12
NT: Acts 2:31; Rev 1:17
Catechism: the sin of pride, 1866, 2094; †Sheol (†Hades) the place of the dead, 633

This chapter presents an †allegory of Egypt's demise: Egypt's history is likened to the rise and fall of a great cedar tree.[15] The RSV-2CE emends the Hebrew text of verse 3 to say "I will liken you to a cedar in Lebanon," but the majority of English translations (e.g., ESV, NRSV, NABRE) and scholars follow the Hebrew text, which says, "Behold, Assyria was a cedar in Lebanon" (ESV).[16] If we accept this reading, then only the first two verses and the final verse of this chapter are directly about Egypt; the rest is a story about the rise, glory, and fall of Assyria, offered as a cautionary tale for what will also befall Egypt. The point of the comparison is this: if Assyria, an empire far greater than Egypt, suffered a devastating collapse, what will be the fate of Egypt when they come up against Nebuchadnezzar?

The allegory of Egypt as a great cedar tree is dated to June 21, 587, just two **31:1–2** months after the previous prophecy. Many in Israel are still hoping that Egypt will come to their rescue and deliver them from the horrors of the siege of Jerusalem, but Ezekiel again declares Egypt to be impotent and unable to come to the aid of Israel. The oracle is addressed directly to **Pharaoh king of Egypt** and his entourage, but the message is primarily intended for the Jewish exiles in Babylon, and possibly also for the people of Israel besieged within Jerusalem. Ezekiel is declaring the weakness of Egypt, and therefore the folly of relying on Egypt to come to Israel's aid. The central question is, **Whom are you like in your greatness?** What does Egypt think about itself? To answer this question, Ezekiel selects the greatest empire of the recent past for comparison—Assyria. The comparison is apt, for Assyria was a great empire, and its fall was within living memory.[17]

The allegory describes a towering cedar like the cedars of Lebanon, greater **31:3–9** than any around it.[18] **Its top** was **among the clouds**, it was well watered by streams and rivers, and in its shadow lived **all great nations** of the earth. The image of a green and growing garden with a great tree at its center functions as a metaphor for the flourishing of Assyrian power. Three times Ezekiel says that this cedar could not be rivaled by trees in the **garden of God** (that is, **Eden**). The Lord God **made it beautiful**, and none could equal its splendor. Surely it would be completely secure in its strength, beauty, and dominance.[19]

But the great cedar tree (Assyria) is suddenly crushed and falls from its **31:10–14** high place. Why did it fall? Because **its heart was proud of its height**. Because

15. Ezekiel (in chap. 17) also uses the image of a great cedar to represent Israel.
16. The Greek translation (†Septuagint) also follows the Hebrew text, naming Assyria as the example to which Egypt is being compared.
17. Despite help from Egypt, Assyria's capital city, Nineveh, had fallen to Babylon in 612 BC, only twenty-five years before Jerusalem was besieged.
18. See Dan 4:10–12 for a similar parable of a great tree representing an eminent political figure (in this case, Nebuchadnezzar) and his empire.
19. †*Targum of Ezekiel* decodes the metaphor, adding historical language of conquest to make the reference to Assyria clear. Levey, *Targum of Ezekiel*, 89–90.

Assyria set its head in the clouds and was boastful, the Lord will give it over to **a mighty one of the nations**—namely, Babylon. And so this great tree was cut down, its branches and boughs all fallen to the ground, deserted by all the nations of the earth. Ezekiel is probably referring to a single event, the battle at Carchemish in 605, where the Assyrians and Egyptians were defeated decisively by the Babylonians. The surrounding nations are meant to give ear and learn the lesson from Assyria's fall: growing tall in pride will only lead to being **given over to death, to the nether world**. The great tree that was fed by waters from "the deep" (v. 4) is now cut down and descends to the deep **Pit**, to Sheol, the place of the dead. As Moshe Greenberg says, "The fate of the towering cedar must be a lesson to all favored ('well-watered') trees. The Assyrian kings' fate is a warning to all mighty kings not to boast in preeminence and grandeur."[20]

31:15–17   The close of the parable brings us to a scene in Sheol: the deep itself (Sheol) and all the nations shall mourn the loss of the great tree (the city): **When it goes down to Sheol I will make the deep mourn for it**. Then **all the trees of Eden, the choice and best of Lebanon,** will be comforted in the world below. They, too, had gone down to Sheol and now were in some way consoled that Assyria, that great and powerful empire, had also been humbled and come down to the place of the dead. Ezekiel uses several similar expressions to refer to the place of the dead: "the nether world" (v. 14), "the Pit" (v. 14), "Sheol" (v. 15), and "the deep" (v. 15). In Sheol, the place of the dead, all are equal, the great and the small. This comfort felt by the humble peoples in Sheol echoes the word of the prophet Isaiah to the proud king of Babylon:

> Sheol beneath is stirred up
> > to meet you when you come,
> it rouses the shades to greet you. . . .
> All of them will speak
> > and say to you:
> "You too have become as weak as we!
> > You have become like us!" (Isa 14:9–10)

31:18   The final verse circles back to the original question regarding Egypt and Pharaoh: **Whom are you thus like in glory and in greatness among the trees of Eden?** Egypt, too, like the great nation Assyria that preceded it, will be brought down to Sheol below and take its place with all the lowly victims of the sword. All this shall befall Pharaoh and his allies because of their pride.

20. Greenberg, *Ezekiel 21–37*, 641.

Sheol, the Abode of the Dead

BIBLICAL
BACKGROUND

This is the first appearance of the term †"Sheol" in the book of Ezekiel. Here and in the following chapter the prophet describes how Egypt will be consigned to the underworld of Sheol as judgment upon its pride. "Sheol" is the most common term in the Old Testament for the place of the dead and was translated into Greek as "Hades." It was the place where seemingly *all* the dead ended up, both the good and the wicked. "For in death there is no remembrance of you; / in Sheol who can give you praise?" (Ps 6:5). The clear expectation of bodily resurrection from the dead emerged in the later writings of the Old Testament (for example, in Dan 12:2–3), but there was no clear promise of resurrection through much of Israel's history.

Still, there are hints of escape from Sheol that begin to point to resurrection. Despite the seeming inevitability of descent to Sheol, there are glimmers of hope for escaping this place of the dead. The book of Proverbs says, "The wise man's path leads upward to life, / that he may avoid Sheol beneath" (Prov 15:24). The psalmist, too, holds out hope for deliverance: "But God will ransom my soul from the power of Sheol, / for he will receive me" (Ps 49:15). Even more strikingly, Ps 16, attributed to King David, speaks of a hope to be delivered from Sheol: "For you will not abandon my soul to Sheol, / or let your holy one see corruption" (Ps 16:10 ESV).[a]

This hope is definitively fulfilled in the person of Christ. When Peter stands up to preach the good news on the day of †Pentecost, he cites this very verse from Ps 16 as testimony that God has raised Jesus from the dead: David "foresaw and spoke of the resurrection of the Christ, that he was not abandoned to Hades, nor did his flesh see corruption" (Acts 2:31). The power of Sheol (Hades)—the place of the dead—is conclusively overcome by Jesus, who opens the way to resurrection and eternal life. In the book of Revelation, John recounts the final triumph of Jesus over death and Hades (the place of the dead): "I died, and behold I am alive forevermore, and I have the keys of Death and Hades" (Rev 1:17).

a. For a detailed study of Sheol in the Old Testament and the hope for eternal life in ancient Israel, see Jon Levenson, *Resurrection and the Restoration of Israel: The Ultimate Victory of the God of Life* (New Haven: Yale University Press, 2006).

Judgment and Lament for Pharaoh and Egypt (32:1–16)

¹In the twelfth year, in the twelfth month, on the first day of the month, the word of the LORD came to me: ²"Son of man, raise a lamentation over Pharaoh king of Egypt, and say to him:

> "You consider yourself a lion among the nations,
>   but you are like a dragon in the seas;

you burst forth in your rivers,
    trouble the waters with your feet,
    and foul their rivers.
³Thus says the Lord God:
    I will throw my net over you
    with a host of many peoples;
    and I will haul you up in my dragnet.
⁴And I will cast you on the ground,
    on the open field I will fling you,
and will cause all the birds of the air to settle on you,
    and I will gorge the beasts of the whole earth with you.
⁵I will strew your flesh upon the mountains,
    and fill the valleys with your carcass.
⁶I will drench the land even to the mountains
    with your flowing blood;
    and the watercourses will be full of you.
⁷When I blot you out, I will cover the heavens,
    and make their stars dark;
I will cover the sun with a cloud,
    and the moon shall not give its light.
⁸All the bright lights of heaven
    will I make dark over you,
    and put darkness upon your land,
        says the Lord God.

⁹"I will trouble the hearts of many peoples, when I carry you captive among the nations, into the countries which you have not known. ¹⁰I will make many peoples appalled at you, and their kings shall shudder because of you, when I brandish my sword before them; they shall tremble every moment, every one for his own life, on the day of your downfall. ¹¹For thus says the Lord God: The sword of the king of Babylon shall come upon you. ¹²I will cause your multitude to fall by the swords of mighty ones, all of them most terrible among the nations.

"They shall bring to nothing the pride of Egypt,
    and all its multitude shall perish.
¹³I will destroy all its beasts
    from beside many waters;
and no foot of man shall trouble them anymore,
    nor shall the hoofs of beasts trouble them.
¹⁴Then I will make their waters clear,
    and cause their rivers to run like oil, says the Lord God.
¹⁵When I make the land of Egypt desolate
    and when the land is stripped of all that fills it,

> when I strike all who dwell in it,
>   then they will know that I am the LORD.

[16]This is a lamentation which shall be chanted; the daughters of the nations shall chant it; over Egypt, and over all her multitude, shall they chant it, says the Lord GOD."

OT: Ps 73:23–24; Isa 14:8–21; 55:11; 65:17; 66:22
NT: Matt 6:19–20; John 14:2; Rev 22:1–5
Catechism: the sin of pride, 1866, 2094; Sheol (Hades) the place of the dead, 633

Ezekiel 32 presents two prophetic oracles against Egypt (vv. 1–16, 17–32). Most of what is contained in them is a repetition and restatement of what Ezekiel has already said about the fate of Egypt. The fact that Ezekiel recounts Egypt's judgment at such length shows his concern with this nation and his conviction that he should announce its downfall at the hand of the Babylonians.

The first oracle is dated to **the twelfth year, in the twelfth month, on the first day of the month** (March 3, 585), two months after Ezekiel received news of the fall of Jerusalem (see 33:21). Ezekiel is told to **raise a lamentation over Pharaoh king of Egypt**, and to announce the judgment of the Lord against the land. Pharaoh touts himself as **a lion among the nations**, but the Lord declares that Pharaoh is really **like a dragon in the seas** that succeeds only in muddying his own waters and fouling his streams.[21] Archaeological evidence shows that Egyptian Pharaohs likened themselves to the crocodile (or dragon) and to a conquering lion,[22] but Ezekiel uses the two images ironically in view of Egypt's upcoming defeat by Babylon. The Lord announces that he will catch this "dragon" in a dragnet and cast it up on the land: **the birds** of prey will feast on it, and **the beasts of the whole earth** will gorge on its flesh.[23] Even the physical world will quake at this judgment: **the heavens** and **their stars, the sun, the moon**, and **all the bright lights of heaven** will grow dark. [32:1–8]

The outcome of all this is that the surrounding nations will see and mourn and fear—they will be appalled and horror-struck: **I will make many peoples appalled at you. . . . They shall tremble every moment, every one for his own life, on the day of your downfall**. Why is this? Because if even this powerful rival empire could not escape the sword of the king of Babylon, what will be the [32:9–16]

---

21. By circling back to the image of Egypt as a dragon, Ezekiel establishes a pair of bookends that mark the beginning and conclusion of the oracles against Egypt (29:3; 32:2). For other biblical references to this dragon or sea monster, see Ps 74:13; Isa 27:1; 51:9–10.

22. For the archaeological evidence, see Greenberg, *Ezekiel 21–37*, 657; Block, *Ezekiel: Chapters 25–48*, 200–201.

23. Scholars identify a parallel here with the ancient Sumerian myth of Marduk and Tiamat, in which Marduk captures Tiamat in a net and spreads her slain body over all the land. See Block, *Ezekiel: Chapters 25–48*, 204.

fate of smaller, weaker nations? The end result will be that the pride of Egypt will fall to ruin, and its leaders will be destroyed. Then the Lord will cleanse the fouled waters of Egypt, and the Egyptians and surrounding peoples will know that he is the Lord. The oracle closes by returning to the theme of lamentation: **the daughters of the nations shall chant** a lament over Egypt because of its great fall.

Egypt Descends to the Place of the Dead (32:17–32)

---

[17]In the twelfth year, in the first month, on the fifteenth day of the month, the word of the LORD came to me: [18]"Son of man, wail over the multitude of Egypt, and send them down, her and the daughters of majestic nations, to the nether world, to those who have gone down to the Pit:

> [19]"Whom do you surpass in beauty?
> Go down, and be laid with the uncircumcised.'

[20]They shall fall amid those who are slain by the sword, and with her shall lie all her multitudes. [21]The mighty chiefs shall speak of them, with their helpers, out of the midst of Sheol: 'They have come down, they lie still, the uncircumcised, slain by the sword.'

[22]"Assyria is there, and all her company, their graves round about her, all of them slain, fallen by the sword; [23]whose graves are set in the uttermost parts of the Pit, and her company is round about her grave; all of them slain, fallen by the sword, who spread terror in the land of the living.

[24]"Elam is there, and all her multitude about her grave; all of them slain, fallen by the sword, who went down uncircumcised into the nether world, who spread terror in the land of the living, and they bear their shame with those who go down to the Pit. [25]They have made her a bed among the slain with all her multitude, their graves round about her, all of them uncircumcised, slain by the sword; for terror of them was spread in the land of the living, and they bear their shame with those who go down to the Pit; they are placed among the slain.

[26]"Meshech and Tubal are there, and all their multitude, their graves round about them, all of them uncircumcised, slain by the sword; for they spread terror in the land of the living. [27]And they do not lie with the fallen mighty men of old who went down to Sheol with their weapons of war, whose swords were laid under their heads, and whose shields are upon their bones; for the terror of the mighty men was in the land of the living. [28]So you shall be broken and lie among the uncircumcised, with those who are slain by the sword.

[29]"Edom is there, her kings and all her princes, who for all their might are laid with those who are slain by the sword; they lie with the uncircumcised, with those who go down to the Pit.

³⁰"The princes of the north are there, all of them, and all the Sidonians, who have gone down in shame with the slain, for all the terror which they caused by their might; they lie uncircumcised with those who are slain by the sword, and bear their shame with those who go down to the Pit.

³¹"When Pharaoh sees them, he will comfort himself for all his multitude, Pharaoh and all his army, slain by the sword, says the Lord GOD. ³²For he spread terror in the land of the living; therefore he shall be laid among the uncircumcised, with those who are slain by the sword, Pharaoh and all his multitude, says the Lord GOD."

OT: Ps 73:23–24; Isa 14:8–21; 25:8; 26:19; 65:17; 66:22
NT: Matt 6:19–20; John 14:2; Rev 22:1–5
Catechism: the sin of pride, 1866, 2094; Sheol (Hades) the place of the dead, 633

The seventh and final oracle against Egypt is dated to **the twelfth year, . . . on**   32:17–18
the fifteenth day of the month, but the Hebrew does not provide a month (the
Greek †Septuagint has "the first month"). Here I follow the NABRE rendering, "On the fifteenth day of that month in the twelfth year," which places this prophecy fifteen days after the prophecy in 32:1 (and so approximately on March 18, 585). The single dominant theme here is the plummeting of Egypt and its armies to the place of the dead, where they will join all the other nations that have gone down to Sheol. This destiny echoes the fate of Tyre (see Ezek 28:8–10) and parallels Isaiah's description of Babylon's descent to Sheol (Isa 14:8–21). Ezekiel presents here perhaps the most developed picture of Sheol in the entire Old Testament (see the sidebar "Sheol, the Abode of the Dead," p. 221).

There is historical evidence that at least Egypt's priests and kings were circumcised, and so for them to be assigned a place with the uncircumcised in the underworld would be a profound degradation. For the Egyptian pharaohs, who spared no expense in preparing themselves for the next world to ensure a high and glorious place in the afterlife, dwelling with the uncircumcised—among the common people—would be especially odious. But here their lot is to descend to the lowest place: "Go down, and be laid with the uncircumcised" (32:19). As Daniel Block observes, "The Egyptians would have found this announcement of their fate shocking. The nation that perceived itself as the epitome of culture, greatness, and glory is hereby sentenced to the most ignominious fate in the netherworld."[24] In striking fashion, Ezekiel is then commanded to *send* Egypt down to the place of the dead by his word: **wail over the multitude of Egypt, and send them down . . . to the nether world**. He is sending them off—bidding them farewell—with a prophetic explanation of their fate. This word also manifests the sovereign power of the Lord God of Israel over *all* the nations of the earth, however powerful in earthly terms. It is the Lord who directs the destiny of the nations.

24. Block, *Ezekiel: Chapters 25–48*, 218.

32:19–30   The conclusion to the oracle portrays a great ingathering of the nations that will join Egypt in the netherworld of Sheol. The nations listed are Assyria, Elam, Meshech, Tubal, Edom, Sidon, and the princes of the north. Ten times in these verses we hear the phrase "**slain** (or **fallen**) **by the sword**." This not only describes a violent death at the hands of enemy combatants, but it points to utter defeat and humiliation. Those "slain by the sword" do not control their own destiny; they have been defeated and sent to the underworld. And by picturing these selected nations gathered in Sheol, now joined by Egypt, Ezekiel brings to a climax his oracles against *all* the nations. After pronouncing a judgment of doom upon each nation in turn, Ezekiel now envisions them all gathered together in Sheol, the place of common judgment.

32:31–32   When Pharaoh sees that he is not alone in Sheol, **he will comfort himself for all his multitude**, on account of all his subjects who share his fate. And yet this is a cold and grim comfort because Pharaoh and all Egypt will **be laid among the uncircumcised** nations that are gathered together, all who have fallen by the sword, because of the Lord's judgment against them.[25] What does this mean for Ezekiel's Israelite audience in exile? They are assured that the mighty nations surrounding Israel, those who dominated Israel and rejoiced in its fall, will be humbled and brought down to the depths of Sheol. Despite appearances, these powerful nations will not always prevail; they will be brought low just as Israel will be raised up. The last major section of the book will take up precisely this "raising up" and restoration of Israel after its fall.

Reflection and Application (32:17–32)

Scholars debate just when the hope of *eternal* life with God became a tenet of faith in Israel. Early in the history of the people of Israel, the expectation was that all people—good and bad—would end up in Sheol, the place of the dead, living a kind of shadowy nonexistence (see the sidebar "Sheol, the Abode of the Dead," p. 221). But we see testimony in the Psalms that a hope for life everlasting with God was emerging: "I am continually with you; / you hold my right hand. / You guide me with your counsel, / and afterward you will receive me to glory" (Ps 73:23–24). The prophet Isaiah declares a day when death will be overcome—"He will swallow up death forever" (Isa 25:8)—and when the bodies of the dead shall rise: "Your dead shall live, their bodies shall rise. / O dwellers in the dust, awake and sing for joy!" (Isa 26:19). Expectation for a "new heavens and a new earth" appears in the final part of the book of Isaiah (65:17; 66:22). In the later history of Israel, the dwelling of faithful souls with

---

25. It is significant that Israel is not found among the nations in this picture of the dead in Sheol. Ezekiel will later speak about dead bones coming to life and the dead coming forth from their graves (chap. 37), indicating a hope of resurrection.

God after death (see Wis 3:1–8) and the hope of bodily resurrection (see Dan 12:2–3) appear with great clarity.

In this passage from Ezekiel (32:17–32), Pharaoh seems to gain a grim comfort in the fact that he is not alone in the depths of Sheol—all the other nations are there with him, keeping him company in the shadow-prison of the underworld (32:31). But God has something far better in store for his people than solidarity and camaraderie in a shadow-existence that is no life at all. We are promised eternal life with God—Father, Son, and Spirit—and with one another: an eternal communion of love and fruitful friendship that has no end, where moth and rust do not consume and where thieves no longer steal (Matt 6:19–20). In Christ, we have received a promise that we will be raised bodily from the dead and share an unbreakable bond of love with God and one another, living in a fruitful garden that is also a glorious city (Rev 22:1–5). How much greater is our hope and comfort than Pharaoh's! We have this promise from Jesus himself: "In my Father's house are many rooms; if it were not so, would I have told you that I go to prepare a place for you?" (John 14:2).

God's Judgment against Israel Completed

Ezekiel 33:1–33

This chapter functions as the hinge between the two main parts of the book. It sums up key themes of Ezekiel's prophesying in chapters 1–32 and brings the first part of the book to a close with the announcement of the fall of Jerusalem. But chapter 33 also initiates a new season of God's action to restore his people. Though the theme of judgment still appears in the chapters that follow (34–48), going forward, Ezekiel's message is mainly one of hope and promise.

Recapitulation of Two Key Themes (33:1–20)

¹The word of the Lord came to me: ²"Son of man, speak to your people and say to them, If I bring the sword upon a land, and the people of the land take a man from among them, and make him their watchman; ³and if he sees the sword coming upon the land and blows the trumpet and warns the people; ⁴then if any one who hears the sound of the trumpet does not take warning, and the sword comes and takes him away, his blood shall be upon his own head. ⁵He heard the sound of the trumpet, and did not take warning; his blood shall be upon himself. But if he had taken warning, he would have saved his life. ⁶But if the watchman sees the sword coming and does not blow the trumpet, so that the people are not warned, and the sword comes, and takes any one of them; that man is taken away in his iniquity, but his blood I will require at the watchman's hand.

⁷"So you, son of man, I have made a watchman for the house of Israel; whenever you hear a word from my mouth, you shall give them warning from me. ⁸If I say to the wicked, O wicked man, you shall surely die, and you do not speak to warn the wicked to turn from his way, that wicked man shall die in his iniquity, but his blood I will require at your hand. ⁹But if you warn the wicked to turn from his way, and he does not turn from his way; he shall die in his iniquity, but you will have saved your life.

¹⁰"And you, son of man, say to the house of Israel, Thus have you said: 'Our transgressions and our sins are upon us, and we waste away because of them; how then can we live?' ¹¹Say to them, As I live, says the Lord GOD, I have no pleasure in the death of the wicked, but that the wicked turn from his way and live; turn back, turn back from your evil ways; for why will you die, O house of Israel? ¹²And you, son of man, say to your people, The righteousness of the righteous shall not deliver him when he transgresses; and as for the wickedness of the wicked, he shall not fall by it when he turns from his wickedness; and the righteous shall not be able to live by his righteousness when he sins. ¹³Though I say to the righteous that he shall surely live, yet if he trusts in his righteousness and commits iniquity, none of his righteous deeds shall be remembered; but in the iniquity that he has committed he shall die. ¹⁴Again, though I say to the wicked, 'You shall surely die,' yet if he turns from his sin and does what is lawful and right, ¹⁵if the wicked restores the pledge, gives back what he has taken by robbery, and walks in the statutes of life, committing no iniquity; he shall surely live, he shall not die. ¹⁶None of the sins that he has committed shall be remembered against him; he has done what is lawful and right, he shall surely live.

¹⁷"Yet your people say, 'The way of the Lord is not just'; when it is their own way that is not just. ¹⁸When the righteous turns from his righteousness, and commits iniquity, he shall die for it. ¹⁹And when the wicked turns from his wickedness, and does what is lawful and right, he shall live by it. ²⁰Yet you say, 'The way of the Lord is not just.' O house of Israel, I will judge each of you according to his ways."

OT: Ezek 3:16–21; 18:21–32
NT: Matt 3:2; 4:15, 17; Acts 2:38
Catechism: warning against spiritual danger, 1033, 1056, 1852; the call to repentance and conversion, 1427–39
Lectionary: 33:7–9: 23rd Sunday in Ordinary Time (Year A)

At the beginning of his ministry Ezekiel heard this call from God: "I have made   **33:1–7**
you a watchman for the house of Israel" (3:17). As this watchman role comes to its conclusion, the Lord now returns to the call of the watchman but extends its reach. Ezekiel addresses the people, describing the role of the watchman who must sound the alarm when he sees enemy troops approaching the city (vv. 1–6). Ezekiel's hearers are now invited into this role of watchman. Only then does the Lord renew the call to Ezekiel himself: **So you, son of man, I have made a watchman for the house of Israel; whenever you hear a word from my mouth, you shall give them warning from me**. These two watchman-words function like "bookends" that bracket Ezekiel's prophetic ministry to warn Israel of the impending judgment.[1]

1. The prophetic role of the watchman is also found in Isa 21:6–9; 56:10; 62:6–7; Jer 6:17; Hosea 9:8; Hab 2:1.

St. Augustine as a Model Watchman over His Flock

LIVING TRADITION

Shortly after St. Augustine's death (in 430), Possidius wrote a biography of the great bishop of Hippo. Using the language of "watchman" from Ezekiel, he presents St. Augustine as an ideal example of what a true watchman over his flock should be:

> In all this he thought of himself as a watchman set by the Lord over the house of Israel; he preached the word in season and out of season, convincing, exhorting, rebuking and teaching with unfailing patience and taking special care to teach in turn those fitted for teaching others. When asked by some to take a hand in their temporal concerns, he wrote letters to various persons for them, but he regarded this occupation as a kind of forced labor that took him away from more important things. His real delight was to speak of the things of God, whether in public addresses or at home in familiar converse with his brothers.[a]

a. *Life of Augustine* 19.5–6 (ACCS 13:99).

33:8–9   The renewal of Ezekiel's call to be a watchman at the conclusion of the judgment †oracles is significant for two reasons. First, it recalls Ezekiel's foundational task as prophet, to warn the people about the Lord's judgment. But second, by revisiting Ezekiel's call as watchman right here as the city falls, the Lord indirectly *commends* Ezekiel for the role that he has played as a faithful watchman (as summarized in chaps. 4–24). Ezekiel's hearers (and readers) are prompted to see that Ezekiel has in fact fulfilled this call faithfully, but the people did not heed his warning; they did not turn from their wicked ways: **but if you warn the wicked to turn from his way, and he does not turn from his way; he shall die in his iniquity, but you will have saved your life**. And so the city has fallen, but the prophet who served as a faithful watchman is not responsible for the blood of his people.

33:10–20   The second section of chapter 33 is a reprise of Ezek 18:21–32, a compelling message about the Lord's justice in dealing with his people and his desire that they should repent and live (see the commentary on 18:1–32 for a fuller explanation of Ezekiel's case studies and main conclusions). Ezekiel restates this word here, but there are new elements that fit this new context. Because the city of Jerusalem has fallen, Israel is deeply discouraged, stricken by the weight of the judgment upon them and conscious that their circumstances are due to their sins. And so they say: **Our transgressions and our sins are upon us, and we waste away because of them; how then can we live?** (v. 10). In the face of this cry of despair, the Lord reminds his people that the way of repentance and restoration to new life is open: **I have no pleasure in the death of the wicked, but that the wicked turn from his way and live; turn back, turn back from your evil ways** (v. 11). The Lord turns the tables on those who are complaining that **the way of the Lord is not just** by showing that **it is their own way that is not just** (v. 17). The Lord declares that by punishing the guilty and forgiving the repentant, who turn from their sin, he is in fact displaying true justice and at the same time opening the way for his people to turn and find life in God.

The Lord is reminding Israel that what they did in the past does not determine their future. One can turn from either way: from death to life or from life to death. St. John of Damascus summarizes this message of life-bringing repentance: "For the wickedness of the wicked shall not hurt him in the day that he turns from his wickedness. If he acts righteously and walks in the statutes of life, he shall surely live; he shall not die."[2] In Ezekiel's powerful restatement of God's justice and mercy, the people of Israel, crushed by the destruction of their city, are *invited* and *entreated* to hear and repent. Though oracles of God's judgment have predominated in the book thus far, this invitation to repent and live is Ezekiel's central message.

In the Light of Christ (33:10–20)

In Ezekiel, a book that seems so full of dark and ominous words of judgment, it is crucial that we recognize the fundamental disposition of God toward human beings: he entreats them to repent and expresses his desire that they should "live." The way of return remains open. Clearly God forgave the sins of Israel in Ezekiel's day—this was one of the main purposes of the offering of sacrifices in the temple. But it is less clear exactly what kind of "life" was promised to them. Certainly it meant having a life-giving relationship with God in the *present* time, but does this include an implicit promise of "eternal life" with God? It seems that God was already pointing to life even after death, though this is not expressly promised in Ezekiel.

The call to repentance has striking parallels with a central theme of the New Testament. The summation of John the Baptist's message is, "Repent, for the kingdom of heaven is at hand" (Matt 3:2). When Jesus begins his public ministry, his message is summed up in exactly the same words (Matt 4:17). On Easter day, the risen Christ renews this ministry of calling for repentance, directing "that repentance and forgiveness of sins should be preached in his name to all nations" (Luke 24:47). When Peter stands up to preach on the day of †Pentecost, he urges his listeners, "Repent, and be baptized every one of you in the name of Jesus Christ for the forgiveness of your sins" (Acts 2:38). This invitation to repentance characterizes

2. *Barlaam and Joseph* 32 (ACCS 13:101).

the message of the †gospel to both Jews and †Gentiles throughout the book of Acts (3:19; 8:22; 17:30; 26:20). But there is something profoundly new in the call to repentance through Jesus. Jesus himself stood in our place. Though sinless, he bore our sins on the cross, even when we were his enemies (Rom 5:8–10), and so won for us an eternal redemption. The way to repentance and *eternal life* has been opened—and that way is Jesus himself (John 14:6). What Ezekiel announces here—God's desire that all turn, repent, and live—has now been fulfilled in the life, death, and resurrection of Jesus.

The City's Fall, God's Judgment, and Ezekiel's Vindication (33:21–33)

²¹In the twelfth year of our exile, in the tenth month, on the fifth day of the month, a man who had escaped from Jerusalem came to me and said, "The city has fallen." ²²Now the hand of the LORD had been upon me the evening before the fugitive came; and he had opened my mouth by the time the man came to me in the morning; so my mouth was opened, and I was no longer mute.

²³The word of the LORD came to me: ²⁴"Son of man, the inhabitants of these waste places in the land of Israel keep saying, 'Abraham was only one man, yet he got possession of the land; but we are many; the land is surely given us to possess.' ²⁵Therefore say to them, Thus says the Lord GOD: You eat flesh with the blood, and lift up your eyes to your idols, and shed blood; shall you then possess the land? ²⁶You resort to the sword, you commit abominations and each of you defiles his neighbor's wife; shall you then possess the land? ²⁷Say this to them, Thus says the Lord GOD: As I live, surely those who are in the waste places shall fall by the sword; and him that is in the open field I will give to the beasts to be devoured; and those who are in strongholds and in caves shall die by pestilence. ²⁸And I will make the land a desolation and a waste; and her proud might shall come to an end; and the mountains of Israel shall be so desolate that none will pass through. ²⁹Then they will know that I am the LORD, when I have made the land a desolation and a waste because of all their abominations which they have committed.

³⁰"As for you, son of man, your people who talk together about you by the walls and at the doors of the houses, say to one another, each to his brother, 'Come, and hear what the word is that comes forth from the LORD.' ³¹And they come to you as people come, and they sit before you as my people, and they hear what you say but they will not do it; for with their lips they show much love, but their heart is set on their gain. ³²And behold, you are to them like one who sings love songs with a beautiful voice and plays well on an instrument, for they hear what you say, but they

will not do it. [33]When this comes—and come it will!—then they will know that a prophet has been among them."

OT: Jer 25:11–12; Ezek 3:26–27; 24:26
NT: Matt 7:21; Mark 4:23
Catechism: God's call on the prophets, 702; hardness of heart, 1859, 1864, 2840

As predicted (Ezek 24:26), a messenger arrives in Babylon to announce the dire　**33:21–22** news about Jerusalem: **The city has fallen**. This is a powerful confirmation of what Ezekiel had prophesied through divine revelation. The date of this messenger's announcement is **the twelfth year of our exile, in the tenth month, on the fifth day of the month** (January 8, 585), leaving a gap of about five months between when the city fell (July–August 586) and when the news arrived in Babylon.[3] Though the news must have been devastating to everyone including Ezekiel, the public announcement of the city's fall vindicates Ezekiel's message and shows him to be a true prophet (see Deut 18:21–22).

In chapter 24 (v. 27), Ezekiel was told that when the messenger arrived to announce the city's fall, "your mouth will be opened to the fugitive, and you shall speak and be no longer mute." This word is now fulfilled, as Ezekiel himself testifies: **he had opened my mouth by the time the man came to me in the morning; so my mouth was opened, and I was no longer mute**. We should recall that at the start of his ministry (3:26–27), the Lord caused Ezekiel to become mute apart from words of judgment that the Lord empowered him to speak.[4] But now his mouth is opened, the time of muteness is past, and a new day of announcing the word of the Lord's restoration is at hand.

Ezekiel has one last word of judgment to those who still hope they will be　**33:23–29** spared punishment for their sins. The city has fallen and many are hopeless and discouraged, but some Israelites who remain among the ruins and remote places in the land are still hoping to retain possession of the land. They are saying: **Abraham was only one man, yet he got possession of the land; but we are many; the land is surely given us to possess**.[5] Who are these **inhabitants of these waste places** who are saying these things? They may include the captains of Israel who remained in the open country and who eventually struck down the Jewish governor Gedaliah and fled to Egypt (see Jer 40–41). But they may also include "the poorest of the land" whom the captain of the Babylonian guard, Nebuzaradan, left behind to take care of the fields (2 Kings 25:12). Scholars estimate that fewer than twenty thousand people may have

---

3. This duration of five months for travel between Jerusalem and Babylon approximates the four months that Ezra and his fellow exiles needed in order to travel from Babylon to Jerusalem (Ezra 7:9).
4. See the commentary on 3:26–27 to explain in what sense Ezekiel was mute, and how this can be consistent with the Lord's command that he speak God's word to the people.
5. See Ezek 11:14–15 for a similar presumptuous claim to the land.

remained in the land.[6] But the Lord negates their false hope: **Shall you then possess the land,** you who, contrary to God's commands, eat blood, worship idols, and commit murder and adultery?[7] No, the people who remain in the land will instead fall prey to various kinds of judgment: the sword, wild beasts, and pestilence. The Lord is determined to make **the land a desolation and a waste** (see Jer 25:11–12), humbling the proud so that they will come to see that God has done this **because of all their abominations.**

33:30–33   The chapter closes with the Lord speaking personally to Ezekiel. The exiles are coming to hear Ezekiel, **and they sit before** him as God's **people** appearing to listen, but they are not *obeying* the word Ezekiel speaks. Exile has not fundamentally changed them. Their hearts are set on personal gain and their own advantage. While the people find Ezekiel's many stories and †allegories to be entertaining, **they will not do** what he tells them—that is, to repent and amend their ways. Ezekiel is among them **like one who sings love songs with a beautiful voice**; the people enjoy listening, but they do not carry out his word. The time will come, however, when the Lord will bring to pass what he has said through Ezekiel, and then the people **will know that a prophet has been among them.**

These two final scenes—the first located in the land of Israel (vv. 23–29) and the second in the land of exile (vv. 30–33)—remind us that true repentance is both possible and necessary. The city has fallen, but the people cannot presume that they can carry on and live as they had before. *The Lord is looking for a humble people that listens to his word and obeys that word.* Ezekiel's message closely follows the words Jesus spoke centuries later: "If anyone has ears to hear, let him hear" (Mark 4:23 ESV), and "Not everyone who says to me, 'Lord, Lord,' shall enter the kingdom of heaven, but he who does the will of my Father who is in heaven" (Matt 7:21).

6. See Block, *Ezekiel: Chapters 25–48,* 259.

7. See Gen 9:4–6 for the double prohibition against eating flesh with blood in it and against shedding human blood.

The Lord God Comes to Shepherd His People

Ezekiel 34:1–31

The judgment has fallen, the tide has turned, and the Lord now announces a season of restoration and the renewal of his †covenant. Chapters 34–37 contain the culmination of God's promises to his people in Ezekiel. The Lord reveals himself as Israel's shepherd-king and promises a glorious return to the land and a resurrection to new life. The deeper purposes of the Lord are disclosed here: a new heart, a new spirit, a renewed covenant, and a life of peace in the land.

Chapter 34 is one of the most compelling and powerful passages in the Old Testament. In response to all that has happened—the continual rebellion of the people and the faithlessness of the leaders (shepherds)—the Lord solemnly promises to come himself and be the shepherd of his sheep. God will come, rescue his people from exile, bring them back to their own land, and feed them with good pasture. It is the announcement of *good news* to the people.

True and False Shepherds (34:1–24)

¹The word of the LORD came to me: ²"Son of man, prophesy against the shepherds of Israel, prophesy, and say to them, even to the shepherds, Thus says the Lord GOD: Ho, shepherds of Israel who have been feeding yourselves! Should not shepherds feed the sheep? ³You eat the fat, you clothe yourselves with the wool, you slaughter the fatlings; but you do not feed the sheep. ⁴The weak you have not strengthened, the sick you have not healed, the crippled you have not bound up, the strayed you have not brought back, the lost you have not sought, and with force and harshness you have ruled them. ⁵So they were scattered, because there was no shepherd; and they became food for all the wild beasts. ⁶My sheep were

scattered, they wandered over all the mountains and on every high hill; my sheep were scattered over all the face of the earth, with none to search or seek for them.

[7]"Therefore, you shepherds, hear the word of the LORD: [8]As I live, says the Lord GOD, because my sheep have become a prey, and my sheep have become food for all the wild beasts, since there was no shepherd; and because my shepherds have not searched for my sheep, but the shepherds have fed themselves, and have not fed my sheep; [9]therefore, you shepherds, hear the word of the LORD: [10]Thus says the Lord GOD, Behold, I am against the shepherds; and I will require my sheep at their hand, and put a stop to their feeding the sheep; no longer shall the shepherds feed themselves. I will rescue my sheep from their mouths, that they may not be food for them.

[11]"For thus says the Lord GOD: Behold, I, I myself will search for my sheep, and will seek them out. [12]As a shepherd seeks out his flock when some of his sheep have been scattered abroad, so will I seek out my sheep; and I will rescue them from all places where they have been scattered on a day of clouds and thick darkness. [13]And I will bring them out from the peoples, and gather them from the countries, and will bring them into their own land; and I will feed them on the mountains of Israel, by the fountains, and in all the inhabited places of the country. [14]I will feed them with good pasture, and upon the mountain heights of Israel shall be their pasture; there they shall lie down in good grazing land, and on fat pasture they shall feed on the mountains of Israel. [15]I myself will be the shepherd of my sheep, and I will make them lie down, says the Lord GOD. [16]I will seek the lost, and I will bring back the strayed, and I will bind up the crippled, and I will strengthen the weak, and the fat and the strong I will watch over; I will feed them in justice.

[17]"As for you, my flock, thus says the Lord GOD: Behold, I judge between sheep and sheep, rams and he-goats. [18]Is it not enough for you to feed on the good pasture, that you must tread down with your feet the rest of your pasture; and to drink of clear water, that you must foul the rest with your feet? [19]And must my sheep eat what you have trodden with your feet, and drink what you have fouled with your feet?

[20]"Therefore, thus says the Lord GOD to them: Behold, I, I myself will judge between the fat sheep and the lean sheep. [21]Because you push with side and shoulder, and thrust at all the weak with your horns, till you have scattered them abroad, [22]I will save my flock, they shall no longer be a prey; and I will judge between sheep and sheep. [23]And I will set up over them one shepherd, my servant David, and he shall feed them: he shall feed them and be their shepherd. [24]And I, the LORD, will be their God, and my servant David shall be prince among them; I, the LORD, have spoken."

OT: Deut 30:4; Jer 23:1–8
NT: Luke 15:3–7; John 10:1–30; Heb 13:20; 1 Pet 5:4
Catechism: Jesus the Good Shepherd, 553, 754, 896, 1548; messianic promise, 528
Lectionary: 34:11–12, 15–17: Solemnity of Christ the King (Year A); 34:11–16: Feast of the Sacred Heart (Year C)

St. Jerome on False Shepherds in the Church

LIVING TRADITION

St. Jerome applies Ezekiel's denunciation of false and unjust shepherds to leaders in the Church who serve themselves rather than the flock of God:

> And what was lost they do not search for, desiring not so much to save the lost as to devour those who are in the churches. . . . This in particular applies to the haughtiness of the bishops, namely, of those who disgrace the dignity of their name by their works, and who adopt a spirit of arrogance in place of humility. Thus they think that they have obtained an honor, not a burden, and they strive to put down any they may see standing out in the church and discoursing on the word of God.[a]

a. *Commentary on Ezekiel* 11.34.1–31, trans. Thomas P. Scheck, ACW (New York: Newman, 2017), 397.

34:1–6 The word of the Lord once again comes powerfully to Ezekiel: he is called to **prophesy against the shepherds of Israel**. The title "shepherd" was used widely among the nations of the ancient world to refer to kings and other rulers. In the Bible as well, kings and other leaders of Israel are often referred to as "shepherds" (Num 27:17–18; 2 Sam 5:2; 1 Kings 22:17; Jer 23:1–4). We tend to think of a shepherd in somewhat sentimental terms, but for the Israelites a "shepherd" was a king or ruler authorized by God to lead the people, punish wrongdoing, and protect the land against aggressors.

What wrongs does the Lord ascribe to these faithless shepherds? They have fed themselves rather than the flock in their charge. They have not taken care of the weak, needy, sick, and lame. This translates into the rulers of Israel not providing food and sustenance for the people, not defending them effectively against their enemies, and not ensuring that the law of God (the †Torah) was followed in the way they governed the people.[1] Instead, **with force and harshness** they have ruled over the people. This language recalls the plight of Israel under harsh Egyptian rule before the exodus (Exod 1:13). The result: the flock has been scattered (in exile) **because there was no shepherd**. In this case, Israel has suffered loss and exile especially because of the sins and failures of their rulers. As the history of Israel reveals (see 1–2 Kings), the actions of leaders have a profound impact on the people's welfare. In this case, because the rulers have been unfaithful to their calling, the people have become food for wild beasts, **with none to search or seek for them**. Significantly, the Lord claims the people

1. When the people of Israel originally asked for a king to be anointed over them, Samuel warned them that their kings would rule them oppressively, taking much of the people's wealth into the king's possession (see 1 Sam 8:8–18).

of Israel as **my sheep** that **were scattered**. They are the Lord's own possession, and the shepherds have failed to care for them as the Lord's own flock.

34:7–10   The Lord pronounces a judgment against these self-serving shepherds. He will hold them responsible for the lives of those they have mistreated, and he will put a stop to their abusive actions; the shepherds will no longer be allowed to feed themselves at the expense of the sheep. Instead, the Lord promises to intervene himself: **I will rescue my sheep from their mouths**.

34:11–16   The Lord now solemnly declares: **I, I myself will search for my sheep, and will seek them out**. The picture here shows the Lord God rising from his throne in heaven, coming down to earth, and personally tracking down all the lost and the strays of his sheepfold.[2] This is just what the Lord promised Moses that he would do if his people sinned and were scattered in exile: "If your outcasts are in the uttermost parts of heaven, from there the LORD your God will gather you, and from there he will fetch you" (Deut 30:4). As a good shepherd, he will bring his flock back into their own land and **feed them with good pasture**. They shall no longer be afraid but shall **lie down in good grazing land**. This would include material provision in the land (crops, food, animals, housing) but also points to the provision of spiritual food, given through the understanding of God's law (see Jer 3:15). If we are in any doubt about the Lord's intention, he repeats this promise and underlines that *he himself* will come: **I myself will be the shepherd of my sheep**. Not only will he care for their needs and bind up their wounds, but he will judge the **fat and the strong** who oppress the sheep. All this is summed up in the deeply consoling phrase **I will feed them in justice**.

In proclaiming this word about the Lord God coming to shepherd his people, Ezekiel may be drawing upon an earlier prophecy given by his older contemporary, Jeremiah: "Then I will gather the remnant of my flock out of all the countries where I have driven them, and I will bring them back to their fold, and they shall be fruitful and multiply" (Jer 23:3). The crucial point is that the Lord is taking the initiative: he will come and act to save his people because they are his sheep and are in great need. The truth is that God has determined to act, and he solemnly promises that he will restore his people to their land, where they will experience both peace and abundance. The intense heart of the Lord for his people is revealed in this ardent declaration that he will come and deliver them. We can only imagine the comfort and consolation these words brought to a defeated people living hundreds of miles from home and suffering a seemingly irreversible misfortune.

34:17–24   The Lord now turns to address his flock directly, declaring that he will come among them and **judge between sheep and sheep**—between the fat sheep who

2. For the Lord God as shepherd of his people, see Gen 49:24; Pss 23:1; 28:19; 80:1; Isa 40:11; Mic 4:6–8; 7:14.

are abusive and the lean sheep who are oppressed. The "fat sheep" are hoarding more than their share and then spoiling the little that remains. As Robert Alter explains, "the fat sheep" clearly refers "to the predatory leaders, so at this point the shepherds have become part of the flock."[3] They deprive the "lean sheep" of their sustenance and then scatter **them abroad**. Once again, the Lord himself promises to come and repair this injustice: **I will save my flock, they shall no longer be a prey; and I will judge between sheep and sheep**.

In a striking and unexpected development, the Lord says that he **will set up** over his flock **one shepherd, my servant David**, who will care for the weak and lean sheep, providing them with good pasture. The title "servant" for David is common in the Old Testament (1 Kings 11:34; 2 Kings 8:19; Pss 36:1; 78:70). In sharp contrast to the previous shepherds, who served only themselves, *this* shepherd will be God's servant who will genuinely provide for the needs of the people. Then in summary of his purpose, the Lord announces to his people, **I, the LORD, will be their God, and my servant David shall be prince among them**. Is Ezekiel expecting King David himself, dead for nearly four hundred years, to come back to life and take up his position as king? Certainly not. The reference to "David" recalls the promise expressed by earlier prophets that a true and faithful heir of David will reign over God's people (see Isa 11:1).[4] Ezekiel is pointing to the coming of the †Messiah, God's anointed one, the son of David. The early Church writer Origen (d. 254) explains that this promise has been fulfilled in Jesus: "For the patriarch David will not be raised up to shepherd the saints, but Christ."[5]

Ancient Israelite readers may have been perplexed by this promise. How is it that God *himself* will shepherd and feed his people (vv. 14–15) and at the same time will appoint his "servant David" to shepherd and feed them (v. 23)? Which will it be? The answer, revealed in Jesus, is that both are true at once. In the person of Jesus, God himself has come down to shepherd his people, and at the same time his Messiah, "David," has been raised up to act as shepherd over them.

In the Light of Christ (34:1–24)

This breathtaking passage from Ezekiel left its imprint on the New Testament presentation of Jesus as the Good Shepherd. Jesus is the Messiah-shepherd prophesied by Micah (Mic 5:4; Matt 2:6). He recognizes that the people are like sheep without a shepherd (Mark 6:34), and he himself seeks and finds the lost

---

3. Alter, "Ezekiel," 1156.
4. For a parallel promise that the offspring of "my servant David" will shepherd God's people, see Jer 33:15–17, 20–21, 25–26.
5. *Commentary on John* 1.146 (ACCS 13:113).

sheep (Luke 15:3–7). Jesus is "the chief shepherd" (1 Pet 5:4) and "the great shepherd of the sheep" (Heb 13:20). For our part, we are like straying sheep that have returned to "the shepherd" of our souls (1 Pet 2:25). And Jesus, the Lamb, is the shepherd who will bring his people fresh water and good pasture in eternal life (Rev 7:17).

The influence of Ezek 34 is most apparent in the depiction of Jesus as the Good Shepherd in John 10. Like Ezekiel, Jesus begins by identifying the "strangers"—the false shepherds—who do not care for the sheep, and then names himself "the good shepherd," who "lays down his life for the sheep" (John 10:11). He promises to give eternal life to his sheep and assures them that "no one shall snatch them" out of his hand (John 10:28). In the person of Jesus the enigma of Ezek 34 is resolved. This is how God himself will come and shepherd his people while at the same time establish "David" his servant—the Messiah—as shepherd over them. Jesus declares, "I and the Father are one" (John 10:30). In Jesus God has come down from heaven to rescue his people. At the same time Jesus is the descendant and heir of David, the one who brings the messianic promise to fulfillment. In the person of Jesus God has come down and David has been raised up to shepherd God's people.

The Covenant of Peace (34:25–31)

[25]"I will make with them a covenant of peace and banish wild beasts from the land, so that they may dwell securely in the wilderness and sleep in the woods. [26]And I will make them and the places round about my hill a blessing; and I will send down the showers in their season; they shall be showers of blessing. [27]And the trees of the field shall yield their fruit, and the earth shall yield its increase, and they shall be secure in their land; and they shall know that I am the LORD, when I break the bars of their yoke, and deliver them from the hand of those who enslaved them. [28]They shall no more be a prey to the nations, nor shall the beasts of the land devour them; they shall dwell securely, and none shall make them afraid. [29]And I will provide for them prosperous plantations so that they shall no more be consumed with hunger in the land, and no longer suffer the reproach of the nations. [30]And they shall know that I, the LORD their God, am with them, and that they, the house of Israel, are my people, says the Lord GOD. [31]And you are my sheep, the sheep of my pasture, and I am your God, says the Lord GOD."

OT: Lev 26:3–13; Num 25:12; Ps 23:1; Isa 54:10
NT: 1 Pet 4:11; 5:2
Catechism: God's redeeming love and covenant faithfulness, 219, 1611

For the first time in Ezekiel, the Lord speaks about establishing a **covenant of**   34:25–31
peace with his people.[6] This recalls God's promise of restoring the "everlasting
covenant" with his people in Ezek 16:60. The two phrases "covenant of peace"
and "everlasting covenant" occur together in 37:26, showing that they point to
the same reality: "I will make a covenant of peace with them; it shall be an everlasting covenant with them." The "covenant of peace" identifies the life-giving
relationship God will have with his people; "the everlasting covenant" indicates
that this will not be a temporary or unstable arrangement but will last forever.

What does this "covenant of peace" mean? Ezekiel lists an array of rich blessings that reflect the covenant blessings promised in Lev 26:3–13. First, **wild
beasts** will be banished from the land. This probably speaks both literally of the
natural world transformed into an Eden-like condition (like Isa 11:6–9; 65:25)
and metaphorically of the exclusion of predatory *human beings*. Second, the
people will **dwell securely** in the land, no longer enslaved or preyed upon by
the surrounding nations. Third, the land itself will be gloriously fruitful: rain
in abundance, a plentiful yield of grain, fruit from the trees, and an end to
hunger. Finally, the crown of all these blessings is a richly renewed relationship
between God and his people, who **shall know that I, the Lord their God, am
with them, and that they, the house of Israel, are my people.**[7] This is the true
heart and center of the renewal of the covenant: God will dwell in peace with
his people in the land. And this marks a decisive turn of events: the people will
know that he is the Lord, not primarily because of the punishment he brings
(as in the first half of the book), but because of the deliverance and blessing
he brings. With great tenderness, the chapter closes with a reaffirmation of the
image of shepherd and sheep: **And you are my sheep, the sheep of my pasture,
and I am your God.**

Reflection and Application (34:1–31)

The revelation of the Lord God as the great shepherd is one of the most
profound expressions of the character of God in the Scriptures. "The Lord is
my shepherd, I shall not want" (Ps 23:1). We rightly stand in awe of how Jesus
the Good Shepherd has come to rescue us and bring us into the good pasture of
eternal life. But 1 Peter takes the figure of the shepherd and reapplies it to "the
elders" in the church.[8] It calls those in leadership to imitate "the great shepherd"
in the way that they care for others. It exhorts them to "shepherd the flock of

---

6. For the phrase "covenant of peace," see Num 25:12; Isa 54:10; Sir 45:24.

7. For the Lord addressing Israel as "my people," see Ezek 11:20; 14:11; 36:28; 37:23, 27. For the
phrase "my people," see also Exod 6:7; Lev 26:12; Jer 11:4; 31:33; 32:38.

8. Peter is following the lead of Jeremiah, who prophesied in the Lord's voice, "I will give you shepherds after my own heart, who will feed you with knowledge and understanding" (Jer 3:15).

God" that is in their charge (1 Pet 5:2 ESV). This is an immensely high calling but one that by the †grace of God they can fulfill.

St. Augustine uses the metaphor of rain, fog, and deep darkness to depict the challenges faced by shepherds: "And it is difficult for the sheep not to go astray in this fog. But the shepherd does not desert them. He seeks them, his piercing gaze penetrates the fog, the thick darkness of the clouds does not prevent him."[9] Using a different metaphor, St. Gregory the Great portrays the faithful shepherd as a salt lick. "We often see a block of salt put out for animals to lick for their well-being. Priests among their people should be like blocks of salt. They should counsel everyone in their flocks in such a way that all those with whom they come in contact may be seasoned with eternal life as if they had been sprinkled with salt."[10]

To be the flock of God that is cared for by so great a Shepherd is an unfathomable blessing. Being called to serve others in the flock as an "undershepherd" is an immense privilege. We can be grateful for the many faithful shepherds who have served God's people through the ages and today. And we know that those who serve fruitfully and faithfully as shepherds can do so only "by the strength which God supplies" (1 Pet 4:11).

9. *Sermon* 46.23 (ACCS 13:109).
10. *Forty Gospel Homilies* 17 (ACCS 13:110).

A New Heart and a New Spirit

Ezekiel 35:1–36:38

Chapters 35 and 36, paired together, present a vivid contrast. The first section (35:1–15) declares the *desolation* of the mountains of Edom; the second section (36:1–15) announces the *restoration* of the mountains of Israel. Edom will be *dispossessed*; Israel will *repossess the land*. Then in 36:16–38 the longed-for renewal of the land and people bursts forth in glorious promises that culminate in the regeneration of the heart and spirit of the people. The promise of the resettlement of the land is a prominent theme, but the true center of Ezek 36 is the interior renewal of the heart and mind of the people that results in the renewal of the covenant relationship between God and his people.

The Desolation of the Mountains of Edom (35:1–15)

¹The word of the LORD came to me: ²"Son of man, set your face against Mount Seir, and prophesy against it, ³and say to it, Thus says the Lord GOD: Behold, I am against you, Mount Seir, and I will stretch out my hand against you, and I will make you a desolation and a waste. ⁴I will lay your cities waste, and you shall become a desolation; and you shall know that I am the LORD. ⁵Because you cherished perpetual enmity, and gave over the people of Israel to the power of the sword at the time of their calamity, at the time of their final punishment; ⁶therefore, as I live, says the Lord GOD, I will prepare you for blood, and blood shall pursue you; because you are guilty of blood, therefore blood shall pursue you. ⁷I will make Mount Seir a waste and a desolation; and I will cut off from it all who come and go. ⁸And I will fill your mountains with the slain; on your hills and in your valleys and in all your ravines those slain with the sword shall fall. ⁹I will make you a perpetual desolation, and your cities shall not be inhabited. Then you will know that I am the LORD.

[10]"Because you said, 'These two nations and these two countries shall be mine, and we will take possession of them,'—although the LORD was there— [11]therefore, as I live, says the Lord GOD, I will deal with you according to the anger and envy which you showed because of your hatred against them; and I will make myself known among you, when I judge you. [12]And you shall know that I, the LORD, have heard all the revilings which you uttered against the mountains of Israel, saying, 'They are laid desolate, they are given us to devour.' [13]And you magnified yourselves against me with your mouth, and multiplied your words against me; I heard it. [14]Thus says the Lord GOD: For the rejoicing of the whole earth I will make you desolate. [15]As you rejoiced over the inheritance of the house of Israel, because it was desolate, so I will deal with you; you shall be desolate, Mount Seir, and all Edom, all of it. Then they will know that I am the LORD."

OT: Gen 36:8; Lev 25:23; Ps 37:7; Hosea 9:3; Obad 13
Catechism: sin manifested in violence, 1851; God's punishment and judgment of sin, 211, 679, 1472–73, 2054

This short chapter, an †oracle against Mount Seir in Edom, would appear to be out of place. We would have expected to find it among the oracles against the nations (in chaps. 25–32), and in fact there is an oracle against Edom that resembles this one (25:12–14). Why would Ezekiel place another oracle against Edom right in the midst of his promises of renewal for Israel? He does so probably to bring to light the great reversal the Lord will accomplish for the sake of his glory: the desolation of the mountains of Edom is contrasted with the restoration of the mountains of Israel. The tables will be turned.

35:1–9   Ezekiel speaks these words against Mount Seir in the name of the Lord: **Behold, I am against you, Mount Seir, and I will stretch out my hand against you, and I will make you a desolation and a waste.** Seir is the mountainous region south of the Dead Sea, on both sides of the rift valley, running south to the gulf of Aqaba. Seir was identified with the nation of Edom (the sons of Esau), who conquered the area and settled there (see Gen 36:8).[1] Why has the Lord set himself against Edom at this time? Because they **cherished perpetual enmity** against the people of Israel and handed Israel over to their enemies **at the time of their calamity**.[2] Not only did Edom support Babylon in the assault upon Israel, but after the Babylonians had devastated the countryside and destroyed Jerusalem, the land of Israel lay open and vulnerable. It appears that Edom took full advantage of this weakness by invading Israel and seizing its undefended land. The psalmist passionately expresses indignation against the nation of Edom for their support of Jerusalem's destruction: "Remember, O LORD, against the Edomites / the day of Jerusalem, / how they said, 'Raze

---

1. Prophetic oracles against Edom appear also in Isa 34:5–17; 63:1–6; Amos 1:11–12; Obad 1–21.
2. As Robert Alter ("Ezekiel," 1158) says, "Edom allied itself with Babylonia and played an eager role in the destruction of Jerusalem, as Ps 137 vehemently recalls."

it, raze it! / Down to its foundations!'" (Ps 137:7). And the prophet Obadiah denounces Edom for taking advantage of his "brother Jacob": "You should not have entered the gate of my people / in the day of his calamity; / you should not have gloated over his disaster" (Obad 13). The consequence of Edom's "anger and envy" (Ezek 35:11) displayed against Israel will be the **perpetual desolation** of the land and cities of Edom.

Ezekiel then amplifies the charges against Edom. Edom envied the **two na-** tions of Israel and Judah and sought to possess them, saying: **we will take possession of them.** While the destruction of Judah (the southern kingdom) is primarily in view here, Ezekiel sees Edom's offense against the *whole* of Israel, the "two nations"—that is, the northern and the southern kingdoms. Edom neglected to recognize that **the Lord was there** in the land (v. 10). It is "the land of the Lord" (Hosea 9:3) that they sought to possess for themselves. "The land shall not be sold in perpetuity, for the land is mine" (Lev 25:23). Because of their arrogant land-grabbing and their enmity against Israel, the Lord declares that Edom will now become desolate: **As you rejoiced over the inheritance of the house of Israel, because it was desolate, so I will deal with you.** The wrong done to Israel, even though Israel itself is under God's judgment, is wrong done to the *God* of Israel. The Lord **heard** Edom's boasts and their **words** against him (vv. 12–13). In consequence, they will receive the same judgment that they meted out to Israel. When this happens, **then they will know that I am the Lord**—in other words, that the God they have mocked and whose people they have dispossessed is the true lord of the universe.

35:10–15

Restoration for the Mountains of Israel (36:1–15)

[1]"And you, son of man, prophesy to the mountains of Israel, and say, O mountains of Israel, hear the word of the Lord. [2]Thus says the Lord God: Because the enemy said of you, 'Aha!' and, 'The ancient heights have become our possession,' [3]therefore prophesy, and say, Thus says the Lord God: Because, yes, because they made you desolate, and crushed you from all sides, so that you became the possession of the rest of the nations, and you became the talk and evil gossip of the people; [4]therefore, O mountains of Israel, hear the word of the Lord God: Thus says the Lord God to the mountains and the hills, the ravines and the valleys, the desolate wastes and the deserted cities, which have become a prey and derision to the rest of the nations round about; [5]therefore thus says the Lord God: I speak in my hot jealousy against the rest of the nations, and against all Edom, who gave my land to themselves as a possession with wholehearted joy and utter contempt, that they might possess it and plunder it. [6]Therefore prophesy concerning the land of Israel, and say to the mountains and hills, to the ravines and valleys, Thus says the Lord God: Behold, I speak in

my jealous wrath, because you have suffered the reproach of the nations; [7]therefore thus says the Lord GOD: I swear that the nations that are round about you shall themselves suffer reproach.

[8]"But you, O mountains of Israel, shall shoot forth your branches, and yield your fruit to my people Israel; for they will soon come home. [9]For, behold, I am for you, and I will turn to you, and you shall be tilled and sown; [10]and I will multiply men upon you, the whole house of Israel, all of it; the cities shall be inhabited and the waste places rebuilt; [11]and I will multiply upon you man and beast; and they shall increase and be fruitful; and I will cause you to be inhabited as in your former times, and will do more good to you than ever before. Then you will know that I am the LORD. [12]Yes, I will let men walk upon you, even my people Israel; and they shall possess you, and you shall be their inheritance, and you shall no longer bereave them of children. [13]Thus says the Lord GOD: Because men say to you, 'You devour men, and you bereave your nation of children,' [14]therefore you shall no longer devour men and no longer bereave your nation of children, says the Lord GOD; [15]and I will not let you hear any more the reproach of the nations, and you shall no longer bear the disgrace of the peoples and no longer cause your nation to stumble, says the Lord GOD."

OT: Gen 1:28; Lev 26:3–13; Deut 30:1–10; Ps 79:1–7
Catechism: restoration from exile, 710; God's redeeming love and covenant faithfulness, 219, 1611

Chapter 36 has a concentric structure that helps us to see the central focus of Ezekiel's message. The structure of the chapter may be expressed as follows:

   A. Restoration of the mountains of Israel: the land repossessed (vv. 1–15)
      B. Sin of Israel and vindication of God's holy name (vv. 16–23)
         C. Renewal of the people in the land: a new heart and new spirit (vv. 24–30)
      B'. Sin of Israel; God acting for his sake (vv. 31–32)
   A'. Restoration and repopulation of the land (vv. 33–38)

Ezekiel begins and ends the chapter (A and A') with a promise of the restoration and repossession of the desolate land and cities. The next layer (B and B') is a sharp reminder of how badly Israel has sinned against the Lord: God is acting to restore them not because they have deserved it but for the sake of his own holy name. At the center of the chapter (section C) is the heart of Ezekiel's message, a promise of the return of the people to the land accompanied by the renewal of the people's heart and spirit.

36:1–7   In a dramatic way, Ezekiel is told to **prophesy to the mountains of Israel**. The personified mountains represent the people, the city, and the land. Because of Babylon's victory over Judah, the hills and mountains have been made **desolate, and crushed . . . from all sides**; they have become **the possession of the**

rest of the nations. Psalm 79 poignantly expresses the plight of Israel crushed under the yoke of surrounding nations: "O God, the nations have come into your inheritance. . . . / We have become a taunt to our neighbors, / mocked and derided by those around us" (Ps 79:1, 4 ESV). Because these nations **gave my land to themselves as a possession with wholehearted joy and utter contempt**, the Lord—speaking in **hot jealousy** and in **jealous wrath**—declares that he will now act on their behalf and cause surrounding nations to **suffer reproach**. The Lord God shows here his profound concern for his people, zealously expressing his determination to recover the land from foreign occupation and resettle his chosen people upon it.

Ezekiel now proclaims the *positive* signs of the renewal of the people and the land using the language of the †covenant blessings (see Lev 26:3–13; Deut 30:1–10). The land will burst into life and bear fruit once again. The people in exile **will soon come home**. This is a stirring reminder that Israel's true home is in the promised land with the Lord dwelling in their midst. Further, the people will multiply in the land. The phrase **they shall increase and be fruitful** recalls the creation story of Adam and Eve (Gen 1:28), soon to be fulfilled in a resettled Israel. The cities will be rebuilt and repopulated, and the people will no longer suffer reproach or disgrace before the nations. The Lord emphasizes that these blessings will come upon **the whole house of Israel, all of it**, both the northern and southern kingdoms.[3] Remarkably, the Lord assures his people: **I . . . will do more good to you than ever before**. The promise of restoration is not meager or partial, a mere shadow of former blessings. Instead, the blessings will be even greater than the blessings God bestowed on his people in the days of their glorious past.

36:8–15

The Sin of Israel and Vindication of God's Holy Name (36:16–23)

[16]The word of the LORD came to me: [17]"Son of man, when the house of Israel dwelt in their own land, they defiled it by their ways and their doings; their conduct before me was like the uncleanness of a woman in her impurity. [18]So I poured out my wrath upon them for the blood which they had shed in the land, for the idols with which they had defiled it. [19]I scattered them among the nations, and they were dispersed through the countries; in accordance with their conduct and their deeds I judged them. [20]But when they came to the nations, wherever they came, they profaned my

---

3. In Ezekiel's day, only two of the original twelve tribes of Israel—Judah and Benjamin—remained in the land. In 722 BC, Assyria conquered the northern kingdom of Israel and exiled the northern ten tribes—and these had not returned to the land. Ezekiel prophesies here the return of "the whole house of Israel," all twelve tribes, and in the closing chapters of the book he reassigns a portion of land to each of the twelve tribes (see Ezek 48:1–29).

holy name, in that men said of them, 'These are the people of the LORD, and yet they had to go out of his land.' ²¹But I had concern for my holy name, which the house of Israel caused to be profaned among the nations to which they came.

²²"Therefore say to the house of Israel, Thus says the Lord GOD: It is not for your sake, O house of Israel, that I am about to act, but for the sake of my holy name, which you have profaned among the nations to which you came. ²³And I will vindicate the holiness of my great name, which has been profaned among the nations, and which you have profaned among them; and the nations will know that I am the LORD, says the Lord GOD, when through you I vindicate my holiness before their eyes."

OT: Exod 15:11; 20:7; Lev 22:32; Ps 115:1; Isa 43:25; 48:11
NT: Matt 6:9; Luke 1:49
Catechism: the holiness of God and of God's name, 208–9, 1424, 2152, 2155, 2794, 2809

36:16–23   The tone of the chapter now shifts from a major to a minor key. It is as if, before the Lord continues to announce the coming blessings, he needs to remind the people of their past sin and emphasize that he is acting not because they deserve his blessing but to display his own holiness and faithfulness. And so Ezekiel recalls how Israel defiled **their own land** through their ways and deeds.[4] Because of their idolatry and bloodshed, the Lord **scattered them among the nations**. The fact that the people of Israel **had to go out of his land** causes the desecration of God's name because the Lord appears in the eyes of the nations as incapable of saving his people from defeat and exile (see 2 Kings 18:32–35). When God delivers Israel from exile, he will vindicate his holiness by proving his power to save his people.

Whether living in the promised land or sent off into exile, the people have done nothing to deserve the mercy and blessing of God. But despite this, the Lord is going to act and restore them. Why? The Lord says that he will act **for the sake of my holy name. . . . I will vindicate the holiness of my great name**. In Isaiah, we find a parallel to this, God acting for the sake of the holiness of his name: "For my own sake, for my wn sake, I do it, / for how should my name be profaned?" (Isa 48:11). This does not mean that the Lord lacks concern for his people, nor does this exclude the Lord also acting to restore his people for their own good. The point here is that God is acting not because Israel deserves restoration—which they clearly do not deserve—but to be faithful to his own promise and his character (his "holiness"). The *holiness* of God predominates in this section: three times the Lord speaks of his "holy name" and twice about the vindication of his "holiness." It is the holiness of the Lord that prompts his saving action.

---

4. For the theme of the defilement of the promised land, see Lev 18:28; Num 35:34; Deut 21:23.

The Holy Name of God

BIBLICAL BACKGROUND

The emphasis God places on acting for the sake of his "holy name" and for the "vindication of his holiness" is a consistent theme in both the Old Testament and the New. In biblical understanding, there is a close connection between the name and the person: to call upon the *name* of the Lord is to call upon *the Lord.* To revere and honor the Lord's name means to revere and honor the Lord himself. When the Lord reveals his name, he is revealing himself and offering profound access to himself, granting to his people the great privilege of calling upon his name.

After the deliverance at the Red Sea, Moses and the people sing in honor of the Lord: "Who is like you, O LORD, among the gods? / Who is like you, majestic in holiness, / awesome in glorious deeds, doing wonders?" (Exod 15:11 ESV). The holiness of the Lord is manifested through his powerful, majestic acts. Not only should God's people praise the holiness of God's name, but they also are obliged to honor his name by the way that they live and speak. In Leviticus, the Lord says through Moses: "And you shall not profane my holy name, that I may be sanctified among the people of Israel" (Lev 22:32 ESV). The obligation to give honor to the name of the Lord is one of the Ten Commandments: "You shall not take the name of the LORD your God in vain" (Exod 20:7). To reverence the name of God as holy means to ascribe all honor and glory to him, both for who he is and for what he has done: "Not to us, O LORD, not to us, / but to your name give glory" (Ps 115:1). "Ascribe to the LORD the glory due his name" (Ps 96:8).

Strikingly, the Virgin Mary †sanctifies the holy name of God in her great prayer, the Magnificat: "For he who is mighty has done great things for me, / and holy is his name" (Luke 1:49). It is no accident that when Jesus instructs his disciples about how to pray, the opening petition is a request that the name of God be "hallowed"—that is, "sanctified" or "treated as holy." Each time we pray the Lord's Prayer, we honor the Lord's name and pray that his name would be revered as holy by all.

When the Lord says that he will "vindicate the holiness" of his name (v. 23), it means that he is going to show who he really is by acting in faithfulness to the †covenant he made with Israel (Lev 26:44–45), even though Israel has broken that covenant repeatedly. They have brought dishonor to the name of the God, which they profess; they have profaned his name among all the surrounding nations by being led away into exile. Despite this, the Lord will act to bring honor to his own name by delivering his people. "I, I am He / who blots out your transgressions for my own sake" (Isa 43:25). The Lord God will display his character through his steadfast love for his people, and then the surrounding nations will know that he is the Lord.

The Promise of Renewal: A New Heart and a New Spirit (36:24–30)

²⁴"For I will take you from the nations, and gather you from all the countries, and bring you into your own land. ²⁵I will sprinkle clean water upon you, and you shall be clean from all your uncleannesses, and from all your idols I will cleanse you. ²⁶A new heart I will give you, and a new spirit I will put within you; and I will take out of your flesh the heart of stone and give you a heart of flesh. ²⁷And I will put my spirit within you, and cause you to walk in my statutes and be careful to observe my ordinances. ²⁸You shall dwell in the land which I gave to your fathers; and you shall be my people, and I will be your God. ²⁹And I will deliver you from all your uncleannesses; and I will summon the grain and make it abundant and lay no famine upon you. ³⁰I will make the fruit of the tree and the increase of the field abundant, that you may never again suffer the disgrace of famine among the nations."

OT: Lev 16:16–19; 26:12; Deut 30:4–6; Ps 51:10; Jer 31:31–33; Lam 5:21
NT: Luke 1:68–72; John 3:5; 10:10–14; Rom 8:1–17; Gal 4:4–7; Rev 21:3, 5
Catechism: restoration from exile, 710; God's redeeming love and covenant faithfulness, 219, 1611; new heart and new spirit, 711, 1432
Lectionary: 36:16–17a, 18–28: Easter Vigil; 36:24–28: infant baptism, confirmation, Mass for the laity, Mass for Christian unity

We now arrive at the central message of this chapter. Ezekiel announces the return from exile, the renewal of the covenant, and the gift of a new heart and spirit in order to follow the Lord's ways. The structure of this subsection, like the overall chapter, has a concentric shape that puts the internal transformation of the people at the center:

> A. Return from exile to the land (v. 24)
> > B. Cleansing from uncleanness (v. 25)
> > > C. A new heart and spirit; the gift of the Spirit and the renewal of the covenant (vv. 26–28)
> > B'. Cleansing from uncleanness (v. 29a)
> A'. Abundance of food and plenty in the land (vv. 29b–30)

36:24–25   The opening promise reveals the Lord's commitment to bring his people back to the land: **I will take you from the nations, and gather you from all the countries, and bring you into your own land**. This points to *a new exodus* from the land of exile, as promised in the book of Deuteronomy: "From there the Lord your God will gather you, and from there he will fetch you; and the Lord your God will bring you into the land which your fathers possessed, that you may possess it" (Deut 30:4–5). But God will do much more than just bring his people back to the land; he will also **sprinkle clean water** upon them and

The Catechism on the Need for a New Heart

LIVING TRADITION

The Catechism speaks eloquently about our need for a new heart as a gift given by God.

> The human heart is heavy and hardened. God must give man a new heart [Ezek 36:26–27]. Conversion is first of all a work of the †grace of God who makes our hearts return to him: "Restore us to thyself, O LORD, that we may be restored!" [Lam 5:21]. God gives us the strength to begin anew. It is in discovering the greatness of God's love that our heart is shaken by the horror and weight of sin and begins to fear offending God by sin and being separated from him. The human heart is converted by looking upon him whom our sins have pierced [John 19:37; Zech 12:10].[a]

a. Catechism 1432.

---

cleanse them from their **uncleannesses**. The people have sinned and need God to bring purification (see Lev 16:16, 19).[5] "I will cleanse them from all the guilt of their sin against me" (Jer 33:8). It is no accident that this purifying action, repeated in verses 25 and 29a, surrounds the central promise of new life (vv. 26–28). The people of God must receive the cleansing action of God if they are to know genuine transformation of heart.

In the central section, the Lord makes a breathtaking promise of interior **36:26–28** transformation to the whole nation of Israel: **A new heart I will give you, and a new spirit I will put within you**. God himself will perform the needed "spiritual surgery," removing the **heart of stone** and supplying a **heart of flesh** that is docile to God's word. These words recall the well-known plea of Ps 51:10: "Create in me a clean heart, O God, / and put a new and right spirit within me." This promise is not new. Moses declared that God himself would bring about a change in the heart of his people: "The LORD your God will circumcise your heart and the heart of your offspring, so that you will love the LORD your God with all your heart and with all your soul" (Deut 30:6). Now through Ezekiel, the Lord renews and deepens this ancient promise of inner transformation.

Above and beyond the promise of a new heart and a new spirit, the Lord promises an even greater gift: **I will put my spirit within you**. He will not only create in his people a new *human* heart and spirit, but he will place *his own Spirit* within them. This gift of the indwelling Spirit will cause the people to walk in God's statutes and laws and to obey the Lord freely from the heart. Then, to clinch this remarkable series of promises, we hear the treasured

---

5. For the sprinkling of water for purification, see Num 8:7; 19:18–21.

covenant formula: **You shall be my people, and I will be your God.**[6] This marks a renewal of the covenant promise God made with Israel in the beginning: "I will walk among you, and will be your God, and you shall be my people" (Lev 26:12).

36:29–30   This great passage ends where it began. The Lord once again declares that he will **deliver** them **from all** their **uncleannesses** (that is, "impurities"). This purification will be God's work. The promised blessing is not limited to spiritual goods but includes a rich, abundant life of grain and fruit in the land, leaving the people free from famine and fear.

With this spectacular bundle of promises, Ezekiel shows how the Lord is fulfilling his promises both old and new. This word fulfills the promise of old in Deut 30:1–10, in which Moses speaks about the gathering of the outcasts of Israel from exile and the circumcising of the heart, so that the people might love the Lord and live in his presence. Moses speaks of a renewal of their heart and soul, while Ezekiel promises a new heart and a new spirit, but the point is the same. God will act *within his people* so that they will be empowered to follow him from their hearts. This passage also completes and expands a theme running through the book of Ezekiel itself. The earlier promise of a new heart and spirit (Ezek 11:19–20) is restated and placed in the context of the renewal of the covenant. The Lord's call for his people to get a new heart and spirit (18:31) is put in a new light. How can the people make for themselves a new heart and a new spirit? Only if they receive these as a gift from God. *It is the Lord who will do this.* God himself will bring his people back to the land; he will cleanse them from their impurity; and he will give them a new heart and spirit through the gift of his own indwelling Spirit. The covenant will be renewed, and God will once again dwell among his people.

One might ask: How have these promises been fulfilled? A partial fulfillment of these promises occurred with the return of the exiles from Babylon and the rebuilding of the temple and the city of Jerusalem in the sixth and fifth centuries BC. This partial fulfillment is recounted in stages by the prophets Haggai and Zechariah and in the books of Ezra and Nehemiah. But this did not include "all" Israel—the northern tribes never returned intact—and it left the people of Israel largely under foreign domination. Further, there is no testimony within the Old Testament itself (the later prophets) that God had fulfilled his promise of delivering a new heart and spirit to his people. In Jewish tradition, this promise was interpreted generally as the renovation of the heart through which God's people are inclined to follow the way of the Lord. One Jewish sage, Moses ben Nachman,[7] applied this passage to the time of the Messiah, when God would re-create human nature to be docile to his law: "The new heart and

---

6. See Jer 31:31–34 and 32:37–41 for covenant renewal combined with the giving of a new heart.
7. Moses ben Nachman (1194–1270) is also known as Nachmanides or Ramban.

the new spirit will insure that, by his very nature, man will want nothing but to walk in God's ways."[8]

In the Light of Christ (36:24–30)

The New Testament does not quote or directly allude to this remarkable passage from Ezekiel about the gift of a new heart and a new spirit. Nevertheless, it may be argued that the message of the New Testament as a whole is that God has begun—and is in the process of bringing about—the true and full restoration he promised through Ezekiel. It *began* when the angel Gabriel appeared to Mary and promised that she would give birth to the †Messiah, the Son of God (Luke 1:32). Zechariah, the father of John the Baptist, prophesies this full renewal: "Blessed be the Lord God of Israel, / for he has visited and redeemed his people" (1:68). The word that God "spoke by the mouth of his holy prophets from of old" is now being fulfilled (1:70). With the coming of Jesus, God is showing "the mercy promised to our fathers" and is remembering "his holy covenant" (1:72).

The decisive fulfillment of these promises occurred through the life, death, and resurrection of Jesus Christ. This fulfillment has already happened in part and will be completed when Christ returns. The promise of return from exile is fulfilled in Jesus, the Good Shepherd, who goes in search of the strays and carries them home (John 10:10–14; Luke 15:3–7). This "return," begun already for those who have a living relationship with Jesus, will be brought to completion when Jesus returns in glory. The promise of being sprinkled with clean water (Ezek 36:25) is fulfilled in baptism: by "water and the Spirit" we are reborn and cleansed from our sins (John 3:5; Titus 3:5–6). The promise of God's own Spirit placed within us is fulfilled at †Pentecost and received by believers in baptism and confirmation (Acts 2:37–38; 8:17–19; 19:5–6). It is because of the indwelling Spirit of God that we know we are God's own sons and daughters (Rom 8:14–17; Gal 4:4–7) and are now empowered to fulfill his commandments from the heart (Rom 8:3–4; 2 Cor 3:3; Gal 5:16, 22–23). The promise that "you shall be my people and I will be your God" is fulfilled even now in the new covenant that Jesus enacted and will be brought to completion in the new age when "he will dwell with them, and they shall be his people, and God himself will be with them" (Rev 21:3). In Jesus and through the gift of the Spirit, the great promises uttered by Ezekiel find their initial fulfillment and will be brought to completion when Jesus comes again.

8. Eisemann, *Ezekiel*, 558.

The Sin of Israel and the Restoration
and Repopulation of the Land (36:31–38)

31"Then you will remember your evil ways, and your deeds that were not good; and you will loathe yourselves for your iniquities and your abominable deeds. 32It is not for your sake that I will act, says the Lord God; let that be known to you. Be ashamed and confounded for your ways, O house of Israel.

33"Thus says the Lord God: On the day that I cleanse you from all your iniquities, I will cause the cities to be inhabited, and the waste places shall be rebuilt. 34And the land that was desolate shall be tilled, instead of being the desolation that it was in the sight of all who passed by. 35And they will say, 'This land that was desolate has become like the garden of Eden; and the waste and desolate and ruined cities are now inhabited and fortified.' 36Then the nations that are left round about you shall know that I, the Lord, have rebuilt the ruined places, and replanted that which was desolate; I, the Lord, have spoken, and I will do it.

37"Thus says the Lord God: This also I will let the house of Israel ask me to do for them: to increase their men like a flock. 38Like the flock for sacrifices, like the flock at Jerusalem during her appointed feasts, so shall the waste cities be filled with flocks of men. Then they will know that I am the Lord."

OT: Gen 3:23–24; Isa 51:3
NT: Eph 2:18; 2 Pet 1:4; Rev 21:5
Catechism: restoration from exile, 710; God's redeeming love and covenant faithfulness, 219, 1611

36:31–38 The final section of chapter 36 is a restatement of what Ezekiel announced in verses 1–15. The Lord reminds Israel that their coming restoration is not based on their merits, for they have acted sinfully (vv. 31–32). God humbles his people even as he promises to deliver them. Ezekiel declares that once God has cleansed Israel of all its **iniquities**, he will cause the land to be restored and **the cities to be inhabited** (vv. 33–38). The land itself shall become **like the garden of Eden**, and the ravaged cities will be **inhabited and fortified**. Ezekiel echoes a similar promise found in the prophet Isaiah: "For the Lord will comfort Zion: / he will comfort all her waste places, / and will make her wilderness like Eden, / her desert like the garden of the Lord" (Isa 51:3). The true recovery of "lost Eden" (Gen 3:23–24) will take place when God makes all things new in the land.[9] When all this happens, the nations roundabout will know and recognize that it is the Lord God of Israel who has fulfilled his covenant promise to his people.

The chapter closes with an echo of the shepherd-flock imagery of chapter 34: the Lord will multiply his people **like a flock,** and the once-devastated cities

9. For references to the garden of Eden elsewhere in Ezekiel, see 28:13; 31:9, 16, 18.

will **be filled with flocks** of people. The Lord, the great shepherd of his people, will cause the people to multiply and will make the waste places flourish once again. **Then they will know that I am the Lord.**[10]

Reflection and Application (36:1–38)

The central theme of this great chapter is the renewal of a broken covenant. Year after year, the Lord warned his people through Ezekiel, urgently calling them to repent and promising dire judgment if they refused. They refused to listen, and so suffered great loss—loss of life, of land, of temple, of kingship, and of hope. Broken and dismembered, the people languished in exile. But the Lord God promised to take action, not because his people were deserving but because of his own holiness and character—because of his faithfulness to the covenant. And so the Lord promises here a glorious return, leading to blessings even greater than Israel possessed in the beginning. He will cleanse his people from their sin, implant in them a new heart and spirit, place his own Spirit within them, and dwell among them as their God.

All this is fulfilled through Jesus and the gift of the Holy Spirit. We are the beneficiaries of these promises, and so have cause for great thanksgiving. As the apostle Peter says, "He has granted to us his precious and very great promises" (2 Pet 1:4). The apostle Paul eloquently announces the great gift of God: through Jesus both Jew and †Gentile have been made new, formed into one body, and now "have access in one Spirit to the Father" (Eph 2:18). This is not just a promise for the future. In Jesus even now we are cleansed from our sins, we receive a new heart and spirit through the giving of his Holy Spirit, and we are brought into the renewal of the covenant (the New Covenant). These blessings are real; we are meant to experience them now in our lives. But they are also only a foretaste, a down payment, of what we shall receive fully in eternal life. Because we experience a share in these good things even now, our spiritual longing is aroused for the day when Jesus will return and renew all things (Rev 21:5).

---

10. For the meaning of this phrase, see the sidebar "'Then You Will Know That I Am the Lord,'" p. 187.

The Covenant of Peace Renewed

Ezekiel 37:1–28

Chapter 37 brings to a climax the great promises of restoration in the book of Ezekiel. It is divided into two distinct parts followed by a summary. The first part (vv. 1–14) is the beloved "dry bones" prophecy: the Lord will bring his people back to life and return them to their land. The second part (vv. 15–23) foretells the reuniting of Israel and Judah into one nation that dwells peacefully in the land. The summary conclusion (vv. 24–28) ties together the entire section (chaps. 34–37), expressing the main themes of God's plan for the restoration and renewal of his people.

The Dry Bones of Israel Come Back to Life (37:1–14)

¹The hand of the LORD was upon me, and he brought me out by the Spirit of the LORD, and set me down in the midst of the valley; it was full of bones. ²And he led me round among them; and behold, there were very many upon the valley; and behold, they were very dry. ³And he said to me, "Son of man, can these bones live?" And I answered, "O Lord GOD, you know." ⁴Again he said to me, "Prophesy to these bones, and say to them, O dry bones, hear the word of the LORD. ⁵Thus says the Lord GOD to these bones: Behold, I will cause breath to enter you, and you shall live. ⁶And I will lay sinews upon you, and will cause flesh to come upon you, and cover you with skin, and put breath in you, and you shall live; and you shall know that I am the LORD."

⁷So I prophesied as I was commanded; and as I prophesied, there was a noise, and behold, a rattling; and the bones came together, bone to its bone. ⁸And as I looked, there were sinews on them, and flesh had come upon them, and skin had covered them; but there was no spirit in them. ⁹Then he said to me, "Prophesy to the spirit, prophesy, son of man, and say

to the spirit, Thus says the Lord GOD: Come from the four winds, O spirit, and breathe upon these slain, that they may live." [10]So I prophesied as he commanded me, and the spirit came into them, and they lived, and stood upon their feet, an exceedingly great host.

[11]Then he said to me, "Son of man, these bones are the whole house of Israel. Behold, they say, 'Our bones are dried up, and our hope is lost; we are clean cut off.' [12]Therefore prophesy, and say to them, Thus says the Lord GOD: Behold, I will open your graves, and raise you from your graves, O my people; and I will bring you home into the land of Israel. [13]And you shall know that I am the LORD, when I open your graves, and raise you from your graves, O my people. [14]And I will put my Spirit within you, and you shall live, and I will place you in your own land; then you shall know that I, the LORD, have spoken, and I have done it, says the LORD."

OT: Gen 2:7; Num 31:14; Deut 28:25–26; Prov 17:22; Jer 8:1–2
NT: Matt 3:11; John 20:22; Rom 5:5; 8:11; 1 Cor 6:19; 12:13
Catechism: resurrection to new life, 992–96; the gift of the Spirit, 733–36
Lectionary: 37:1–14: Pentecost Vigil; 37:12–14: 5th Sunday of Lent (Year A)

The "dry bones" prophecy is divided into three acts. In act 1 (vv. 1–6), the Lord transports Ezekiel to the valley of dry bones and tells him to prophesy to the parched bones. In act 2 (vv. 7–10), Ezekiel prophesies to the bones and the bones are joined together and come back to life. In act 3 (vv. 11–14), the Lord gives Ezekiel the interpretation of this extraordinary vision.

As the passage opens, Ezekiel comes under a prophetic anointing: **The hand**   37:1–6
of the LORD was upon me.[1] Ezekiel is transported **by the Spirit of the LORD**
and set down **in the midst of the valley** that **was full of bones**. Most probably, Ezekiel was not transported bodily but *in his spirit*. In Ezekiel's original vision (3:22–23), the Lord took him to "the valley," where he witnessed the glory of the Lord manifested in the †divine chariot. Now in the same valley the Lord appears once again, this time to re-create and restore his people. The narrative, however, is reversed: the first valley-vision pointed to the coming judgment; the second valley-vision reverses the judgment and points to the restoration of the nation and new life for the people.

Now situated in the valley, Ezekiel sees **very many** bones, and they are **very dry**—no life remains in them.[2] In the ancient world, including Israel, there was a horror of dying and remaining unburied. The image of scattered bones lying unburied on the surface of the land recalls Jeremiah's prophecy (Jer 8:1–2)

---

1. The expression "the hand of the LORD was upon me" is common in Ezekiel, appearing also in 1:3; 3:14, 22; 8:1; 33:22; 40:1.

2. The Jewish rabbis taught that there was a residue of life within each person's bones that would be the nucleus of the body at the time of the resurrection. Because the bones in Ezekiel's vision were "very dry," they lacked this residue of life and so needed life (the spirit or breath) to come from the outside in order to be resurrected. See Rosenberg, *Book of Ezekiel*, 2:321.

The Dry Bones and the Resurrection from the Dead

LIVING TRADITION

In the Christian tradition, Ezekiel's prophecy of the dry bones was interpreted by some as the return of Israel's exiles to the land and by others as the final resurrection of the dead. St. Jerome (d. 420) believes Ezekiel is prophesying here specifically about the return of the exiles to the land of Israel: "From this it is clear that we are not denying the resurrection, but asserting that these things [in Ezek 37] are not written about the resurrection. Rather, by means of a parable of a resurrection, he is prophesying the restoration of Israel, who at the time was captive in Babylon."[a] Gregory of Nyssa (d. 395), however, interprets the dry bones prophecy as describing the future general resurrection of the dead: "Ezekiel, with prophetic spirit, has surpassed all time and space and with his power of prediction has stood at the very moment of the resurrection. Seeing the future as already present, he has brought it before our eyes in his description."[b]

a. *Commentary on Ezekiel* 11.37.1–14, trans. Thomas P. Scheck, ACW (New York: Newman, 2017), 420.
b. *On the Soul and Resurrection* (ACCS 13:122).

of scattered and dried-up bones of Israel, lying on the surface of the ground unburied under the sun. Building on this picture, Ezekiel prophesies their regathering and reanimation. The vision of scattered bones also calls to mind the dire †covenant curse in Deut 28:25–26: "The LORD will cause you to be defeated before your enemies. . . . Your dead body shall be food for all the birds of the air, and for the beasts of the earth."

The Lord now poses a question to Ezekiel: **Can these bones live?** The obvious and expected answer would be, "Of course not." But instead of answering, Ezekiel directs the question back to the Lord—**O Lord GOD, you know**—leaving room for God to do the impossible: to bring dead bones back to life. The Lord then commands Ezekiel to prophesy *to the bones*: **Prophesy to these bones. . . .** What word is Ezekiel called to speak on God's behalf? **I . . . will cause flesh to come upon you, and cover you with skin, and put breath in you, and you shall live**. The bones will be reconnected, with flesh, sinews, and skin covering them once again. The key term "breath" (Hebrew *ruach*), which can mean "spirit," "breath," or "wind," occurs ten times in verses 1–14. The Lord God says that he will cause "breath" or "spirit" to enter into these reconstituted bodies and so cause them to live. There is a clear echo here of the creation of Adam (Gen 2:7), when the Lord took dust of the ground, formed it into a man, and breathed into his nostrils. In the present case, however, this is not the original creation of the human race but a *re-creation* of those who have died and left behind only dead and dry bones.

Ezekiel obeys: he prophesies to the bones, and the word of promise is fulfilled: **So I prophesied as I was commanded**. He is not just a bystander watching the sovereign action of God, but he actively cooperates with God through his words. As Ezekiel speaks, the word takes effect. The process of restoration comes in two stages that parallel the two-stage creation of Adam in Gen 2:7. In the first stage, the form of the human being is fully restored: the bones are joined back together, connected with sinews, and covered with flesh. In the second stage, Ezekiel calls the breath or spirit from the four corners of the earth to come: **Come from the four winds, O spirit, and breathe upon these slain, that they may live.**[3] Ezekiel is making use of the various meanings of the word *ruach* (breath, spirit, wind) to beautifully illustrate this scene. The four directions from which the spirit is summoned correspond to the locations of the exiles scattered through the whole earth. The breath enters into the restored human forms, and they stand and become **an exceedingly great host** (ESV, "great army"). The result is the reanimation not only of a *people* but of an *army*.[4] Just as the people of Israel were shaped into a fighting force in the wilderness under Moses (Num 31:14), so once again they are raised up as an army in the wilderness. Lifeless, scattered, dry bones become a veritable fighting force through the work and power of God.

In the third act the Lord gives the interpretation of this vision to Ezekiel (and to us as readers). The bones, says the Lord, represent **the whole house of Israel**. This includes the people of both the northern and southern kingdoms, each of which tasted the grief of exile. The people in exile have been crying out in lament that their **bones are dried up**, that their **hope is lost**, and that they have been **clean cut off** from the presence and the blessings of the Lord. They have been utterly crushed and so wail in their agony. In them is fulfilled the proverb, "A crushed spirit dries up the bones" (Prov 17:22 ESV). In response to this lament, the Lord God promises: **I will open your graves, and raise you from your graves, O my people**. The metaphor has subtly changed here from *unburied* bones lying open on the surface of the ground to *buried* bones raised from their graves.

As the crown of all, the Lord adds: **I will put my Spirit within you, and you shall live**. This is nearly identical to the promise in the previous chapter (36:27): "And I will put my Spirit within you, and cause you to walk in my statutes." This shows that the "dry bones" prophecy is closely connected to the promise of a new heart and new spirit. The vision of the dry bones coming back to life

37:7–10

37:11–13

37:14

---

3. For the four winds of heaven, see Jer 49:36; Zech 6:5.

4. The Hebrew phrase "great host" or "great army" occurs earlier in Ezekiel (17:17), where it refers to Pharaoh and his great army. See also Ezek 29:18; 32:31; 38:15 for the term "host" indicating an "army."

is a different presentation of the same work of God promised in chapter 36. The gift of God's Spirit represents the primary strategy for restoring the people. God will place *his own Spirit* within them, producing *a new heart and spirit* in the people that will enable them to live and to keep the ways of the Lord. This is the fundamental remedy: the gift of God's Spirit creating a new spirit within his people.

In the Light of Christ (37:1–14)

The "dry bones" prophecy is not cited explicitly in the New Testament, but what Ezekiel saw in vision has been beautifully fulfilled in Christ through the Spirit. When John the Baptist distinguishes his ministry from Christ's, he points to the one coming who will baptize with the Holy Spirit and with fire (Matt 3:11). When Jesus appears to the twelve on Easter evening in the upper room, his first act is to "breathe" on them and say, "Receive the Holy Spirit" (John 20:22). They become animated with God's own Spirit and receive a new heart and spirit within them. When the apostle Paul presents our new life in Christ, he says that by one Spirit we have been baptized into one body and have all drunk of one Spirit, receiving the Spirit into our inner being (1 Cor 12:13). One of the greatest gifts we have as Christians is God's own Spirit dwelling within us: "Do you not know that your body is a temple of the Holy Spirit within you, which you have from God?" (1 Cor 6:19). And because God's love has been poured into our hearts through the Spirit (Rom 5:5), we now have a power within us that enables the "just requirement of the law" (Rom 8:4) to be fulfilled in us, just as Ezekiel promised. In a way unparalleled in the Old Testament, Ezekiel announces the great gift of God's Spirit that we now experience in the New Covenant as disciples of Jesus Christ.

The question is often posed: Is the prophecy of the dry bones genuinely a prediction of the resurrection of the dead, or is it really just a parable describing the reanimation of *living* people who are in exile in Babylon and elsewhere? The fact that the Lord enters into a dialogue with a broken and dispirited people (v. 11) shows that they are still in some sense "alive" and capable of making a complaint to the Lord. And the result of the bones coming to life is the return of the people to the land (v. 12), a reference to return from exile. So, in a primary sense, the dry bones prophecy describes the reanimation and restoration of *living* exiles who experience a new heart and spirit—a new hope put within them. But the dry bones prophecy can also be understood spiritually as a promise of the resurrection of the dead. The change in the metaphor in verses 12–13, which speak of people being raised from their *graves*, points toward a final resurrection from the dead. Just as the Lord God created the human race in the beginning, breathing his life into it (Gen 2:7), so he will resurrect the human race by raising the dead from their graves through the power of the Spirit: "He who raised Christ Jesus from the dead will give life to your mortal bodies also through his Spirit who dwells in you" (Rom 8:11). And so, this prophecy points in the first place to the return of the exiles to the land, but also has a wider fulfillment when God will raise his people from death and dwell with them forever (see Rev 21–22).[5]

The Two Kingdoms Reunited in a Covenant of Peace (37:15–28)

[15]The word of the LORD came to me: [16]"Son of man, take a stick and write on it, 'For Judah, and the children of Israel associated with him'; then take another stick and write upon it, 'For Joseph (the stick of Ephraim) and all the house of Israel associated with him'; [17]and join them together into one stick, that they may become one in your hand. [18]And when your people say to you, 'Will you not show us what you mean by these?' [19]say to them, Thus says the Lord GOD: Behold, I am about to take the stick of Joseph (which is in the hand of Ephraim) and the tribes of Israel associated with him; and I will join with it the stick of Judah, and make them one stick, that they may be one in my hand. [20]When the sticks on which you write are in your hand before their eyes, [21]then say to them, Thus says the Lord GOD: Behold, I will take the sons of Israel from the nations among which they have gone, and will gather them from all sides, and bring them to their own land; [22]and I will make them one nation in the land, upon the mountains of Israel; and one king shall be king over them all; and they shall be no longer two nations, and no longer divided into two kingdoms. [23]They shall not defile themselves any more with their idols and their detestable things, or with any of their transgressions; but I will save them from all the backslidings in which they have sinned, and will cleanse them; and they shall be my people, and I will be their God.

[24]"My servant David shall be king over them; and they shall all have one shepherd. They shall follow my ordinances and be careful to observe my statutes. [25]They shall dwell in the land where your fathers dwelt that I gave to my servant Jacob; they and their children and their children's children shall dwell there for ever; and David my servant shall be their prince for ever. [26]I will make a covenant of peace with them; it shall be an everlasting covenant with them; and I will bless them and multiply them, and will set my sanctuary in the midst of them for evermore. [27]My dwelling place shall be with them; and I will be their God, and they shall be my people. [28]Then

5. For the interpretation of the "dry bones" vision in the Jewish †rabbinic tradition, see Eisemann, *Ezekiel*, 562–71. Rabbi David Kimchi (d. 1235) sees the prophecy of the dry bones as first of all describing the return of Israel from exile but also possibly pointing to the future resurrection of the dead. See Rosenberg, *Book of Ezekiel*, 2:318.

the nations will know that I the LORD sanctify Israel, when my sanctuary is in the midst of them for evermore."

OT: Gen 28:13–15; Jer 30:3; Zech 10:6
NT: Luke 1:67–69; John 4:1–42; Acts 8:4–25; 13:20; Rev 21:3–4
Catechism: restoration from exile, 710; God's redeeming love and covenant faithfulness, 219, 1611
Lectionary: 37:15–19: Mass for Christian unity

37:15–22   The Lord calls Ezekiel to perform another prophetic †sign-act, the final one in the book. The number one appears ten times in this subsection, signaling the theme of unity and oneness. Ezekiel is told to **take a stick** and to **write** upon it, **for Judah, and the children of Israel associated with him**, and then to **take another stick** and to write upon it, **for Joseph (the stick of Ephraim) and all the house of Israel associated with him**. Then he is told to **join them together into one stick** so that **they may become one in your hand**. The northern kingdom (identified here variously as "Israel," "Ephraim," and "Joseph") was conquered by Assyria in 722 BC, and its people were scattered in exile.[6] The southern kingdom (Judah), conquered by Babylon in 586 BC, also saw its people sent into exile. Through this prophetic action, Ezekiel is signifying that the Lord is going to **take the sons of Israel from the nations among which they have gone, and will gather them from all sides, and bring them to their own land.** This includes the regathering of *all* the people of Israel, north and south, into one nation, and **one king shall be king over them all**. This is a clear echo of the promise in Ezek 34:23–24 that there will be a single shepherd over Israel.

Crucially, the Lord says that he will do this **that they may be one in my hand.** It is *God* who will bring back the scattered exiles and take them into his hand and make them one again (34:15–16). Like the "dry bones" vision, this prophetic sign-act predicts the return from exile but under a new metaphor, the joining of two sticks. The focus here is on reuniting the two kingdoms into one, a reality not in place since the death of Solomon. The reuniting of the northern and the southern kingdoms was also an important component of Jeremiah's prophetic message: "For behold, days are coming, says the LORD, when I will restore the fortunes of my people, Israel and Judah, says the LORD, and I will bring them back to the land which I gave to their fathers" (Jer 30:3).[7]

37:23   When the Lord accomplishes this unification of the two kingdoms, then the people will no longer defile themselves as they have in the past (which was the cause of the two exiles). The Lord will **save them from all the backslidings** (or "apostasies") and cleanse them. Once again they shall be his people, and he

---

6. Because the tribe of Ephraim, Joseph's son, had become the most numerous, the northern kingdom was often named poetically "Joseph" or "Ephraim." For the name "Joseph" as a designation for the northern kingdom, see Ps 77:15; Amos 5:15; 6:6; Obad 18; Zech 10:6. For the name "Ephraim" as designation of the northern kingdom, see Isa 7:2–9; Hosea 5:3–9; Zech 9:10, 13.

7. For this theme of the unity of the two kingdoms in Jeremiah, see also 3:18; 31:31; 33:14–16; 50:4–5.

will be their God: the †covenant between the Lord and his *entire* people will be restored and renewed.

In the Light of Christ (37:15–23)

A question that confronts Christian readers is whether the promise of the reuniting of the two kingdoms has been fulfilled, in part or in full. In other words, do we find in the postexilic writings of the Old Testament or in the New Testament any indication about how the reunification of the kingdoms has happened (or will happen)? In fact, we do not find explicit testimony in either the Old or the New Testament concerning the fulfillment of this promise. We know that a significant number of exiles returned from Babylon in the late sixth century BC, but there is only limited testimony about the return of some members from the northern tribes who were exiled by Assyria in 722 BC (see 2 Chron 30:10–12). When the reuniting of the two kingdoms is mentioned (for example, in Zech 10:6), its fulfillment lies still in the future. In the New Testament, Jesus comes to save "Israel" (see Luke 1:16, 54), but there is no direct reference to Jesus uniting the two kingdoms and bringing them together in unity. Zechariah's great prophecy (Luke 1:67–79) announces that Jesus will fulfill what the prophets have foretold and that he will renew the covenant with God's people, Israel, but there is nothing specifically about the *two kingdoms* being reunited in the promised land.

Some Christian interpreters see a partial fulfillment of Ezekiel's promise that the two kingdoms would be united in one body in the evangelization of the Samaritans (see John 4:1–42; Acts 8:4–8, 14–25), since the Samaritans were related by blood to the former tribes of the northern kingdom.[8] Other interpreters propose that, because the northern tribes were assimilated among the †Gentiles and so lost their identity as Israelites, the only way to fulfill this promise of reuniting the northern and southern tribes was to bring *the Gentiles* into union with the Jews in Christ. According to this proposal, as Jew and Gentile become one body in Christ (Eph 2:11–22), the lost tribes, dispersed among the Gentiles, are now reunited to the Jews (through the Gentiles)—and this is how God has fulfilled his promise to reunite all the tribes of Israel into one body under "one shepherd" (Ezek 37:24), who is Jesus Christ. While both of these proposals have some plausibility, it remains unclear how and when God will fulfill his promise to unite the two kingdoms in the promised land. Notably, the apostle Paul says that in the end "all Israel will be saved" (Rom 11:26), echoing Ezekiel's own references to "the whole house of Israel" (Ezek 36:10; 37:11), but there is no explicit reference to the two kingdoms or

---

8. When the Assyrians exiled the northern tribes of Israel in the eighth century, a remnant of the Israelite people who were left behind intermarried with the foreign peoples that the Assyrians introduced. The result was a new people—the Samaritans—who occupied the former land and cities of the tribe of Ephraim (2 Kings 17:22–34).

the return of all twelve tribes. It may be that the fulfillment of this promise will occur only in the age to come.

〰〰〰〰〰〰〰〰〰〰〰〰〰〰〰〰〰〰〰〰〰〰〰〰〰〰〰〰〰〰〰〰〰〰〰〰〰〰〰

37:24–28   These verses serve as a recapitulation of chapters 34–37 by highlighting the main fruits of God's saving action. All that the Lord has promised his beleaguered people comes together in one final synopsis. The emphasis is on the promises of the Lord lasting *forever*. First, the Lord renews the promise of the messianic king: **My servant David shall be king over them; and they shall all have one shepherd.** He will be **their prince for ever.** This recalls the promise of David as the one shepherd in 34:23–24. Second, the people **shall follow** all the ways of the Lord—the **ordinances** and **statutes**—and so be obedient from the heart. This recalls the fruit of the new heart and spirit in 36:27 (and 11:19–20). Third, the people **shall dwell in the land**, they and their descendants forever, and will **multiply** in the land in fulfillment of the promise given to Jacob (Gen 28:13–15). This brings to mind the promise of multiplication in 36:37. Fourth, the Lord promises to **make a covenant of peace with them; it shall be an everlasting covenant.** This recalls the promise of the covenant of peace in 34:25 and the everlasting covenant in 16:60.

Finally, the Lord promises to set his **sanctuary in the midst of them for evermore**: his **dwelling place shall be with them** once again.[9] This is in fact a new promise in the book of Ezekiel, the first time the Lord promises to rebuild the sanctuary and dwell again in their midst. Chapters 40–48 will present in great detail the new sanctuary and temple in the midst of a restored Israel. And so this last promise sets the stage for the final part of the book. This powerful summary concludes with the covenant formula that represents the heart of the book: **I will be their God, and they shall be my people.** The presence of the Lord among his people, leading to a life of ongoing communion, is the end-goal of God's saving purpose.

In the Light of Christ (37:24–28)

Ezekiel presents a picture of life with God that reflects the major covenants given to Israel. All of them will be fulfilled: the covenant promises to Abraham, Isaac, and Jacob of a people multiplied and dwelling in the land; the covenant of the law on Sinai through Moses, in which God will dwell with his people and enable them to keep his law from the heart; and the covenant with David, in which the true heir of David will reign as king and shepherd in righteousness over his people. All these covenants are embraced and taken up in the everlasting, eternal covenant

---

9. †*Targum of Ezekiel* inserts the word †Shekinah here for "dwelling" (Levey, *Targum of Ezekiel*, 104). See the sidebar "'Shekinah' in Jewish and Christian Tradition," p. 74.

of peace promised through Ezekiel—and this finds its fulfillment in Jesus Christ and the New Covenant he establishes. Jesus is the true offspring of Abraham (Gal 3:16) through whom the blessing of God will come to all the nations (Gal 3:14). He is the mediator of a new and better covenant (Heb 7:22; 9:15). He is the true "son of David" who will reign over his flock (Matt 21:9). He is "the great shepherd of the sheep" who by his blood inaugurated "the eternal covenant" of God with his people (Heb 13:20). In Jesus, all the purposes of God, summed up in Ezek 37, reach their completion and fulfillment.

Reflection and Application (37:1–28)

Most of us experience times when we feel like "dry bones" that have no life in them. Whether we have suffered great personal loss, the heavy burden of sin, or some other trial, we find ourselves in "exile" without much hope for the future, and we wonder if God still cares for us. We may ask: Is there anything good that I can look forward to? Can these dry bones live? This was exactly the plight of the exiles in Babylon. God met his dispirited people with the promise of his *word* and his *power*. In Ezekiel's prophetic vision, the Lord God re-forms his people—puts them back together and sets them on their feet—and breaths his own Spirit into them. *And they come back to life.* This vision has inspired believing Jews and Christians of every generation who live in the midst of deep suffering and discouragement to place their hope in God's future salvation.

Ezekiel 37 is also a great text for the seasons of Lent and Easter. The promise of a "return" accompanied by blessing and fruitfulness provides a powerful message to Christians as we repent of our sins and seek the Lord. In a time of division and disunity, the pledge of the Lord to unite his people under "one shepherd" is also a word of profound hope. And in the midst of death—of loved ones and friends—the joyful promise of resurrection from our graves offers hope in a time of bereavement. The Lord is aiming at much more than merely giving us a longer life; his purpose goes far deeper. He is intent on nothing less than bringing us back from our exile to the "land" of his own presence, so that he can genuinely be our God and we can be his people, both in this age and in the age to come: "Behold, the dwelling place of God is with men. He will dwell with them, and they shall be his people, and God himself will be with them" (Rev 21:3–4).

The Great Battle: Gog and Magog

Ezekiel 38:1–39:29

These chapters are among the most obscure and mysterious in the Bible and have given rise to much speculation in both the Jewish and Christian traditions. The chronicle of the war against Gog and Magog is different in tone from anything else we have seen in Ezekiel. Rather than being rooted in the historical events of sixth-century Judah and Babylon, these chapters speak about events that concern distant nations in a time far off. Although Ezekiel had many unusual visions, this prophecy is unique and is often described as †apocalyptic writing—that is, a genre of prophecy that makes use of symbolic language to reveal mysteries of the invisible world or of the future (often of the end times).

Chapters 38–39 present, in two parallel panels, a single great war against Israel revolving around the adversarial figure Gog of Magog. This is a war waged in the future against a restored Israel already dwelling securely and at peace in the land. Structurally, these chapters appear as an intrusion "out of the blue."[1] The end of chapter 37 (the promise of God dwelling among his people) flows naturally into the beginning of chapter 40 (the vision of the renewed temple). Inserted between them we encounter this mysterious chronicle of a future time when the nations will gather to assault the people and the land of Israel. But the Lord God promises that he will intervene sovereignly to deliver Israel and to vindicate his holiness in the sight of the nations. The relationship of this future conflict to historical events and the significance of this vision within the book of Ezekiel remain perplexing questions.

The First Account of the Battle against Gog and the Nations (38:1–23)

¹The word of the LORD came to me: ²"Son of man, set your face toward Gog, of the land of Magog, the chief prince of Meshech and Tubal, and

---

1. Some scholars believe chaps. 38–39 are a later addition to the book, perhaps inserted here by Ezekiel himself.

prophesy against him [3]and say, Thus says the Lord GOD: Behold, I am against you, O Gog, chief prince of Meshech and Tubal; [4]and I will turn you about, and put hooks into your jaws, and I will bring you forth, and all your army, horses and horsemen, all of them clothed in full armor, a great company, all of them with buckler and shield, wielding swords; [5]Persia, Cush, and Put are with them, all of them with shield and helmet; [6]Gomer and all his hordes; Beth-togarmah from the uttermost parts of the north with all his hordes—many peoples are with you.

[7]"Be ready and keep ready, you and all the hosts that are assembled about you, and be a guard for them. [8]After many days you will be mustered; in the latter years you will go against the land that is restored from war, the land where people were gathered from many nations upon the mountains of Israel, which had been a continual waste; its people were brought out from the nations and now dwell securely, all of them. [9]You will advance, coming on like a storm, you will be like a cloud covering the land, you and all your hordes, and many peoples with you.

[10]"Thus says the Lord GOD: On that day thoughts will come into your mind, and you will devise an evil scheme [11]and say, 'I will go up against the land of unwalled villages; I will fall upon the quiet people who dwell securely, all of them dwelling without walls, and having no bars or gates'; [12]to seize spoil and carry off plunder; to assail the waste places which are now inhabited, and the people who were gathered from the nations, who have gotten cattle and goods, who dwell at the center of the earth. [13]Sheba and Dedan and the merchants of Tarshish and all its villages will say to you, 'Have you come to seize spoil? Have you assembled your hosts to carry off plunder, to carry away silver and gold, to take away cattle and goods, to seize great spoil?'

[14]"Therefore, son of man, prophesy, and say to Gog, Thus says the Lord GOD: On that day when my people Israel are dwelling securely, you will bestir yourself [15]and come from your place out of the uttermost parts of the north, you and many peoples with you, all of them riding on horses, a great host, a mighty army; [16]you will come up against my people Israel, like a cloud covering the land. In the latter days I will bring you against my land, that the nations may know me, when through you, O Gog, I vindicate my holiness before their eyes.

[17]"Thus says the Lord GOD: Are you he of whom I spoke in former days by my servants the prophets of Israel, who in those days prophesied for years that I would bring you against them? [18]But on that day, when Gog shall come against the land of Israel, says the Lord GOD, my wrath will be roused. [19]For in my jealousy and in my blazing wrath I declare, On that day there shall be a great shaking in the land of Israel; [20]the fish of the sea, and the birds of the air, and the beasts of the field, and all creeping things that creep on the ground, and all the men that are upon the face of the earth, shall quake at my presence, and the mountains shall be thrown down, and the cliffs shall fall, and every wall shall tumble to the ground.

> [21]I will summon every kind of terror against Gog, says the Lord GOD;
> every man's sword will be against his brother. [22]With pestilence and blood-
> shed I will enter into judgment with him; and I will rain upon him and his
> hordes and the many peoples that are with him, torrential rains and hail-
> stones, fire and brimstone. [23]So I will show my greatness and my holiness
> and make myself known in the eyes of many nations. Then they will know
> that I am the LORD."

OT: Gen 10:2; Pss 18:12–13; 120:5; Isa 30:30; Jer 1:13–15
Catechism: God's punishment and judgment of sin, 211, 679, 1472–73, 2054

38:1–6 The †oracle begins with the Lord telling Ezekiel to prophesy against **Gog, of
the land of Magog, the chief prince of Meshech and Tubal**. There is no con-
sensus on the identity of Gog or the location of Magog, either in Jewish and
Christian tradition or in contemporary scholarship. This is the only instance
of the name "Gog" in the Old Testament; "Magog" is the name of Japheth's
second son (Gen 10:2; 1 Chron 1:5). Some scholars link the figure of Gog to
Gyges, king of Lydia (668–631 BC), whose great-grandson was a contemporary
of Ezekiel. The †*Targum of Ezekiel* identifies Gog with Rome and the Roman
emperor, an indication that Gog came to symbolize Israel's great enemies.[2] The
lands of "Meshech and Tubal" appear in Ezekiel's list of the trading partners
of Tyre (Ezek 27:13) and among the nations found in †Sheol (Ezek 32:26).
Meshech and Tubal are identified as the *brothers* of Magog in the list of the
sons of Japheth (Gen 10:2; 1 Chron 1:5). Meshech also appears in Ps 120:5 as a
place of exile. Some commentators, rejecting all historical references, conclude
that "Gog of Magog" stands symbolically for an ancient mythological figure
or the personification of darkness. As Paul Joyce summarizes, "Neither Gog
nor Magog has ever been satisfactorily identified."[3] The lack of clear historical
referents for Gog and Magog supports the idea that they function primarily
as symbolic figures.

The Lord says that he has set himself against Gog and will provoke him to
come out in battle against his people: **I will bring you forth**. We are not told
why the Lord has provoked Gog to draw him into battle. The situation here is
similar to when the Lord drew Pharaoh out at the Red Sea in order to gain glory
over him. In any event, Gog appears arrayed for battle in league with nations
coming from the east, north, and south—Persia, Cush, Put, Gomer, and Beth-
togarmah—showing that "Israel was invaded by all its surrounding nations."[4]
The total number of these nations (seven) matches the number of the nations

---

2. Levey, *Targum of Ezekiel*, 108.
3. Joyce, *Ezekiel*, 214.
4. Jacob Milgrom and Daniel I. Block, *Ezekiel's Hope: A Commentary on Ezekiel 38–48* (Eugene, OR:
Cascade Books, 2012), 10. According to the list of nations in Genesis (10:2–3), Gomer is the brother of
Meshech, Tubal, and Magog and the father of Togarmah.

named in chapters 25–32, indicating the symbolic nature of these numbers: they stand for the totality of surrounding nations set against Israel.

The prophet speaks to the armies of Gog, calling them to remain in readiness for attack upon a restored Israel. The Lord God is the one summoning the attack by Gog, but he is also the one who is being attacked, because Gog is attacking God's own people, who dwell in his land. Notably, the prophecy says that all this will happen **after many days** and **in the latter years**, indicating that the great battle will not take place soon but at some distant time.[5] All this will happen when Israel has been dwelling securely in the land for some time and living in peace. **38:7–9**

The Lord now reveals the *motives* of Gog: thoughts arise in Gog's mind that prompt him to **devise an evil scheme**. He sees in Israel a vulnerable nation ripe for plunder, easy pickings for his great army: **I will fall upon the quiet people who dwell securely, all of them dwelling without walls . . . to seize spoil and carry off plunder**. The absence of city walls in Israel points to a people that is secure and without fear of external attack.[6] At this point, Ezekiel clarifies for his hearers that Israel is now back from exile, secure in the land, and blessed with a rich store of livestock and crops. The blessings promised in chapters 34–37 have come to pass, and Gog and his allies greedily look upon Israel for their own gain. Certain nations in league with Gog (Sheba, Dedan, and Tarshish) ask if Gog has in fact come to conquer and carry off plunder, probably hoping to share in the spoils. Strikingly, Ezekiel identifies the people of Israel as those who **dwell at the center of the earth**.[7] This reflects an earlier passage in Ezekiel: "This is Jerusalem; I have set her in the center of the nations, with countries all around her" (Ezek 5:5 NRSV). The place where God has chosen to make his dwelling *is* de facto the center of all things. **38:10–13**

The Lord speaks directly to Gog, drawing Gog out to battle so that the Lord may gain glory over the proud, conquering nations. Significantly, the Lord identifies Israel as **my people** who dwell in **my land**. They are the Lord's covenant people, and he abides among them. By attacking Israel, Gog is defying the Lord himself. And so in the face of Gog's aggressive posture, the Lord declares: I will **vindicate my holiness before their eyes**, so **that the nations may know me** (see the sidebar "The Holy Name of God," p. 249). **38:14–16**

We now hear the declaration of the Lord's defeat of Gog and the armies of the nations. Ezekiel begins by asking whether Gog's attack is a fulfillment of **38:17**

5. For a similar expression, "in the latter days," see Isa 2:2; Jer 23:20; Ezek 38:16; Dan 2:28; 10:14; Mic 4:1.
6. The prophet Zechariah foresees a day when Jerusalem will be without walls because the Lord "will be to her a wall of fire round about" (Zech 2:5).
7. In the Greek Old Testament (the †Septuagint), this was rendered "navel of the earth." Jewish texts from the †Second Temple period (250 BC–AD 100) and later †rabbinic texts also adopted this notion of Israel as the "navel" of the world (see Block, *Ezekiel: Chapters 25–48*, 447).

Origen on the Purpose of God's Wrath

Origen of Alexandria (d. 254) describes the various purposes of God's wrath—to rebuke, chasten, and improve—but underlines God's aim to heal and restore.

But there may perhaps be someone who takes offense even at the term "wrath" and objects to it with reference to God. We will respond to him that God's wrath is not so much wrath as necessary governance. Hear what the action of God's wrath is for: to rebuke, to chasten, to improve: "Lord, rebuke me not in your wrath, nor chasten me in your fury" (Ps 6:1). The one who says these things knows that God's fury is not without usefulness for healing. On the contrary, the reason it is administered is to cure the sick, to improve those who have despised listening to his words. . . . Everything that comes from God that seems to be bitter is advanced for instruction and healing. God is a physician, God is a Father, he is a Master, and he is not a harsh but a mild Master.[a]

a. *Homily* 1.2, in *Homilies 1–14 on Ezekiel*, trans. Thomas P. Scheck, ACW 62 (New York: Newman, 2010), 27–28.

God's previous predictions of those who would come against Israel: **Are you he of whom I spoke in former days by my servants the prophets of Israel?** Ezekiel does not answer this question directly, and it is unclear what previous prophetic words Ezekiel is referencing. He is probably referring to past declarations by the prophets, that God will judge his people by means of the surrounding nations (see Jer 1:13–15). Some commentators believe the implied answer to this question is "yes," that Gog is the one who fulfills earlier prophetic words of judgment. But others conclude that the implied answer is "no," because Nebuchadnezzar fulfilled these predictions of judgment.[8] The latter conclusion seems best, because Gog is presented not as the Lord's instrument for judging his people, but rather as the one through whom the Lord will reveal his holiness and power.

38:18–23   Ezekiel now predicts the Lord's complete victory over Gog on the day when he **shall come against the land of Israel**. The Lord promises to act out of **jealousy** (that is, his zeal) for his people and in **blazing wrath** against the unrighteous nations. Signs in the natural world—earthquakes, hailstones, fire and sulfur—will accompany the Lord's assault against the armies of Gog. These may refer to actual physical phenomena, or they may be metaphorical descriptions of the severity of the judgments that God will bring. The Lord **will summon**

8. See Jer 6:22–26 and 25:9 for Jeremiah's statement that Nebuchadnezzar is fulfilling God's prophetic word of judgment.

every kind of terror against Gog, and the swords of the attacking nations will be turned against each other. Gog will experience **pestilence and bloodshed**, accompanied by **torrential rains and hailstones, fire and brimstone**—all common biblical metaphors for God's manifestation of himself in judgment (see Ps 18:12–13; Isa 30:30). The outcome of this intervention is threefold: the nations will perceive the Lord's **greatness**, they will perceive his **holiness**, and they will come to **know** who the Lord is.

The Second Account of the Battle against Gog and the Nations (39:1–20)

¹"And you, son of man, prophesy against Gog, and say, Thus says the Lord GOD: Behold, I am against you, O Gog, chief prince of Meshech and Tubal; ²and I will turn you about and drive you forward, and bring you up from the uttermost parts of the north, and lead you against the mountains of Israel; ³then I will strike your bow from your left hand, and will make your arrows drop out of your right hand. ⁴You shall fall upon the mountains of Israel, you and all your hordes and the peoples that are with you; I will give you to birds of prey of every sort and to the wild beasts to be devoured. ⁵You shall fall in the open field; for I have spoken, says the Lord GOD. ⁶I will send fire on Magog and on those who dwell securely in the islands; and they shall know that I am the LORD.

⁷"And my holy name I will make known in the midst of my people Israel; and I will not let my holy name be profaned any more; and the nations shall know that I am the LORD, the Holy One in Israel. ⁸Behold, it is coming and it will be brought about, says the Lord GOD. That is the day of which I have spoken.

⁹"Then those who dwell in the cities of Israel will go forth and make fires of the weapons and burn them, shields and bucklers, bows and arrows, handpikes and spears, and they will make fires of them for seven years; ¹⁰so that they will not need to take wood out of the field or cut down any out of the forests, for they will make their fires of the weapons; they will despoil those who despoiled them, and plunder those who plundered them, says the Lord GOD.

¹¹"On that day I will give to Gog a place for burial in Israel, the Valley of the Travelers east of the sea; it will block the travelers, for there Gog and all his multitude will be buried; it will be called the Valley of Hamongog. ¹²For seven months the house of Israel will be burying them, in order to cleanse the land. ¹³All the people of the land will bury them; and it will redound to their honor on the day that I show my glory, says the Lord GOD. ¹⁴They will set apart men to pass through the land continually and bury those remaining upon the face of the land, so as to cleanse it; at the end of seven months they will make their search. ¹⁵And when these pass

through the land and any one sees a man's bone, then he shall set up a sign by it, till the buriers have buried it in the Valley of Hamon-gog. ¹⁶(A city Hamonah is there also.) Thus shall they cleanse the land.

¹⁷"As for you, son of man, thus says the Lord God: Speak to the birds of every sort and to all beasts of the field, 'Assemble and come, gather from all sides to the sacrificial feast which I am preparing for you, a great sacrificial feast upon the mountains of Israel, and you shall eat flesh and drink blood. ¹⁸You shall eat the flesh of the mighty, and drink the blood of the princes of the earth—of rams, of lambs, and of goats, of bulls, all of them fatlings of Bashan. ¹⁹And you shall eat fat till you are filled, and drink blood till you are drunk, at the sacrificial feast which I am preparing for you. ²⁰And you shall be filled at my table with horses and riders, with mighty men and all kinds of warriors,' says the Lord God."

OT: 2 Kings 9:30–37; Isa 12:6; 54:5; Jer 7:33
NT: 2 Thess 2:8; Rev 16:14; 19:17–21; 20:7–10
Catechism: God's punishment and judgment of sin, 211, 679, 1472–73, 2054; †sanctification of God's name, 2814

39:1–6a   Ezekiel restates here what he just declared (in 38:1–6), speaking in the Lord's name directly to the figure of Gog. God is the primary actor in this scene. Though Gog for his part greedily seeks to plunder the vulnerable nation of Israel, in his own way the Lord will drive Gog forward, bring him **from the uttermost parts of the north**, and lead him **against the mountains of Israel**. There the Lord will strike down Gog and his army, knocking his weapons from his hand. Gog and his troops will perish on the mountains of Israel, and their unburied corpses will be devoured by **birds of prey of every sort** and by **the wild beasts**, bringing great shame on the slain armies of Gog. To be left unburied was greatly degrading, a sign of God's intense judgment, as seen in the example of the body of Jezebel consumed by the dogs (2 Kings 9:30–37). In addition to this, the Lord will **send fire on** the land of **Magog** and on all who dwell along the coasts. In sum, the Lord will gain complete and utter victory over Gog and bring ruin to his land. It is striking that Ezekiel does not describe a human battle or refer to Israel going to war. It seems that the Lord defeats this great army by himself; the people of the land simply clean up afterward.

39:6b–8   The main result of this triumph is that the nations will come to a true knowledge of the Lord: **and they shall know that I am the Lord**. But in addition, the Lord acts so that his **holy name** will no longer be profaned and derided. Both the people of Israel and the surrounding nations **shall know that I am the Lord, the Holy One in Israel**. This is the singular instance in Ezekiel (and in the Bible) of the title "the Holy One in Israel." A similar title, "the Holy One of Israel," occurs frequently in Isaiah (see Isa 12:6; 54:5). The Lord is not only Israel's God but he dwells among them *in Israel*. He is the Holy One *in and among* the people of Israel.

39:9–20

This section narrates the complete destruction of Gog and his allies. It functions as a restatement of 38:14–23 but makes three additions to the story. The first addition (vv. 9–10) concerns the cache of weaponry taken as booty. So many weapons will be recovered that **they will make fires of them for seven years** in Israel. Israel will **despoil those who despoiled them, and plunder those who plundered them**, a kind of fitting justice. The second addition (vv. 11–16) emphasizes that the number of the slain will be so great that it will take a full seven months just to gather the slain and bury them, **in order to cleanse the land**. To bury all the corpses, an entire valley will be set aside, named **the Valley of the Travelers**, also called **the Valley of Hamon-gog**, which means "the horde of Gog." The bodies of the dead were devoured by birds of prey and wild beasts (v. 4), but the bones would remain and would require burial. The use of the number seven (seven years, seven months) probably signifies the completeness of the victory that God will win over the enemies of his people.

The third addition (vv. 17–20) is the Lord's invitation to the birds of the air and beasts of the field to come to **the sacrificial feast** prepared for them on the mountains of Israel. They will feed upon the bodies of the slain from Gog's army.[9] With this grim image of the carrion birds feasting upon the slain, the oracles against Gog conclude. What is the purpose of this renarration of the great battle with these additions? It serves to demonstrate how complete and conclusive the victory of the Lord will be.

The great battle against Gog of Magog is one of the most enigmatic and mysterious passages of the Bible. To what does it refer? Is Ezekiel describing a *literal* battle of human armies, or is this a *symbolic* narrative of God's final victory over his enemies? In Jewish tradition, the rabbis understood Ezek 38–39 to describe a future historical event, but they were cautious about peering too closely into the details. They believed, however, that the battle against Gog was connected to the coming of the messianic age and that "dark days are to precede the coming of the †Messiah."[10]

In the Light of Christ (38:1–39:20)

At the close of his public ministry, Jesus solemnly warned his disciples about a great trial that would come before his return (see Matt 24:3–51; Mark 13:3–37; Luke 21:5–36). Paul also spoke of the coming of "the lawless one," whom Jesus would defeat "with the breath of his mouth" at his second coming (2 Thess 2:8). But

9. This picture of carrion birds feeding upon the slain also appears in Jer 7:33 and in the book of Revelation when it depicts the final battle between Christ and the kings of the earth (see Rev 19:17–21).

10. Eisemann, *Ezekiel*, 577. Eisemann describes a tradition among the rabbis that recognizes two distinct Messiahs, the first from the house of Joseph (Ephraim) who would begin the redemption of Israel and the second from the house of David who would bring the messianic age to fulfillment (577–80).

neither Jesus nor Paul spoke of a final battle using the language and imagery that we find in Ezekiel. It is in the book of Revelation that we find an explicit reference to Ezekiel (chaps. 38–39) to describe the final assault by †Satan and his servants against Christ and his disciples. As Peter Williamson observes, "The visions at the end of Revelation provide a prophetic interpretation of the last chapters of Ezekiel and follow the same sequence."[11] Revelation 16:14 makes use of Ezekiel's language when describing the "kings of the whole world," who are assembled "for battle on the great day of God the Almighty" (see Ezek 38:14–16). In Rev 19:17–21, after relating the appearance of Christ as the warrior riding into battle on a white horse, John describes the feast of the great carrion birds on the bodies of the dead soldiers in language that echoes Ezek 39:1–5 and 17–20. Most explicitly, Rev 20:7–10 identifies the final battle as against "Gog and Magog," in which the armies of the nations march on Israel and surround the city of Jerusalem. But "fire came down from heaven and consumed them" (Rev 20:9), just as Ezekiel describes (Ezek 39:6). To sum up: the book of Revelation explicitly refers to Ezek 38–39 when depicting the final battle and the decisive victory of God over his enemies.[12]

Summation of the Message of the Book (39:21–29)

[21]"And I will set my glory among the nations; and all the nations shall see my judgment which I have executed, and my hand which I have laid on them. [22]The house of Israel shall know that I am the LORD their God, from that day forward. [23]And the nations shall know that the house of Israel went into captivity for their iniquity, because they dealt so treacherously with me that I hid my face from them and gave them into the hand of their adversaries, and they all fell by the sword. [24]I dealt with them according to their uncleanness and their transgressions, and hid my face from them.

[25]"Therefore thus says the Lord GOD: Now I will restore the fortunes of Jacob, and have mercy upon the whole house of Israel; and I will be jealous for my holy name. [26]They shall forget their shame, and all the treachery they have practiced against me, when they dwell securely in their land with none to make them afraid, [27]when I have brought them back from the peoples and gathered them from their enemies' lands, and through them have vindicated my holiness in the sight of many nations. [28]Then they shall

11. Peter Williamson, *Revelation*, CCSS (Grand Rapids: Baker Academic, 2015), 315n12.
12. The question arises: Are Rev 19 and 20 describing two distinct battles, or are they depicting the same battle from two different angles? The two battle accounts are probably best understood as two distinct presentations of the *same* event. We recognized that Ezek 38–39 is best understood as depicting *one battle scene* in two parallel narratives. The fact that John refers to Ezek 38–39 in *both* battle scenes in Rev 19–20 suggests that the closing chapters of the book of Revelation are also depicting one final confrontation in two distinctive ways.

know that I am the LORD their God because I sent them into exile among the nations, and then gathered them into their own land. I will leave none of them remaining among the nations any more; [29]and I will not hide my face any more from them, when I pour out my Spirit upon the house of Israel, says the Lord GOD."

OT: Lev 26:40–42; Deut 30:1–10
NT: John 15:8; Acts 2:17, 33; Rom 8:14–17; 1 Cor 12:4–11; Gal 5:22–23; Eph 2:18
Catechism: restoration from exile, 710; God's redeeming love and covenant faithfulness, 219, 1611; the gift of the Spirit, 733–36

The final section of chapter 39 acts as a summation of the message of the book thus far. It answers the question: Why did the Lord judge his people by letting them be conquered and sent into exile? Was he just lacking in power? The answer given is "no." The Lord acted in this way in order to correct his people and treat them as their sins deserved in order to purify them. Nevertheless, God will show his love and covenant faithfulness to his people by gathering them from the nations, revealing himself to them, and pouring out the Spirit on them.

The first part is directed to the nations. **All the nations** will recognize the   39:21–24
Lord's glory through the **judgment** he brings upon them. Remarkably, the Lord will not only return in his glory to dwell among his people Israel but will also **set** his **glory among the nations**. Here we can perceive an indication, a kind of promise, that God will come to dwell among the nations of the earth. Further, the nations will also come to understand why Israel was sent into exile by their God—namely, **for their iniquity**. Because God's people were unfaithful to their †covenant with the Lord, the Lord hid his face from them and handed them over to their adversaries: **I dealt with them according to their uncleanness and their transgressions, and hid my face from them.**

The second part is directed to the people of Israel. The Lord declares that he   39:25–29
will restore them by his own hand: **Now I will restore the fortunes of Jacob, and have mercy upon the whole house of Israel; and I will be jealous for my holy name**. This recalls the promises of restoration in chapters 34–37. The emphasis falls here on the *whole* of Israel; all the tribes will be included, from the north and from the south. When God brings his people back from exile, then they **shall forget their shame** and their long history of unfaithfulness. They will dwell securely in the land, where no one can make them afraid.

In the final statement (vv. 28–29), the Lord sums up the message of the book. Because Israel sinned, he **sent them into exile among the nations**. But because of his own holiness and faithfulness, he will gather **them into their own land**, leaving none behind. He will no longer hide his face from his people. This pattern of exile and regathering follows the precise contours of the †covenant blessings, curses, and restoration promised to Israel of old (see Lev 26:40–42; Deut 30:1–10). As the culmination of his work, the Lord says that all this will happen **when I pour out my Spirit upon the house of Israel**. God will not only deliver his people; he will pour out his Spirit upon them so that they can live faithfully as his covenant people.

This presents a striking contrast to the first part of the book. During the time of judgment, Ezekiel questioned whether the Lord would destroy his people by pouring out his wrath: "Ah, Lord GOD! will you destroy all that remains of Israel in the outpouring of your wrath upon Jerusalem?" (9:8). In answer to this plea, the Lord now promises to pour out his own Spirit as the ultimate blessing that enables his own people to live and flourish in the promised land.[13]

This magnificent summary of God's promises to his people was partially fulfilled when the exiles returned from Babylon in the sixth century BC. The prophets Haggai and Zechariah testify to this return and the rebuilding of the temple. Nehemiah and Ezra oversaw the rebuilding of Jerusalem and a return to the practices of the law. The people of Israel were once again settled in the land of promise. But plainly the promises of Ezekiel as expressed here and elsewhere in the book were not completely fulfilled. Other postexilic Jewish writings show that the Jewish people were keenly aware of this fact (for example, Neh 9:36–37; Sir 36:1–17). Israel remained under foreign rule, and the people were waiting for the promised Messiah, who would bring to completion all that Ezekiel prophesied.

Reflection and Application (39:21–29)

The good news for us is that this has decisively occurred through Jesus, the Messiah of Israel and savior of the whole world. Specifically, on the day of †Pentecost, the Spirit was definitively poured out on the house of Israel, fulfilling Ezekiel's prophecy. Peter stands up among the people and, citing the prophet Joel, says: "And in the last days it shall be, God declares, / that I will pour out my Spirit upon all flesh" (Acts 2:17). Proclaiming salvation through Jesus, Peter explains: "Being therefore exalted at the right hand of God, and having received from the Father the promise of the Holy Spirit, [Jesus] has poured out this which you see and hear" (Acts 2:33). The messianic age has begun, the Spirit has been poured out, and Christians now experience the fruits of the gift of the Spirit. Through Jesus the Messiah of Israel, the nations (†Gentiles) have been included in the promises given to Israel, receiving the Spirit of adoption (Eph 2:11–22).

Do we recognize and appreciate all that we have received through the Spirit? Through the gift of the Spirit, we have returned from our exile—we are adopted sons and daughters who now live in our Father's house (Rom 8:14–17). We have full access to the presence of the Lord God, able to call upon him in worship,

13. For the outpouring of God's Spirit in the Old Testament, see Isa 32:15; 44:3; Joel 2:28; Zech 12:10.

praise, and supplication (Eph 2:18). Because the Spirit has been poured into our hearts, we experience the love of God (Rom 5:5). And we have received both the fruit of the Spirit (Gal 5:22–23) and the gifts of the Spirit (1 Cor 12:4–11), enabling us to live Christ's way of life and so bring glory to the Father (John 15:8). While it is true that the complete fulfilment of Ezekiel's promises will occur only when Christ returns in the age to come, even now the Spirit has been poured out. Those who belong to Christ, Jew and Gentile both, are heirs of Ezekiel's prophetic promises.

The New Temple

Ezekiel 40:1–42:20

The final part of Ezekiel is about the refounding of the temple and the resettlement of the land of Israel. This fulfills the promises of chapters 34–37 and accomplishes the reversal of the Lord's departure from the temple described earlier in the book. Structurally, Ezekiel appears to follow the threefold pattern set by Moses in the †Pentateuch: (1) Moses first narrates the construction of the tabernacle (Exod 25–40); (2) then he delivers prescriptions for the temple and its worship (Lev 1–Num 10); (3) finally, he apportions the land to the twelve tribes (Num 34–35). Ezekiel follows the same pattern in chapters 40–48: (1) chapters 40–42 describe the dimensions of the new temple; (2) chapters 43–46 outline the prescriptions for the new temple and its worship; and (3) chapters 47–48 describe the reapportioning of the land.[1] Following the great calamity of the Babylonian captivity, Ezekiel sees in a vision nothing less than the refoundation of the temple and the resettlement of the people in the land.[2]

In this first section (chaps. 40–42), Ezekiel is given an extensive tour of the new temple that culminates in the return of God's presence and glory to the temple (43:1–5). This tour sharply contrasts with an earlier tour when Ezekiel was shown all the corrupt practices occurring in the house of God and witnessed the ominous departure of the presence of the Lord from the temple (chaps. 8–11).

---

1. Block, *Ezekiel: Chapters 25–48*, 498, proposes that "these parallels provide an early clue that Ezekiel is functioning as a second Moses."

2. Scholars are divided over whether Ezekiel himself is the author of all the material in chaps. 40–48. One view sees a layering of later sources added to Ezekiel's own testimony; another view sees a fundamental unity in these chapters and argues that Ezekiel himself is the author. I will assume a fundamental unity to this final section of the book, though some later additions are certainly possible. The fact that so little of Ezekiel's design went into the actual reconstructing of the †second temple suggests that this design comes from Ezekiel's time, before the temple was rebuilt.

Ezekiel's Temple in Jewish Tradition

LIVING
TRADITION

Readers of Ezekiel perennially ask: Does Ezekiel offer an architectural plan intended for the building of a real temple? In other words, is Ezekiel providing a blueprint for the temple's literal reconstruction? On the one hand, the concern for precise measurements and the allocation of spaces and rooms for concrete day-to-day functions all seem to point to a physical, functioning temple, not just a symbolic vision. On the other hand, Ezekiel does not give enough detail for the actual construction of a new temple; his measurements are partial and incomplete, and many temple features are missing. Further, Ezekiel's enormous concern for precise symmetry, with measurements based on multiples of 5, 25, 50, and 100, points in the direction of a symbolic representation of the new temple. Scholars are divided on the question, but most view Ezekiel's temple as predominantly symbolic. John Bergsma and Brant Pitre, for example, conclude that "Ezekiel's Temple is intended to represent a miraculous and †*eschatological* reality, not merely a natural stone building."[a] According to the historical record, the actual reconstruction of the second temple, which took place under Zerubbabel (in 520–516 BC), did *not* follow Ezekiel's model of the temple—Ezekiel's design was never used for actual construction.

According to some rabbis, Ezekiel's design for the new temple was not used by the exiles returning from Babylon because the second temple was destined to fall, while Ezekiel's design was for the temple that would last forever. In Jewish tradition, the predominant interpretation of the rabbis was that Ezekiel's temple would be built only when the †Messiah would come and bring the final redemption.[b]

a. John Bergsma and Brant Pitre, "Ezekiel," in *A Catholic Introduction to the Bible*, vol. 1, *The Old Testament* (San Francisco: Ignatius, 2018), 863.

b. Maimonides (d. 1204) taught that Ezekiel's temple would actually be built by human hands when the Messiah appeared; Rashi (d. 1105) said that this temple would be made of fire and would descend directly from heaven. See Eisemann, *Ezekiel*, 603–7, for the variety of †rabbinic views on Ezekiel's temple.

It will be helpful to gain an overview of Ezekiel's temple before engaging the tour that Ezekiel's guide directs. At the center of the entire temple complex is the temple itself, a relatively small enclosed (roofed) building. Around the temple building is an inner court, and this is surrounded by a large outer court. Three gates connect the inner and the outer courts (on the south, east, and north), and three connect the outer court to the outside world (on the south, east, and north). The outer court is surrounded by a series of rooms around the perimeter of the temple complex, with an outer wall separating the entire temple area from the outside world (see fig. 8, p. 283).

Measurement of the Outer Courts (40:1–27)

[1]In the twenty-fifth year of our exile, at the beginning of the year, on the tenth day of the month, in the fourteenth year after the city was conquered, on that very day, the hand of the LORD was upon me, [2]and brought me in the visions of God into the land of Israel, and set me down upon a very high mountain, on which was a structure like a city opposite me. [3]When he brought me there, behold, there was a man, whose appearance was like bronze, with a line of flax and a measuring reed in his hand; and he was standing in the gateway. [4]And the man said to me, "Son of man, look with your eyes, and hear with your ears, and set your mind upon all that I shall show you, for you were brought here in order that I might show it to you; declare all that you see to the house of Israel."

[5]And behold, there was a wall all around the outside of the temple area, and the length of the measuring reed in the man's hand was six long cubits, each being a cubit and a handbreadth in length; so he measured the thickness of the wall, one reed; and the height, one reed. [6]Then he went into the gateway facing east, going up its steps, and measured the threshold of the gate, one reed deep; [7]and the side rooms, one reed long, and one reed broad; and the space between the side rooms, five cubits; and the threshold of the gate by the vestibule of the gate at the inner end, one reed. [8]Then he measured the vestibule of the gateway, eight cubits; [9]and its jambs, two cubits; and the vestibule of the gate was at the inner end. [10]And there were three side rooms on either side of the east gate; the three were of the same size; and the jambs on either side were of the same size. [11]Then he measured the breadth of the opening of the gateway, ten cubits; and the breadth of the gateway, thirteen cubits. [12]There was a barrier before the side rooms, one cubit on either side; and the side rooms were six cubits on either side. [13]Then he measured the gate from the back of the one side room to the back of the other, a breadth of five and twenty cubits, from door to door. [14]He measured also the vestibule, twenty cubits; and round about the vestibule of the gateway was the court. [15]From the front of the gate at the entrance to the end of the inner vestibule of the gate was fifty cubits. [16]And the gateway had windows round about, narrowing inwards into their jambs in the side rooms, and likewise the vestibule had windows round about inside, and on the jambs were palm trees.

[17]Then he brought me into the outer court; and behold, there were chambers and a pavement, round about the court; thirty chambers fronted on the pavement. [18]And the pavement ran along the side of the gates, corresponding to the length of the gates; this was the lower pavement. [19]Then he measured the distance from the inner front of the lower gate to the outer front of the inner court, a hundred cubits.

Then he went before me to the north, [20]and behold, there was a gate which faced toward the north, belonging to the outer court. He measured its length and its breadth. [21]Its side rooms, three on either side, and its jambs and its vestibule were of the same size as those of the first gate; its length was fifty cubits, and its breadth twenty-five cubits. [22]And its windows, its vestibule, and its palm trees were of the same size as those of the gate which faced toward the east; and seven steps led up to it; and its vestibule was on the inside. [23]And opposite the gate on the north, as on the east, was a gate to the inner court; and he measured from gate to gate, a hundred cubits.

[24]And he led me toward the south, and behold, there was a gate on the south; and he measured its jambs and its vestibule; they had the same size as the others. [25]And there were windows round about in it and in its vestibule, like the windows of the others; its length was fifty cubits, and its breadth twenty-five cubits. [26]And there were seven steps leading up to it, and its vestibule was on the inside; and it had palm trees on its jambs, one on either side. [27]And there was a gate on the south of the inner court; and he measured from gate to gate toward the south, a hundred cubits.

OT: Exod 12:3; 25–31; 35–40; Josh 4:19; Isa 2:2
NT: Rev 1:15; 2:18
Catechism: vision of God, 294, 1720, 1726, 2519; centrality of the temple, 576, 583–86, 2580–81

This is the last dated †oracle in the book (v. 1). The date given is **the twenty-** **40:1–2**
fifth year of our exile, at the beginning of the year, on the tenth day of the month, in the fourteenth year after the city was conquered (April 28, 573 BC). The "beginning of the year" is probably the month of Nisan, the month of the †Passover feast. "The tenth day of the month" coincides with when the people of Israel crossed the Jordan River and arrived in the promised land (Josh 4:19). It was also the day on which the Passover lambs were selected (Exod 12:3). This date, then, may signify in Ezekiel's vision the return of Israel to the land and the renewal of sacrifice to the Lord. The fact that Ezekiel calls attention to "the twenty-fifth year of our exile" is also significant. Twenty-five is half the span of the †Jubilee (fifty years), and Ezekiel refers to the Year of Jubilee (the fiftieth year) as the "year of liberty" (46:17). "Thus, symbolically, Israel has reached the turning point in its exile in Babylonia; henceforth, they can expect to receive good news of their impending return to their land."[3]

Once again, consistent with other main visions in the book, **the hand of the** LORD is upon Ezekiel, and **in the visions of God** he is brought to **a very high mountain** opposite a **city** (Jerusalem), where he will see and hear what the

---

3. Milgrom and Block, *Ezekiel's Hope*, 61.

St. Gregory the Great on the High Mountain as a Type of Christ

LIVING
TRADITION

Pope Gregory the Great offers an †allegorical reading of Ezek 40:1–4, seeing in the "very high mountain" a †type of Christ himself:

Therefore, whom does the high mountain signify if not the Mediator of God and men, the Man Jesus Christ? He is indeed from the earth but beyond the earth because the flesh of this same Savior of ours contains material from the depths but excels on the heights because of His power. … He was made not only Man but by the conception of this same humanity which was assumed by Him, He became God/Man, not only Man beyond men but also Man above the Angels.[a]

a. *Homilies on the Book of the Prophet Ezekiel,* trans. Theodosia Tomkinson, 2nd ed. (Etna, CA: Center for Traditionalist Orthodox Studies, 2008), 262.

Lord calls him to proclaim.[4] Jerusalem is never named in these final chapters, but it is clear throughout that Ezekiel is referring to the Holy City.[5] The reference to "a very high mountain" echoes Isa 2:2: "The mountain of the house of the LORD / shall be established as the highest of the mountains." The vision of the high mountain also links back to the promise in Ezek 20:40 that the Lord would regather his people on his holy mountain: "For on my holy mountain, the mountain height of Israel, says the Lord GOD, there all the house of Israel, all of them, shall serve me in the land." As we shall see, Ezekiel places the newly constructed temple on the north of the Temple Mount, outside the city, with Jerusalem lying to the south.

40:3–4   When Ezekiel arrives in vision on the high mountain, he finds there **a man, whose appearance was like bronze, with a line of flax and a measuring reed in his hand.**[6] This heavenly guide, similar to the one described earlier in the book (8:2–3; 9:2–4, 11; 10:2, 6–7), will accompany Ezekiel in an extensive tour of the temple. In chapters 8–10, a heavenly guide revealed to Ezekiel the corruptions occurring in the temple; now a heavenly attendant leads him on a tour of the new and purified temple. The fact that the guide's "appearance was like bronze" points to his supernatural identity (see Rev 1:15; 2:18); the "line of flax" (a linen cord) and the measuring rod are instruments for longer and shorter measures respectively. They will be used to calculate the dimensions of the new temple. Impressively, Ezekiel is told to embrace the vision with his

4. The phrase "visions of God" links this vision to those beginning in 1:1 and 8:3 and signals the inauguration of a significant new vision.
5. For example, in Ezek 43:3 it is clear that by "the city" he means the city of Jerusalem.
6. The prophet Zechariah also saw in a vision "a man with a measuring line in his hand" (Zech 2:1).

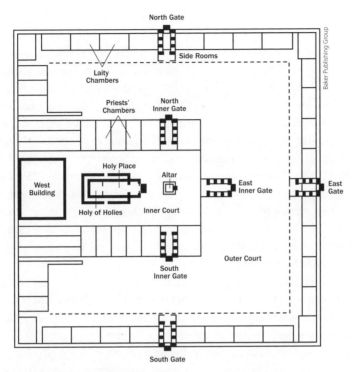

Figure 8. Ezekiel's temple and courts

whole being: **look with your eyes, and hear with your ears, and set your mind upon all that I shall show you.** He is meant to *see*, *hear*, and *pay attention to* all that God will reveal to him. But this is not for Ezekiel's sake alone: his task is to **declare all that** he sees **to the house of Israel**. To fulfill his prophetic commission, Ezekiel must consecrate all his faculties—sight, hearing, and understanding—to what God is revealing, so that he can faithfully convey the vision to the people.

Ezekiel now begins a long, patient description of the new temple that takes up the next three chapters. We may wonder why Ezekiel relates all the precise details of the tour and records the exact measurements of the structure. For contemporary readers this may seem like unimportant detail, akin to the long lists of ancestors in the biblical genealogies. But the background for what Ezekiel presents is the painstaking detail of the plan for the wilderness tabernacle that Moses received (Exod 25–31; 35–40). Ezekiel follows a similar pattern, though with far *less* detail overall. As we shall see, the precise details and the intense symmetry that mark this temple plan symbolize the perfection of the dwelling of God among his people.

The tour of the temple area begins and ends at the eastern gate (40:6; 42:15), but it is the outer temple wall that receives first and last notice (40:5; 42:20): **there**

40:5–16

was a wall all around the outside of the temple area.[7] This wall separates what is holy from what is common (42:20). The wall's height and thickness are equal to the length of the measuring rod, **six long cubits**, approximately three meters or about ten feet.[8] The guide then takes the measure of the east gate and the chambers within it (vv. 6–16). There are six chambers along this vestibule, three on each side. The purpose for these chambers is not described, but they probably serve as guardrooms where security personnel would be stationed. To give a sense for the size of the temple, the east gate opening is 10 cubits (17 feet) wide, and the length of the vestibule leading to the outer court is 50 cubits (86 feet). In total, the horizontal dimensions of this east gate and vestibule are 25 cubits wide and 50 cubits long. "The 25 × 50 spatial dimensions give this gateway a perfectly proportioned rectangular shape."[9] What is lacking in this plan are the vertical dimensions (the height of the gate and vestibule). The result is a two-dimensional view of the temple area, indicating that Ezekiel was not intending to give a full blueprint usable for building.

40:17–27   Ezekiel and his guide then ascend the steps that lead up from the east gate and proceed to measure the **outer court** of the temple and its **chambers** ("rooms") (vv. 17–19). Ezekiel identifies thirty chambers in the outer wall of the temple area, located proportionately along the four inner walls of the outer court. He also identifies a lower pavement, probably a raised walkway, that ran around the circumference of the outer walls, probably enabling access to the chambers. Finally the guide measures the north and the south gates, identical in structure and dimensions to the east gate (vv. 20–27), and records the distance (100 cubits) between each gate as it opens into the outer court. The number of steps leading up to each gate is "seven," the number of completeness and perfection: **and seven steps led up to it**. The number of steps (seven) and the precise symmetry of the dimensions (25 × 50 × 100) are probably intended to reveal symbolically the glory and perfection of God in his presence among the people.[10]

Measurement of the Inner Courts (40:28–49)

---

[28]**Then he brought me to the inner court by the south gate, and he measured the south gate; it was of the same size as the others; [29]Its side rooms,**

7. By "temple area" is meant everything contained within the outer temple wall, including the outer courts, the inner courts, the various chambers, and the temple building itself.
8. The measuring rod makes use of the "long cubit." The normal cubit was six handbreadths (17.6 inches); the long cubit, used here, was 20.5 inches.
9. Block, *Ezekiel: Chapters 25–48*, 522.
10. Milgrom and Block, *Ezekiel's Hope*, 75, identify the number twenty-five as "the base number of Ezekiel's architectural system."

its jambs, and its vestibule were of the same size as the others; and there were windows round about in it and in its vestibule; its length was fifty cubits, and its breadth twenty-five cubits. ³⁰And there were vestibules round about, twenty-five cubits long and five cubits broad. ³¹Its vestibule faced the outer court, and palm trees were on its jambs, and its stairway had eight steps.

³²Then he brought me to the inner court on the east side, and he measured the gate; it was of the same size as the others. ³³Its side rooms, its jambs, and its vestibule were of the same size as the others; and there were windows round about in it and in its vestibule; its length was fifty cubits, and its breadth twenty-five cubits. ³⁴Its vestibule faced the outer court, and it had palm trees on its jambs, one on either side; and its stairway had eight steps.

³⁵Then he brought me to the north gate, and he measured it; it had the same size as the others. ³⁶Its side rooms, its jambs, and its vestibule were of the same size as the others; and it had windows round about; its length was fifty cubits, and its breadth twenty-five cubits. ³⁷Its vestibule faced the outer court, and it had palm trees on its jambs, one on either side; and its stairway had eight steps.

³⁸There was a chamber with its door in the vestibule of the gate, where the burnt offering was to be washed. ³⁹And in the vestibule of the gate were two tables on either side, on which the burnt offering and the sin offering and the guilt offering were to be slaughtered. ⁴⁰And on the outside of the vestibule at the entrance of the north gate were two tables; and on the other side of the vestibule of the gate were two tables. ⁴¹Four tables were on the inside, and four tables on the outside of the side of the gate, eight tables, on which the sacrifices were to be slaughtered. ⁴²And there were also four tables of hewn stone for the burnt offering, a cubit and a half long, and a cubit and a half broad, and one cubit high, on which the instruments were to be laid with which the burnt offerings and the sacrifices were slaughtered. ⁴³And hooks, a handbreadth long, were fastened round about within. And on the tables the flesh of the offering was to be laid.

⁴⁴Then he brought me from without into the inner court, and behold, there were two chambers in the inner court, one at the side of the north gate facing south, the other at the side of the south gate facing north. ⁴⁵And he said to me, This chamber which faces south is for the priests who have charge of the temple, ⁴⁶and the chamber which faces north is for the priests who have charge of the altar; these are the sons of Zadok, who alone among the sons of Levi may come near to the Lord to minister to him. ⁴⁷And he measured the court, a hundred cubits long, and a hundred cubits broad, foursquare; and the altar was in front of the temple.

⁴⁸Then he brought me to the vestibule of the temple and measured the jambs of the vestibule, five cubits on either side; and the breadth of the

gate was fourteen cubits; and the sidewalls of the gate were three cubits on either side. [49]The length of the vestibule was twenty cubits, and the breadth twelve cubits; and ten steps led up to it; and there were pillars beside the jambs on either side.

OT: Lev 1:1–17; 4:1–35; 5:1–6; Num 18:20–24; Deut 10:8; 2 Sam 15:24–29
Catechism: vision of God, 294, 1720, 1726, 2519; centrality of the temple, 576, 583–86, 2580–81

40:28–37   Ezekiel is now escorted from the outer court through the south gate to the **inner court** and its chambers, and he then proceeds to the east **gate** and the north gate. The gates leading from the outer court to the inner court of the temple area are measured: they are identical in size and structure (25 × 50 cubits) to the gates and vestibules leading into the **outer court**. The one difference is that the stairways leading up to the inner court at each gate have **eight steps**. This additional number probably expresses the greater holiness of the inner court: "Its greater holiness is also marked by its elevation, eight steps—one step higher than the seven-step lower platform."[11]

Scholars debate whether a wall separated the outer court from the inner court. Some assume that it must have been there but is not mentioned; others believe that in this new temple there is no need for a wall of separation, for the people have all been renewed with a new heart and spirit. The only wall of separation identified in Ezekiel's temple is the *outer* wall, which divides the clean from the unclean.[12]

40:38   At this point (vv. 38–43), the tour pauses as Ezekiel describes the areas within the inner court, where the priests minister. This is where **the burnt offering was to be washed**, before being slaughtered and laid out on tables. It appears that the animals were received by the Levites in the outer court and brought up the stairs and through the inner gate on the north side, where they were washed and then prepared for slaughter on four tables set up at the entrance at the north vestibule.[13]

40:39–43   In verse 39, Ezekiel names three of the main sacrifices that were offered in the temple.[14] **The** (whole) **burnt offering** is the entire unblemished animal given to the Lord as a sign of wholehearted devotion (see Lev 1:1–17). The **sin offering** deals primarily with moral impurity. It makes atonement for sin and brings about forgiveness in the one who presents the offering (see Lev 4:1–35). The **guilt offering** is similar to the sin offering but serves especially to bring

11. Milgrom and Block, *Ezekiel's Hope*, 75.
12. See Milgrom and Block, *Ezekiel's Hope*, 43–44, for the view that there was no wall of separation between the outer and inner courts of Ezekiel's temple.
13. See 2 Chron 4:6 for the practice of washing sacrificial animals within the temple precincts.
14. In Leviticus, five main sacrifices are described. Ezekiel refers to three of them here (burnt offering, sin offering, guilt offering) but does not refer to the remaining two: the cereal or grain offering (Lev 2) and the peace offering (Lev 3).

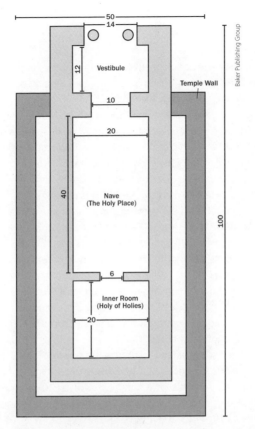

Figure 9. The temple building

about the cleansing of a guilty conscience in the case when a sin or infraction is hidden from someone but then becomes manifest. The worshiper presents an offering to be cleansed from guilt (see Lev 5:1–6).

In the next stage of the tour, Ezekiel reviews the **chambers** on the north   40:44–46 and south sides of **the inner court**. The first is reserved for the priests who have charge of the temple, the second for the priests who have charge of the altar. This distinction probably refers to a division of labor among the Zadokite priests—guarding the temple and guarding the altar—not to a distinction between two kinds of priests (see the sidebar "The Zadokite Priesthood," p. 288).[15]

In the next stage of the tour, Ezekiel comes to **the vestibule of the temple**   40:47–49 building. We are told that the inner **court** (v. 47)—where Ezekiel is standing—is a perfect square, one hundred cubits long and wide, with the altar placed in the center of the inner court in front of the temple building itself (the altar

15. See also Ezek 43:19; 44:15; 48:11 for reference to priests from the house of Zadok.

The Zadokite Priesthood

Ezekiel refers to "the sons of Zadok" in 40:46, saying that they alone among the "sons of Levi" are authorized to "come near to the Lᴏʀᴅ to minister to him." In other words, only the family of Zadok among the families of the tribe of Levi is qualified to serve as priests in the temple. The tribe of Levi was set aside (consecrated) in the time of Moses to serve as attendants in the worship of the Lord: "At that time the Lᴏʀᴅ set apart the tribe of Levi to carry the ark of the covenant of the Lᴏʀᴅ, to stand before the Lᴏʀᴅ to minister to him and to bless in his name, to this day" (Deut 10:8; see also Num 18:20–24). This privileged service was granted to the tribe of Levi because of the faithfulness they showed to Moses and to the Lord when many Israelites worshiped the golden calf (see Exod 32:25–29). Among the Levites, the family of Aaron was specially chosen to serve as priests to offer sacrifice before the Lord in the newly constructed sanctuary (see Exod 28:1–4; Num 3:3–10).

In the reign of King David, when Absalom led a rebellion against his father, Zadok and Abiathar were the priests who stood by David and were faithful to him even when others turned away (2 Sam 15:24–29). Crucially, Zadok stood by David's choice of Solomon to succeed him (1 Kings 1:39), while Abiathar supported Solomon's rival, and so Zadok emerged as the one true faithful high priest for David and Solomon (1 Chron 29:22). The lineage of Zadok thus became the faithful line of high priests in Israel and Judah (2 Chron 31:10). Ezekiel validates this role for the house of Zadok, identifying this line as the true priesthood in Israel (see also Ezek 43:19; 44:15; and 48:11).

will be described in detail in 43:13–17). Then Ezekiel's guide begins to measure the dimensions of the temple building itself, here giving the dimensions of the vestibule (vv. 48–49). To gain a sense for the whole building, there are three rooms in sequence: a vestibule, a great hall, and the inner sanctum (holy of holies). **Ten steps** lead up to the temple building, elevating this structure above all else around it. Here we should recall that seven steps led from the gate into the outer court, and then a further eight steps into the inner court. To go from the inner court to the temple building, one must now ascend a further ten steps. The increased "ascent" at each level indicates the increasing holiness as one approaches the Lord's presence. When added together, the total number of stairs someone would climb to go from the outer gate to the temple building itself was twenty-five. This number (twenty-five) is important for Ezekiel, signaling the holiness and perfection of the dwelling of God among his people. In short, the measurements communicate the profound *holiness* of Ezekiel's temple.

The Inner Sanctuary, Wider Temple, and Furnishings (41:1–26)

¹Then he brought me to the nave, and measured the jambs; on each side six cubits was the breadth of the jambs. ²And the breadth of the entrance was ten cubits; and the sidewalls of the entrance were five cubits on either side; and he measured the length of the nave forty cubits, and its breadth, twenty cubits. ³Then he went into the inner room and measured the jambs of the entrance, two cubits; and the breadth of the entrance, six cubits; and the sidewalls of the entrance, seven cubits. ⁴And he measured the length of the room, twenty cubits, and its breadth, twenty cubits, beyond the nave. And he said to me, "This is the most holy place."

⁵Then he measured the wall of the temple, six cubits thick; and the breadth of the side chambers, four cubits, round about the temple. ⁶And the side chambers were in three stories, one over another, thirty in each story. There were offsets all around the wall of the temple to serve as supports for the side chambers, so that they should not be supported by the wall of the temple. ⁷And the side chambers became broader as they rose from story to story, corresponding to the enlargement of the offset from story to story round about the temple; on the side of the temple a stairway led upward, and thus one went up from the lowest story to the top story through the middle story. ⁸I saw also that the temple had a raised platform round about; the foundations of the side chambers measured a full reed of six long cubits. ⁹The thickness of the outer wall of the side chambers was five cubits; and the part of the platform which was left free was five cubits. Between the platform of the temple and the ¹⁰chambers of the court was a breadth of twenty cubits round about the temple on every side. ¹¹And the doors of the side chambers opened on the part of the platform that was left free, one door toward the north, and another door toward the south; and the breadth of the part that was left free was five cubits round about.

¹²The building that was facing the temple yard on the west side was seventy cubits broad; and the wall of the building was five cubits thick round about, and its length ninety cubits.

¹³Then he measured the temple, a hundred cubits long; and the yard and the building with its walls, a hundred cubits long; ¹⁴also the breadth of the east front of the temple and the yard, a hundred cubits.

¹⁵Then he measured the length of the building facing the yard which was at the west and its walls on either side, a hundred cubits.

The nave of the temple and the inner room and the outer vestibule ¹⁶were paneled and round about all three had windows with recessed frames. Over against the threshold the temple was paneled with wood round about, from the floor up to the windows (now the windows were covered), ¹⁷to the space above the door, even to the inner room, and on the outside. And on all the walls round about in the inner room and the nave were carved likenesses ¹⁸of cherubim and palm trees, a palm tree between cherub and cherub. Every cherub had two faces: ¹⁹the face of a man toward the palm tree on the one side, and the face of a young lion toward the palm tree on the other side. They were carved on the whole temple round about; ²⁰from the floor to above the door cherubim and palm trees were carved on the wall.

²¹The doorposts of the nave were squared; and in front of the holy place was something resembling ²²an altar of wood, three cubits high, two cubits long, and two cubits broad; its corners, its base, and its walls were of wood. He said to me, "This is the table which is before the Lord." ²³The nave and the holy place had each a double door. ²⁴The doors had two leaves apiece, two swinging leaves for each door. ²⁵And on the doors of the nave were carved cherubim and palm trees, such as were carved on the walls; and there was a canopy of wood in front of the vestibule outside. ²⁶And there were recessed windows and palm trees on either side, on the sidewalls of the vestibule.

OT: Exod 25:23–40; 26:33; 30:1–10; Lev 24:5–9; 1 Kings 6:1–10; 2 Macc 8:1–8
NT: Heb 9:1–14
Catechism: centrality of the temple, 576, 583–86, 2580–81

41:1–4   In chapter 41, the tour of the temple continues with a description of the temple building itself: its measurements, rooms, and decorations. Following the pattern set by Solomon, Ezekiel's temple has three adjoining rooms; the dimensions of the two main rooms (the holy place and the holy of holies) match exactly the measurements of these rooms in Solomon's temple (see 1 Kings 6:1–10). But nearly all of the furnishings found in Solomon's temple go unmentioned here.

Ezekiel is escorted into the inner temple (see fig. 9, p. 287), moving from the outer vestibule into **the nave**. This room was called "the holy place" in the tabernacle constructed by Moses (Exod 26:33). Both the vestibule and the nave are carefully measured. Ezekiel's guide then enters into **the inner room** and measures its dimensions, but Ezekiel himself does not enter. The guide tells Ezekiel that this is **the most holy place** (the holy of holies), where no unauthorized person may enter. As one proceeds through the three rooms, the entryways become increasingly narrow (from fourteen to ten to six cubits), indicating that access to God's glorious presence is more and more restricted as one draws closer. The symmetry of the rooms, carefully measured and recorded, communicates the full and perfect holiness of the Lord.

In the Light of Christ (41:1–4)

Ezekiel refers to the two main rooms of the temple building: the holy place (what Ezekiel calls the "nave") and the most holy place (the holy of holies). According to the instructions given to Moses, the first room (the holy place) contained (1) a table on which was set the "bread of the Presence" (Exod 25:23–30), (2) the golden lampstand (25:31–40), and (3) the altar of incense (30:1–5). Here the priests went about their daily round of duties, tending the lampstand, offering incense, and changing the bread of the Presence.

The Letter to the Hebrews also refers to these two rooms (Heb 9:1–7) and shows how, in a manner unknown to the prophet Ezekiel, Christ has fulfilled all the sacrifices offered of old through his one, perfect sacrifice of himself to the Father. The second inner room, the holy of holies, which housed the ark of the covenant, could be entered only by the high priest once per year on the solemn Day of Atonement (Heb 9:3–5, 7). The author of Hebrews tells us that this arrangement, ordained by God through the Law, brings about only an imperfect sacrifice for sin (9:8–10). But Christ Jesus has broken through and opened the way for us all to have full access to the Father. He did not, like an earthly priest, enter into the earthly sanctuary, but he entered heaven itself, into the true most holy place, and there offered his own blood as a perfect once-for-all sacrifice that truly brings reconciliation with God and full access to his presence (9:11–14).

In this section, Ezekiel's guide takes precise measurements of the side rooms **41:5–12** that surround the inner temple, the connecting stairways, and an adjoining building. The details are challenging to follow. The entire temple building stands on **a raised platform** six cubits high (v. 8). The description of the **three stories** of **side chambers** closely tracks the design for these found in Solomon's temple (see 1 Kings 6:5–8). There is also a second wall, surrounding the inner wall, that supports side rooms on three sides of the inner temple (north, south, west). There are three stories of ten rooms each (a total of thirty rooms) on each side. Thus, Ezekiel's description portrays a total of ninety small rooms. We are not told what the function of these side rooms was. Possibly they served as storage rooms for all the materials needed for sacrifice in the temple and for support of its personnel, but they may also have served as "storehouses for temple treasures."[16]

When we add together the various measurements, the length of the temple building adds up to one hundred cubits, and the width to fifty cubits. We are presented again with a perfectly dimensioned rectangle (100×50) that makes use of multiples of twenty-five.

Ezekiel's guide now painstakingly measures each dimension of the temple **41:13–20** building and its side chambers (vv. 13–15a): it is a perfect square, **a hundred cubits** on each side (see fig. 9, p. 287). The remainder of chapter 41 provides further details of the decorations and sacred objects in the temple building. The details of the plan are obscure; it is not easy to be certain how things are arranged. We are told that all three rooms in the temple building—the **vestibule**,

16. Block, *Ezekiel: Chapters 25–48*, 552.

the nave (the holy place), and **the inner room** (the holy of holies)—are paneled with wood from top to bottom. Carved †**cherubim** and **palm trees** adorn the temple walls: **they were carved on the whole temple round about; from the floor to above the door cherubim and palm trees were carved on the wall** (see Exod 26:1, 31; 1 Kings 6:29, 32). Unlike the four-headed cherubim of Ezekiel's earlier visions (chaps. 1, 10), each carved cherub here has just two faces: the face of a man facing one way and the face of a lion facing the other (vv. 18–19).

41:21–26   Ezekiel then refers to **an altar of wood, the table which is before the Lord**. This may refer to the table that holds the bread of the Presence, the continual offering of twelve freshly baked loaves of bread that were placed before the presence of the Lord each week (see Lev 24:5–9). But it may refer to the golden altar of incense, upon which the priests were commanded to burn incense twice daily, in the morning and in the evening (see Exod 30:1–10). Finally, Ezekiel tells us that the entrances to both the nave and the most holy place are marked by double swinging doors, following the design in Solomon's temple (1 Kings 6:34).

The most notable aspect of Ezekiel's description of the inner temple (the holy place and the holy of holies) is the *absence* of the ark of the covenant. Speculation abounds as to why the ark does not appear in Ezekiel's temple: (1) because the ark was destroyed during the reign of Manasseh; (2) because the ark could not be present apart from the actual glorious presence of the Lord; (3) because the prophet Jeremiah hid the ark, and it is to be rediscovered only when God reveals its hiding place (2 Macc 8:1–8); or (4) because the glorious presence of the Lord now replaces the ark of the covenant (Jer 3:16). As we shall see (Ezek 43:6–9), the fourth explanation most persuasively accounts for the absence of the ark in Ezekiel's holy of holies.

The Priestly Rooms and Final Measurements (42:1–20)

¹Then he led me out into the inner court, toward the north, and he brought me to the chambers which were opposite the temple yard and opposite the building on the north. ²The length of the building which was on the north side was a hundred cubits, and the breadth fifty cubits. ³Adjoining the twenty cubits which belonged to the inner court, and facing the pavement which belonged to the outer court, was gallery against gallery in three stories. ⁴And before the chambers was a passage inward, ten cubits wide and a hundred cubits long, and their doors were on the north. ⁵Now the upper chambers were narrower, for the galleries took more away from them than from the lower and middle chambers in the building. ⁶For they were in three stories, and they had no pillars like the pillars of the outer court; hence the upper chambers were set back from the ground more

than the lower and the middle ones. [7]And there was a wall outside parallel to the chambers, toward the outer court, opposite the chambers, fifty cubits long. [8]For the chambers on the outer court were fifty cubits long, while those opposite the temple were a hundred cubits long. [9]Below these chambers was an entrance on the east side, as one enters them from the outer court, [10]where the outside wall begins.

On the south also, opposite the yard and opposite the building, there were chambers [11]with a passage in front of them; they were similar to the chambers on the north, of the same length and breadth, with the same exits and arrangements and doors. [12]And below the south chambers was an entrance on the east side, where one enters the passage, and opposite them was a dividing wall.

[13]Then he said to me, "The north chambers and the south chambers opposite the yard are the holy chambers, where the priests who approach the LORD shall eat the most holy offerings; there they shall put the most holy offerings—the cereal offering, the sin offering, and the guilt offering, for the place is holy. [14]When the priests enter the holy place, they shall not go out of it into the outer court without laying there the garments in which they minister, for these are holy; they shall put on other garments before they go near to that which is for the people."

[15]Now when he had finished measuring the interior of the temple area, he led me out by the gate which faced east, and measured the temple area round about. [16]He measured the east side with the measuring reed, five hundred cubits by the measuring reed. [17]Then he turned and measured the north side, five hundred cubits by the measuring reed. [18]Then he turned and measured the south side, five hundred cubits by the measuring reed. [19]Then he turned to the west side and measured, five hundred cubits by the measuring reed. [20]He measured it on the four sides. It had a wall around it, five hundred cubits long and five hundred cubits broad, to make a separation between the holy and the common.

OT: Exod 19:6; 29:33; Lev 2:1–10; 6:14–18; 10:10–11; 20:24–26
NT: 2 Cor 7:1; Gal 3:28; Eph 2:13; 1 Pet 1:15; 2:9; Rev 21:15–16
Catechism: centrality of the temple, 576, 583–86, 2580–81; holiness of God, 208–9, 2012–16, 2809

Chapter 42 completes the initial tour of the temple and concludes by placing Ezekiel and his guide back at the east gate, where they began, positioned for the return of the Lord's glorious presence (in 43:1–4).

This opening section describes **the chambers** or sacristies in the outer court   42:1–14 where the priests would go to eat the holy offerings and to robe themselves for their priestly duties. Because of textual difficulties and the use of unknown architectural terms, there are many different interpretations concerning where these chambers were located, how they were accessed, and how to understand the specific features within them. As Daniel Block observes, "Virtually every detail concerning the design and appearance of the chambers is open to debate, and any reconstruction is tentative."[17] But knowing all the architectural details is not critical; understanding the point behind the dimensions and the details described is more significant for interpreting the book of Ezekiel.

What Ezekiel sees are two buildings, one on the north of the temple building and one on the south, each one having three stories that are connected by an inner spiral staircase. Each building is a hundred cubits long and fifty cubits wide, thus following the symmetrical design of the perfect rectangle built on multiples of twenty-five.[18] The function of these chambers is clearly stated: **The north chambers and the south chambers opposite the yard are the holy chambers, where the priests who approach the LORD shall eat the most holy offerings**. In the burnt offering the animal was utterly consumed by the fire, but for most offerings a part or the whole of the sacrifice was consumed by the priests after it was offered to the Lord. These chambers functioned as the place where the holy offerings were brought and consumed—and so they needed to be holy and separate from common use: **there they shall put the most holy offerings—the cereal offering, the sin offering, and the guilt offering, for the place is holy**. This closely follows the teaching of Leviticus that directs how the priests were to eat a portion of these offerings—the grain, sin, and guilt offerings (Lev 2:1–10; 6:14–18; 7:7–10; Num 18:8–19). This provision is recalled in Ezek 44:29: "They shall eat the cereal offering, the sin offering, and the guilt offering."

And so, when the priests traveled from the **holy place**, they were able to access these holy chambers by an inner pathway, so that they would not have to enter the outer court, where the people gathered. In short, the priests remained within the inner court (and so remained in that holy space) while they were completing the offering of the sacrifices by eating them in holy garments, as the priests were instructed in the book of Exodus: "They shall eat those things with which atonement was made, to ordain and consecrate them . . . because they are holy" (Exod 29:33). After this was completed, they put on common clothing before going out and mixing with the people: **they shall put on other garments before they go near to that which is for the people**.

42:15–19   With the conclusion of the measurement of **the interior of the temple area**, the tour of the temple area is effectively completed (except for a tour of the priestly and lay kitchens in 46:19–24). Ezekiel and his heavenly guide now make their way back to their original starting point, to **the gate which faced east**. The tour began with the thickness and height of the outer wall of the temple (40:5); the tour concludes by taking the measurement of the full perimeter of that outer wall. Each section of the wall measures 500 cubits (about 830 feet), making a perfect square of the temple complex, 500 × 500 cubits. Daniel Block

17. Block, *Ezekiel: Chapters 25–48*, 564.
18. Milgrom and Block, *Ezekiel's Hope*, 99, see in the combined dimensions of the two buildings (which together form a perfect square) a sign of the holiness and perfection of the temple design: "Together they would form a square, 100 × 100 cubits—a guarantee of holiness."

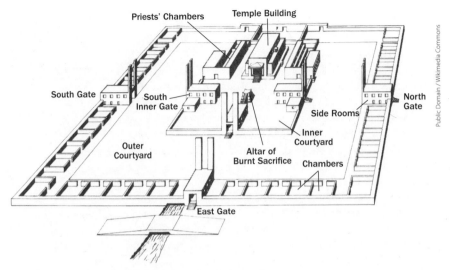

Figure 10. Three-dimensional representation of Ezekiel's temple

notes the significance of this design: "The shape and size of the entire complex reflect a lofty theological and spiritual ideal, according to which the residence of Yahweh must be perfectly proportioned."[19] In a similar way, the book of Revelation presents the angelic guide measuring the heavenly Jerusalem as a perfect cube (Rev 21:15–16), indicating by this the perfection of the eternal dwelling place where God will live among his people.

The purpose of this outer wall is **to make a separation between the holy and the common** or "to separate the sacred from the profane" (NABRE). Holiness and separateness are distinctive characteristics of Ezekiel's temple. Earlier in the book, Ezekiel accused the priests of failing to distinguish between what is holy and what is common: "Her priests have done violence to my law and have profaned my holy things; they have made no distinction between the holy and the common, neither have they taught the difference between the unclean and the clean" (22:26). The outer temple wall expresses and preserves this division.

42:20

Reflection and Application (42:15–20)

Talk of separating "the holy from what is common" lands awkwardly in our contemporary context. To our ears this sounds like everything bad that characterized primitive religion. We prize inclusion and equality, and so wince when the Bible speaks about walls that separate one group of people from another.

19. Block, *Ezekiel: Chapters 25–48*, 570.

Separation of the Holy from What Is Common or Unclean

BIBLICAL BACKGROUND

In chapter 42, Ezekiel the priest underlines the requirement of holiness in the new temple, both for the people and for the priests who minister at the altar. This is a return to the holiness that Israel was called to pursue from the beginning. As the Lord forged the family of Israel into a nation in the desert, the call to holiness was central to their identity: "You shall be to me a kingdom of priests and a holy nation" (Exod 19:6). The *entire* nation of Israel was called to be holy, even though one tribe (Levi) and one family (Aaron) were designated for special priestly service within this holy nation. The core meaning of "holiness" is to be set apart, separated from what is common and especially from what is unclean or impure. To be holy is to be set apart for God and his purposes—this was the call on Israel as a nation: "I am the LORD your God, who have separated you from the peoples. . . . You shall be holy to me; for I the LORD am holy, and have separated you from the peoples, that you should be mine" (Lev 20:24, 26). The priests were given a special commission to be holy (that is, separated) by refraining from certain practices[a] and by teaching the people about the requirement of holiness: "You are to distinguish between the holy and the common, and between the unclean and the clean, and you are to teach the people of Israel all the statutes that the LORD has spoken to them by Moses" (Lev 10:10–11 ESV). This call to holiness is a central feature of Ezekiel's new temple. God's people are set apart for the Lord so that the nations will recognize the greatness and holiness of the Lord: "And the nations will know that I am the LORD, says the Lord GOD, when through you I vindicate my holiness before their eyes" (Ezek 36:23).

a. To preserve their ritual purity, priests were forbidden (1) to have contact with dead bodies, (2) to trim their beards, and (3) to marry widows (see Lev 21:1–7, 14).

And in fact, the New Testament celebrates the equal access that all people—Jew and †Gentile, male and female, slave and free—now share in Christ (see Gal 3:28). Paul says that Christ "has broken down the dividing wall of hostility" (Eph 2:14) that divided Jew and Gentile, bringing about peace and equal status in the body of Christ.

But this does not in any way diminish the call to holiness for each and every member of the Christian people. Paul exhorts us all—Jew and Gentile alike—to "cleanse ourselves from every defilement of body and spirit, and make holiness perfect in the fear of God" (2 Cor 7:1). Echoing the book of Leviticus, Peter tells us: "As he who called you is holy, be holy yourselves in all your conduct" (1 Pet 1:15). Remarkably, Peter, echoing Exod 19:6, extends the status of "holy nation" to both Jew and Gentile in the body of Christ: "But you are a chosen race, a royal priesthood, a holy nation, God's own people" (1 Pet 2:9). Following Ezekiel's pattern closely, John, too, has a vision of the new Jerusalem in which the city walls mark a separation between what is holy and what is unclean: "Nothing unclean shall enter it" (Rev 21:27). Access to the living God through Christ is now equally available to all people. But the call to holiness has only deepened because now we have the "Holy" Spirit dwelling within us, producing in us— with our active cooperation—greater and greater likeness to Christ himself.

The New Law of the Temple

Ezekiel 43:1–46:24

Ezekiel's vision of the glorious return of the Lord's presence (43:1–9) functions as a bridge connecting what comes before with what follows. The temple was prepared and measured for just this event: the return of the holy and glorious presence of God among his people. This return brings to completion Ezekiel's guided tour of the temple precincts (chaps. 40–42) and opens the way for the laws and prescriptions of the new temple (chaps. 43–46).

We should recognize the solemnity, hopefulness, and joy of this great event. The book of Ezekiel has been leading up to this climactic occurrence: the Lord God returns to his people! Now they will have his blessing, protection, guidance, and holy presence.

The Return of the Lord's Glorious Presence to the Temple (43:1–9)

¹Afterward he brought me to the gate, the gate facing east. ²And behold, the glory of the God of Israel came from the east; and the sound of his coming was like the sound of many waters; and the earth shone with his glory. ³And the vision I saw was like the vision which I had seen when he came to destroy the city, and like the vision which I had seen by the river Chebar; and I fell upon my face. ⁴As the glory of the LORD entered the temple by the gate facing east, ⁵the Spirit lifted me up, and brought me into the inner court; and behold, the glory of the LORD filled the temple.

⁶While the man was standing beside me, I heard one speaking to me out of the temple; ⁷and he said to me, "Son of man, this is the place of my throne and the place of the soles of my feet, where I will dwell in the midst of the sons of Israel forever. And the house of Israel shall no more defile my holy name, neither they, nor their kings, by their harlotry, and by the dead bodies of their kings, ⁸by setting their threshold by my threshold and

their doorposts beside my doorposts, with only a wall between me and them. They have defiled my holy name by their abominations which they have committed, so I have consumed them in my anger. [9]Now let them put away their idolatry and the dead bodies of their kings far from me, and I will dwell in their midst forever."

OT: Exod 40:34–35; 1 Kings 8:27; Pss 98:6; 99:1; Isa 66:1; Jer 3:16–17
NT: John 1:14; Col 2:9; Rev 21:3, 22–23
Catechism: glory of God, 293–94, 1722, 2809; Jesus as the new temple, 593, 1179, 1197, 1543; †sanctification of God's name, 2814
Lectionary: 43:1–2, 4–7a: dedication of a church

Standing at the east gate where the tour of the temple began and ended, Ezekiel **43:1–3b**
in vision now beholds the **the glory of the God of Israel** coming **from the east**, the direction from which Ezekiel saw it depart (see Ezek 11:22–25). The Lord's arrival is accompanied by **the sound of many waters**, and **the earth shone with his glory**. Ezekiel immediately links this vision with the two previous visions of the Lord's chariot throne (in 1:4–28 and 10:1–22; 11:22–25). It is a vision of the same reality, but the direction is now reversed. The Lord, who abandoned his own temple, now returns to dwell there once again in glory. Just as in the days of Moses and Solomon, God's presence enters his dwelling place only after it has been prepared, although in this case, preparation has been accomplished only in a vision.[1]

Once again (see Ezek 1:28), Ezekiel falls down upon his face before the **43:3c–5**
overwhelming glory of the Lord. As he does so, the Lord's presence enters through the east **gate** of the temple. At this point, Ezekiel himself is lifted up by the Spirit (see 2:2) and brought to **the inner court**, where he testifies to what he sees: **the glory of the LORD filled the temple**. Ezekiel's vision recalls the cloud of God's glory filling the tabernacle in the wilderness (Exod 40:34–35) and filling the temple built by Solomon (1 Kings 8:10–11). It is from this place, with Ezekiel standing before the glorious presence of the Lord, that God will speak to him.

With the guide who measured the dimensions of the temple (40:3–4; 42:15– **43:6–7a**
20) standing beside him, Ezekiel hears the Lord's voice coming now from the midst of the inner temple: **Son of man, this is the place of my throne and the place of the soles of my feet, where I will dwell in the midst of the sons of Israel forever**. Despite Israel's grave sins, God has chosen to dwell among them again. This is where his *throne* is set: the Lord will dwell as king over his people. Strikingly, the Lord says that he will place the soles of his feet in this place. God, of course, does not have literal feet, but he speaks in metaphor of sitting on the throne with his feet upon the ground in order to communicate

---

1. For the glory of the Lord filling Moses's tabernacle in the desert, see Exod 40:34–35; for the glory of the Lord filling Solomon's temple, see 1 Kings 8:10–11; 2 Chron 5:13–14; 7:1–2.

The Temple Sanctuary as the Lord's Throne   **BIBLICAL** BACKGROUND

In the Old Testament, when the Lord came to dwell in the tabernacle and temple, this was pictured as the Lord seated on his throne in the midst of Israel, bestowing blessing and giving judgment. Israel recognized that the Lord was not contained spatially inside the temple, as Solomon acknowledges: "Behold, heaven and the highest heaven cannot contain you; how much less this house which I have built!" (1 Kings 8:27). The prophet Isaiah reminds Israel that the Lord is not contained in an earthly house but reigns from heaven: "Heaven is my throne / and the earth is my footstool; / what is the house which you would build for me, / and what is the place of my rest?" (Isa 66:1). Yet when the glorious presence of the Lord settled upon the tabernacle and temple, he came to dwell there among his people in a special way. The Psalms express the presence and kingship of the Lord in the temple with great fervor: "With trumpets and the sound of the horn / make a joyful noise before the King, the LORD!" (Ps 98:6). "The LORD reigns; let the peoples tremble! / He sits enthroned upon the †cherubim; let the earth quake!" (Ps 99:1). Furthermore, the temple sanctuary was conceived as the Lord's "footstool." The psalmist urges the faithful: "Extol the LORD our God; / worship at his footstool! / Holy is he!" (Ps 99:5). "Let us go to his dwelling place; / let us worship at his footstool!" (Ps 132:7; see also 1 Chron 28:2). When Ezekiel describes the temple as the place the Lord will set the soles of his feet, he is building on the Old Testament imagery of the temple as God's throne that serves also as his footstool.

the *reality* of his dwelling among his people. In a sense, the Lord's throne takes the place of the ark of the covenant, which is absent in Ezekiel's description of the future temple. This accords with a prophetic promise from Ezekiel's older contemporary, Jeremiah: "They shall no more say, 'The ark of the covenant of the LORD.' It shall not come to mind, or be remembered, or missed; it shall not be made again. At that time Jerusalem shall be called the throne of the LORD, and all nations shall gather to it, to the presence of the LORD in Jerusalem" (Jer 3:16–17). The Lord God reveals a great and consoling truth here: he has come to dwell among his people forever. This is very good news.

43:7b–9   This holy presence of the Lord calls forth and requires the holiness of the people: **And the house of Israel shall no more defile my holy name**. The Lord soberly reminds his people that in the recent past he judged them for their sins. Now they must abide in holiness: **let them put away their idolatry and the dead bodies of their kings far from me, and I will dwell in their midst forever**. According to the laws of ritual purity (Lev 21:11; Num 19:13), contact with corpses defiles a person. The "dead bodies of their kings" probably refers either to the tombs of the kings that were located close to the temple precincts or to rites for the dead kings that were practiced within the temple precincts.

In the Light of Christ (43:1–9)

What are we to make of the Lord's promise to Ezekiel that he will plant the soles of his feet in the new temple, and so make this his dwelling place? On one level, it is a marvelous example of ascribing human qualities to God in order to express concretely how *real* the Lord's presence will be among his people. At the same time this imagery anticipates the †incarnation of the Word of God in Jesus of Nazareth. When the Gospel of John describes the birth of Jesus, it uses temple language to describe God's coming among us: The Word who is God takes on our flesh—that is, he becomes a human being—and "dwells" among us (John 1:14). The Greek verb translated "dwell" (*skēnoō*) is derived from the word "tent" (*skēnē*).[2] Moses was commanded to build a tent for God to dwell in (Exod 25:8–9); according to John, the eternal Word of God has "pitched his tent" among us by taking on our nature. And just as in Moses's day the people beheld the glory of God dwelling in the tent of meeting, so we now behold the fullness of the glory of God residing in the Son (Col 2:9). When the three disciples witnessed the transfiguration, they were beholding the glorious presence of God (the †Shekinah) in Jesus Christ (see the sidebar "'Shekinah' in Jewish and Christian Tradition," p. 74).

In a way that could not have been anticipated, God has indeed planted the soles of his feet among us. Jesus himself *is* the glory of God manifest in human flesh (2 Cor 4:6). According to the book of Revelation, in the age to come, in the new creation, God will dwell intimately with his people: "Behold, the dwelling ["tent," *skēnē*] of God is with men. He will dwell [*skēnoō*] with them, and they shall be his people" (Rev 21:3). But he will not come to dwell *in* a temple. The Lord God and Jesus the Lamb of God *are* the new temple in whose presence we will live forever (Rev 21:22–23).

The Law of the Temple and the Altar of Sacrifice (43:10–27)

[10]"And you, son of man, describe to the house of Israel the temple and its appearance and plan, that they may be ashamed of their iniquities. [11]And if they are ashamed of all that they have done, portray the temple, its arrangement, its exits and its entrances, and its whole form; and make

---

2. The word "dwell" in John 1:14 (*skēnoō*) is also closely related to the verb "dwell" used in the Greek version of Ezek 43:7, 9 (*kataskēnoō*).

known to them all its ordinances and all its laws; and write it down in their sight, so that they may observe and perform all its laws and all its ordinances. [12]This is the law of the temple: the whole territory round about upon the top of the mountain shall be most holy. Behold, this is the law of the temple.

[13]"These are the dimensions of the altar by cubits (the cubit being a cubit and a handbreadth): its base shall be one cubit high, and one cubit broad, with a rim of one span around its edge. And this shall be the height of the altar: [14]from the base on the ground to the lower ledge, two cubits, with a breadth of one cubit; and from the smaller ledge to the larger ledge, four cubits, with a breadth of one cubit; [15]and the altar hearth, four cubits; and from the altar hearth projecting upward, four horns, one cubit high. [16]The altar hearth shall be square, twelve cubits long by twelve broad. [17]The ledge also shall be square, fourteen cubits long by fourteen broad, with a rim around it half a cubit broad, and its base one cubit round about. The steps of the altar shall face east."

[18]And he said to me, "Son of man, thus says the Lord God: These are the ordinances for the altar: On the day when it is erected for offering burnt offerings upon it and for throwing blood against it, [19]you shall give to the Levitical priests of the family of Zadok, who draw near to me to minister to me, says the Lord God, a bull for a sin offering. [20]And you shall take some of its blood, and put it on the four horns of the altar, and on the four corners of the ledge, and upon the rim round about; thus you shall cleanse the altar and make atonement for it. [21]You shall also take the bull of the sin offering, and it shall be burnt in the appointed place belonging to the temple, outside the sacred area. [22]And on the second day you shall offer a he-goat without blemish for a sin offering; and the altar shall be cleansed, as it was cleansed with the bull. [23]When you have finished cleansing it, you shall offer a bull without blemish and a ram from the flock without blemish. [24]You shall present them before the Lord, and the priests shall sprinkle salt upon them and offer them up as a burnt offering to the Lord. [25]For seven days you shall provide daily a goat for a sin offering; also a bull and a ram from the flock, without blemish, shall be provided. [26]Seven days shall they make atonement for the altar and purify it, and so consecrate it. [27]And when they have completed these days, then from the eighth day onward the priests shall offer upon the altar your burnt offerings and your peace offerings; and I will accept you, says the Lord God."

OT: Lev 4:25; 11:44–45; 1 Kings 1:50–51
Catechism: centrality of the temple, 576, 583–86, 2580–81; call to share in God's holiness, 773, 2012–15

43:10–12   This short section introduces **the law of the temple.** "Law" in Hebrew is †*torah*, which also means "teaching." In other words, this is the teaching—that is, the instruction—about the temple. Moreover, the temple itself—its measurements, entrances and exits, and ordinances—is like a "torah" for the people, a guide to their holiness. If sin brings moral chaos, then holiness does the opposite: it brings moral order. The architectural order here symbolizes the moral and spiritual order of the torah.

Ezekiel is told to describe the details and plan of the temple, so that the people **may be ashamed of their iniquities**. The Lord tells them that *if* they are ashamed of their past sins, then Ezekiel should portray the full plan for the new temple. The idea seems to be that by communicating a thorough knowledge of the temple and its functioning, the people will be led to obey the precepts of the Lord and so pursue holiness. Ezekiel, therefore, is told to make known to the people **all its ordinances and all its laws**, and further to **write it down in their sight**. The direction to "write down" the laws confirms the view that Ezekiel not only spoke these words but also wrote them down as a reminder for the people (see "Authorship" in the introduction, pp. 17–18).

The first and fundamental law of the temple is that **the whole territory** of the Temple Mount **shall be most holy** (literally, "holy of holies"). There is an expansion of God's holiness at work here. The inner room of the temple sanctuary is properly the "most holy place" (the "holy of holies"), but now this quality of being "most holy" is applied to the *entire* Temple Mount. Jacob Milgrom observes that "Ezekiel's spatial notion of holiness is fluid: strong holiness will spill over its bound and affect the contiguous area."[3] If the Lord is to dwell among his people, they must be holy as he is holy (Lev 11:44–45). All the ordinances and laws that follow are a *means* to this end—namely, that the people should live a holy and blameless life in the presence of the Lord.

In the descriptions that follow, Ezekiel and his guide are no longer in view. 43:13–17 We are simply given the measurements of the altar of sacrifice and the laws for its functioning. During the earlier tour of the inner court (40:47), the altar of sacrifice was identified, but no description was given; now full attention is given to its dimensions and functioning (see fig. 11, p. 304). Though similar to the dimensions of Solomon's altar, the measurements here are not precisely the same. The Jewish rabbis struggled to reconcile the measurements and prescriptions of Ezekiel's temple with the original provisions given to Moses and then to Solomon.[4]

The base around the altar, the trench in which it sits, is measured first. Here the blood and remains of the sacrifice would be collected. The altar has two further levels of support—a **smaller ledge** and a **larger ledge**—on which is set **the altar hearth**, the upper level of the altar, which is a perfect square, 12 × 12 cubits. In addition, the altar has **four horns**, one on each corner. The horns were used for purifying the altar: "Then the priest shall take some of the blood

---

3. Milgrom and Block, *Ezekiel's Hope*, 117.

4. For the altar of sacrifice built by Solomon, see 2 Chron 4:1–4. For the smaller altar built by Moses for the tabernacle, see Exod 20:24–26; 27:1–8.

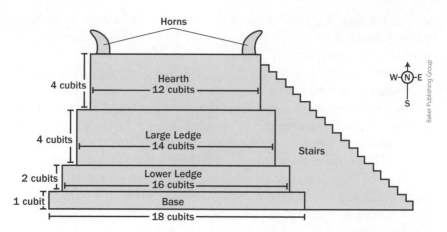

Figure 11. The altar of sacrifice

of the sin offering with his finger and put it on the horns of the altar of burnt offering" (Lev 4:25). The horns of the altar also served as sites of refuge for those who had committed manslaughter or murder: they could seize the horns of the altar when seeking protection from their pursuers (see 1 Kings 1:50–51). Finally, from the **east** side of the altar rises a set of stairs by which the priests ascend and offer sacrifice.[5]

43:18–27   Next we are given the prescribed **ordinances** for the use of the altar of sacrifice. The first is for the purification of the altar itself, to make it worthy and acceptable to serve in an ongoing way: **thus you shall cleanse the altar and make atonement for it**. The task of purifying the altar falls to **the Levitical priests of the family of Zadok**.[6] Specific instructions follow for the offering of bulls, goats, and rams, mixed with salt, as a sin offering and burnt offering to the Lord (vv. 19–24). **Seven days shall they make atonement for the altar and purify it, and so consecrate it**. Ezekiel's direction to "make atonement for" and to "consecrate" the altar reflects the direction Moses received in Exod 29:37: "Seven days you shall make atonement for the altar, and consecrate it, and the altar shall be most holy."[7] The language of atonement in this context sounds strange in our ears. How can an altar require atonement? The word "atone," which normally describes cleansing from sin, is used here in an analogous sense to describe ritual cleansing and purification.

5. This provision for stairs appears to contradict the prescription given by Moses: "And you shall not go up by steps to my altar, that your nakedness be not exposed on it" (Exod 20:26).

6. The phrase "Levitical priests" first appears in Deuteronomy (17:9, 18; 18:1) to designate those who serve at the altar. Jeremiah identifies the "Levitical priests" as those who will continue in the service of the Lord's temple (Jer 33:18–22), but it is Ezekiel who limits the priesthood to the family of Zadok. See the sidebar "The Zadokite Priesthood," p. 288.

7. The seven-day purification of the altar here also parallels the seven-day purification of the altar mandated for Solomon's temple (2 Chron 7:9). See also Lev 8:10–15 for the consecration of the altar.

Figure 12. Four-horned altar

Ezekiel makes use of several related words—"cleanse," "purify," "atone for," and "consecrate"—to describe how the altar of sacrifice is to be prepared for use. The first three all describe how the altar is to be made *fit* for use: it must be made ritually pure by the blood that is put on the four horns of the altar. The last term, "consecrate," refers to the setting-aside of the altar for special use: to be the *holy place* where sacrifices will be offered to the Lord God.[8] When the seven-day purification is completed, **then from the eighth day onward the priests shall offer upon the altar your burnt offerings and your peace offerings**.

Why is so much attention given to the purification of the altar of sacrifice in the temple? Because this enables the worship of the Lord to commence. It is by means of the worship offered through the various sacrifices offered on the altar that the people maintain and renew their relationship with the Lord and receive his blessings.

Temple Ordinances and the Role of the Levites (44:1–14)

[1]**Then he brought me back to the outer gate of the sanctuary, which faces east; and it was shut. ²And he said to me, "This gate shall remain shut; it shall not be opened, and no one shall enter by it; for the LORD, the God of Israel, has entered by it; therefore it shall remain shut. ³Only the prince**

8. For a description of how sacrifices of the Old Covenant could convey †grace and holiness, see the "In the Light of Christ" section for 18:30–32, pp. 141–42.

may sit in it to eat bread before the LORD; he shall enter by way of the vestibule of the gate, and shall go out by the same way."

⁴Then he brought me by way of the north gate to the front of the temple; and I looked, and behold, the glory of the LORD filled the temple of the LORD; and I fell upon my face. ⁵And the LORD said to me, "Son of man, mark well, see with your eyes, and hear with your ears all that I shall tell you concerning all the ordinances of the temple of the LORD and all its laws; and mark well those who may be admitted to the temple and all those who are to be excluded from the sanctuary. ⁶And say to the rebellious house, to the house of Israel, Thus says the Lord GOD: O house of Israel, let there be an end to all your abominations, ⁷in admitting foreigners, uncircumcised in heart and flesh, to be in my sanctuary, profaning it, when you offer to me my food, the fat and the blood. You have broken my covenant, in addition to all your abominations. ⁸And you have not kept charge of my holy things; but you have set foreigners to keep my charge in my sanctuary.

⁹"Therefore thus says the Lord GOD: No foreigner, uncircumcised in heart and flesh, of all the foreigners who are among the people of Israel, shall enter my sanctuary. ¹⁰But the Levites who went far from me, going astray from me after their idols when Israel went astray, shall bear their punishment. ¹¹They shall be ministers in my sanctuary, having oversight at the gates of the temple, and serving in the temple; they shall slay the burnt offering and the sacrifice for the people, and they shall attend on the people, to serve them. ¹²Because they ministered to them before their idols and became a stumbling block of iniquity to the house of Israel, therefore I have sworn concerning them, says the Lord GOD, that they shall bear their punishment. ¹³They shall not come near to me, to serve me as priest, nor come near any of my sacred things and the things that are most sacred; but they shall bear their shame, because of the abominations which they have committed. ¹⁴Yet I will appoint them to keep charge of the temple, to do all its service and all that is to be done in it."

OT: Lev 21:6–8; 22:25; Num 16:1–35; Deut 18:1–7; Neh 13:1–9
NT: John 1:18
Catechism: glory of God, 293–94, 1722, 2809; holiness of God, 208–9, 2012–16, 2809; Levites and Old Testament priests prefiguring ordained ministry in the Church, 1541

In chapter 44, Ezekiel continues his description of "the law of the temple" with attention given to three areas: (1) the permanent closure of the east gate (vv. 1–3), (2) restrictions for access to the temple (vv. 4–14), and (3) rules for the priests (vv. 15–31).

44:1–3   The heavenly guide escorts Ezekiel back to the east gate of the temple complex. The Lord tells him: **This gate shall remain shut; it shall not be opened, and no one shall enter by it**. Why is this gate to be permanently shut? Because **the LORD, the God of Israel, has entered by it**. Because God's holy presence

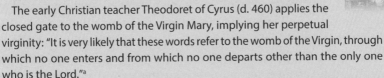

The Closed Gate Applied to Christ and Mary — LIVING TRADITION

Early Christian teachers applied the "closed gate" in chapter 44 to both Christ and the Virgin Mary. Origen of Alexandria (d. 254) applies the "closed gate" to the things that only Christ knows because he is the only begotten Son of the Father (John 1:18): "But there is a gate, one only, and one that is closed, through which 'no one passes.' For there are certain things unknown to the whole creation and known only to one; for whatever the Son knows he has not disclosed to the world."

The early Christian teacher Theodoret of Cyrus (d. 460) applies the closed gate to the womb of the Virgin Mary, implying her perpetual virginity: "It is very likely that these words refer to the womb of the Virgin, through which no one enters and from which no one departs other than the only one who is the Lord."[a]

a. Origen, *Homily* 14.2, in *Homilies 1–14 on Ezekiel*, trans. Thomas P. Scheck, ACW 62 (New York: Newman, 2010), 168; Theodoret of Cyrus, *Commentary on Ezekiel* (ACCS 13:141).

---

has passed through, this gate is especially holy, no longer available for common entrance and exit. **Only the prince** is allowed access through a side entrance **to eat bread before the Lord**. The prince is accorded a special privilege of eating the sacrificial meal ("bread") in the vestibule of the eastern gate.[9] But he may not enter through the east gate; this remains closed because it was the Lord's own pathway.

In the final section of Ezekiel (chaps. 40–48), the rulers in Israel are given the title "prince," not "king." Scholars debate whether Ezekiel intentionally uses the title "prince" in order to show a reduced role for the "kings" in a restored Israel, largely due to their grievous failures leading up to the Babylonian exile. But when we examine Ezekiel's use of "king" and "prince" throughout the book, he seems to use the two terms largely interchangeably. In the first part of the book, Israel's rulers are called both "king" and "prince" (1:2; 12:10; 17:16; 21:25). The rulers of Tyre (28:2, 12) and Egypt (30:13, 21) are also called both king and prince. And most notably, the messianic figure "David" is called "king" (34:24; 37:22, 24) and then "prince" in the very same context (37:25), without any sense that the title "prince" conveys a lower status or role.

With the east gate shut, Ezekiel circles around to the north gate and re-enters **44:4–5** the temple area. There he beholds **the glory of the Lord** filling **the temple of the Lord**. Once again, Ezekiel falls upon his face at the sight of this great glory (see 1:28; 43:3). This glorious presence of God is the basis for the prescriptions

---

9. In Leviticus, the food offerings and even the animal sacrifices offered by the priests are called "the bread of your God" (see Lev 21:6, 8; 22:25).

that follow: because the Lord, the holy God, has chosen to dwell here, the people must closely adhere to **the ordinances of the temple of the Lord and all its laws**.

44:6–9   The tone now shifts to one of rebuke. The Lord solemnly tells Ezekiel that, because of past failures by both the people and the Levites, access to the temple is to be strictly limited. The Lord condemns Israel for past failures when they allowed foreigners not just to have admittance to the outer court but even to *minister* in the inner temple (vv. 7–8).[10] Who were these foreigners who served in the sanctuary? They may have been armed temple guards hired to keep peace in the temple area.[11] Whatever the exact cause, the result is a sharp restriction of access: **no foreigner, uncircumcised in heart and flesh . . . shall enter my sanctuary**. This restriction on foreigners was enforced during the restoration under Ezra and Nehemiah (see Neh 13:1–9) and remained in place during the time of Jesus.[12] There was an outer court that †Gentiles could enter, but only Israelites were allowed to enter the inner court of the temple.

44:10–14   The Lord then rebukes the Levites for their past unfaithfulness: **But the Levites who went far from me, going astray from me after their idols when Israel went astray, shall bear their punishment**. Because of this past failure, Ezekiel declares that the Levites are limited to serving as attendants to the priests in the outer temple court and are forbidden to enter the inner court or to serve as priests: **they shall not come near to me, to serve me as priest, nor come near any of my sacred things and the things that are most sacred**. This striking statement raises two questions. First, when did the Levites go astray after idols? There is no clear record of this in the †canonical books of the Old Testament. The leading view is that Ezekiel is referring to Korah's rebellion (Num 16:1–35), when some Levites rebelled against Moses, claiming the right of priesthood. But Ezekiel could also be referring to a more recent failure of the Levites, not described in the historical or prophetic books, that contributed to idolatry under the later kings.

Second, Ezekiel's prohibition against the Levites serving as priests seems to assume that there was some expectation that they would (or could) do this. But in the law of Moses, the Levites were clearly distinguished from the priests, who were from the house of Aaron and served at the altar. Why does Ezekiel seem to be demoting them from a role that apparently they never had? The reason for this remains unclear. Jacob Milgrom suggests that Ezekiel is presupposing the approach to "Levitical priests" as found in Deuteronomy, where it seems that

---

10. In Lev 22:25, foreigners are forbidden to offer sacrifice at the temple.

11. Milgrom and Block (*Ezekiel's Hope*, 140) believe that Ezekiel is referring to foreign guards who were hired in the place of Levites to provide protection within the temple precincts (see 2 Kings 11:4–8; Num 18:3–4).

12. Paul the apostle was falsely accused of bringing uncircumcised foreigners into the temple area, the penalty for which was death (see Acts 21:27–31).

all Levites served at the altar (see Deut 18:1–7).[13] Whatever the reason might be for Ezekiel's direction to the Levites, the result is that in the restored temple of Ezekiel's vision, the Levites are given a restricted but important role: **to keep charge of the temple, to do all its service and all that is to be done in it.**

The Role of the Priests (44:15–31)

[15]"But the Levitical priests, the sons of Zadok, who kept the charge of my sanctuary when the people of Israel went astray from me, shall come near to me to minister to me; and they shall attend on me to offer me the fat and the blood, says the Lord GOD; [16]they shall enter my sanctuary, and they shall approach my table, to minister to me, and they shall keep my charge. [17]When they enter the gates of the inner court, they shall wear linen garments; they shall have nothing of wool on them, while they minister at the gates of the inner court, and within. [18]They shall have linen turbans upon their heads, and linen breeches upon their loins; they shall not clothe themselves with anything that causes sweat. [19]And when they go out into the outer court to the people, they shall put off the garments in which they have been ministering, and lay them in the holy chambers; and they shall put on other garments, lest they communicate holiness to the people with their garments. [20]They shall not shave their heads or let their locks grow long; they shall only trim the hair of their heads. [21]No priest shall drink wine, when he enters the inner court. [22]They shall not marry a widow, or a divorced woman, but only a virgin of the stock of the house of Israel, or a widow who is the widow of a priest. [23]They shall teach my people the difference between the holy and the common, and show them how to distinguish between the unclean and the clean. [24]In a controversy they shall act as judges, and they shall judge it according to my judgments. They shall keep my laws and my statutes in all my appointed feasts, and they shall keep my sabbaths holy. [25]They shall not defile themselves by going near to a dead person; however, for father or mother, for son or daughter, for brother or unmarried sister they may defile themselves. [26]After he is defiled, he shall count for himself seven days, and then he shall be clean. [27]And on the day that he goes into the holy place, into the inner court, to minister in the holy place, he shall offer his sin offering, says the Lord GOD.

[28]"They shall have no inheritance; I am their inheritance: and you shall give them no possession in Israel; I am their possession. [29]They shall eat the cereal offering, the sin offering, and the guilt offering; and every devoted thing in Israel shall be theirs. [30]And the first of all the first fruits of

---

13. Milgrom and Block, *Ezekiel's Hope*, 161. Other scholars interpret Ezek 44:10–14 as indicating that right up to the Babylonian exile, *all* Levites served as priests, and that it is only with Ezekiel that the house of Zadok came to be the sole priestly family.

all kinds, and every offering of all kinds from all your offerings, shall belong to the priests; you shall also give to the priests the first of your coarse meal, that a blessing may rest on your house. [31]**The priests shall not eat of anything, whether bird or beast, that has died of itself or is torn."**

OT: Exod 3:5; 19:21; Lev 10:1–3; 21:1–8; 2 Sam 6:6–7; Ps 16:5–6
NT: 1 Cor 11:29–30; 2 Cor 3:18; Eph 2:18; Heb 12:28–29
Catechism: holiness of God, 208–9, 2012–16, 2809; Levites and Old Testament priests prefiguring ordained ministry in the Church, 1541

44:15–16   Ezekiel now turns his attention to the priests—**the Levitical priests, the sons of Zadok**—who are responsible to offer sacrifice in the temple.[14] At the point when the people and the Levites **went astray** from the Lord, the sons of Zadok remained faithful and so retained the privileged role of acting as priests at the altar and as judges for the people. The Lord says of them: **They shall enter my sanctuary, and they shall approach my table, to minister to me**.

44:17–22   The provisions that follow express the holiness required of the priests. They are to be set apart in their clothing, their grooming, their food and drink, and their manner of entering marriage (see Lev 21:1–8 for a similar set of regulations). When serving the Lord at the altar, the priests are to be robed only in linen garments. When they finish their priestly service, they must change into common clothing before going out among the people, so that they do not **communicate holiness to the people with their garments**.[15] What is wrong with communicating holiness? Ezekiel's concern is to keep the people from the harm that they would suffer by coming into contact with a manifestation of God's holy presence that they were not chosen and prepared to encounter. In a similar way, the Lord warned Moses on Mount Sinai, "Go down and warn the people, lest they break through to the LORD to gaze and many of them perish" (Exod 19:21). God's holiness in the biblical account is not "safe"; to come into contact with God's holiness without being sufficiently purified can be deadly (see Reflection and Application below).

44:23–27   An important element of the vocation of the priest is to teach the people **the difference between the holy and the common** and to help them distinguish between what is clean and unclean. In this role they are to **act as judges** for the people, ruling according to the law of the Lord. Further, they are to ensure that Israel follows all the **appointed feasts** and keeps the **sabbaths holy**. If the priests incur ritual defilement, they must quarantine themselves for seven days and then present a sin offering to the Lord for their own cleansing. In Ezekiel's vision as in the law of Moses, the Levitical priests are the caretakers—the

---

14. For background to the house of Zadok, see the sidebar "The Zadokite Priesthood," p. 288.

15. For priests wearing linen garments when serving at the altar in service, see Exod 28:42–43 and Lev 16:4. Aaron was commanded to lay his linen garments aside as he exited the inner sanctuary (Lev 16:23).

guardians—of the way of life of the people. They are to teach and model how to live in holiness.

Just as was true since the days of Moses, the Levitical priests **shall have no**   44:28–31
inheritance in the land like the other tribes. Why not? Because of the astonishing truth that the Lord proclaims: **I am their inheritance. . . . I am their posses-sion.**[16] Because the priests have no land or herds, they are given portions of the various offerings of the people (cereal, sin, and guilt offerings). But in a special way they belong to the Lord God; he is their "land" and their "inheritance." It is from the Lord himself that they receive what they need. This unique and intimate relationship is effectively expressed in Ps 16:5–6: "The LORD is my chosen portion and my cup; / you hold my lot. / The lines have fallen for me in pleasant places; / yes, I have a goodly heritage."

Reflection and Application (44:1–31)

According to the testimony of the Scripture, it was considered a great privilege to come into God's presence, but it could also be dangerous. Why is this? Because God is holy and his presence is powerful, awe-inspiring, and even dangerous to mere mortals. Moses was told to remove his shoes before the burning bush because the holy presence of God was there (Exod 3:5). When Aaron's sons offered unauthorized incense to the Lord, fire came forth and consumed them (Lev 10:1–3). When Uzzah unfittingly put out his hand to steady the ark of the Lord, he was struck down (2 Sam 6:6–7). Similarly, the people of Israel begged Moses to go up the mountain in their place because they were afraid to come too near to the Lord (Exod 20:18–21). In the New Testament, the apostle Paul warns the Corinthians to approach the reception of the Eucharist with rever-ence and a proper disposition, or else they will be liable to ill effects: "For any one who eats and drinks without discerning the body eats and drinks judgment upon himself. That is why many of you are weak and ill, and some have died" (1 Cor 11:29–30).

Paul also recalls for the same Corinthian believers how Moses put a veil over his face to shield the people from seeing the fading glory of the Lord reflected in his face (see Exod 34:29–35). But now in Christ, Paul says, the veil is removed (2 Cor 3:12–16). Because of Christ's cleansing action in our lives, we have been called and consecrated (John 17:19; 1 Cor 1:2; 6:11), to stand in the holy presence of God. He writes, "And we all, with unveiled face, beholding the glory of the Lord, are being changed into his likeness from one degree of glory to another" (2 Cor 3:18). Through the Holy Spirit, we are joined to Christ and now have full, confident access to God our Father (Eph 2:18). This is the

16. In the original distribution of land, neither the tribe of Levi nor the house of Aaron was given an inheritance in the land. The Lord God and his service was to be their inheritance (see Num 18:20–24; Deut 10:8–9; 18:1).

great blessing of the New Covenant. This does not mean abandoning reverence when we enter God's presence. As the Letter to the Hebrews exhorts us: "Let us offer to God acceptable worship, with reverence and awe; for our God is a consuming fire" (Heb 12:28–29). Nonetheless, we are encouraged to draw near to God *with confidence* (Heb 10:19), because Christ has chosen and qualified us to stand in the presence of our heavenly Father and worship him confidently as sons and daughters.

Land for the Priests, the People, and the Prince (45:1–9)

¹"When you allot the land as a possession, you shall set apart for the LORD a portion of the land as a holy district, twenty-five thousand cubits long and twenty thousand cubits broad; it shall be holy throughout its whole extent. ²Of this a square plot of five hundred by five hundred cubits shall be for the sanctuary, with fifty cubits for an open space around it. ³And in the holy district you shall measure off a section twenty-five thousand cubits long and ten thousand broad, in which shall be the sanctuary, the most holy place. ⁴It shall be the holy portion of the land; it shall be for the priests, who minister in the sanctuary and approach the LORD to minister to him; and it shall be a place for their houses and a holy place for the sanctuary. ⁵Another section, twenty-five thousand cubits long and ten thousand cubits broad, shall be for the Levites who minister at the temple, as their possession for cities to live in.

⁶"Alongside the portion set apart as the holy district you shall assign for the possession of the city an area five thousand cubits broad, and twenty-five thousand cubits long; it shall belong to the whole house of Israel.

⁷"And to the prince shall belong the land on both sides of the holy district and the property of the city, alongside the holy district and the property of the city, on the west and on the east, corresponding in length to one of the tribal portions, and extending from the western to the eastern boundary of the land. ⁸It is to be his property in Israel. And my princes shall no more oppress my people; but they shall let the house of Israel have the land according to their tribes.

⁹"Thus says the Lord GOD: Enough, O princes of Israel! Put away violence and oppression, and execute justice and righteousness; cease your evictions of my people, says the Lord GOD."

OT: Num 26:53–56; 35:1–8; Josh 18:6–10; 21:1–3
Catechism: the gift of the land, 1222, 2795

Now for the first time in Ezekiel the allotment of land comes into focus. The full apportioning of the land will come in chapters 47–48; here we encounter an initial provision of land allotted to the sanctuary, the Levitical priests, the prince, and the people dwelling in the Holy City.[17]

The very first portion of land is set aside *for the Lord*: **When you allot the**   45:1–6
land as a possession, you shall set apart for the Lord a portion of the land as a holy district. This is hugely significant: the Holy Land is not first of all for the priests or Levites but for the Lord and the worship of the Lord. The apportioning of land begins from the sanctuary and goes out from a holy center to the periphery. Everything is defined in terms of its relation to the Lord and his presence among the people.

The dimensions of this holy tract of land are substantial: the whole area is 25,000 cubits long (8 miles) and 20,000 cubits broad (6.5 miles), many times larger than the entire city of Jerusalem at the time of the Babylonian exile.[18] **It shall be holy**—that is, set apart—**throughout its whole extent**. In the center is a square plot (500 × 500 cubits) for the sanctuary itself, with a 50-cubit perimeter surrounding it. The land to the south—half of the holy tract—is marked out for the priests: **It shall be a place for their houses and a holy place for the sanctuary**. A strip of equal size to the north is set aside for the Levites.[19] A final section of land (25,000 × 5,000 cubits), further to the south, is marked out for the Holy City; **it shall belong to the whole house of Israel**. The entire sacred area, with the city included, is a perfect square (25,000 × 25,000 cubits), matching the symmetry of the temple area itself. The temple right at the center functions as a "holy of holies" within the new, wider sacred tract of land in which Israel will dwell near to the presence of the Lord. Paul Joyce calls this layout of land "an exercise in theological geography, a map whose heart and focus is the temple and the worship of the God of Israel."[20]

Only at this point does Ezekiel allot land to the prince of Israel: **to the prince**   45:7–9
shall belong the land on both sides of the holy district. The prince is given a portion of land to the east and to the west of the sacred district (see fig. 13, p. 314). **It is to be his property in Israel**. But the chief purpose of this allocation in fact is to *limit* the prince's land so that he will no longer oppress the people and rob them of their rightful portion of land: **And my princes shall no more oppress my people**. In the spirit of the true shepherd of the people (chap. 34), the Lord sternly exhorts the princes of Israel to **put away violence and oppression, and execute justice and righteousness; cease your evictions of my people**.

---

17. For the apportioning of the promised land under Moses and Joshua, see Num 26:53–56; 33:50–54; Josh 18:6–10. For the boundaries of the land, see Num 34–35.

18. The Hebrew †Masoretic Text lists the breadth as 10,000 cubits, but most modern translations follow the Greek †Septuagint version, which has 20,000 cubits of breadth.

19. This portion of land serves as a replacement for the cities that the Levites were given in the original settlement of the land (see Num 35:1–8; Josh 21:1–3).

20. Joyce, *Ezekiel*, 234.

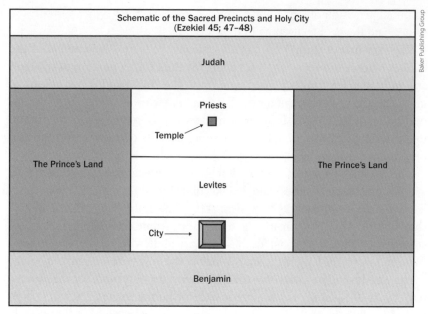

Figure 13. The holy precincts

Weights, Measures, and Rules for Festivals (45:10–25)

[10]"You shall have just balances, a just ephah, and a just bath. [11]The ephah and the bath shall be of the same measure, the bath containing one tenth of a homer, and the ephah one tenth of a homer; the homer shall be the standard measure. [12]The shekel shall be twenty gerahs; five shekels shall be five shekels, and ten shekels shall be ten shekels, and your mina shall be fifty shekels.

[13]"This is the offering which you shall make: one sixth of an ephah from each homer of wheat, and one sixth of an ephah from each homer of barley, [14]and as the fixed portion of oil, one tenth of a bath from each cor (the cor, like the homer, contains ten baths); [15]and one sheep from every flock of two hundred, from the families of Israel. This is the offering for cereal offerings, burnt offerings, and peace offerings, to make atonement for them, says the Lord GOD. [16]All the people of the land shall give this offering to the prince in Israel. [17]It shall be the prince's duty to furnish the burnt offerings, cereal offerings, and drink offerings, at the feasts, the new moons, and the sabbaths, all the appointed feasts of the house of Israel: he shall provide the sin offerings, cereal offerings, burnt offerings, and peace offerings, to make atonement for the house of Israel.

[18]"Thus says the Lord GOD: In the first month, on the first day of the month, you shall take a young bull without blemish, and cleanse the sanctuary. [19]The priest shall take some of the blood of the sin offering and put

it on the doorposts of the temple, the four corners of the ledge of the altar, and the posts of the gate of the inner court. [20]You shall do the same on the seventh day of the month for anyone who has sinned through error or ignorance; so you shall make atonement for the temple.

[21]"In the first month, on the fourteenth day of the month, you shall celebrate the feast of the passover, and for seven days unleavened bread shall be eaten. [22]On that day the prince shall provide for himself and all the people of the land a young bull for a sin offering. [23]And on the seven days of the festival he shall provide as a burnt offering to the LORD seven young bulls and seven rams without blemish, on each of the seven days; and a he-goat daily for a sin offering. [24]And he shall provide as a cereal offering an ephah for each bull, an ephah for each ram, and a hin of oil to each ephah. [25]In the seventh month, on the fifteenth day of the month and for the seven days of the feast, he shall make the same provision for sin offerings, burnt offerings, and cereal offerings, and for the oil."

OT: Exod 12:1–28; Lev 19:36; Num 28:16–25; Deut 25:15
NT: Matt 5:17, 21–22; 17:24–27; Luke 19:13–25
Catechism: Jesus as the fulfillment of Old Testament sacrifices and offerings, 522, 606–17, 1330

The theme of justice (45:8–9) leads naturally into laws for weights and measures.[21]   **45:10–17** Ezekiel tells the people: **you shall have just balances** regarding quantities: the ephah and bath for dry goods, the homer and cor for liquid goods, the shekel and mina for weights.[22] This closely echoes the teaching of Moses in the †Pentateuch: "A full and just weight you shall have, a full and just measure you shall have; that your days may be prolonged in the land which the LORD your God gives you" (Deut 25:15). Additionally, the people are told to give the proper portion of their goods to the Lord as an offering: wheat, barley, oil, and sheep. All these make up the sacrificial elements for the **cereal offerings, burnt offerings, and peace offerings** that serve **to make atonement** for the people. There is a reciprocal relationship between the people and the prince: the people are to supply the prince with portions of these same goods, while the prince is to provide all that is needed for the various sacrifices **at the feasts, the new moons, and the sabbaths, all the appointed feasts of the house of Israel**. The fact that offerings in the new temple will be needed **to make atonement for the house of Israel** shows that in the era of the new temple "sin will continue to be a problem for the nation," and this sin will need to be remedied through sacrifice.[23]

21. For prohibitions against false weights and measures in the Old Testament, see Lev 19:36; Deut 25:15; Prov 16:11; Hosea 12:7; Amos 8:5–6; Mic 6:10–11.
22. The ephah (for dry goods) and the bath (for liquid goods) were measures of volume; ten ephahs were equal to one homer, ten baths to one cor. The shekel was a measure of weight (not a coin) in ancient Israel; fifty shekels were equal to one mina. For shekels and minas in the New Testament, see Matt 17:24–27; Luke 19:13–25.
23. Block, *Ezekiel: Chapters 25–48*, 659. See also Milgrom and Block, *Ezekiel's Hope*, 198, for agreement with and expansion of Block's summary.

The question arises: If there is need for atonement for sin in Ezekiel's vision of the new temple, how is this consistent with an †eschatological temple and the messianic age? It is clear that Ezekiel envisions the new temple as including animal sacrifices and the keeping of the feasts. While there are symbolic elements in Ezekiel's description of the renewed temple (for example, the symmetrical measurements), it is nonetheless a real "working" temple that Ezekiel describes. Traditional †rabbinic Jewish commentary typically viewed Ezekiel's temple as pertaining to the coming messianic age, but even in the messianic age, the temple with the full set of sacrifices would still be in operation.[24]

45:18–25   In this final section of the chapter, Ezekiel outlines the designated offerings for four distinct occasions. The first sacrifice described—a sin offering of an unblemished bull—is made on the first day of the first month for the purification of the sanctuary, the altar, and the temple itself, in order to **cleanse the sanctuary**. The same sacrifice is then to be offered on the seventh day of the first month for any who have sinned in ignorance or error.[25] The third occasion is the fourteenth day of the first month, when the people gather to **celebrate the feast of the passover, and for seven days unleavened bread shall be eaten**. Ezekiel underlines the responsibility of the prince: he is to provide the animals—bulls, rams, and goats—for the seven days of public sacrifice. Here Ezekiel has in view the public convocation of the people for †Passover (Num 28:16–25)—which took place on the first full day of the feast—not the household celebration with the Passover lamb (Exod 12:1–28), which occurred on the evening before. The fourth and final occasion is the fourteenth day of the seventh month, which is the Feast of †Tabernacles (though not named). The prince again is obliged to provide all that is needed for the sin offerings, burnt offerings, and cereal offerings of the feast.

In the Light of Christ (45:10–25)

The Jewish rabbis struggled to align Ezekiel's directions and provisions for the new temple with those found in the law of Moses (Exod 25–30; Lev 1–7) and in the construction of Solomon's temple (1 Kings 6–7). Because of minor discrepancies between the two versions, some rabbis concluded that Ezekiel's temple and its provisions would only come to pass during the times of the †Messiah, when the practices of the law (the †halachah) would also be changed.[26] In this interpreta-

---

24. See Eisemann, *Ezekiel*, 709–11, for the views of the rabbis on Ezekiel's temple in the messianic age.
25. The Greek †Septuagint modifies this date to the first day of the seventh month, which more closely aligns this sacrifice with the traditional Day of Atonement (see Lev 16).
26. For a summary of the discrepancies between Ezekiel's renewed temple and the temple as given through Moses, and an account of the various rabbinic strategies for reconciling them, see Eisemann, *Ezekiel*, 715–20; Block, *Ezekiel: Chapters 25–48*, 673–76.

tion, there is an expectation that the Messiah—when he comes—will have the authority to bring about a new way of living God's law.

This is in fact what we see when Jesus applies and interprets the law of Moses in the Sermon on the Mount. He firmly upholds the law and claims only to bring about its fulfillment: "Do not think that I have come to abolish the law and the prophets; I have come not to abolish them but to fulfil them" (Matt 5:17). Then he takes several provisions of the law and gives a deeper and broader understanding of their meaning and application: "You have heard that it was said, . . . but I say to you . . ." (Matt 5:21–22). Jesus, however, not only teaches what the new law is but also fulfills all the sacrifices and makes atonement for our sin. In his saving words and actions, Jesus, the Messiah of Israel, brings about the perfect fulfillment of the law of Moses and of the sacrifices performed in the temple.

Regulations for the Prince and Allocations for the Priests (46:1–24)

[1]"Thus says the Lord GOD: The gate of the inner court that faces east shall be shut on the six working days; but on the sabbath day it shall be opened and on the day of the new moon it shall be opened. [2]The prince shall enter by the vestibule of the gate from without, and shall take his stand by the post of the gate. The priests shall offer his burnt offering and his peace offerings, and he shall worship at the threshold of the gate. Then he shall go out, but the gate shall not be shut until evening. [3]The people of the land shall worship at the entrance of that gate before the LORD on the sabbaths and on the new moons. [4]The burnt offering that the prince offers to the LORD on the sabbath day shall be six lambs without blemish and a ram without blemish; [5]and the cereal offering with the ram shall be an ephah, and the cereal offering with the lambs shall be as much as he is able, together with a hin of oil to each ephah. [6]On the day of the new moon he shall offer a young bull without blemish, and six lambs and a ram, which shall be without blemish; [7]as a cereal offering he shall provide an ephah with the bull and an ephah with the ram, and with the lambs as much as he is able, together with a hin of oil to each ephah. [8]When the prince enters, he shall go in by the vestibule of the gate, and he shall go out by the same way.

[9]"When the people of the land come before the LORD at the appointed feasts, he who enters by the north gate to worship shall go out by the south gate; and he who enters by the south gate shall go out by the north gate: no one shall return by way of the gate by which he entered, but each shall go out straight ahead. [10]When they go in, the prince shall go in with them; and when they go out, he shall go out.

¹¹"At the feasts and the appointed seasons the cereal offering with a young bull shall be an ephah, and with a ram an ephah, and with the lambs as much as one is able to give, together with a hin of oil to an ephah. ¹²When the prince provides a freewill offering, either a burnt offering or peace offerings as a freewill offering to the LORD, the gate facing east shall be opened for him; and he shall offer his burnt offering or his peace offerings as he does on the sabbath day. Then he shall go out, and after he has gone out the gate shall be shut.

¹³"He shall provide a lamb a year old without blemish for a burnt offering to the LORD daily; morning by morning he shall provide it. ¹⁴And he shall provide a cereal offering with it morning by morning, one sixth of an ephah, and one third of a hin of oil to moisten the flour, as a cereal offering to the LORD; this is the ordinance for the continual burnt offering. ¹⁵Thus the lamb and the meal offering and the oil shall be provided, morning by morning, for a continual burnt offering.

¹⁶"Thus says the Lord GOD: If the prince makes a gift to any of his sons out of his inheritance, it shall belong to his sons, it is their property by inheritance. ¹⁷But if he makes a gift out of his inheritance to one of his servants, it shall be his to the year of liberty; then it shall revert to the prince; only his sons may keep a gift from his inheritance. ¹⁸The prince shall not take any of the inheritance of the people, thrusting them out of their property; he shall give his sons their inheritance out of his own property, so that none of my people shall be dispossessed of his property."

¹⁹Then he brought me through the entrance, which was at the side of the gate, to the north row of the holy chambers for the priests; and there I saw a place at the extreme western end of them. ²⁰And he said to me, "This is the place where the priests shall boil the guilt offering and the sin offering, and where they shall bake the cereal offering, in order not to bring them out into the outer court and so communicate holiness to the people."

²¹Then he brought me forth to the outer court, and led me to the four corners of the court; and in each corner of the court there was a court— ²²in the four corners of the court were small courts, forty cubits long and thirty broad; the four were of the same size. ²³On the inside, around each of the four courts was a row of masonry, with hearths made at the bottom of the rows round about. ²⁴Then he said to me, "These are the kitchens where those who minister at the temple shall boil the sacrifices of the people."

OT: Exod 29:38–41; Num 28:3–8, 9–15; 29:6
NT: Rom 12:1; 1 Cor 10:11; 2 Tim 3:16; Heb 12:28–29
Catechism: Jesus as the fulfillment of Old Testament sacrifices and offerings, 522, 606–17, 1330; Jewish and Christian feasts, 583, 593, 1096, 1164, 2581

46:1–3   Chapter 46 concludes Ezekiel's regulations for worship in the new temple. The role of the prince in worship is the center of attention, but the worship of the people is also in view. The outer east gate of the temple has been permanently closed (44:1–3). Ezekiel now mandates that the **gate of the inner court that faces east** will be shut **on the six working days**, but on the sabbath day and the day of the new moon this gate shall be opened. On these special days, the prince shall enter by the inner east gate, ascend the steps, and present his offerings to the priests in the vestibule. The priests will then offer the prince's burnt offerings and peace offerings on the altar of sacrifice, while the prince stands in worship **at the threshold of the gate** and then exits by the way he came. Meanwhile, **the people of the land** will stand outside the inner east gate and worship the Lord on the sabbath and new moon. Ezekiel carefully orchestrates how the prince, the priests, and the people have access in worship with varying levels of proximity to the presence of the Lord.

Ezekiel next delineates the sacrifices that the prince shall offer on the sabbath and the day of the new moon. Notably, this description of the sacrifices is in apparent conflict with the Mosaic regulations for these two feasts (see Num 28:9–15; 29:6).[27] Once again, the rabbis developed different strategies for reconciling the two accounts, some attempting to harmonize them and others proposing that there will be a new set of regulations in force for the third temple in the days of the Messiah.   46:4–8

Ezekiel now choreographs the entrances and exits of the people and the prince when they come to worship at the great feasts. These feasts include the sabbath, the new moon, †Passover, and Tabernacles, and possibly also the Feast of Weeks (†Pentecost). In short, prince and people are to enter and exit together. If they enter by the north gate, they shall leave by the south gate (and vice versa): **no one shall return by way of the gate by which he entered, but each shall go out straight ahead**. The reason for this direction is probably for the sake of good order and crowd control. Jacob Milgrom concludes that "two lines are formed, moving in opposite directions to regulate traffic."[28]   46:9–11

In a further provision (v. 12), whenever the prince offers **a freewill offering** to the Lord, he shall enter and exit the temple area by the inner east gate. The freewill offering is a free and voluntary sacrifice offered by the worshiper to the Lord. In addition, the prince is required to provide a lamb **for a burnt offering to the LORD daily; morning by morning he shall provide it . . . for a continual burnt offering**. This is the perpetual morning sacrifice offered each day to the Lord. Notably, Ezekiel offers no provision for the *evening* sacrifice, as in the Mosaic ordinances (Exod 29:38–41; Num 28:3–8). This may indicate a shift to one daily sacrifice, or it may be that Ezekiel chose to describe the morning offering and is assuming the same for the evening.   46:12–15

27. For a detailed comparison of the ordinances of Moses with those of Ezekiel, see Block, *Ezekiel: Chapters 25–48*, 673–74; Milgrom and Block, *Ezekiel's Hope*, 219–20.

28. Milgrom and Block, *Ezekiel's Hope*, 212.

46:16–18   To conclude this section, Ezekiel lays down the rule for how the prince's land may be distributed. In short, the land allotted to the prince may not be given to others in perpetuity but will revert to the prince in the Year of †Jubilee. At the same time, **the prince shall not take any of the inheritance of the people** as happened during the earlier monarchy. The prince can only give his own land to his sons; he cannot acquire land that belongs to the people, and then give this land to his offspring. This regulation protects the inheritance of the tribes from dispossession by the princes, so that **none of** the **people shall be dispossessed of his property**.

46:19–24   In this final section, the tour of the temple resumes with a description of the temple kitchens. This is the first we have heard of Ezekiel's tour guide since 44:1–3. The point of this description is to underline the levels of sanctity that separate the priests from the people, the Levites being identified with the people. Ezekiel is first escorted to the place where the sacrifices are "cooked" for the priests: the meat is boiled and the cakes are baked. The priests are required to prepare and consume the sacrifices in the inner court to avoid improperly communicating their **holiness to the people** in the outer court (v. 20). This same concern was first raised in 44:19. It sounds odd to us that the priests are to avoid "communicating holiness" to the people, but the purpose behind this is not only to demarcate what is holy from what is common (44:23) but also to *protect* the people from contact with a level of holiness that they are not called or consecrated to experience (see the Reflection and Application section for 44:1–31, pp. 311–12).

To conclude, Ezekiel is then shown a further set of kitchens in the outer court where the remains of the sacrifices are prepared for consumption by the Levites, **those who minister at the temple**. This is where the Levites and the people who made the offering prepare and eat the sacrificial food and so share in the blessing of the sacrifices that have been offered. As Joseph Blenkinsopp observes, the details here reflect "the concern for order and holiness which, according to the priestly theology, must permeate the whole of life."[29]

In the Light of Christ (Ezek 40–46)

As we come to the close of Ezekiel's visionary design for the new temple, it may be helpful to compare and contrast Ezekiel's vision (chaps. 40–46) with the vision of John in the book of Revelation (chaps. 20–21).[30] Clearly, John made ample use of the imagery from Ezekiel's vision, as the following list of similarities shows:

29. Joseph Blenkinsopp, *Ezekiel*, Interpretation (Louisville: John Knox, 1990), 230.
30. See Block, *Ezekiel: Chapters 25–48*, 502–3, 741, for the similarities and differences between Ezekiel and Revelation.

- transport of the prophet to a very high mountain (Ezek 40:2; Rev 21:10)
- the assistance of a heavenly guide who measures the temple in Ezekiel (Ezek 40:3–4) and the Holy City in Revelation (Rev 21:15–17)
- the presence of God dwelling with his people (Ezek 43:4–5; 48:35; Rev 21:3)
- the holiness of the people in the presence of God (Ezek 43:7–12; Rev 21:27; 22:14–15)[31]

But alongside these striking parallels, we must also recognize significant differences. The first fundamental difference is that Ezekiel primarily describes the dimensions and qualities of the new *temple*, while John portrays the dimensions and qualities of the new *city*, where he sees no temple. Further, while the measurements in Ezekiel and John both display a high degree of symmetry, Ezekiel offers a *two*-dimensional picture of the *temple* (Ezek 40:5–16), while Revelation offers a *three*-dimensional view of the *Holy City* (Rev 21:10–16). Finally, in Ezekiel's vision the temple, the city, the prince's dwelling, and the land allocated for each tribe are clearly separated from one another (48:21–22); in Revelation, everything comes together in one united, integrated "dwelling": the Lord God and the Lamb, who are the new temple, dwell with the redeemed people in the new and expanded city forever (Rev 21:2–4). John sees no temple because the new Jerusalem and the new creation are the new temple where God dwells with his people. John creatively makes use of many elements from Ezekiel's vision but recasts them to portray a distinctive vision of the marriage feast of the Lamb (Rev 19:9) and the dwelling of God with his people (Rev 21:3).

Reflection and Application (46:1–24)

Passages of Sacred Scripture like Ezek 46 are difficult for us to digest. We wonder why such attention is given to detailed regulations and rules for sacrifices. We tend to have little patience with descriptions concerning the number of animals, the weight and measure of each item offered, and the careful delineation of roles between the priests, the Levites, the prince, and the people. In fact, we are unsure why animal sacrifices are part of the worship of God in the first place. All of this can seem just a crude, primitive form of belief and practice that we are glad to be done with; it seems like a relic of the past that has no possible interest for us.

But if we take seriously St. Paul's teaching that "all Scripture is †inspired by God and profitable for teaching, for reproof, for correction, and for training in

---

31. See the "In the Light of Christ" section for Ezek 47:1–12 (pp. 327–28) for further parallels (a river flowing from the temple, the leaves of the trees for healing).

righteousness" (2 Tim 3:16)—and Paul is referring here to the *Old Testament*—and if we believe that the Old Testament narratives "were written down for our instruction" (1 Cor 10:11), then we should be actively searching to discover God's wisdom in these provisions for worship and sacrifice in Ezekiel's temple.

Here are three insights that we can glean from chapter 46. First, the detailed descriptions of temple worship communicate that God seeks to instruct us about who he is and how we are to worship him. The Lord God is *holy*, and we are meant to approach him reverently and with care. The liturgy of the Mass reflects this concern for holiness, order, and a precision of language, all of which teach us about the God that we are worshiping. This does not mean that worship is meant to be dry and merely "correct." From reports we have in the ancient sources, temple worship in Israel was in fact a joyful affair, often accompanied by musical instruments, singing, shouts of praise, and blessings from God. Our ordered worship should also be expressive and joyful.

Second, the precious sacrifices (animal, grain, oil) show that the gifts the people had received were offered by them to God as part of their worship. So we, too, offer what we have received (the bread and wine brought to the altar), which by God's powerful word becomes for us spiritual food and drink (the body and blood of Christ) that nourishes us to eternal life. Christian worship also entails giving generously of the material blessings God has given us for the needs of the poor, the needs of the Church, and the advance of the gospel (2 Cor 8–9; Phil 4:15–18; Heb 13:16). Crucially, we also offer *ourselves* "as a living sacrifice, holy and acceptable to God" (Rom 12:1).

Third, the limitations of access to the Lord imposed on the people of Israel should cause us to stand in wonder that, now in Christ, *all* baptized believers have full access in the Holy Spirit (Eph 2:18) to the true temple, to the heavenly holy of holies (Heb 10:19, 22; 12:22–24), because Christ is there and he has joined us to himself. Our liturgy on earth is a participation in the liturgy of heaven. As Paul proclaims in his letter to the Ephesians, God the Father has made us alive with Christ, and spiritually has "raised us up with him, and made us sit with him in the heavenly places" (Eph 2:5–6).

The New Land

Ezekiel 47:1–48:35

Ezekiel concludes his book by turning our attention to *the land*. The glorious presence of God has returned to the temple, but now the entire land needs to be cleansed and made new so that the people can dwell once again fruitfully in the land of promise. And so the stream of water flowing from the temple—from the presence of the Lord—sanctifies the land, bringing life and fruitful abundance.

This final section is divided into three parts. The first part (47:1–12) memorably describes the river flowing from the temple to the east, with all the effects of that river for the flourishing of life; the second part (47:13–23) designates the outer boundaries of the land (east, west, north, and south); the third part (48:1–35) describes the reapportioning of the land to the twelve tribes of Israel. The parts are logically linked. The land must be made fruitful again as a prelude to its distribution among the tribes returned from exile.

The River of Life and the Boundaries of the Land (47:1–12)

¹Then he brought me back to the door of the temple; and behold, water was issuing from below the threshold of the temple toward the east (for the temple faced east); and the water was flowing down from below the right side of the threshold of the temple, south of the altar. ²Then he brought me out by way of the north gate, and led me round on the outside to the outer gate, that faces toward the east; and the water was coming out on the right side.

³Going on eastward with a line in his hand, the man measured a thousand cubits, and then led me through the water; and it was ankle-deep. ⁴Again he measured a thousand, and led me through the water; and it was knee-deep. Again he measured a thousand, and led me through the water;

and it was up to the loins. ⁵Again he measured a thousand, and it was a river that I could not pass through, for the water had risen; it was deep enough to swim in, a river that could not be passed through. ⁶And he said to me, "Son of man, have you seen this?"

Then he led me back along the bank of the river. ⁷As I went back, I saw upon the bank of the river very many trees on the one side and on the other. ⁸And he said to me, "This water flows toward the eastern region and goes down into the Arabah; and when it enters the stagnant waters of the sea, the water will become fresh. ⁹And wherever the river goes every living creature which swarms will live, and there will be very many fish; for this water goes there, that the waters of the sea may become fresh; so everything will live where the river goes. ¹⁰Fishermen will stand beside the sea; from En-gedi to En-eglaim it will be a place for the spreading of nets; its fish will be of very many kinds, like the fish of the Great Sea. ¹¹But its swamps and marshes will not become fresh; they are to be left for salt. ¹²And on the banks, on both sides of the river, there will grow all kinds of trees for food. Their leaves will not wither nor their fruit fail, but they will bear fresh fruit every month, because the water for them flows from the sanctuary. Their fruit will be for food, and their leaves for healing."

OT: Gen 2:10; Lev 2:13; Pss 46:4; 65:9; Joel 3:18; Zech 14:8
NT: John 7:37–39; 19:34; Rev 22:1–2
Catechism: the gift of the Spirit, 733–36; water of baptism, 694
Lectionary: 47:1–9, 12: infant baptism; 47:1–2, 8–9, 12: dedication of the Lateran Basilica

47:1–2 Ezekiel's guide now escorts him to the inner court facing the door of the temple. There he sees water **issuing from below the threshold of the temple toward the east**. This flow of water, coming from the throne of God, streams out from the east end of the temple past the altar of sacrifice and continues through the inner and outer gates on the east side of the temple. Ezekiel and his guide circle around through the northern gate (because the east gate is closed) and arrive at the outer gate of the temple that faces east. There Ezekiel sees **water . . . coming out on the right side** of the east gate (see fig. 8, p. 283).[1]

47:3–5 Ezekiel's guide, **with a line in his hand**, then leads the prophet into the water, and as they wade toward the east, the water increases in depth. After one thousand cubits, it is **ankle-deep**; then after the same length it is **knee-deep**; in another one thousand cubits it is **up to the loins** (waist-deep). Finally, after a fourth interval of one thousand cubits, it is **a river that I could not pass through**. What does all this signify? First, the water flowing from the temple represents the very life of God, flowing out from his presence in the temple, a

1. In Jewish tradition, the outer east gate of the temple was called "the water gate" because it was through this gate that water was brought into the temple during the Feast of Tabernacles. The rabbis speculated that this same gate would see the outflow of the abundance of God's river in ⁺messianic times (Eisemann, *Ezekiel*, 734–35).

Water Flowing from the Temple

While the Gihon spring (2 Chron 32:30) supplied water to the City of David and to the pool of Siloam, there was no actual spring or river flowing from the Temple Mount in Jerusalem. Nevertheless, biblical tradition speaks of a river that flows from the throne of God and provides life and sustenance for the people. The Psalms proclaim this current of water that comes from the throne of God: "There is a river whose streams make glad the city of God, / the holy habitation of the Most High" (Ps 46:4; see also 65:9). The prophet Joel foresees a day when "the mountains shall drip sweet wine, / and the hills shall flow with milk, / and all the stream beds of Judah / shall flow with water; / and a fountain shall come forth from the house of the Lord / and water the Valley of Shittim" (Joel 3:18). The prophet Zechariah likewise announces a day to come when "living waters shall flow out from Jerusalem, half of them to the eastern sea and half of them to the western sea. It shall continue in summer as in winter" (Zech 14:8). Ezekiel is probably also drawing on the picture of a river flowing from the garden of Eden to water the surrounding territory: "A river flowed out of Eden to water the garden, and there it divided and became four rivers. . . . The name of the second river is Gihon" (Gen 2:10, 13). In Ezekiel's vision, the new temple and the renewed land bring to fulfillment the original creation in Eden. God will once again dwell with his people in the "garden" watered by the Lord.

life that bears fruit in great abundance. Miraculously, the flow of water, without additional tributaries, becomes deeper as it flows—the divine life of God is superabundant and inexhaustible. Ezekiel and his guide wade into the water to demonstrate the increasing depth, and they walk downstream. Their example serves as an invitation to God's people to wade in and immerse themselves ever more deeply in God's abundant life.

At the point where the water has become too deep to walk through, Ezekiel's **47:6–7** guide poses the question: **Son of man, have you seen this?** Ezekiel and his guide then make their way to the bank of the river, where Ezekiel sees **very many trees** on both sides of the river. Clearly the ever-deepening river was meant as a sign—a sign of God's ever-increasing provision for his people. The guide's question recalls a similar question posed earlier in the book (in 8:15) when Ezekiel was asked: "Have you seen this, O son of man?" At that time Ezekiel was shown the abominations occurring in the temple precincts; now he is witnessing the healing waters pouring from the temple. The Lord God has reversed the fortunes of his people, and Ezekiel is called as a witness to this transformation.

The guide now offers the interpretation of what Ezekiel has seen, using lan- **47:8–12** guage that recalls the creation narrative in Gen 1, with swarming creatures and

Latin Hymn "Vidi Aquam"

LIVING
TRADITION

From Easter to †Pentecost, the Latin hymn "Vidi Aquam" may be sung during the sprinkling of water at the beginning of the liturgy during the penitential rite. The sprinkling signifies the baptism of the faithful and the new life that has come through the resurrection of Christ. This ancient hymn, drawn directly from Ezekiel's vision of the water flowing from the temple (47:1–2), identifies this water with the baptismal water through which Christ's own saving life is communicated to the believer.

> *Vidi aquam egredientem de templo, a latere dextro, alleluia:*
> *Et omnes ad quos pervenit aqua ista, salvi facti sunt,*
> *Et dicent: alleluia, alleluia.*

> I saw water flowing from the temple, from its right side, alleluia:
> And all to whom that water came were saved,
> And they shall say: alleluia, alleluia.

fruit-bearing trees. The river of water flowing from the temple will flow to the east, **into the Arabah,** the arid land extending southward from the Jordan valley and the plains of Jericho, and then on into the Dead Sea.[2] The two sites named, **En-gedi** and **En-eglaim,** are oases on either side of the Dead Sea. Astonishingly, when the water flows into the sea, it will make the sea *fresh.* Given the intense saltiness of the Dead Sea and the absence of fish, this is a great miracle. Wherever the river flows, there fish will teem: **everything will live where the river goes.** Fishermen will draw out fish of every kind from the former Dead Sea, just as they do from the Mediterranean Sea on the west and the Sea of Galilee in the north. However, the **swamps and marshes** that branch off from the river **will not become fresh** but will **be left for salt.** Why is this? Probably because salt is necessary for life, and this valuable mineral would be preserved in the swamps and marshes for use by the people.[3] Salt was also required for the temple sacrifices and so contributed to the worship of the Lord (Lev 2:13; Ezek 43:24). Moshe Eisemann eloquently expresses the meaning of this vision of the life-giving river of God flowing from the temple: "Water, the life force of God's creation, would have its source in that very Holy of Holies in which God Himself allows His Shechinah to rest. All life will derive from this holy source

2. There is a traditional †rabbinic interpretation, probably influenced by Zech 14:8, that conceives of the waters of the river divided into three parts, the first flowing to the Sea of Galilee, the second into the Dead Sea, and the third to the Mediterranean. See Block, *Ezekiel: Chapters 25–48,* 698; Milgrom and Block, *Ezekiel's Hope,* 233–34.

3. †*Targum of Ezekiel* supports this view by specifying that "they shall be left for salt mines." Levey, *Targum of Ezekiel,* 126.

as the tiny trickle of water turns into a mighty river, and brings the healing touch of sanctity to all the world's waterways."[4]

To close the vision, our gaze returns to the trees on the banks of the river: **on the banks, on both sides of the river, there will grow all kinds of trees for food**. Strikingly, the trees along the banks of this river will provide fresh fruit **every month** of the year, a thing that does not happen in fruit trees as we know them. At the same time, the leaves of the trees, which **will not wither**, are **for healing**, for medicinal use to treat the sicknesses of the people. The trees, then, represent the provision of the Lord for the sustenance and the healing of his people.

In the Light of Christ (47:1–12)

Ezekiel's vision of water flowing out from the temple is fulfilled in at least three ways in the New Testament. The first is related to the Feast of †Tabernacles. During this great autumn feast, for seven days a procession of priests descended from the Temple Mount to the spring of Gihon, which fed the pool of Siloam; gathered water in a golden pitcher; and returned to the temple. The water was poured out onto the ground as a sacrificial offering in recognition of God's miraculous provision of water for the Israelites in the desert and as a prayer for rain in the present time.[5] Jesus, standing in the temple on the eighth and final day of the Feast of Tabernacles, takes advantage of this occasion to declare: "If anyone thirsts, let him come to me and drink. Whoever believes in me, as the Scripture has said, 'Out of his heart will flow rivers of living water'" (John 7:37–38 ESV). John tells us that Jesus is referring here to the gift of the Holy Spirit (7:39): the water that will flow from the temple refers to the gift of the Spirit that will flow out from the hearts of those who believe.

The second fulfillment occurs just after Jesus dies on the cross. John testifies that he saw blood and water flowing from the side of Christ: "But one of the soldiers pierced his side with a spear, and at once there came out blood and water" (John 19:34). The flow of blood signifies Jesus's sacrifice of his life for our salvation, while the water points to Jesus as the "new temple" from whom living water—the Holy Spirit—flows out to give life to the world.

The third fulfillment appears in the final chapter of the New Testament. Building directly upon Ezekiel's vision, the book of Revelation portrays eternal life with God in terms of the same imagery of the river flowing from the presence of God and the trees that yield fruit and healing for all the nations: "Then he showed me the river of the water of life, bright as crystal, flowing from the throne of God and of

4. Eisemann, *Ezekiel*, 735.

5. Francis Martin and William Wright IV, *The Gospel of John*, CCSS (Grand Rapids: Baker Academic, 2015), 145.

the Lamb through the middle of the street of the city; also, on either side of the river, the tree of life with its twelve kinds of fruit, yielding its fruit each month; and the leaves of the tree were for the healing of the nations" (Rev 22:1–2). In Revelation, however, there is no temple building; the throne of God and the Lamb *is* the new temple from which the river of life flows eternally.

The Boundaries of the Land (47:13–23)

[13]Thus says the Lord GOD: "These are the boundaries by which you shall divide the land for inheritance among the twelve tribes of Israel. Joseph shall have two portions. [14]And you shall divide it equally; I swore to give it to your fathers, and this land shall fall to you as your inheritance.

[15]"This shall be the boundary of the land: On the north side, from the Great Sea by way of Hethlon to the entrance of Hamath, and on to Zedad, [16]Berothah, Sibraim (which lies on the border between Damascus and Hamath), as far as Hazer-hatticon, which is on the border of Hauran. [17]So the boundary shall run from the sea to Hazar-enon, which is on the northern border of Damascus, with the border of Hamath to the north. This shall be the north side.

[18]"On the east side, the boundary shall run from Hazar-enon between Hauran and Damascus; along the Jordan between Gilead and the land of Israel; to the eastern sea and as far as Tamar. This shall be the east side.

[19]"On the south side, it shall run from Tamar as far as the waters of Meribath-kadesh, thence along the Brook of Egypt to the Great Sea. This shall be the south side.

[20]"On the west side, the Great Sea shall be the boundary to a point opposite the entrance of Hamath. This shall be the west side.

[21]"So you shall divide this land among you according to the tribes of Israel. [22]You shall allot it as an inheritance for yourselves and for the aliens who reside among you and have begotten children among you. They shall be to you as native-born sons of Israel; with you they shall be allotted an inheritance among the tribes of Israel. [23]In whatever tribe the alien resides, there you shall assign him his inheritance, says the Lord GOD."

OT: Lev 19:33–34; Num 34:1–12
NT: Matt 5:13; Gal 5:22–23; Eph 2:11–19; Col 1:9–10
Catechism: the gift of the land, 1222, 2795

47:13–14   The Lord God now speaks to Ezekiel about the apportioning of the land as an **inheritance among the twelve tribes of Israel**. In chapters 47–48, Ezekiel refers to the "tribes of Israel" (47:13, 21, 22; 48:19, 29, 31; see also "the tribes" in 48:1, 23) instead of his more common expression "house of Israel," because he is concerned here with the specific inheritance of each tribe in the land. **Joseph shall have two portions** of land, following the original allotment to the sons of Joseph (Ephraim and Manasseh) under Joshua. And the land shall be divided **equally** between the tribes. What this means is that every tribal portion will be equal to the others; there is an egalitarian quality to this reapportioning of land in Israel that was not true of the original allotments under Joshua, in which each tribe's allotment of land was proportional to its population size. Notably, there is no need for conquest as we find in Joshua: the land will simply be given by the Lord to his people in fulfillment of the Lord's promise whereby he **swore to give . . . this land . . . to** the **fathers** of Israel (Abraham, Isaac, Jacob).[6]

Ezekiel marks out the outer boundaries of the land (east, west, north, and south). The boundaries roughly follow those given in Num 34:1–12 but expand the territory to the north and to the east above the river Jordan. The northern boundary receives the greatest extension beyond the traditional borders of Israel. It includes most of modern-day Lebanon, including the ancient cities of Tyre, Sidon, and Byblos. The eastern boundary stretches into modern Syria and includes the city of Damascus, but then narrows to follow the line of the river Jordan down to the Dead Sea. Notably, this eastern border, for reasons unknown, *excludes* the land in the Transjordan that was originally given to the tribes of Reuben and Gad and the half-tribe of Manasseh. The southern and eastern borders roughly follow the boundaries of the original settlement of the land under Joshua. 〔47:15–20〕

The chapter concludes with an important practical provision made for **the aliens who reside** and settle among the tribes of Israel. They are to be adopted by the tribe among which they dwell: **they shall be to you as native-born sons of Israel.** This practice is consistent with the generous treatment shown to sojourners in Lev 19:33–34: "When a stranger sojourns with you in your land, you shall not do him wrong. The stranger who sojourns with you shall be to you as the native among you, and you shall love him as yourself; for you were strangers in the land of Egypt." Sojourners from the †Gentile nations are to have an equal inheritance in the land with the native-born tribes of Israel.[7] When interpreted in the light of Christ, this equal treatment of non-Israelite sojourners foreshadows the full membership in the people of God extended to Gentile believers in Christ (Eph 2:11–19). 〔47:21–23〕

Reflection and Application (47:1–23)

Ezekiel's vision of the river of water streaming out from the temple provides a treasure trove of images for application to the spiritual life. In the early Christian

---

6. For the promise of the land to Israel, see Exod 6:8; 13:5; 32:13; Deut 1:8; 6:10.
7. Provision for the sojourner in the land is also found in Isa 56:3–8 and Jer 22:3.

tradition, Ezekiel's stream of water was associated with baptism and with the entire growth of the Christian believer through various stages, such that each stage brings a greater depth of relationship with God.[8] The Christian life, begun in the waters of baptism, grows ever deeper as we wade progressively into the life of God, to the point where we are entirely encompassed and overwhelmed. The life of God in us is not like a stream that gradually diminishes and dries up as it moves away from its source. Rather, the Spirit of God, the source of our life, is like a stream of water within us (John 7:37–39) that continually deepens as we walk in the Spirit, watering the dry, arid parts of our lives and bearing fruit in every season (Gal 5:22–23; Col 1:9–10). Even Ezekiel's vision of the "salt" that remains in the marshes and swamps (47:11) could be spiritually applied to Christ's call for Christians to be "the salt of the earth" (Matt 5:13). This illuminates our missionary role in the world and our impact on the culture around us, where the stranger and the sojourner are embraced and welcomed into the full inheritance of the people of God (47:22–23). In Ezekiel's vision of the river of God we possess profound images of the spiritual life that develops and advances through the course of our lives.

Apportioning of the Land and the Gates of the Holy City (48:1–35)

[1]"These are the names of the tribes: Beginning at the northern border, from the sea by way of Hethlon to the entrance of Hamath, as far as Hazar-enon (which is on the northern border of Damascus over against Hamath), and extending from the east side to the west, Dan, one portion. [2]Adjoining the territory of Dan, from the east side to the west, Asher, one portion. [3]Adjoining the territory of Asher, from the east side to the west, Naphtali, one portion. [4]Adjoining the territory of Naphtali, from the east side to the west, Manasseh, one portion. [5]Adjoining the territory of Manasseh, from the east side to the west, Ephraim, one portion. [6]Adjoining the territory of Ephraim, from the east side to the west, Reuben, one portion. [7]Adjoining the territory of Reuben, from the east side to the west, Judah, one portion.

[8]"Adjoining the territory of Judah, from the east side to the west, shall be the portion which you shall set apart, twenty-five thousand cubits in breadth, and in length equal to one of the tribal portions, from the east side to the west, with the sanctuary in the midst of it. [9]The portion which you shall set apart for the LORD shall be twenty-five thousand cubits in length, and twenty thousand in breadth. [10]These shall be the allotments of the holy portion: the priests shall have an allotment measuring twenty-five

8. For the application of the ever-deepening stream to the stages of the spiritual life, see Block, *Ezekiel: Chapters 25–48*, 699; Joseph Blenkinsopp, *Ezekiel*, Interpretation (Louisville: John Knox, 1990), 232.

thousand cubits on the northern side, ten thousand cubits in breadth on the western side, ten thousand in breadth on the eastern side, and twenty-five thousand in length on the southern side, with the sanctuary of the LORD in the midst of it. [11]This shall be for the consecrated priests, the sons of Zadok, who kept my charge, who did not go astray when the people of Israel went astray, as the Levites did. [12]And it shall belong to them as a special portion from the holy portion of the land, a most holy place, adjoining the territory of the Levites. [13]And alongside the territory of the priests, the Levites shall have an allotment twenty-five thousand cubits in length and ten thousand in breadth. The whole length shall be twenty-five thousand cubits and the breadth twenty thousand. [14]They shall not sell or exchange any of it; they shall not alienate this choice portion of the land, for it is holy to the LORD.

[15]"The remainder, five thousand cubits in breadth and twenty-five thousand in length, shall be for ordinary use for the city, for dwellings and for open country. In the midst of it shall be the city; [16]and these shall be its dimensions: the north side four thousand five hundred cubits, the south side four thousand five hundred, the east side four thousand five hundred, and the west side four thousand five hundred. [17]And the city shall have open land: on the north two hundred and fifty cubits, on the south two hundred and fifty, on the east two hundred and fifty, and on the west two hundred and fifty. [18]The remainder of the length alongside the holy portion shall be ten thousand cubits to the east, and ten thousand to the west, and it shall be alongside the holy portion. Its produce shall be food for the workers of the city. [19]And the workers of the city, from all the tribes of Israel, shall till it. [20]The whole portion which you shall set apart shall be twenty-five thousand cubits square, that is, the holy portion together with the property of the city.

[21]"What remains on both sides of the holy portion and of the property of the city shall belong to the prince. Extending from the twenty-five thousand cubits of the holy portion to the east border, and westward from the twenty-five thousand cubits to the west border, parallel to the tribal portions, it shall belong to the prince. The holy portion with the sanctuary of the temple in its midst, [22]and the property of the Levites and the property of the city, shall be in the midst of that which belongs to the prince. The portion of the prince shall lie between the territory of Judah and the territory of Benjamin.

[23]"As for the rest of the tribes: from the east side to the west, Benjamin, one portion. [24]Adjoining the territory of Benjamin, from the east side to the west, Simeon, one portion. [25]Adjoining the territory of Simeon, from the east side to the west, Issachar, one portion. [26]Adjoining the territory of Issachar, from the east side to the west, Zebulun, one portion. [27]Adjoining the territory of Zebulun, from the east side to the west, Gad, one portion. [28]And adjoining the territory of Gad to the south, the boundary shall run from Tamar to the waters of Meribath-kadesh, thence along the Brook of Egypt to the

Great Sea. ²⁹This is the land which you shall allot as an inheritance among the tribes of Israel, and these are their several portions, says the Lord GOD.

³⁰"These shall be the exits of the city: On the north side, which is to be four thousand five hundred cubits by measure, ³¹three gates, the gate of Reuben, the gate of Judah, and the gate of Levi, the gates of the city being named after the tribes of Israel. ³²On the east side, which is to be four thousand five hundred cubits, three gates, the gate of Joseph, the gate of Benjamin, and the gate of Dan. ³³On the south side, which is to be four thousand five hundred cubits by measure, three gates, the gate of Simeon, the gate of Issachar, and the gate of Zebulun. ³⁴On the west side, which is to be four thousand five hundred cubits, three gates, the gate of Gad, the gate of Asher, and the gate of Naphtali. ³⁵The circumference of the city shall be eighteen thousand cubits. And the name of the city henceforth shall be, The LORD is there."

OT: Exod 33; Josh 13–21; Isa 62:2, 4; Jer 33:16
NT: Matt 28:20; John 10:11–16; Rev 21
Catechism: the gift of the land, 1222, 2795; the presence of God and of Jesus among the faithful, 208, 788, 1039, 1374, 2781

48:1–7 Now that the outer boundaries of the land have been established, Ezekiel re-apportions to each tribe its share within the land, beginning from the north and working his way to the southern boundary. Ezekiel begins: **These are the names of the tribes.** What follows is a roll call whereby each tribe is named and granted its portion of land (see fig. 14). While the same twelve tribes receive an allocation of land as they did under Joshua (see Josh 13–21), the actual details of the land distribution differ in significant ways. First, no land is allotted in the Transjordan region east of the Jordan River. The tribes that were located in the Transjordan under Joshua—Gad, Reuben, and the half-tribe of Manasseh—now have portions to the west of the Jordan River. Second, Judah's portion is now located north of Benjamin's allotment (previously Benjamin was placed north of Judah). Third, Issachar, Zebulun and Gad, previously located in the north, are now given land to the south of the Holy City.

Interestingly, the new allocations appear to favor the tribes descended directly from the wives of Jacob (Leah and Rachel)—they are closest to the temple and city, four on either side—while the tribes descended from their maids are at the furthest extremes, north and south (Dan, Asher, Naphtali, Gad). Ezekiel's allocation of land has a kind of mathematical symmetry, whereby each tribe is given a strip of land running from east to west in a manner that pays little attention to real geographical features. Judah remains, however, in a privileged position, located directly above the central portion of land dedicated to the Lord.[9]

---

9. Milgrom and Block, *Ezekiel's Hope*, 250, propose that Ezekiel's new allocation of the land is intended to limit the royal power of the king and to provide all the tribes with roughly equal portions of land and access to the Holy City.

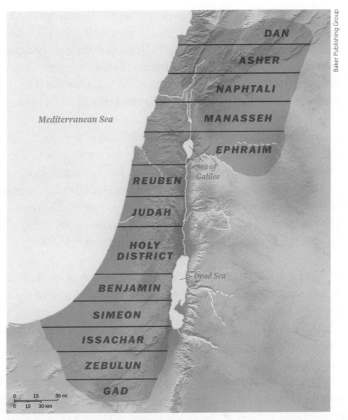

Figure 14. The new distribution of the land

In this section, Ezekiel revisits and develops his earlier description of this **48:8–14** central **portion** of land (see 45:1–9), located *between* the tribal portions, set aside for the sanctuary and its ministers and for the city and the prince. The word "portion" (or "district") is literally the word for "offering" (Hebrew *terumah*). This indicates that this special holy portion of land is to be an "offering" set aside in a special way for the Lord. The details of the allocation are complicated and best viewed visually (see fig. 13, p. 314). The entire central portion is twenty-five thousand cubits square, approximately eight miles on each side (v. 8). Once again we see Ezekiel's concern for symmetry: just as the temple area itself is a perfect square, so is the holy portion of land set aside for the Lord and his ministers. The larger, upper section (twenty thousand cubits in breadth, north to south) is devoted to the Lord (v. 9). Half of this section (ten thousand cubits in breadth) is set aside for the Zadokite priests (vv. 10–12). Notably, **the sanctuary of the Lord** is **in the midst of it**. Where the Lord dwells is the heart of the land. Just as there is a "most holy place" within the temple itself, so this portion of land functions as a "most holy place" for the priests: **it shall belong to them as a special portion from the holy portion of the land, a most holy place**. Adjoining the land for the priests is the land set aside for the Levites (vv. 13–14). This encompasses the other half of the land devoted to the Lord (ten thousand cubits in breadth). Ezekiel does not say whether this land is to the north or the south of the land dedicated to the priests, but the land remains **holy to the Lord**, and so cannot be sold or exchanged.

48:15–20   Next, a smaller portion of the central plot of land (5,000 cubits in breadth) is set aside for the Holy City and those who care for its needs. Ezekiel first referred to this "holy district" of land in 45:6. In the center stands the Holy City, Jerusalem. It encompasses a portion of land 4,500 cubits square with a "green belt" of 250 cubits surrounding it on all four sides. The remaining territory to the east and west (10,000 cubits in each direction) is designated for farming: those who work in the city can cultivate this land and use it for their food.

48:21–22   Finally, the land on either side of this central portion is marked out for the prince: **What remains on both sides of the holy portion and of the property of the city shall belong to the prince** (see Ezek 45:7–8). The prince, then, has his own land, distinct from tribal allotments. The fruits of this land not only supply the needs of the prince and his household but also provide the grain and animals needed for the sacrifices in the temple.

One noteworthy feature of this land allocation is that the Holy City is separated from the temple precincts by a considerable distance (approximately ten to fifteen thousand cubits, or about five miles). Solomon constructed the first temple next to the Holy City, close to his own dwellings. In Ezekiel's vision, the temple and the city are widely separated, and the land set aside for the prince is separated from both. The reason for these separations is uncertain; Jacob Milgrom proposes that the distancing of the Holy City from the temple and the lands of the prince shows that in a special way "the city belonged to the people."[10] In this respect, Ezekiel's vision stands in contrast to the vision in the book of Revelation (chaps. 21–22), where everything is centered in the new city, the heavenly Jerusalem: the Lord God and the Lamb (Jesus), who *are* the new temple (Rev 21:22), dwell with the people of God in the Holy City forever (21:3).

48:23–29   With the allocation of the central portion of land finished, Ezekiel returns and completes the apportioning of land to **the rest of the tribes**. The remaining five tribes—Benjamin, Simeon, Issachar, Zebulun, and Gad—each receive their strip of land running from east to west down to the southern border. Benjamin receives the best portion, directly adjoining the land dedicated to the Holy City. Ezekiel concludes the allocation of the land with a formal declaration: **This is**

---

10. Milgrom and Block, *Ezekiel's Hope*, 256.

the land which you shall allot as an inheritance among the tribes of Israel, and these are their several portions, says the Lord GOD.

To close the book, Ezekiel directs our gaze to the walls and gates of the Holy City. Expanding on the description of the Holy City in 48:16, he declares that there will be three **exits** (or gates) on each of the four sides of the square city. These twelve gates, three on each side, are **named after the tribes of Israel.** Levi is now included, and Joseph receives just one gate (whereas Joseph had two portions of land through his sons, Manasseh and Ephraim, and Levi received none). Typically an ancient city would have just a few gates for entrance and exit, though Jerusalem had up to seven gates in the time of Ezekiel.[11] Designating a gate for each tribe underlines that this is the *people's* city. Jerusalem is no longer just "the city of David" but a holy city that belongs equally to all the tribes. The city "shall belong to the whole house of Israel" (45:6).[12]

The final sentence of the book provides an eminently fitting conclusion and climax to the book: **And the name of the city henceforth shall be, The LORD is there.** Beginning with chapter 40, Ezekiel never refers to the Holy City by its name, Jerusalem. He calls it simply "the city." Now the city receives a name, "the LORD is there" (Hebrew †YHWH *shammah*). By giving Jerusalem a new name, Ezekiel follows closely in the footsteps of Isaiah and Jeremiah. Isaiah promises a time when Jerusalem will be called by a new name: "You shall be called My delight is in her" (Isa 62:4). Jeremiah, speaking of the days of the Messiah to come, also gives a new name to Jerusalem: "And this is the name by which it will be called: 'The LORD is our righteousness'" (Jer 33:16). The *name* of the city that Ezekiel gives is in fact the *name* of the LORD (YHWH), signifying his presence *there* with his people.[13] This is the great end-goal: the Lord God dwelling among his people provides the fullest life imaginable.

Up to this point, Ezekiel has focused almost exclusively on the temple as the locus of God's presence. But now, as the book closes, he announces that the Lord is "there" *in the Holy City*. The Lord will establish his presence not only in the new temple but also in the newly rebuilt city, showing his accessibility to the entire people of God. And where God dwells, there is life, blessing, and abundance. It is obvious that this new Holy City in Ezekiel's vision is not yet a reality, but points to a day to come when God in his holy presence—his Shekinah—will dwell among his people.[14]

48:30–35a

48:35b

11. Block, *Ezekiel: Chapters 25–48*, 736.
12. Block, *Ezekiel: Chapters 25–48*, 738–39.
13. Joyce, *Ezekiel*, 241, calls this "a magnificently theocentric note for this most God-centered of biblical books to end on!"
14. †*Targum of Ezekiel* adds a line, indicating that it is the glorious presence of the Lord—his †Shekinah—that will dwell in the Holy City: "And the name of the city, designated from the day that the Lord makes His Shekinah rest upon it, shall be: The Lord is there." Levey, *Targum of Ezekiel*, 129.

In the Light of Christ (48:35)

The prophet Isaiah, speaking of the city of Jerusalem, announced a day to come when the Holy City "shall be called by a new name / which the mouth of the Lᴏʀᴅ will give" (Isa 62:2). Ezekiel gives the Holy City a new name, "the Lᴏʀᴅ is there," but it is only in the book of Revelation that we see the ultimate fulfillment of this promise. Whereas Ezekiel presents a vision of a temple and a city separate and distinct from one another, Revelation combines the two into one. No longer will there be a separate temple (building or structure), "for its temple is the Lord God the Almighty and the Lamb" (Rev 21:22). In the new Jerusalem envisioned by John, Ezekiel's name for the city ("the Lᴏʀᴅ is there") is fully realized. "Behold, the dwelling of God is with men. He will dwell with them, and they shall be his people, and God himself will be with them" (Rev 21:3). As in Ezekiel's vision, the twelve gates of the new city will be named after the twelve tribes of Israel: "It had a great, high wall, with twelve gates, . . . and on the gates the names of the twelve tribes of the sons of Israel were inscribed" (Rev 21:12). But the city wall also has twelve foundations, "and on them [are written] the twelve names of the twelve apostles of the Lamb" (21:14). Through the apostolic preaching the new Jerusalem has been enlarged to include not only Israel but all the nations: "By its light shall the nations walk" (21:24). The "good shepherd" (John 10:11) is gathering up not only his sheep from within Israel but "other sheep, that are not of this fold" from among the nations, so "there shall be one flock, one shepherd" (10:16). And "the Lᴏʀᴅ is there" among them all.

Reflection and Application (48:1–35)

Ezekiel is a book marked by dark and frightening scenes, but it begins and ends with the same awe-inspiring vision: the presence of the Lord among his people. The book opens with Ezekiel's vision of the glorious presence of the Lord on his mobile throne. Despite living in the sorrow-laden land of exile, Ezekiel experiences the *presence* of God and hears his word. The book concludes with a vision of the Lord dwelling among his people, with his holiness and life flowing out from the temple: *the Lord is there*. This recalls a remarkable dialogue between Moses and the Lord upon Mount Sinai. The Lord tells Moses that he will send his angel to accompany the people into the land but says, "I will not go up among you, lest I consume you in the way" (Exod 33:3). Moses responds: "If your presence will not go with me, do not bring us up from here" (33:15 ESV). Moses is profoundly aware that the *presence of the Lord* is what they most need. This is why the †incarnation of the Word is so central to the entire biblical narrative: in Jesus the Word made flesh, God has come to dwell definitively among his people. He pitched his tent in our midst and allowed us to see his face. He is Immanuel, God with us. Ezekiel's witness points to this truth: *God present in our midst is our life and salvation.* We experience the presence of God in this life in many ways—"I am with you always, to the close of the age" (Matt 28:20)—but we also long and pray for the glorious return of Jesus, so that we may dwell in his presence forever and know the fullness of his divine life. Maranatha, Come Lord Jesus!

Suggested Resources

From the Jewish and Christian Tradition

Eisemann, Moshe. *Yechezkel/Ezekiel: A New Translation with a Commentary Anthologized from Talmudic, Midrashic, and Rabbinic Sources.* 3 vols. New York: Mesorah Publications, 1977, 1979, 1988. This work presents a wide variety of Jewish interpretations of Ezekiel through the centuries.

St. Gregory the Great. *Homilies on the Book of the Prophet Ezekiel.* Translated by Theodosia Tomkinson. 2nd ed. Etna, CA: Center for Traditionalist Orthodox Studies, 2008. St. Gregory offers a wide-ranging spiritual interpretation of Ezekiel and applies it to the individual believer and to the Church.

St. Jerome. *Commentary on Ezekiel.* Translated by Thomas P. Scheck. ACW. New York: Newman, 2017. St. Jerome offers an in-depth commentary on Ezekiel, making use of both the Hebrew and Greek.

Levey, Samson H., trans. *The Targum of Ezekiel.* Aramaic Bible 13. Wilmington, DE: Michael Glazier, 1987. The English translation of this ancient Aramaic translation of Ezekiel offers illuminating insights into the early Jewish understanding of the book.

Origen of Alexandria. *Homilies 1–14 on Ezekiel.* Translated by Thomas P. Scheck. ACW 62. New York: Newman, 2010. Origen's homilies are among the earliest on Ezekiel in the Christian tradition and provide a wealth of spiritual application.

Rosenberg, A. J., trans. *Ezekiel.* 2 vols. Mikraoth Gedoloth. New York: Judaica Press, 1991, 2000. This commentary preserves the interpretation of Ezekiel by the renowned rabbi Rashi and also draws upon other selected rabbis to present a traditional rabbinic commentary on the book of Ezekiel.

Stevenson, Kenneth, and Michael Glerup. *Ezekiel, Daniel.* ACCS: Old Testament 13. Downers Grove, IL: IVP Academic, 2008. A collection of short excerpts from a variety of the Church Fathers offering brief comments mostly on well-known passages in Ezekiel.

Scholarly Commentaries

Alter, Robert, trans. *The Hebrew Bible*, vol. 2, *Prophets*, 1047–197. New York: Norton, 2019. This skilled Jewish translator provides insightful commentary on the meanings of words and historical background.

Block, Daniel I. *The Book of Ezekiel, Chapters 1–24; The Book of Ezekiel, Chapters 25–48.* New International Commentary on the Old Testament. Grand Rapids: Eerdmans, 1997, 1998. This two-volume commentary from a Protestant scholar provides one of the most thorough studies of Ezekiel to date, and a wealth of knowledge about the text.

Greenberg, Moshe. *Ezekiel 1–20; Ezekiel 21–37.* Anchor Bible 22, 22A. New York: Doubleday, 1983, 1997. An in-depth commentary on Ezekiel from a renowned Jewish scholar that presents the book as a unified work.

Joyce, Paul M. *Ezekiel: A Commentary.* Library of Hebrew Bible/Old Testament Studies 482. New York: T&T Clark, 2007. A concise study of Ezekiel that helpfully presents the main options for interpretation.

Milgrom, Jacob, and Daniel I. Block. *Ezekiel's Hope: A Commentary on Ezekiel 38–48.* Eugene, OR: Cascade Books, 2012. An in-depth commentary on the final section of Ezekiel aimed at completing the two-volume commentary begun by Moshe Greenberg.

Popular and Pastoral Commentaries

Bergsma, John, and Brant Pitre. "Ezekiel." In *A Catholic Introduction to the Bible*, vol. 1, *The Old Testament*, 837–74. San Francisco: Ignatius, 2018. A concise background introduction to the book of Ezekiel that provides the reader with a wealth of understanding about the text and its main themes.

Jenson, Robert W. *Ezekiel.* Brazos Theological Commentary on the Bible. Grand Rapids: Brazos, 2009. A theological commentary on Ezekiel that connects Ezekiel's message with contemporary theological issues.

Klein, Ralph W. *Ezekiel: The Prophet and His Message.* Columbia: University of South Carolina Press, 1988. A topical presentation of Ezekiel with helpful background material and attention given to central themes.

Taylor, John B. *Ezekiel: An Introduction and Commentary.* Tyndale Old Testament Commentaries. Downers Grove, IL: InterVarsity, 1969. A sound, accessible commentary on Ezekiel that helps the reader follow the main story line of the book.

Glossary

allegory (from the Greek, "to say other things," meaning to say one thing in order to mean another): a symbolic narrative that is intended to convey a meaning not contained in the narrative.

apocalyptic: a distinctive type of ancient Jewish and Christian literature that professes to reveal mysteries of the future or of the heavenly realm using symbolic language and images.

Aramaic: a Semitic language related to Hebrew, adopted by the Jews after their exile in Babylon. It was the ordinary language spoken by Jews in first-century Palestine.

call-narrative: the description of how a given prophet in Israel is called by God to speak his word to the people.

canon (canonical): the list of books discerned by the Church as belonging to Sacred Scripture.

Chaldeans (Chaldean empire): an ancient Semitic people native to present-day southern Iraq; in reference to biblical history, "the Chaldean empire" refers primarily to the Neo-Babylonian Empire (626–539 BC), which conquered Judah and exiled its people in 586 BC.

cherubim: the rank of angels that appear in the temple of the Lord, surrounding the divine presence. In Ezekiel's vision, the cherubim also pilot the divine chariot, which houses the glorious presence of the God of Israel.

Church Fathers: the renowned teachers and leaders in the first seven centuries of the Church, marked by their orthodox teaching, holiness of life, and approval by the Church.

covenant: a sacred kinship bond established between God and his people, involving a mutual commitment of love and fidelity. God formed a covenant with Abraham and later with his descendants, the people Israel, through Moses. Through his passion, death, and resurrection, Jesus established the new and eternal covenant, which fulfills the old.

covenant blessings and curses: the collection of blessings and curses found in Leviticus 26 and Deuteronomy 28–30, outlining what will happen to Israel if they follow the covenant (blessings) or if they are unfaithful to the covenant (curses).

Dead Sea Scrolls: a collection of ancient manuscripts dating from ca. 250 BC to AD 70, discovered first in 1947 in the caves near Qumran, near the northwest shore of the Dead Sea.

Deist (Deism): a religious belief in the existence of a supreme being (God) who does not intervene or reveal himself in the world.

divination: the practice of determining the future or the cause of events by the interpretation of omens or by the aid of supernatural powers.

divine chariot: the vehicle, seen by the prophet Ezekiel in a vision (Ezek 1), that houses the divine presence and moves throughout the world at the prompting of the cherubim who pilot the chariot.

eschatology (eschatological) (from Greek *eschata*, "last things"): all that concerns the end of human history, the final tribulations, the coming of Jesus, the last judgment, and the resurrection of the dead. For the New Testament, the end begins with Jesus's passion and resurrection, the transition from the former age to the new and final age of salvation history.

fuller sense (*sensus plenior*): a deeper meaning of the biblical text, intended by God but not clearly expressed by the human author.

Gentile(s): peoples of non-Jewish descent. The biblical Hebrew and Greek words that are translated as "Gentiles" are also sometimes translated as "nations."

Gnostics, Gnosticism: a second-century movement composed of varying groups that posed a threat to Christianity by assimilating Christian elements into its ideas of a secondary creator god responsible for the material creation.

gospel (the Gospels): the message (literally, "good news") about salvation through the death and resurrection of Jesus Christ preached by the apostles to Jews and Gentiles, summoning all to faith and repentance. "Gospel" later came to refer to one of the four canonical narratives of the life of Jesus.

grace (Greek *charis*): (1) a disposition of favor, generosity, or magnanimity; (2) a gift, benefit, or other effect that results from this attitude. The distinguishing character of "grace" is that it is freely given, not earned.

Hades: in Greek mythology, the underground abode of the dead, where the souls of all the dead came to rest. It is the equivalent of "Sheol" in Hebrew thought. While it is a place of sadness and gloom, it does not normally have the element of everlasting punishment that came to characterize the later Jewish and Christian conception of hell.

halachah: the laws and ordinances, based on biblical commandments, drawn from both the written and oral Torah, that regulate religious observances and the daily life and conduct of the Jewish people.

Holiness Code: the collection of laws found in Leviticus 17–26 that emphasizes the call to priestly holiness for the people of Israel.

hyperbolic (hyperbole): refers to an extravagant statement not intended to be taken literally; an expression of speech that is intentionally exaggerated for effect.

incarnation (from Latin *incarnatio*; literally, "enfleshment"): the eternal Son of God's taking on of human nature in the womb of Mary.

inspired (inspiration): the quality pertaining to the sacred authors of the books of the Bible, and to the books they composed under the inspiration of the Spirit, by virtue of which these books have God as their primary author.

Johannine books: a term used to refer to the biblical writings attributed to the apostle John.

Jubilee: in Israel, the Jubilee Year is the fiftieth year in a fifty-year cycle. It was set aside for the forgiveness of debts, the return of land to its original owner, and the release of indentured slaves (see Lev 25).

Masoretic Text: the traditional Hebrew text of the Old Testament (Jewish Scriptures), codified between the sixth and tenth centuries AD.

Merkabah mysticism: a school of mysticism that emerged in rabbinic Judaism after the destruction of the second temple in AD 70, based on the vision of the chariot throne that includes stages of ascent to God.

Messiah (messianic) (from Hebrew *mashiah*, "anointed one"; Greek *Christos*): the descendant of King David promised by God, who many Jews of Jesus's day hoped would come to restore the kingdom to Israel.

oracle: a message understood to be directly from God, normally delivered orally. A judgment oracle conveys a message of God's impending judgment; a salvation oracle communicates God's promise of deliverance.

Passover: the Jewish feast, held in the first month of the calendar year, that celebrates the deliverance of the Israelites from Egypt.

Pentateuch (literally, "five scrolls/books"): the first five books of the Bible (the books of Moses): Genesis, Exodus, Leviticus, Numbers, and Deuteronomy.

Pentecost: also known as "the Feast of Weeks," the Jewish feast celebrated fifty days after the Feast of Firstfruits, which marked the beginning of the barley harvest and commemorated the giving of the law on Sinai (Lev 23:15–22). It was on the Feast of Pentecost that the Holy Spirit was poured out on the first disciples (see Acts 2).

rabbinic (Judaism, tradition): the main form of Judaism that developed after the destruction of the second temple (AD 70). The rabbinic Jewish tradition upholds an oral law, codified in the Talmud, that serves as a commentary on the written law.

sanctification (sanctify, sanctified): the process of being made holy or set apart for God.

Satan (the devil) (Hebrew for "adversary"): in the Old Testament, a member of the heavenly court who accused or opposed God's people (1 Chron 21:1; Job

1:6–12). In the New Testament, Satan is the prince of demons, the invisible spirits who oppose God's plan and seek to destroy humanity.

second temple: the temple erected after the destruction of the first temple in 586 BC. Begun in the late sixth century BC and finally completed only during the reign of Herod the Great (first century BC), the second temple was destroyed by the Roman armies in AD 70.

Septuagint: the Greek translation of the Old Testament begun around the third century BC. The name comes from the Latin *septuaginta* ("seventy"), based on a legend that seventy-two scholars uniformly translated the Hebrew text into Greek. It is the version most often used by New Testament authors when they quote from the Old Testament.

Shekinah: a postbiblical Hebrew word that became popular in early rabbinic Judaism and means "dwelling" or "presence," signifying the presence of the God of Israel.

Sheol: in the Old Testament, the underground abode of the dead where the souls of all the dead came to rest. While being a place of sadness and gloom, it does not normally have the element of everlasting punishment that came to characterize the later Jewish and Christian conception of "hell."

sign-act: an action designed to communicate a message; the Lord calls Ezekiel on numerous occasions to act out a "sign" for the exiles in Babylon.

Tabernacles (also "Booths" or "Sukkoth"): the autumn harvest feast in Israel, which commemorates Israel's sojourn in the wilderness when they dwelt in "booths" and experienced the Lord providing water from the rock and leading them with the pillar of cloud and fire.

Targum of Ezekiel: an Aramaic translation and paraphrase of the book of Ezekiel written down by the Jewish rabbis in the early centuries of the common era (AD).

theophany: a manifestation of God (literally, "appearance of God") to his people, often powerful and glorious.

Torah (Hebrew for "instruction" or "law"): the first five books of the Old Testament, also called the Pentateuch or the Law of Moses. "Torah" can also refer to all God's instructions for living a holy life for those in covenant with the Lord.

type: a person, place, institution, or event in an earlier stage of God's plan that foreshadows God's action at a later stage in Christ, the Church, the sacraments, or the future kingdom.

Yhwh: the proper name of the God of Israel revealed to Moses at the burning bush (Exod 3:14). The form "Yhwh" is called the "Tetragrammaton," meaning "four letters." According to ancient custom, Jews refrain from pronouncing this divine name ("Yahweh") out of reverence, and substitute for it the title "the Lord" (Hebrew *Adonai*). In most English Bibles the name Yhwh in Hebrew is rendered Lord in small capital letters.

Index of Pastoral Topics

This index indicates where topics that may be useful for evangelization, catechesis, apologetics, or other forms of pastoral ministry are mentioned in Ezekiel.

Index of Sidebars